# one-

# AMERICA

**Continuing the Destructive
Path of Division**

# one-
# America

## Continuing the Destructive
## Path of Division

### By Shawn Paul Cosner

one-America HARDCOVER **ISBN:** 978-1-7375918-2-5
one-America PAPERBACK **ISBN:** 978-1-7375918-1-8
one-America EBOOK **ISBN:** 978-1-7375918-0-1

Self-published
Printed in the United States of America
First Edition Published
05/12/2022
Last Copy Edit
08/05/2022

To those who are lost, confused, and equally powerless to stop our collective demise—I feel your pain.

# one-
# AMERICA

"The truth is born, nurtured, and reaches full maturity in those who create somethingness out of nothingness. Its existence is not contingent on being factually accurate, respectful to logic, or in consideration of rational thoughts."

"Its only purpose, its only design is to infect, based on how consumable it is and pursued to that end. An emboldened lie will eventually become a deep-rooted dogma. Therefore, vigilance in accepting the truth is needed as there exists nothing except the truth a person is willing to accept."

"For if the truth ever becomes untrue, it will consume the ignorant, destroy any civilization that compromises with it, and unleash war upon the innocent who encounters such a denial. Throughout the history of humanity, societies have faced numerous reckonings for the sake of protecting these lies."

"Better known as Existential Consequences."

# Contents

# America's Love for Hate Creates Unity of a Destructive Kind.

# *Thank You*

First and foremost, I would like to thank God for the path of destruction that I had to endure so my life would have meaning. It is the path that must receive credit for what was created. Left to my own device, I would have blessed myself with what I wanted; not what I needed.

Second, the love of my life—Gigi Mesfin. You were sent from heaven, are a blessing, and the reason I will continuously pursue truth over emotion, personal growth over mediocrity, and selflessness over selfishness. You are my best friend and a person I can look to when in need. You always extend understanding without fear of judgment.

I am a flawed man, but you look to empathize before you criticize even when it is understandably difficult and logically disastrous. Thank you for what you have done and will do in our future. I have only been in love once; she is you. I have found my equal, my soulmate, and the one I wish to hold my hand with as I slowly fade away from this world.

It is my hope many years pass before the day comes my expiration breaks your heart. Let us forever enjoy what we know because what we do not, will destroy us both. The time lost finding each other was necessary, as was the many sufferings we had to endure. I would not change a thing nor deny the pain suffered because the path to you was surely necessary and my worthiness of such a person, essential.

You give me the courage necessary to be a better man. Your presence is instrumental in ensuring my existence is one of love, not hate; peace, not destruction; empathy, not apathy. You give me the strength to tolerate myself and the power to be more. You are the best part of me.

Third, my son. Given the opportunity to create a child with a checklist, I could not have created a more kind, loving, intelligent version of who you are becoming. Your person, who you are, warms my heart. When the opportunity presents itself and the time comes for you to be the man you are destined to be—never run, never falter, and never doubt. Succeed where our fathers failed. Deep in your soul is the man the world needs. Remember that!

God made you the way you are because God made you perfect. He put in you what was needed to overcome, only what you could manage, and only what you could achieve. As what is contained inside you, is special.

Only ever able to live in your being as a physical entity and in your soul as a spiritual entity.

The love we share, what we have been through, and our relationship all represent proof of such a wonderful gift. Nothing will ever change who you are to me, how much you mean to me, and what your birth did for me. Nor can I extinguish the sadness I carry, forever filling a void in my heart. The hole, the emptiness, it is lonesome, refuses what is, and is angry at a world blinded by an unjust system. This is the time that is lost to us both. Your absence was the hardest life lesson a broken man could ever endure. But I am forever a greater man for knowing you, as you are everything I could never be, representing everything I wish you to be.

Fourth, those who are my friends and family. The list is not as long as it should be or once was. This recognition is for those who know the acknowledgment is for them. Those who wanted the best for me, expected the best of me, and supported me in my pursuits. Your commitment to keep my words kind and ensuring my actions always matched my words, will never slip my mind. I have finally figured out the type of people who belong in my life. Respect is not always reciprocal—a lesson I will not soon forget.

Finally, anyone who had the opportunity to influence me to be a better person. It was by your actions I turned into the man I am today. Negative or positive, agreed with or disagreed with, liked or disliked, your selfish and selfless behavior is now a part of me. A part that I will always be or a part that I will never be.

# Thank You

Yonas,

The time, the care, and your complete honesty will never be forgotten. It warms my heart that a piece of you is included in this book— አመሰግናለሁ.

An American is not a place, a race, or a birthright. An American is greater than and transcends those identifiers. Though the term "American" has been given many definitions in the past, it always represents an ideological preference attached to a simple premise worth dying for—

**Autonomy over Control**

# _Preface_

A thought continues to reoccur, attacking a premise I once lived by. A belief system I was willing to surrender everything for in the event it was necessary. A notion I would have died for, something I felt required even. This thought, the one that continues to haunt my existence—It seems America may very well be a failed nation. Would I still give my life to defend such a divided people?

Yes, a failed Nation. It is not reflective of such a descriptor in its current state, but only because those without good sense continue to push the limits of peace between dangerous, willing people. I see the potential to end such a beautiful way of life. Once understood by me, Americans represented—strength of unity through differences—is now characterized by—strength of unity through similarities.

Though the term "American" has been given many definitions in the past, it now represents a disastrous unfavorable chess match of specific intent played by foolish child-like leaders aiming to conquer what they perceive as their enemy. Uniting their followers through division and enticing them through half-truths, removing any version of dissent. Once the fulfillment of hate has reached the desired level, respect will disappear along with peace between free people. But is this new? Or is it only new to my generation?

Has the internal desire to create a society by likeness always been hidden, disguised by, and promoted with the illusion of freedom? It is a selfish desire that each hides from the rest in hopes that people will never figure it out. Maybe that was always the case. What people crave and what they desire is a nation reflective of such a premise. It is a belief that collectively the Nation is superior and only correct if it contains an absolute identity. A reflection representing nothing but a singular thought of likeness or an identity inconsiderate of competing interests, lifestyles, or differing points of view; their conception of "one-America."

Am I presently watching the beginning of the end for democracy because the division has again created enough momentum to make another stain in history? Has it been developing since the conclusion of the American Revolutionary War, or is it an absolute: never changing from the spark of self-awareness reinforced by a need to surround oneself with similarities? Does peace only exist through an illusion of control? Does our participation matter, or is it a ruse to control the masses? Whatever it is, I fear our Nation will be destroyed by the selfish endeavors of the few but paid for by the blood of the many. Caution we all should heed as our wonderful Nation is collapsing from the inside.

Our leaders practicing petulance as they contain zero integrity, and possess little or no vision; unless, of course, the vison contains their likeness. These divisive characters invaded our system with a specific purpose. As a result, we are presently watching the decline of America and quite possibly the beginning of the end. Although, it could be argued this is what democracy looks like. However, this is our fault. We allow such nonsense to control our world because we are too scared to stand for decency and hold those accountable who created this rift.

The loudest, most vulgar, and least capable are changing our system because those who were incompetent failed to prove that they possessed any real value. Instead, those tasked with protecting people's best interests did precisely the opposite and helped create the worst versions of ourselves.

Screaming, yelling, conflating issues because we can never really understand the truth as its availability is too costly and ignorance a viable, much cheaper alternative. So, all citizens of this Nation are continuously manipulated into the falsities being spoon-fed by their people. From the prophets unto the disciples and later into the mouths of the willing—zealotry.

It matters not one bit what is said or spread. And if "it" is found to resemble even the slightest thought circling our mind—game, set, match. We do not even blink nor see a need to submit to the grander idea of due diligence verifying if it is true. "Thank you, may I have another." It, at this point, does not matter what is said. We have succumbed to the extent that our ideologies are the truth.

Ignorance controls the ignorant. Not that being ignorant is wrong, as I am undoubtedly unaware of many things. But the commitment to maintain this type of posture is detrimental to our civility, our people, and our Nation. So, where do we go from here? I imagine it will be the same song and dance targeting those we dislike because someone told us to.

The greatest lie speaks to the most gullible because it is easy to influence the masses. What is essential is never based on actuality, only what is consumable for the most significant amount of people. Of course, when our identity and lifestyle is attacked, or an agreeable preference is limited, our basic instinct is to defend. Which, rightfully, is a correct response.

But the continued cycle of political misinformation, especially the disinformation, clouds our better judgment. Our emotions take control, and the rational thought needed to defeat lies or the desire to confirm what is being repeated is no longer present. The threat to democracy is always us. And the defenders of democracy are the same ignorant people.

The viability of our freedoms has met its match. I am unsure if it is fixable. In my mind, this position we put our Nation in is further than I thought we could go. Not because civil war is not plausible or the destruction of our institutions is not possible, but I thought we knew better. I figured we understood what happens when our better selves are absent. I was wrong. Theoretically, we all would rally together and defeat the threat, but it seems identifying the cause is the cause.

History is mercilessly in command, and we submit to its authority. Unfortunately, we never question what we should because being the person who disagrees is left out of the pack, and in earlier times, this was a death sentence. It is also problematic today as consequences of not agreeing to a forced truth can ostracize even the most liked person. So, we embrace the pack mentality simply to belong. Even if belonging is detrimental, we cannot see it because acceptance is a powerful effect of our addiction. And intolerance is the drug of choice for our people.

As the beacon of hope for individuality and freedom of choice in America collapses, so too will the ability of the rest of the world to prevent a similar plunge. This is a guarantee because people will always define themselves as correct, forcing absolutism upon society. No matter the diversity, difference, or distinction between people, the desire to categorize by superiority will destroy what should have never been threatened.

Regardless of your type, someone in America believes you do not belong. It seems soon a people, a type, an ideology will no longer be welcome in a place that welcomes freedom. Where can the innocent, the peaceful, and the persecuted find protection if not America?

# Introduction

I consider myself blue-collar, decently educated and typically have conservative (apolitical) views that I live by. I would rather live in the countryside than in the city, even though I enjoy visiting a city every chance I get. I find agreement in myself with solitude and a sense of peaceful safety when away from people. I have always enjoyed the peace of mind that results from firewood or pursuing any type of outdoor manual labor resulting in this peace.

I grew up in West Virginia on a dirt road surrounded by family and the beautiful Appalachian Mountains. Coopers Rock State Forest bordered Pisgah, a small community in Preston County where my mother's family lived. It was 10 minutes away from a small town named Bruceton Mills, with no stoplights and no cops. As a child, I sat on my grandfather's tailgate and fished at the trout pond or the hunting club pond.

As a younger man my friends and I burned old tires from Mitchell's auto shop, hay bales in Peter's field, or the empty property county cops had yet to chase us from drinking our daddy's beer or the beer we talked our older cousins and their friends into buying for us. "Yes sir" and "yes ma'am" was required in my upbringing. Church was not mandatory, although I enjoyed going with my grandfather even though I hadn't realized it until he was gone. It was a chance to be around family and forget my life.

I was not a fan of school. I hated it and loathed it, even though, later in life, I developed an insatiable appetite for learning. I graduated high school with a 1.4 GPA in a five-year span, unfortunately owning the moniker—Super-Senior. I never thought I would be able to leave that place. So often did I awake to nightmares being short the required credit hours come graduation time but graduate I did. My laziness, foolishness, and inability to see the importance of education made my life more challenging but later gave me a greater purpose and a desire to find the truth.

Being disciplinarians out of respect for their military experiences, both parents created rules, regulations, and a code of conduct not ignorable by those within their household. Like many other children subjugated to disciplinarians such as my parents, it was always readily available when a hands-on approach was necessary. Although my son would never experience what I did, I believe my father tried to do the same, and he succeeded for the most part. This created a deterrent of a sort, discipline through fear. I didn't mind so much as it was a challenge to control me and most likely I benefited from the wall-to-wall counseling my behavior warranted.

Decency was mandatory as was respect for others. My parents were nowhere close to being perfect people or perfect parents, but they did understand and recognize what was required for such a pursuit. Their children were always required to respect others and treat people with kindness, which we all still practice.

Because common decency towards fellow man was taught, it allowed me to develop a strong understanding of right and wrong as I embarked into the world as a child, an adolescent, and later a young man. Not that I was free of errors, nor am I a perfect representation of correctness, but because I was taught right and wrong, I was equipped to find fault in the wrong and possessed the ability to see agreeance in the right.

I had family and mentors who stuck with my shortcomings and never gave up on me, something not all children or adults have. Ornery was the word used to describe mischievous kids such as myself. My behavior represented every aspect of that word. Even at times, I sure made it easy for them to quit on me; regardless of my transgressions, I was blessed and loved, always given a lesson in acceptable behavior.

I was not without mistakes and boy did I always find a way to achieve some sort of reconstructive training from my father. Even when I was doing wrong, I knew I shouldn't, it hurt my insides, and I felt horrible. Not for the hands-on punishment of my father but because I recognized something was wrong with me and my actions. How can I do wrong, know it was wrong, and still do it regardless? What is wrong with me?

I would like to pretend that my deviancy was beaten out of me as an adolescent, but the truth is, it stuck with me well into my adult life. Although I finally outgrew it, the stains of anger, regret, and the yesterdays I wish to forget, control what other people still think of me. But I was blessed to have a few people in my life setting examples of correct behavior and the type needed to become a man.

Because of this, I turned out to be a decent man, but I was not prepared for a world in which adults acted like children. Neither was I equipped for the lack of accountability to which society has grown accustomed or the incompetence possessed by those who must lack this cancerous fault. It saddens me, and the exposure to such selfish behaviors made me want to quit life on two separate occasions.

My life seemed unbearable, and my existence seemed unimportant to those I wanted it to matter to. I know what it feels like to be overwhelmed, lost, and incomplete—hopeless. Because of this, I also understand what metal in my mouth tastes like. The taste of bitterness that is left from a barrel of a gun and the shame of such a selfish thought when blessings are abundant. But I was given something so many people did not have—a chance. It cannot be explained. I was granted an opportunity, a light, something I have been drawn to believing in and following ever since I decided to ignore such a violent ending.

Why write a book?

I have something to say, and I believe others feel the same way. As an American and with my understanding of what America represents, I am not pleased by the landscape of our current reality nor the reality of the world. I am also disgusted by society and how our elected leaders continue to divide the populous into factions or tribes. I see flaws in such behavior with the potential to create cataclysmic consequences. A one-sided America should be met with great aggression.

I am paralyzed, unable to move or plan a future because what I see is a reality that will forever alter what we know and destroy anything worth having. It leaves me unable to plan, decide, or figure out what to do with my life. Leaving me with no direction, no purpose, and absolutely no answers.

I find myself crying often and feel so small in a world that seems to have lost the ability to be kind. I feel sick to my stomach watching, reading, and observing the unnecessary rhetoric hurled at the identities people claim are the enemy. I often am without words to describe the atrocities I recognize are coming foreshadowed by the ignorant, incompetent, and influential hateful people controlling the minds of the willing.

I have grown tired of people abusing their positions to take advantage of innocent people. Unscrupulous lawyers, politicians, business owners, doctors, and influential people hurt those I love and others who deserve better from professionals in professions that demand better. Finally, I am sickened by the selfish, hurtful, and ignorant people who have the luxury of opening their mouths to intentionally demean people or say untrue rhetoric without consequences.

Somehow these imbeciles have made it through life, never being punched in the mouth for their intolerant unkind words to make their unimportant lives matter more. I guess I am just tired, hurt, and lost because my expectations of people are so much greater than what we all suffer from.

To continue, and be quite honest, I am tired of the self-prescribed ethically superior and the morally elite making others feel bad for who they are or what they believe in. Assuming a way of life that is different from theirs is flawed because they cannot understand it or feel it. Even though their mindset, what they stand for, can be similarly applied against their own identity, they care naught. Believing differences are somehow wrong and not a proper way to live is—asinine. Doing so creates nothing more than an inferiority cycle destined to repeat, divide, and destroy.

Somehow people believe a higher power, unknown to others, has ordained them and other individuals like them, with unbridled power to decide the rules for all others. These great ones arbitrarily force their will onto those differences they disagree with and attempt to cancel what they perceive as a threat to their America.

I have always been amused by absolutism and the pursuit of such an atrocious endeavor. In this book, my thoughts are not a pursuit to silence competing views, nor am I trying to prove people wrong by submitting any viewpoints as absolute or superior. It is quite the opposite. I rather enjoy expansive thought and always find victory in pursuing what I cannot understand.

Additionally, this is not an attempt to prove which examples of current or past reckless behaviors are at fault. Or which short-sighted illogical thoughts are more wrong but a push to highlight that these, in fact, do exist, and we must prevent this ignorance from consuming reality.

As freedom is congruent with perspective and the American way of life, a commitment to defend all Americans must be present. Differing thoughts must exist in harmony, no matter the level of subjective-triggeredy created to establish victimhood. I will highlight the absurdity of hypocrisy and address the unwavering commitment from differences to hate each other. I will, however, offend many, and that is okay too.

My intent is not to insult, although who and where I offend, I will also defend. But the offense taken will occur because that was the useless emotional response sought without understanding one-America in its entirety. My interpretations are from a belief in merit over identity and accountability over feelings. I am doing nothing but seeking answers to discover the truth. These are the questions I ask myself that I do not understand, and I criticize myself before criticizing others. This is my way of describing actions or behaviors that are counterproductive, even detrimental to society.

I can easily identify flaws or limits with the constant use of the critical perspective. Not addressing these flaws as incorrect but highlighting incompleteness. Mostly, I identify errors in other people's logic, decisions, or issues that cannot be reconciled but for a subjective understanding as it is removed from the critical perspective and heavily influenced by the absolutism of a personal kind. I cannot make it make sense.

It is not that they are wrong; their truth encompasses a more biased representation of carnality [grossness of the mind] instead of impartially viewed actuality [the quality or state of being actual]. As I look through my lens of subjectivity, these tend to be in the form of inferences unreconcilable by available understood logic that I recognize. Someone gave them permission to feel, act, and believe accordingly.

In other words, individuals believe 2+2=10, but the integers can be replaced with many different flawed beliefs (subjectively applied), and the equation is always incorrectly correct based on the value prescribed. The comprehension of truth is always limited by the understanding and perception of individuality. Believing self-correctness is everything destroys togetherness and cohesion. It is complicated to solve the present problems with the minds of the past. Yet our collective growth and progressed evolution continue to be limited by thoughts with expiration dates or thoughts outside what is scientific, logical, or required.

It concerns me that people cannot grasp the consequences of such selfish ways. It angered me and affected my life so much that I wanted to address the flaws around me and change everything so it could operate more efficiently and possess operational consistency—offending none yet empowering all. I forced myself to be comfortable in places I knew I did not belong to gain insight and create opportunities in hopes I could alter what threatens the peaceful stability our Nation requires.

I am aware that education has power. It can create influence and establish legitimacy; more importantly, it can remove ignorance, an honorable pursuit by itself. Knowing this, I learned as much as possible to affect change one day. Not all knowledge is learned in school; because of this, I have learned more from my relationships with people and life experiences than from any higher learning institution. Not that these places are without value; however, each seems less essential and without purpose if the human element is ignored or not considered when what must be understood is being evaluated.

I do not pursue a selfish endeavor of being right where others are wrong. I simply seek to be as factually accurate and as understanding as possible regarding the truth. And to be honest, this book is an attempt to empty my mind and combat the restlessness and helplessness I seem to be a part of. At times I am unable to sleep, and I lose my ability to stay focused or concentrate on tasks because my mind is mentally hijacked by the absurdities occurring in the world.

My thoughts drift off into a realm focused solely on discovering solutions while creating a cognitive bliss but paralyzing my existence at the same time—pensivity. Or I am in a constant state of internally controlled rage—a cancerous soul. This sadness and anger cycle is so far from peace I am fearful I will never know what it's like to not hurt anymore.

I think part of the reason I am plagued with a vicious cycle of thoughts is because of the lack of accountability and the absence of truth. It stems from the operating flaws in a system built to protect the hypocrisy in everything from the government to news agencies and the availability of the truth or lack thereof. Included are the irresponsible people who consume lies as a nutritional supplement starving themselves of knowledge yet gorging themselves on ignorance. Accountability must never be applied conveniently, nor should the application of truth be a subjective endeavor.

Who would have guessed the world is not what it seems, and its actors are mostly self-serving liars? Many are hell-bent on a deity's mission to recreate a one-America representative of "their likeness." Destroying all and any caught in their path of self-importance as they become the billboard of misguided intent represented by tragic indulgences just as it had once plagued institutional religion.

We are taught from a young age about right, wrong, just, unjust, virtue, righteousness, and how to treat one another. I was and still am ill-equipped to deal with the gravity of those fabrications. It seems as if people who try to do the right thing are playing by a different set of rules than the selfish, ego-driven monsters controlling society and dictating double standard proclamations.

Those who choose to live a life through understanding are doomed as the rest of society participates in a similarly misguided form of Game of Thrones consuming power for a purpose, not influence for absolution. A tragedy our children will observe and repeat because no one showed them any different.

Somehow, a standard of decency has been removed from our society, but lately, I am questioning if it ever really existed. It is hard to believe that people accept a lesser version of themselves, a lesser version of society, and a lesser version of what America could be. America's new reality is as perplexing as it is toxic.

The system is not operating adequately or at the very least equitably. Are people not interested in solving our society's issues? Do its citizens crave the possibility of conflict? Why is society still openly debating concurrent issues from generations past without addressing a resemblance of truth to solve these known shortcomings?

I try to understand everything, and since everything has a purpose, it also must have operational consistency. When people, politicians, and those within our government operate outside of their allowable parameters, that behavior should immediately be attacked as unacceptable, and the support of these bad actors, including their behavior, must cease. I cannot understand why it continues, nor am I able to accept the corruption it represents. A system such as this prevents the change necessary and destroys the ability to coexist.

W.E.B. Du Bois said, "The ruling of men is the effort to direct the individual actions of many persons toward some end. This end theoretically should be the greatest good of all, but no human group has ever reached this ideal because of ignorance and selfishness."

People do not seek peace, equality, or equity because they do not attempt to inflict equitable administration of the law. They instead choose power over peace, control over delegation, and absolutism over understanding, ignoring what could be for what never will be.

It is nothing more than a continuation of what was, what is, and what shall remain. Those who have the power to choose; select likeness for support, ignorance over knowledge, and feelings in place of logic. Accomplishing nothing but a continuation of nonsense, participating and playing the same game our species has done since the beginning of time.

It fails to register as an acceptable type of behavior, creating an effect of stress and the desire to correct or point out the deficiencies. I am fully aware that bad people will do bad things, but even those who get paid to represent good seem to blur that line.

I continue to try and minimize my limits to continue to grow as a person. These uncomfortable truths always lead to growth spurts which are necessary changes for the man I hope to be. I know my faults, and because of this, I recognize what I need to change, so I may be a better man. Every person brings their own unique perspective of life and what it contains. My life and the understanding of my surroundings are from a viewpoint only I can share. I hope to enlighten you as my life experience and others have enlightened me.

I sought knowledge to remove my ignorance in hopes of one day being better equipped to address recognized threats, at least for myself. Unfortunately, I am still forced to have some exceedingly difficult conversations about who I am. Fortunately, I continue to grow, causing the deaths of my many demons because I choose this path.

Recognizing that we are all to blame can create a sense of joint responsibility and allow the reconstructive process to collectively begin. I sincerely plea that you create more questions than this book offers and find solutions to both. Thoughts of an inquisitive nature may instill enough doubt to interrupt what allows us to hate. The current lack of respect festering between our people will soon create an ending of some sort, and it will carry unforeseen consequences for generations. Each one of us has an assigned duty to our future. Please take the responsibility to create a better tomorrow a bit more serious.

In conclusion, this book represents a journey of tolerance, the destruction of intolerance, and a lesson for those who continue to ignore history and a great many mistakes belonging solely to those who came before us. This book contains a continued theme of tolerance used to create a tolerant mindset. It may offer a path forward for a society divided due to its differences. Society finally has evidence of measurable consequences, and it has the empirical data necessary to change what is known to cause these issues. It is likely that the system only needs a few changes to create the best outcome. Substantial change and growth are always within our grasp; are we willing?

I do things my own way and always have. This is a reason for most of my trauma, guilt, or the self-inflicted suffering in my youth, including a bit as an adult and some unnecessary pain I currently struggle with today. Although it is a path of many mistakes, I have learned quite a lot about life, especially people. But one thing I have kept through it all is to never stop growing, asking why, and certainly, I never settle for an answer that cannot satisfy my inquiry or the thirst for what is true.

I can never respect the status quo or the authority of another instructing me how to do something because they said so or that's the way it's been done before. Nor can I accept an answer when it cannot correctly address my concerns. It tickles me when others get in line and nod like simpletons to agree with whoever has the talking stick. A good friend of mine refers to these people as "halfwits."

I told you this because I wanted the readers to know my words are my own. Not a single person instructed me how to write this book, what words to include or omit, nor am I targeting a specific demographic to read this text. Knowing this will allow the reader to understand my style—the way I write, what I am saying, how I tell my story, and its format—is mine; it's me and mine alone. I did this my way because I didn't want people telling me I couldn't do it like this, I was wrong for doing it like this, or these people will not like those words.

I am trying to be genuinely honest and uniquely me, uninhibited without influence. I did not want to be told I could not ask why, question the purpose, or be prevented from explaining what about this world makes absolutely zero sense to me. I never wanted my words censored because that would make me a liar and an opportunist driven by fear or money, which is the same thing—a person who betrays the truth.

Mostly I am looking for peace in hopes more people feel the way I do. I would also like to explain what I think the issues are in hopes of creating a more perfect union or at least encouraging a sort of kindness and decency our world is slowly losing. I wanted to do it my way. At the end and upon the conclusion of my book, right or wrong, support or no support, agreed with or disagreed with; this is how I feel.

Writing one-America was relatively straightforward as the book represents a part of me—who I am, what I believe in, and my understanding of the world around me. However, what I found extremely difficult, while also taxing on my emotions and my mental health, was the pursuit to make it perfect or flawless. I wanted my message to be fair and resonate with as many people as possible. Therefore, as I attempted to edit the message, I tried to convey it in a way that my words could not insult.

The truth is that nothing, especially people, can be perfect, and because of this, what is created by people will always contain flaws no matter the number of misguided followers who believe the human construct created. Insult will always exist simultaneously with acceptance. I can never make it right because it will always be wrong but what is included is a truth that I am unable to hide.

I am not trying to convince people to believe or accept my words. On the contrary, I wish for nothing but for people to accept me for who I am. I want people to know what I believe is real to me. As is my truth for my life. It is as natural to me as is their life to them. Our experiences, identities, and existence create separate but similar interpretations that are unique and true only because we are neither perfect nor identical. This permits individuals to be considered both right and wrong depending on the person's subjectivity in perceiving the message.

No matter what I write, no matter the time I take to defend my positions, no matter the consideration I give others, people will always find fault because their existence is perfect, their truth is correct, and their life experiences created an absolute irrefutable to others allowing them to always pass judgments upon differences. And because they can never be wrong, what I believe will never be right or perfect to anyone other than me. And I am finally okay with that.

Because what is true to me does not need to be true to them. I exist, believe, and feel; therefore, I am. Since my thoughts, words, and expressions are real, this allows my truth to be honest. I tried to convince myself I was wrong to find the truth. I am left alone in my thoughts and at times in my life because even those closest to me cannot see what I see or feel. But the many truths I have can only ever be understood by me because my life has only ever been lived by me.

I believe this is true from my perspective and my truth. The words in this book represent the most straightforward way I can explain how I think, my thought process, and what I believe. This means my identity is not open for interpretation, nor should I be considered right or wrong, only an extension of thought encompassing logical application represented by my life experiences and what I understand.

These are justifiable and reasonable inferences established by my critical thought. I showed my work by explaining intelligible defined terms connecting coherent meaning with logical understanding. Some thoughts or ideas may be incomplete or need more work, but it is a start in the right direction. If I am wrong, I am always willing to correct the deficiency because I am searching for truth. Ignorance is for fools and those who enjoy selfishness.

It is likely as I chase down more tomorrows, many of my thoughts will change or evolve because the level of what I know will change or evolve as well. This book is everything I believe or was willing to accept as the truth up to my current station in life, concerning the topics discussed by using my current level of intelligence, education, and the lessons my life experiences provided.

I am sure there were far more teachable moments than the ones I was able to obtain and more growth that I could not achieve, but I lacked the proper level of emotional and intellectual maturity needed to create a better version of myself. Anything learned and understood is represented by the level of selfishness a person keeps in their heart and the level of ignorance a person keeps in their mind.

This is the mess in my head. I write the way I speak, affecting how my words are interpreted or understood. At times, the sentence structure may seem as if it is a run-on sentence, but in my mind, it is a continuous singular thought. It may not make sense to everyone, but it makes sense to me.

My apologies for the added difficulty; however, I believe there is always more than one way to do something, especially when what is known limits what can be. What we are unable to comprehend in the present seems to be better understood with each passing day and the acceptance of what this additional blessing brings.

The book in its entirety is complete as a combined piece of work because its purpose was to quickly encourage and hopefully spark conversations by sharing what I believe in and what makes me, Me. However, it is incomplete as many of the included thoughts are not finished separately and must be expanded on independently, providing a more complete thought and solution for each, respectively.

Could my words have been written differently? Quite possibly. With better grammar or more accurate sentence structure? Absolutely. Rearranged more appropriately reflective of something someone intellectually superior to my ability would have written? Most likely. But there is a reason another writer would have written this book differently—they are not the ones writing it, and these are not their words.

But this book, from the beginning to the end, is me and only me. I created something, and I hope my creation allows for conversations that people are afraid to engage in. This is an expression, extension, and explanation of what I see, what I learned, and a great many things awaiting a broken people. What is not said, explained, and clarified in this book, has already begun in "The First Addendum." Always create a place for your thoughts, even if others fail to see the purpose.

God bless America, her people, and the many fantastic people around the world.

This is my understanding of life...

# CHAPTER I

## *A Taste of Insanity*

**W**hat a strange reality people are suffering. It is abundantly clear that humanity lacks rational thought, which ultimately paves the way for reasonable discourse. The truth is missing; it has been replaced by people who decided to lick a Brillo pad for answers. The outcome was not that of cognitive growth culminating in knowledge, but a maddening craze of delirium and hysteria used to divide.

People presently armed with opinions believe themselves to be experts because they buy into the nonsense spuing from the ones they have anointed and faithfully follow and the filth that flows from their mouths. They somehow believe themselves to be intellectually superior to those who are not like-minded or have differing identities. So they identify and target people as enemies for not agreeing to the premise they offer. And these people, the ones who may differ in thought, are considered wrong for possessing a contrasting point of view, and undoubtedly the cause of America's decline or the reason a path forward is absent.

It is a paradox of absolutes not vetted but absentmindedly consumed by the unaware. Understanding self-importance through unearned confidence and perceived legitimacy[1] has created a type of alternate reality in the form of "The Outer Limits," allowing the inept to influence the masses.

"You must believe this way, act this way, or support this lifestyle, and if you don't...."

Subjugation through absolutes and forced participation through power is nothing more than virtue signaling for acceptance, purity testing for

---

[1] A belief that greatness has been acquired, respect must be given, and what is spoken must be accepted without hesitation.

membership, and a type of exclusion through hate. The intolerance of and unacceptable posture against self-expression has found its way to the doorsteps of a free people. Forcing others to accept certain truths without discussing or understanding the idiom "it is a free country" is against the principles of controlling documents in place to prevent such atrocities.

Although social norms are governed separately, it is only a matter of time before the malady is transmitted to government actors creating a police state, one that abuses in the name of a subjective absolute and is correct in its premise to control the ones unwilling to accept the new world order. In many ways, it is already occurring as examples of this abuse and overreach are visible in all states and in all administrations regardless of if these are republican or democrat held. Representing nothing more than demagogues as they spread misinformation to create a platform, lie to maintain power, and sow hate to establish clearly recognizable enemies, but these tactics are also used to align the troops in the event their existence is necessary.

The many blemishes of history have shown what occurs when people allow such sickness to control, compel, and eventually conquer. It is irresponsible and reckless to ignore these people. When they choose this path and are allowed to choose this path, it will inevitably re-enact humanity's violent past; once again completing the cycle our species is unable to break.

Does the very meaning of insanity encompass a want and a need for such a fool's errand? Is this not what the word insanity means—repeatedly doing the same thing, expecting a new and different result? To what end do they speak? What path does those with power wish to create?

It would be unwise to assume those who choose to divide want anything other than their likeness to control. Any or all such mindless flirtations of the ignorant kind should never influence a rational society and its people. History has not been kind to those with such selfish endeavors, and it would be foolish to assume their plight for chaos will have a resemblance to a differing outcome:

> "But when a long train of abuses and usurpations, pursuing invariably the same Object evinces a design to reduce them under absolute Despotism, it is their right, it is their duty, to

throw off such Government, and to provide new Guards for their future security."

The words in the Declaration of Independence and the Constitution are not exclusive to Americans and must not be ignored by the unfaithful. The strength these words create is not for a single race, religion, location, or people. Applicability is for the human species.

Do not continue in the way of the past. Be forewarned that intolerance is thriving, irritability growing, and violent conflict is brewing. Failing to heed the warnings of the past by ignoring the indicators that catastrophe may be imminent is reckless, as once it is upon us, it will spread like wildfire burning out of control.

Failures related to ignorance from weak societal leadership cause failed nations, governments, or any other system in place used to control people. Continuing the same behavior repeatedly with the anticipation of a different result is nothing more than the death penalty for freedoms and the consequences of mediocrity represented by insanity.

Modern society is not exempt nor immune to such a destructive force, including America and her people. America literally has participation awardees running the country, influencing children, and leading when they should be following.

The strongest and best of the population must control, influence, and lead. Not those who are propped up satisfying a selfish desire in hopes of being perceived as kinder and more tolerant because somehow strength has been made offensive. But am I wrong?

Am I wrong for wanting to follow strength? Am I wrong to believe strength represents a more appropriate way to lead? Am I wrong for characterizing weakness as rendering one incapable of leading? Is my desire for the strongest to lead, the strongest to guide, and the strongest to represent strength incorrect? I do not wish to follow weakness, nor should weakness be allowed to lead me. What is wrong with that statement? Weakness and strength either destroy or create, corrode or protect, kneel or stand. This book will define both by identifying the differences between creating and solving the problem.

Who decides the correct way to live a life? If two competing thoughts are in conflict or in disagreement, what does society direct people to do?

What is the right conclusion regarding different opinions on how to live? Is society forced to choose one group of people over another to assign correctness? How must society decide who is correct? More importantly, who is incorrect? Or does forcing people to live a life, not of their choosing represent a sin against humanity?

When people believe or assume their lifestyle is the only permissible version, it creates monsters. These thoughts of their own devising prevent progress, enslave, and cripple any drive or determination to achieve peace. This establishes more distance between diversity in a free nation. This behavior is used by influential people as a selfish endeavor to destroy cohesiveness. These people tell others who to hate and why to hate them. Are they right? Who is responsible for causing fractures in our society? Is it the democrats or the republicans? Is it the liberals or the conservatives? Is it [assign your own fault] or [assign your own fault]? I believe it is all of us, but Am I wrong?

Am I wrong for not understanding ideas I cannot comprehend or may disagree with? Am I any less of a person because I think differently than someone else? Why would I be attacked for being different or supporting differences? How can I be attacked for thinking differently or supporting different thoughts? Do I not have a right to express free thought of preference, free thought of who to believe, and free thought of who to follow?

I guess if it were that easy to be free, society would have reached a consensus on which people to hold responsible for the apparent decline and looming loss of the efficacy of American politics, but it most likely has always been this way, and blame is always projected towards the one enemy that is in conflict with our truth.

Truth. It is not easy to find the truth, and it is not easy to see the truth. What adds to the difficulty of such a task? Is it ourselves? Do we prevent cohesiveness just to feel better about our own flavor? I feel as if I am looking for the truth, but I am failing to find what is considered acceptable to my own mind. This is a consequence of attempting to answer a multiple-choice question that does not have the correct answer as part of the choices. The choices are unreconcilable with the critical perspective and the logical thought required to become an absolute answer—**all but one** is wrong.

Does this mean everyone is wrong? The truth is obtainable but giving up is intolerance at its finest. People choose to ignore alternatives as viable when these alternatives do not agree with their understanding or comprehension. I believe the majority of Americans are innocent. They are simply trying to survive but are placed into the category of wrong as inclusion is forced upon their identity, but they gladly accept their role to further their identity to fit in whatever category they feel the most comfortable in. Are they wrong, am I wrong, are we all wrong?

Respect is and always should be reciprocal. When this statement fails to be true, peace usually ends, and aggression begins when competing ideas lose respect for one another. It is not violent at first, only rhetoric from the weak. But eventually, when reciprocity to respect differences is no longer present, the need or want of a people to start killing differences occurs. This is the final step in the cycle of destruction—the acceptance of a belief that represents the need to defend their differences against a perceived threat to their lifestyle becomes consequently necessary and unavoidable. What does that acceptance feel like, and when does it occur?

Did the people from history's past recognize it? Did they decide not to prevent it? Is it a feeling of pain, fear, or hopelessness? Is it the thought of the unknown in combination with what could happen? What does it mean for a society when this occurs? At what moment do the many varying truths belonging to the many varying people destroy cohesiveness? Will I recognize when it is time? The most important question is, will I be brave to take a stand to stop what must be defeated?

Consider 2020, what it was, what it represented. People may have felt a need or want to change the outcome. The association of detriment, the representation of an ending, the undeniable conclusion that selfishness controls the majority. This control is used to destroy as it underlies the creation of our worst fears. These feelings are hazardous when weaponized by desire but cloaked in the guise of leadership. This is where peace is created, and this is why peace is destroyed.

People need to believe in something collectively as a group. It does not matter what it is. Religion, government, a constitution, or anything people are willing to protect. What people need is a nation that represents all. A place to be free, a place with protections, a place with justice. It is not essential where this nation is or what people are included, only that the people involved believe.

The willingness to live side by side, hand in hand, in unison, representing one likeness with or without any likeness surviving, protecting, and growing as a single unit. Bettering life for all while encouraging others to do the same is how I define such a place. That is how I define America. This is what she has the power to create—believing in something collectively inspires believing in others subjectively.

Society and what it represents is falling apart because people chose to forget the value of our most treasured possession. The Rule of Law is required to control chaos and sustain peace—the absence of conflict. But unfortunately, a substantial number of people are doing nothing to protect it. Instead, most people are substituting logic with actions or thoughts that are inconsiderate and even detrimental to people and the freedoms Americans share. It is occurring because certain leaders encourage civil unrest and discourage discourse.

Being inconsiderate of others and their differences is detrimental to peace, and it serves only to cause destruction. Deciding to criticize differences without first understanding them adds to the stew of poison simmering in people's hearts. Allowing people's truths to conflict with differences is why what is factually accurate matters. This is what happens when a person lets bias control irrational thoughts.

The inferior/superior complex is born of necessity in response to people's actions. The need to build some form of protection, a place where likeness can survive against the pursuit of absolutism. The logical response of self-preservation combined with the illogical response of group-preservation to create an inclusive but exclusive form of America represented and protected by a purity test known as one-America[2].

If you don't fit our mold, you do not belong in the toy box.

Born of need, separative in its intent, similarly incoherent, the introduction of insanity through the vessel of flawed logic is used to protect likeness, exclude differences, and ignore consequences. It has taken hold, and an antidote may never exist to slow such a virus or prevent such a process. Americans are creating enemies because people live differently and express different opinions. Application of one fallacy being superior

---

[2] A belief and movement designed to create a country of likeness without consideration of tolerance for differences or respect of independent thought.

to another is destroying truth and creating a pack mentality amongst our citizens.

People are called racists for supporting police officers. Anti-police for wanting due process or justice in response to egregious behavior. Accused of being a liberal and anti-Christian for supporting any alphabet of the LGBTQ kind. Racist for suggesting that proper identification should be required to vote. People are public enemy number one for supporting the 2nd Amendment.

People are considered in error for supporting labor groups, unions for protections and controlled wages, or a merit shop based on the individual's worth representing production and outcome—value. One is considered stupid for supporting socialism for believing the rich accumulated too much money as the poor and those without are suffering needlessly.

Others judge harshly, implying a total bar from identities speaking on racial divides because skin tone insinuates victimhood, and privilege prevents understanding. A particular sex is not allowed to be an advocate for causes involving the opposite sex because opinions originating from the opposite sex are presumed to be toxic. One's identity or likeness is the only defining characteristic or quality required to be considered competent. It is easy to be considered ignorant, intolerant, or racist when what is placed in this category is conveniently a competing viewpoint.

It is even more of an insult to logic when the only people permitted to criticize your behavior share in the same likeness, same thought, or same voting record—even though the much-needed criticism of our own identities seldom occurs. Again, a selfish understanding motivated by a selfish need, ignoring the opportunity to look inward.

Maybe that is what all people should do. Find a way to be selfish and allow their mind to create an endless echo chamber full of vacuumed, incoherent misconceptions only understood and processed by their brain and other brains like it. Is that peace? Being oneself and unapologetic to those who may be offended. Emboldened by their differences because someone gave them the permission to act the way they feel. Continuing to shove beliefs down the opposition's throat because you will never have to go to war to defend your words. The weak say what they want, knowing that someone other than them will face the consequences.

I wish I knew what that felt like. I wish I could speak my mind publicly and openly express my thoughts without the fear of someone accusing me of hate or telling me—I am or my opinion is wrong simply because of identity. Somehow I am supposed to believe that my views and thoughts are irrelevant because the standard for the logical interpretation of correctness is beyond my mental capabilities, my sex, and the color of my skin. People must accept differences and competing thoughts as this prevents groupthink. On the contrary, similarities and a refusal to accept competing ideas encourage groupthink.

How does society fix the issues destroying the cohesive structure[3] needed to maintain peace? First, people must create a necessary proactive posture or an equal but effective reaction to solve the issues society is suffering from. This task has always been one for our political leaders, a responsibility that has largely been ignored thus far. People must be as neutral as possible to promote balance in a societal structure that is starving for it.

This does not mean that you should surrender your convictions or what motivates you but that learning to tolerate differences by abandoning adherence to selfish thoughts will increase the efficacy and cohesion of America. This will help mend what divides us all. However, I think the division also has to do with the citizenry value[4] our people lack or have, which complicates our cohesive structure from the onset.

Doing what we want and treating people how we want is the problem, as selfishness is the motivation. It is problematic, extraordinarily divisive, and counterproductive to peace when people fail to allow intellectual debates or differing opinions to coexist. Many people believe in and follow flawed logic only to defend the same behavior they claim to be against. The continuous power struggle of a two-sided idiot coin will eventually remove the truth from those who need it and the society that must have it. Fighting over irrelevant identity politics or instigating a cultural war does nothing but further divide a society destroying its cohesive structure.

Because people fail to pick a side based on likeness, they become less respected and hated by their peers. Their similarities, in their entirety, must be defended above all else—no matter what. By creating a line of enematic

---

[3] Represented by the type of unity present in citizens.

[4] An impartial rating of a nation's citizens willingness to participate in its form of governance and the benefit or cost objectively represented.

characteristics[5] not to be crossed, likeness must align itself with a similar ideology as this becomes the only way to protect their identity. Even with a shared likeness, those who are not easily influenced are perceived to be and treated as the enemy. The absence of truth starts this process. The design of fascism is to create loyalty above all else. The exclusivity of differences and the ease of identifying enemies create a vessel for hate. A way to protect and destroy most efficiently.

These thoughts, different from the thoughts espoused by the group and unique to the person, are contrary to what is allowed by the one-America demagogues[6] and their followers who created the rules. The policies of the hateful are rather easy to understand for their loyal followers. If the person is different—they are part of the problem because they do not vote along party lines, they are part of the problem if they have an identity shared by others yet believe differently, they are part of the problem because their ability to remain neutral threatens the efficacy of absolutism; including those who look like us but do not think like us. These types attack our credibility and make it difficult for us to continue our group's intolerance and hate.

Application of lines based on thoughts and likeness does nothing for peace, does nothing for freedom, and it does nothing for America. Instead, what it creates is divisiveness. Society needs a system to hold people accountable for creating problems where problems do not and should not exist. Or at the very least, make their anti-American views known for what they truly are and what they represent as their endgame. Their end goal is a selfish desire to destroy peace. Selfishness consumes as selfishness creates, and its prevalence is apparent, yet protective measures aimed at thwarting its spread are nearly non-existent due to a lack of strong leadership.

Things will continue to worsen since our leaders and those with influence cannot comprehend the consequences of their actions. When a shared truth is no longer present, a lie takes its place, division increases, and conflict begins to loom on the horizon. This is not new, nor is it unique to our current state. It is a cycle of behavior created by selfishness and

---

[5] The negative visual or known characteristics of the enemy
[6] An individual or entity who/that believes in a one-America ideological absolutism

ignorance, designed to create, maintain, or remove power. Human beings as a species are flawed creatures.

Unfortunately, it seems as if people will continue to relive the mistakes of the past because history fails to be useful, educational, and enlightening for the ignorant.

Over-populated + Over-stimulated + Hyper-sensitive + Hyper-divided = **Unsustainable**

It will eventually collapse, society will be destroyed, and what is, will no longer be. Its cause—is a lack of empathy for and from competing viewpoints. Each side operates under the same irrational absolutism theory. To see how far off-track Americans have become, ask any person in this country or the world, for that matter, if they would be happier with a country or a world full of likeness—democrats or republicans, conservatives or liberals, Christians or members of any religion, or any other identities they represent.

Their answer will most likely be yes. If it is that thought, that belief, that is the **PROBLEM**. These people are a traitor to a thought greater than their existence. That exact thought process is why we are so divided as people both currently and throughout the history of our species. If they say no, that is what people must believe to be an asset for America and the world. I am not saying never disagree, nor am I saying believe whatever people are forcing down your throat, but differences are a part of our species, and acknowledging this can help change the world for the better.

This is kindness. And precisely what is needed to save freedom. Those people, the ones willing to engage without compromising their beliefs, the ones who are willing to try and understand, are Americans. Those people are patriots. Those people are absolutely the change necessary to end conflicts. They also represent the answer to how we change the trajectory of our insane reality. It is time to not only coexist but coexist by understanding people and their positions a bit more. People must get rid of ignorance and gain the knowledge needed to prevent themselves from making the same mistakes made by every civilization of times past.

Each nation is diverse regardless of the likeness it may represent. Whether the diversity originates from their outer differences or inner differences. People must understand that at an individual level, all people have personal convictions or a separate identity that is all their own. And that should be celebrated. So why would it ever be appropriate to have only one likeness or encourage groupthink?

The more populated the world becomes, the faster peace will break down; this is true regardless of the society people belong to. Human minds evolve too slowly to cope with the rapid population growth and the amount of knowledge created from uniqueness. The differences they are stimulated by cause friction. The resulting responses represent behaviors rooted in hate and acceptance or resting somewhere in between on the tolerance continuum. People's intelligence levels vary too much and are too different to support the necessary efficacy to counter the negative effects of population increases and the need for representation.

Or people are just mean, and what is encouraged is simply inconceivable, incomprehensible, and goes against a truth that has since been made insulting because the hate policies of the group demanded concessions from weak leadership trying to keep power, achieve power, or desire to be treated as a person. The way people view things says a lot about our issues. Perspective is the darndest thing.

The varying beliefs contained on the Infinite Spatial Growth Chart[7] are the cause and represent consequences of diversity. The chart is used to measure the existing gap in intellectual thought between society, the ruling class, and representation motivated for or against competing identities. It represents the lack of growth required to correctly evolve in a measurement applicable to sustainable peace in society. It is a straight-line representing truth and moving further away from the center represents moving further away from the truth. It undeniably contains more lies, falsities, and eventually the creation of existential consequences completing the cycle of destruction.

Whether the measurement is generational, in the context of the cycles of human life, a society's existence, a civilization's existence, all members of the generational thought causing conflict must pass [death] to end whatever less evolved mindset, or thought is no longer appropriate for the

---

[7] A chart used to show the gap between similar intellectual growth patterns among the human species

tree of life[8] in the respective timeline. This occurs through evolutionary progress by members of society. It changes through the following two means; 1) the increase of tolerance for one another as a result of expansive progressive thought or 2) forced by conflict destroying one of two truths or one of two lies depending solely on the subjectivity of those willing to kill or willing to die for what they believe in.

The pursuit of knowledge and application of tolerance adopted by some, yet needed and required for all, will increase differences' success in living peacefully together. However, what are they to do when people continue to represent and push a one-America idea on those who do not represent their likeness? Thinking deeply seems to only produce a constant emotional crisis unresolvable by the current landscape of America's divisive politics and her divisive people.

Why is it that; the short-sighted, the cognitively lazy, and the unintelligible assume power over all others? Is it only when peace is abundant? Do these villains of critical perspective exist because weakness grows like a weed when diligence is lacking when the strong cannot be bothered, or are they not needed to prevent such an atrocity? Are most people too preoccupied with distractions to stop it from happening? Is it the necessities of survival that interrupt the ability to prevent these consequences from occurring because we are all too busy? Will it always be too little too late to stop weak leadership from assuming these positions?

It seems to be the case that those who encourage divisiveness are here out of some consequence. To the detriment of compromise and peace, these divisive actors seem unable to empathize with any identity or viewpoint originating outside of their likeness. Despite its form or position in society, a stance against compromise always has the same degree of potency. Hopelessness can invade civilizations at any time, but when the detrimental actions of the many create a rift in peaceful coexistence, it seems to be magnified in the hearts of those who want to prevent such a stain on history.

---

[8] A reference to an upward and outward growth pattern of intellectual thought by society and those represented by the applicable or measured timeline

It is the responsibility of all to care for and nurture peace. Do not be inconsiderate or callous in caring for others or their differences. It is a wise and fruitful endeavor to practice tolerance to aid in preventing and eradicating hate. Hate can only control when it is allowed to do so by those who have the power to prevent it. And this hate will give influence to an illusion of correctness.

These fictitious controlling arms are created by the powerful, and the masses have zero choices but to be a part of it, play a part in it, and agree that it is the best way, or be branded an insurrectionist and a traitor. Politicians, the government, and a select few business owners control the masses through the media's absence of truth and unconscious influence.

They can accomplish this by convincing people they do not have the resources necessary to change the power dynamic or alter the status quo, although history will show and prove otherwise. Still, those with influence do what they do best—control the masses, ignoring what should be done by doing what benefits them the most. It is all done for the sake of self-preservation, self-dealing, and self-enriching. In addition to creating and protecting a system that benefits themselves, they also create an echo chamber among their subjects while degrading those who are not willing to step into the vacuum.

Criticizing, further dividing, and even encouraging the occasional occurrence of civil unrest or even an accompanying violent act. Although they walk it back under the guise of their words being taken out of context or that it was a misunderstanding arising due to the weaponization of their words by their enemies. And in the event that it must be defended legally, the 1st Amendment offers excellent protection to idiots and the words they utter. It also creates a campaign questioning what should be protected under free speech by the opponents of who said what.

The people who understand this are most likely involved with influencing and convincing others to not only be a part of a system that is broken but emphasize that protecting the system is essential and that it should be carried out through the adoption of whatever half-truth required to preserve the status quo. Of course, the same people are responsible for countless inequities and other life-altering events, but the problem we face as a people seeking equity can be contrasted to those faced by those seeking to maintain power and promulgate division. We are so divided that our ideology becomes the enemy, not the individuals with influence who make our society toxic; they just weaponize it through opportunity.

The sheep are many and are surrounded by vicious predators disguised as competent herders. They have become tyrants who will never relinquish power unless it is taken by them by force. The two-party political system in America is the controlling entity and props itself up by preventing any outside independent voices from being heard. They control the system, and the money and will prevent any type of alternative from removing them from power. Or is it the puppet masters controlling them? Whatever it is, it is killing the American dream by not allowing her people to be free to choose independent thought over partisan interests. This keeps the power dynamic in the hands of those whose coffers are filled with gold.

And people willingly give them control forever, preventing any real substantial change. These parties divide and pit Americans and the world against each other. It is killing us all. Our problems, divisions, the cause, and the consequences of what is occurring are worth more to them than the solution is to us. The people have power, the people have control, and the people are responsible for the change. In addition, they are also responsible for what is allowed, tolerated, and continued.

It is sickening to observe what people have grown accustomed to and the level of acceptance they have resigned themselves to regarding the cycle of rot and decay that is paraded in the faces of the innocent. We are all innocent, and we are all victims. We, the people, should remain substantially higher in value and importance than a profit margin or an entity designed to control. We are the ones who are victims, those who are raped of their dignity as the wealth gap increases growing out of control. We are the ones who are victims, those who are without justice when corruption assumes a standard. We are the ones who are persecuted and made into an enemy for no reason. Those who have power are creating victims in a society built to prevent such atrocities from ever occurring.

The right props up the rich, and the left props up the lazy, but they both prop up each other because they consist of both. If either party would learn to stand for those who want to live in peace and expect others to be held to the same standard of accountability, we all could prosper together; united. Ideas and beliefs must overlap, or representation without purpose creates division with purpose.

Remove party lines and remove the problem. America has and always will be independent; her citizens somehow were brainwashed to believe differently. Americans are the keepers of peace; Americans are the protectors of the vulnerable; Americans are those who must stay vigilant against internal corruption.

It is us and only us; we have the power to rise against ignorance to shut down the injustices of the system our politicians strengthen. Instead, Americans are losing their chance as the government is getting too powerful, and the American people are too divided. Americans are losing their privacy; Americans are losing their freedom; Americans are losing their liberty.

Make no mistake, the future will require a revolution to rectify the corruption of the past. It is simple; inflict change at all costs. The tree of liberty must be refreshed with the blood of patriots and tyrants. Patriots and those who value freedom must remember that tyrants evolve and change their masks over time, but their actions inevitably have the same detrimental outcome—tyranny.

The fragility of true freedom has always been at the individual level and will only be able to be defended by those who understand this. If you are willing to save it, you must first be willing to see it. Do not falter, do not be blinded by the illusion of competency when it is nothing more than mere arrogance. The powerful will always prevent you from seeing the truth. We all must defend freedom in addition to our daily lives. This is non-negotiable. Freedom has a cost that is far less than what the absence of freedom would cost. We all have a duty and responsibility as citizens of this great Nation. If you are unwilling to accept the duties required of you as a citizen, you are unworthy of enjoying those rights reserved for the citizens of this great nation.

The downfall of America will be a lack of shared efficacy as we draw lines and categorize people in likeness. This will do nothing but create a purity test only your type can belong to. Motivated by hate and selfishness, people effectively remove any hope of a sustainable free society as those different from them can never truly belong. Human beings are flawed creatures and may never be able to coexist. But what if they never knew how? What if the instructions were never given to society? This sounds pretty absurd as the teachings of many religions have always spoken of loving thy neighbor. Even if one is not religious, it is hard to argue against the golden rule.

Mutual respect, dignity, and understanding without a hypocritical double standard are what can mend the divide people are all responsible for in this wonderful Nation and even the world. If people become a bit more selfless, the future may mend what was and continues to be broken.

What society does next will change the world. What direction people decide to embark on will guide society to a determinative outcome or a successful resolution. Is it a continued course focused solely on a cataclysmic event forever changing and destroying the progress those before us created? Or is it a more sustainable and tolerant future?

Knowledge and ignorance occur because people will always be both knowledgeable and ignorant. I am not sure this will ever change. All the available knowledge is overwhelmingly exhausting, especially when each competing idea attacks the other. What is true when a person does not find either side convincing? How can any person be correct, or an idea be true when the same problems seem to never disappear? Economics, race, religion, and government create the same cycle of destruction repeatedly. Is this the big ugly beast?

What I mainly learned; people use the truth to hide lies and create a system that will always fail because it will always protect one and not all. However, it is necessary to continue learning so people can communicate thoughts, ideas, and beliefs because these have a chance to alter what is known or what is believed, creating change. Protecting dissent, expression, and the ability to attack ideas, not people, can remove ignorance. Even if I forget most of what I learned, I may remember a small piece, something valuable.

Even if knowledge is soon forgotten, people must continue to express themselves regardless of a competing interest finding fault in what is shared. This will create a more complete thought allowing for the ease of explaining, and eventually, the work created turns reflexive when a person is justifying their opinion or clarifying their theory to others.

This is a handy tool because ignorance can destroy peace, forever altering freedom. But ignorance is brutal to remove outside of oneself, especially when people do not see a need to seek knowledge. What happens if people know, learn, and believe lies? What happens if these lies create hate, and this hate creates more lies?

Growth must continue if we expect peace, as its existence is fleeting and always ready to implode at any moment. Division destroys while unity creates. Blaming the group rather than the individuals responsible will do nothing but push the divide deeper while encouraging and even emboldening counterproductive consequences. People will always defend their likeness even when faced with undeniable adversarial truths of such behavior or beliefs. Subjectively, it is hard to imagine they did something or anything wrong.

It may prove challenging to change, as personally, it is always hard for people to see and recognize that the world may very well have other identities, differences, or truths that are counterintuitive and actually just as important as or equal to their own. But unfortunately, close-mindedness and ignorance pave a path for more of the same.

Uncomfortable truths lead to, uncomfortable questions, which lead to the solutions to every crisis our species has faced and is responsible for. But first, people must look inward to see their own limits, selfishness, and what truths they hold onto. Failing to do this serves only to stand in the way of the eradication of ignorance.

Every group we assign likeness to includes fantastic and beautiful people, but those groups also contain the worst of our species. Therefore, a broad generalized application and assignment of responsibility for detrimental behavior must never be used strictly against identities only. This is the birthplace of hate, the destruction of tolerance, and the ending of what we very well may never be able to obtain in this world again; unity and peace through and protected by freedoms.

Or am I naive for believing that society and its members had it? Do people seek it, or is it only talked about frivolously, never allowing the possibility to coexist to ever manifest into existence? It seems society's only purpose is to quickly divide themselves into a likeness, gathering resources and power in case a conflict emerges between differences to ensure survival over all or any other. And then the conflict occurs. We hate what we are not, even though we are all the same.

I do not see race or gender when I look at someone or any other identifying features for that matter. I see people and a likeness that I am willing to die for no matter the difference. Accepting hate speech, hateful acts, and a hateful self only adds to our cancerous stew. Part of the problem may be that those who push for progress are philosophical thinkers, ideological dreamers simply trying to live and improve things in the real world. It looks good on paper but is neither realistic nor applicable. Maybe it's time for the real world to start living in a philosophical one. It is definitely time to recognize the influence of the negative kind.

America has always been united through hate because what we hate, we destroy...

# A Place for Your Thoughts:

# CHAPTER II

## *United Through Hate*

In the aftermath of the 2020 presidential election and the circus that followed, I was highly disappointed in the behavior of grown men and women acting unbecoming of what is required for sustainable peace and prosperity.

What our leaders, voters, and citizens exhibited were completely unacceptable and detrimental to our cohesive unity. Many thoughts appeared simultaneously in my mind. Most were what I considered the beginning of the end and what that means for a society in denial.

It also made it possible to reflect on the consequential behaviors I have witnessed my entire life. I was angry because the ones who need to represent a standard, the people who must maintain decorum, and those who protect the truth were failing and have been since I could remember. Where should I seek guidance in a world without leadership? Where are the people who stand and fight for decency, the truth, a standard of leadership no matter the cost? What happened to character, integrity, and righteousness? Where are the leaders, the strong, the selfless, those I look up to? The leaders who represent greatness outside their identity and represent decency within their character—**Honorable**.

A few may exist, but they are far, and few between as the standard of blurring the line for selfishness controls the metamorphosis, turning even the most promising candidate into the monsters required to play the game. These people are now absent from society, if they ever existed at all. The positions of authority and influence are filled, but I would not follow a single one of them. I see nothing but one-America demagogues jockeying for power, stepping on whoever is in the way to achieve their selfish pursuits. Each ignores a better way simply to maintain the old way.

They do not represent the standard I hold myself to; they may not even represent a standard at all. What I believed, how I lived, and the patriotism burning in my heart was not reflected in America's leadership. This was the first time I felt alone in my life. The first time I recognized that America is no longer what she should be. I was heartbroken because the symbol I had created myself to represent was a lie. Those people I had faith in were undeserving. And my purpose, or what gave my being meaning, ideology, and admiration of my country, has been weakened.

Everything I stood for, all that is good in me, the lies I told my son, the standard I told him to represent was non-existent in the world. I was hurt and lost. I cried, cussed, and screamed at anyone in the direction of my projected anger. If a person has ever experienced a murder in their family or had a friend taken by this selfish act, that was the feeling akin to what I felt and experienced. Not the loss or heartache but more complete and better understood by the unexpected tragedy experienced. Sorrow, betrayal, and disgust. It elicits a very recognizable version of hate, especially directed at the ones who are believed to be responsible.

I was wrong for expressing my anger towards those not responsible, but the cause and creation of my anger were justified, and it finally had a face. It represented all the people who decided to divide instead of uniting, all who believed decency was unnecessary, and all who represented selfishness. I hated them and everything they stood for. I wrote a Facebook post on my wall out of anger at what my identity represented.

It read:

> The reason we are divided is because we quit being Christians.
>
> It is Christians who forgot what it was like to be human.
> It is Christians who forgot what it was like to be hated.
> It is Christians who forgot what it was like to be persecuted.
> It is Christians who forgot what it was like to be crucified.
> It is Christians who forgot what it was like to be murdered.
>
> You failed as your inconsideration of others triumphs.
> You failed as you lack decency.
> You failed our savior, you failed Jesus Christ, and you failed yourself.
> You failed because you judged while having no

authority.

You judged a scared woman, a woman who may not know what the best choice is regarding a human life. You judged a people who feel targeted because of their skin color.

You judged a people who had nothing to do with your position of life. You judged a people because they succeeded where you stopped. You judged a people for kneeling without trying to understand what they were saying.

You judged a profession for trying to serve and protect. You judged people for trying to protect their jobs. You judged people trying to protect the environment. You judged people for loving someone.

You judged people for being patriotic. You judged people for voting for the best interests of their family. You judged people for being an American. You judged the innocent.

More importantly, you judged differences. We are better than this. We are all God's creation. It is you who judged without authority, and it is you who created this divide. The enemy is not they it is we; all of us collectively as a people.

We are divided because we are the enemy. We are divided because we are selfish. We are divided because we choose to be.

It is our intolerance as a people that collapsed this Nation.

We quit being considerate of others because we quit being Christians. The system does not promote decency anymore. Society became hateful creatures angry at easily identifiable differences.

Maybe, just maybe,
decency never really existed in the first place. As people
try to prevent the collapse of society by keeping peace
so true is the opposite. Others encourage the collapse
of society by creating conflict. Which one are you?

Is anyone else watching? Do they care or at the very least recognize what is occurring? Are they blinded to the truth because it does not promote self-preservation? I was trying to appeal to someone for help or, at the very least, validate my emotions. Regardless of what it was or why I posted it. I knew what the cause was. I knew that no matter what a person believes, there is a standard of right and wrong; people choose not to care.

Knowing full well people are ignoring a standard of decency; they were doing whatever they pleased, I blamed everyone. We wanted this, and this is what shall be. If people were not willing to criticize themselves or hold themselves to a standard, I was going to do it. What is the use of a standard if we don't abide by it, reach for it, and hold others accountable when they fail to maintain such an achievable condition?

Quite a few people responded. Some called me judgmental, pot calling the kettle black, self-righteous much. Others defended me, offering encouraging words but most of the 1000+ people Facebook identifies and defines as my friends did not reply. Instead, they probably muted me or blocked my posts because they felt I used Facebook as a bulletin board of morality.

I am that guy, the one who likes to inquire into the meaning of a divisive post or propaganda being spread indiscriminately. I always found a flaw in spreading misinformation. I never understand why it is believed or, at the very least, not verified before a like or share occurs. What is more cowardly is the disinformation used by those for the exact consequences it creates. Call me crazy, but I believe the truth is essential in preventing chaos and lies are fabricated to create chaos.

The best response, the one I appreciated the most, was from a man I met by chance and connected with over good conversations.

It read:

"In terms of our collective ability to solve problems as a species, the sons of Abraham have been killing each other over possession of the Gaza Strip for the last 2000 years. I doubt that a few keyboard warriors are going to solve racism(fear) by blacking out their profile pictures on social media because it's the latest pray for Paris bs. The problem is more than skin color; it's culture, history, government, poverty, flock mentality, fear, greed, resentment, and tradition all rolled into one ugly beast that won't die until we are all blended into one ethnicity and by then people will find something else to hate about each other. The only real change that can be accomplished is at a personal level. That's my thinking on the problem/solution. Fight me!"

It gave me great joy to read yet great fear to comprehend. I still today disagree with him, and his answer made me angry. Not because he said anything untrue, nor is his answer in opposition to what I believe; it is more of a belief that we all can change together. But if he is right, why haven't people been trying to figure out why it occurs and how it occurs to prevent it from occurring? Why are we unable to stop it from occurring? What is preventing us from solving the issue of the big ugly beast he described?

It is likely because people are instructed only to focus on what they can change. After all, the more important the endeavor, the harder it becomes, and the less likely it is to occur. But does that not by itself make the pursuit that much more important? I believe it does. I think we can prevent anything we choose to because we can change anything we choose to.

He invited me to engage in his understanding of life. What I realized, the system, no matter what a person believes to be true, is broken. The big ugly beast is winning, and it is using hate as a weapon. The standard of decency in the controlling arms of society has long been forgotten if it ever existed in the first place.

Hate must be eradicated before anything can be rendered sustainable and for what is important to have meaning. However, what is important represents value, and at times value has no worth complicating or exacerbating what prevents the destruction of hate. Value represents the standard of what is sought, not the worth contained. Therefore, I am always up for a good fight, especially if it means the protection of something I value as I know it has worth.

This is my identity, what I believe, and who I am:

I am not white—I had no choice in that.
I am not a male—I had no choice in that.
I am not hetero-sexual—I had no choice that.
I am not American—I had no choice in that.

I am however a combination of those things reflective of my decisions.

I chose to be a patriot—A defender of freedom.
I chose to be a soldier—A defender of the weak.
I chose to be a Christian—A defender of righteousness.
I chose to be honest—A defender of the truth.
I chose to be tolerant—A defender of peace.

Because I choose these things, these are what I represent. These are what define me. And these are my convictions—the meaning I encompass that accurately defines me. So how can the things I represent make people angry or even hate me? Do their beliefs, experiences in life, and definitions of words change the meaning of what I represent? Do they recognize a problem with those identities I cannot alter? Do they see something I do not? Does my likeness or what I represent disgust them, allowing them to hate me? Is it hate for no reason?

I am not sure I can explain what people think when they hate or what motivates them to hate. I tried to figure it out. To be honest, I even allowed people to hate by permitting them to because hate is justified and honestly needed in some cases. This type of hate is more of a reactive variation not accompanied by an emotion but more of a need in the sense of survival. But maybe that is what all hate is, survival.

However, I cannot explain or conclude that hate is anything other than a choice. We all fail, motivated by a selfish quest used to apply an inaccurate account of what people do or do not represent. It is a cycle that is destined to be repeated because all the knowledge in the world will not deter the wicked, the evil, or the willing. Their intent, their desire, and their need to target are more potent than their need to see, understand, to empathize.

What these vile people represent is in no way associated with the truth. Creating and sowing destruction because they want to use language for that purpose—words to divide and words to deceive. It is odd when people use words and terms to describe things and identify things they cannot comprehend or are inappropriately applying meaning to. It is equally bizarre but more troublesome when people become attached to a triggered emotional response disconnected from reality to create hostility via that meaning. Society is full of people repeating half-truths, spreading untrue theories, and forcing differences to hate one another.

One of the biggest problems occurs when the group or the group's identity is silent, relating to indecent, toxic, or deviant behavior. This could be insulting language, discriminatory or harassing actions, or criminal conduct. One group is waiting for the other group to denounce, what they feel, needs to be denounced. But it seems as if people make excuses or ignore accountability because what if it's true? What does that say about us; more importantly—what does it say about me.

Hate is such a strong emotion—a way to describe an intense feeling against. Emotional trauma creates a cognitive response through experience, or a lesson taught from one generation to another. It is later projected and manifested through words and possible actions towards what people deem to be a threat to their existence or their happiness. But what does hate mean?

Subjectively at this moment and concerning this book, it means a need for an entire chapter because "hate" must be understood by its purpose, its value, and its worth to describe its design. The incoherent mess that follows is equally represented by the incoherent mess of what hate is. If it does not make much sense, it is because I was unable to make hate—make that much sense.

What is hate? What is hate on a personal level? What is hate on a group level? What causes this irrational/rational human emotion?

Defined by observations, this is an explanation of what it means to hate or be intolerant. It is defining hate in my own way, proving intolerance creates hate because it is valuable to people. This is what hate is and why it is so easy to participate in these forms of expression. It has a purpose but creates detrimental unity, and a cycle that once started may never end.

It forms because weak-minded people allow incompetent leaders who influence with the intent to divide.

People must be willing to define, describe and understand what terms represent by their own means through their own creation. Not distorting reality but applying firsthand experience and applicable knowledge, closely representing a logical account of the truth that can be undeniable and irrefutable as such. Do not depend on strangers to be honest. They may never apply the same truth required to understand what words, terms are, or the meaning of experiences and what they represent. People should refrain from using terms that do not accurately reference what is being described. This allows for misinterpretation and strengthens ignorance. Likewise, it may prove to be an eye-opening experience if you define yourself as well.

By using identity factors[9] a person can accurately discover what needs to be discovered. Understanding fire is hot does not occur from reading or being a recipient of information gathered by others. It is from recognizing fire as hot due to discovering this truth through firsthand experience. To be independent and possess true autonomy, it is essential to self-define and self-realize. This allows detrimental influence to remain minimal and self-discovery of truth maximized. Ignore the fear of assumed originality[10] and discover the truth for yourself. Life has meaning separate from the meaning given to it by others and must be defined by each one of us. Let your life create progressional knowledge that benefits humanity and allows personal growth.

It is important to recognize the opportunity to self-define but not get carried away by self-importance or the illusions of grandeur from an elitist mentality. Stay closely grounded in reality, protected by the critical perspective. A reality logically connected to meanings through the eyes of a child. With an inquisitive nature, a quantifiable result, and a childlike lens—seek nothing but the truth free from emotion. Listen with your eyes. This is why children represent the best of us because they have the want, the need, and the desire to discover the truth.

---

[9] Used to create self, knowledge, and truth by being stimulated with influinci in combination with the senses of design and senses of emotion

[10] The internal belief that a person's thoughts in relation to external factors are original and should be considered original

They are not covering up or altering facts to benefit their world. They want to know what is real, why it is real, for the sake of knowing real. They possess something pure, and something lost in the adult world they will eventually become a part of. They are looking for something that pushes them to know the truth, something that adults do not possess. Selfishness is what eventually destroys children and adults alike. This is why children grow up to change the world to counter the destructive behavior of adults.

When these creatures see adults acting in a way that is counter to what they have been told, their age, influence, and power later in life create the change they felt the world needed. Children feel things and are more in tune with their emotions than their aged counterparts. This is why childhood trauma is difficult to overcome. They are conditioned to be subordinate and have zero autonomy but often feel unsure what to believe.

What they experience through sight and sound with their emotions during an experience has a chance to alter perceptions and can develop empathy if they are taught such a thing. As the child grows and views the adult world through their childlike lens, they eventually demand change. Because empathy is the solution to counter selfishness, it is a way to find the truth and eradicate hate. Something we must encourage our children to do. We must condition them to be better than we are at all costs.

When using empathy, people practice patience through understanding from an individual perspective but also from the perspective of others. Practicing the consideration of empathy will not only generate a process to discover the truth but, in so doing, can create an empathetic will, strengthening the cohesive structure of society. Applying what is accurate speaks to the truth and is neither influenced by ignorance nor emotion. It limits emotions and maximizes truth. Emotion is very important but not the irrational discharge it creates. Therefore, factual accuracy is superior to the pursuit of being correct. Both represent truth, but the former destroys fallacies and can limit the emotional baggage used to instill, infuse, and inspire bigotry.

Discovering a cure for hate is the last piece of the puzzle to change the world. In doing so, respect will be reciprocal, care and consideration the norm, and equality through equity—systematic. It will occur without recognition because people will be taught the correct way to treat one another. However, it is not love that will eradicate hate. The possession of empathy can exist without love, and hate can exist with love, but hate cannot exist with empathy. That is why hate is such a big part of politics because it sows fear, the most accessible form of control.

The leaders who practice such a desperate perversion are too lazy to express any form of self-thought or are too inept at representing something substantive. It is a charade used to hide the inability to solve the problems afflicting the people they represent. Weaponizing an emotion for the sake of claiming legitimacy is not hard.

Many foolish self-proclaimed chosen ones throughout history have used this technique to gain popularity as the ease with which they can convince those who are willing grows with every broad-brush stroke used to paint an untrue generalization of the target. And when a made-up half-truth premise takes hold, it gives birth to a particular set of consequences.

Hate then is formed into a survival instinct and is maintained through our species through necessity. The self-realization of hate elicits a unique feeling. An acquiescence to hate is solely focused on the things that are not understood or on those things seen in the light of preexisting prejudices. Finally, the reason to express the desire to hate—self-preservation.

Every stereotype, which is a basis of dislikes and prejudices, waits to be purposely selected to take center stage only to reinforce what people already suspected to be true. It isn't until the majority of likeness believes it that it becomes problematic. It is not until they are told, "you need to save yourself and others like you," that it becomes dangerous. That is where the division begins and what can cause peace to end.

A reason why genuinely honest people who have good hearts are, more often than not, absent from politics; it is harder to be a fair person representing empathy than it is to be an ignorant person representing hate. Hate is easier to wield, easier to create, and has a faster emotional response than logic. They are making it the weapon of choice when seizing power or emboldening ignorance.

Recognizing hate will never end and why hate will always control is hard to swallow. By a simple half-truth and out of a motivational need or a survival instinct, humans developed hate to be stronger than love. People are fans of hate because it creates unity. Hate always controls people and their lack of free will. Hate tends to hide truths, uncomfortable ones at that.

At the start of the 2016 presidential campaign and at the end of 2020, it was clear that 1) our system is on the brink of collapsing, 2) Americans generally hate each other, and 3) it is likely that 2021 and beyond will progressively become worse. A collapse is imminent because reasonable people do not have anyone to follow. It is difficult because, even when people stand for something honorable and decent, it does not mean the person is honorable or decent, no matter the nature of intentions behind the act or the importance of the stand.

As I try to understand why or to what end, it occurs to me that society is and always has been doomed. Not because of the actions of one individual but due to what we chose to do collectively as a people; humanity created every conflict purposefully. Not that they chose this path over a more sustainable one, but the truth is—people very seldom possess the ability to see the actual consequences of their behavior and actions. More importantly and sadly, people may not care for what is different or how harmful their actions are to those differences and the peace society benefits from as a whole.

Most lack the ability to see past their selfishness, being unable to fully contemplate the limits of what they choose. Every action, every time a choice is made, a new ripple and a new result occur because people unintentionally put things in motion that they did not fully understand. The butterfly effect is a general term used to describe what I am referring to; however, it is nothing more than cognitive laziness and a choice to be as about as selfish as a person can be. This happens because all individual decisions are an impulse that does not require a deeper understanding of what may be the unintended consequences of each decision.

Furthermore, people do not care enough about those around them to form a better model of decision-making. As they choose what behavior is acceptable, it forms their self-identity represented by their group-identity. However, the process can force an internal conflict if the person is willing to be honest with themselves. This in turn, can alter detrimental behavior, but being willing and aware may prove to be too difficult for most people.

People know what behavior is considered less than or in conflict with decency. Because of this, a deviation from the standard that all reasonable people share can be understood as willful. People choose to be the worst version of themselves. Although it is rather easy to ignore what is decent for something a bit more convenient, known and trusted—something comforting even.

As people grow, they watch and observe others in their environment who influence everything they do. Their mirror neurons fire, creating what at first is an objective way to act subjectively, allowing self-discovery to slowly conform to what is known. As people assume the observed behavior is normal or acceptable, it soon becomes something more consequential. These behaviors form the subjective process of growth when people choose to create themselves, accepting whatever is presented for consumption. And it is hard to overcome being a product of your environment.

Repeatedly I see people willingly and knowingly choosing to be a lesser version of themselves. They ignore a more appropriate way to act and choose instead to violate norms society has in place to create cohesion. Why? What motivates people to be themselves, and why do people decide upon a particular choice over another one? I always ask myself, "What is the "purpose" behind an "individual's" "actions?""

People must have a reason why they do something. Is it motivation by an external factor others cannot see because they are blind, lazy, or too selfish to see the truth in its entirety? Are people unable to break from the cycle of bad decision-making? Are people created to be selfish as an instinctive measure of self-preservation?

On the other hand, are people so caught up in themselves that they believe they are the standard of appropriateness? Is it a gift from an unknown source that ushers in authority to criticize what is deemed subjectively inferior? Does their truth stand against anything that does not share in their likeness? Do they make decisions because they do not care enough to adopt a critical perspective before choosing? Are they eager to learn?

Is it preventable, and can anyone truly possess the authority to hold others accountable objectively to their subjective standards? Is there a person in society who people can look to for the answers representing what is clearly a correct way to live? Is it too easy and wrong to judge others? Or are people correct to pass judgment upon those who are different? Is it acceptable for people to believe others are "less than" while creating an "us versus them" type of society?

Maybe understanding motivation and the purpose of a person's decisions requires a deeper empathetic view of individual actions tied to oneself and the history of their group-identity. The willingness to view actions and only associate these acts to the individuals themselves will create a better understanding of those around us. It may also be the reason we fail as a species as we associate decisions with the group the person identifies with instead of the individual who made those decisions.

People shift blame from the individual to the category the person belongs to, the sort they dislike the most. The one that is easiest to attach enematic characteristics to, so their group-identity is strengthened. It is now clear what this group is—the enemy. The one competing existence,[11] whether it is whites, blacks, cops, gays, Muslims, Christians, Mexicans, republicans, democrats, or any other group imagined or created that we want to turn into a scapegoat. Their use of selective creation encourages grouped-isolationism[12] But also detrimental unity furthering singular progression.[13] Each lie, each fabrication, each attack destroys our Nation's cohesive structure.[14]

Our selfishness once again manifests without consideration of what will later be divisive rhetoric to make us feel better about the group we belong to. Using ignorance to misapply responsibility to achieve accountability is an odd way to seek the truth. It is unfair to force restitution upon the innocent or assign blame to a competing group for wrongs unrelated to their actions or intentions. That is not equity. That is not what people should seek; it is quite the opposite.

It is appropriate to seek justice. It is always good policy to hold others accountable and responsible for actions, but retribution will do nothing for our cause. It is a form of irrational hijacking[15] causing a forced cultural belief[16] that will destroy peace in a time we must have unity to survive.

It is no different if I were to say, "I imagine it brings a sense of relief and happiness to people when they can finally find someone to blame

---

[11] The continuing struggle and relationship of the governed participants in society

[12] A flawed belief that groups do not need each other in a diverse society. Arising as a condition associated with the failure of assimilation by minority groups and lack of acceptance by majority groups.

[13] The promotion of one identity over all others

[14] Represented by the type of unity present in citizens.

[15] A form of deceptive discourse to create and maintain detrimental unity among the population of a people

[16] An increasingly detrimental way of thinking reinforces the need for division between diversity and fracturing the cohesive structure of society

other than themselves for the consequences they are suffering. Especially when that blame reinforces a subjective truth of the ignorant sort." This ignores the truth in its entirety but establishes drawn lines of intolerance that clearly lack the required empathetic will needed for peaceful coexistences. This does nothing to help the situation only worsens the severity of the sickness inside us all, as does ignoring the truth, which all people seem to accept more and more, adding to the probability of conflict.

A hard part of life is accepting truths. Especially when those truths are detrimental to a subjective point of view, it begs the question, are we striving towards something we are incapable of achieving? Can our species create a society and respect differences, no matter how hateful? Is that not what people must do—be accepting and tolerant? Do people truly want peace? Is it possible people secretly long for chaos and violence aimed at those who are different? Does it finally give their identity legitimacy and their life purpose in a world where people have moved on from that conflict and have discovered a new purpose?

Are we motivated by what we can never have? Is it our inability to create a utopian society that pushes the bounds of what our society should look like? Do people push for an all-inclusive society, or are they only interested in including the likeness they deem acceptable? Is peace inherently a fool's quest? Are we all driven by intolerance?

These questions made me confront a dystopian conclusion; it may not be possible to live peacefully with differences. A recognition that the cycle of violence and conflict will always be our identity. One of a personal nature, owned and created by the species itself for a specific breed for a specific purpose.

Suppose people cannot get along with those they share the most likeness with. How can we ever eradicate selfishness and hate to become a better version of ourselves, or society for that matter—at the very least, respect those who are different? People's selfishness and the need for acceptance in the group forces people to choose irrelevancies in a world filled with vital similarities.

As an example, what identities are truly important? Who are people in general? Are they their race, religion, gender, or sexual orientation? Are they a citizen of the country they reside in? Are they a direct reflection of the amount of money they make or the profession they are a part of?

Is that the value people possess? Or is it just a costume people wear to create a sense of self-worth and self-importance by using achievements to separate themselves from those considered to belong to a lower class? Are these superficial tags mere examples of identities people seek for the privilege of belonging to a group? What should be considered higher value, identities people cannot choose or the ones they can?

These are questions that can only be answered and understood by the person required to respond. An internal reflection will give the proper understanding of truth. But when influencing factors give people the opportunity to choose the identity they seek, others may never comprehend their decision as rational. The influinci[17] present in society can form a dangerous reality, one that is often filled with half-truths or none at all.

Comprehension of actions and choices is limited to the individual choosing. It is not grasped by or available to spectators. People may never understand why a person feels the way they do or why they choose A over B. Nevertheless, pleasing the group or identity we want to belong to, or an ideology over what is decent may be the motivating factor of all selfishness. Selfishness will always control even if decisions are made as a group.

Justifying a group's behavior or their bad actions and accepting whatever they do for cohesiveness amongst members will eventually create enemies out of those who are not like them. Societal self-preservation is a product of this behavior.[18] This is the inferiority cycle[19] used to target people who are different by promoting hate to strengthen one identity by reinforcing the enemy through internalization.

The group gives identities strength and legitimacy yet can also destroy credibility. An individual's bad behavior creates unnecessary consequences for the group. Because of this a very illogical phenomenon called detrimental tolerance[20] occurs, creating a never-ending cycle of defending the indefensible. Not only are people unwilling to recognize their own

---

[17]Stimulating factors influencing growth

[18] The decision to survive with those who represent likeness the most. A point in history always presents itself for self-preservation

[19] An internal group identity belief used to discredit another group identity

[20] Allowing behavior to occur within a group that is not and would not be tolerated but for shared likeness.

faults, but they also very often let others around them act in ways unbecoming of decency. Why do people fail to criticize those within the group yet defend an attack from people who do not share likeness even though the criticism is more than deserving? Social group-identity sensory blindness[21] prevents accountability and is a catalyst that destroys peace.

The selfishness to avoid conflict by ignoring the truth when weighed harshly against the ones closest to us has created an alternate reality. This encourages the removal of logic just so people can keep peace in something they can control; to balance what they cannot control by creating the habit of defending the indefensible simply because an attack on their group is an attack on their identity. People make excuses for those they know, act like, look like, or support, allowing them to be the worst versions of themselves.

Think about the people in your life who say they love you and those you choose to be around in your daily routine. To be more specific, your family and close friends or co-workers, for that matter. The people you love and choose to associate with are the same people you secretly know to be flawed, but you accept them anyway, no matter the consequences. Remove all prior knowledge and history with those closest to you and allow for an objective view of those in your life.

Do your family ties or intimacy with those people around you create and promote the growth of ignorance and tolerance for behavior that should be unacceptable? Ask yourself, "Would the choices and beliefs of those individuals be acceptable to you if you were to remove the bind that ties you together?"

In other words, would you be associated with those people if not for history, shared likeness, or the blood in your veins? Or is this the reason their behavior is tolerated? I imagine it is easier to be in a relationship with people when less is known about them and a lot easier when tolerance for detrimental behavior is allowed because you know them.

People tend to make excuses for those around them because we decided to use love to justify accepting lesser versions of one another. And it may very well be true that preventing conflict by ignoring faults brings a

---

[21] A type of sensory blindness to behaviors, actions, and words used to encourage detrimental tolerance.

type of peace the alternative would destroy. This short-sighted removal of conflict destroys the standard of what can be viewed as being universally decent.

But, when it is something so fundamentally egregious, people draw the line. I can finally understand the Civil War idiom "Brother vs. Brother," as it speaks to the limit of what people are willing to accept and the means by which people are willing to seek, to destroy what they hate. At that moment, people finally remove respect, and what was used to keep the peace was thrown away, justifying conflict. A decision to ignore peace because it may never be achievable allows for a different type of society to emerge. People will use hate to justify all actions to eliminate differences— justifying the means of whatever end is sought.

All civilizations and societies eventually break down and are destroyed by our inability to coexist. It is about to occur once again because the cause or issue is an incurable disease carried by all people. It is the human species' ability to hate, and we are without an antidote. Collectively, the human species has always created more harm than good. People must rely on strangers and the expectation that they will do the right thing, hoping they embrace a resemblance of kindness or decency, yet it never really materializes.

Sure, society and history are littered with spurts of greatness, but a lack of shared efficacy and intolerance towards visual differences confines sustainable growth. People all are literally stuck in their skin and cannot, no matter how hard they fight it, ever change. They are bound by their past and limited by their identities.

People cannot fight for one another as their identities limit what they can accomplish. What is viewed and measured differently must represent a more accurate understanding of character. Acceptance through the content of this cognitive identity defined by intelligence without considering what people look like will allow the human species to achieve sustainable peace.

People lose themselves because their realities and lives are never really in their own hands. Simply put, our species craves acceptance through similarities ignoring faults for happiness. They seek likeness to gain acceptance to avoid loneliness. This allows for the tolerance of detrimental behavior by removing accountability to create cohesiveness. This is how peace is destroyed. Eventually, the cost of the consequences comes due.

When viewing history, it is beneficial to look at the plight of human existence as a cycle. History has a way of repeating itself, and in no way, shape, or form, can the consequential results be altered. Does it not seem strange that even in societies where all people are similar in every way, our species still finds a way to hate one another and create conflict?

People crave conflict. They even seek it within their own likeness. White people hate white people, black people hate black people, Asians hate Asians, males hate males, women hate women, Christians hate Christians, and Muslims hate Muslims, so on and so forth. It seems the problem and the "purpose" of such behavior are in people's DNA. They cannot alter what they cannot control. Because of this, they subconsciously remove respect which ultimately leads to the demise of whatever society the species belongs to in its specific timeline.

The timeline for such a catastrophic change is not measured by a single human lifetime. Instead, it is measured by peace in whatever society is governing most of the world at the time. Peace comes to an end because a division between the ruling parties becomes too much to overcome, and eventually, the peace contained within the timeline runs its course.

It is very hard for people to even comprehend or see the end coming as most are too blinded by a misconception that their way of life cannot be altered. And most people are extremely ignorant to history's perversion of power that is never balanced but shaped by the intoxication of control and self-importance.

It may be by choice, accident, or it may be a coping mechanism that our species has to prevent mass suicide. It could be the incompetency of some people or just the inability to see it. Undoubtedly, it somewhat can be attributed to the fact human beings are creatures of necessity, only doing what is required to survive and never altering behaviors until they are without choice.

Whatever it may be, it makes the species weaker than it should be. The inability to adapt and perceive threats leads to the extinction of people and the eventual collapse of whatever society those who fail to adapt belong to. It is more difficult to be a part of such a societal altering shift when you not only recognize it is occurring but are watching it unfold before your eyes and are powerless to stop it from consuming everything around you. All you want is for those in power to stand for what is fair. Defending what is right and to die preventing the demise of the society you are a part of; however, they choose instead to destroy it.

The cataclysmic consequences do not have the same feeling as reading about it in history books. Reading about the rise of Hitler is very different from experiencing the rise of Hitler. It is not an overnight thing; it is a cancer that consumes the hearts of willing occurring over years, if not decades.

Watching life-altering events unfold in real-time is an extremely difficult thing to be a part of and something emotionally, mentally, and physically devastating, as anyone who actually lived during the last decade up to 2021 can attest to. What occurs next, if only consumed by an author's pen, will surely be consumed and understood differently than those who were unfortunate enough to live through such a destructive time.

People are under the impression that as technology advances and the calendar year passes into a larger number, people are somehow getting better and will always create progress as a species. To be completely honest, I, too, am naïve in believing that people have the ability to continue to progress and evolve into something greater than what we are currently or presently, regardless of the timeline our species resides.

Are we more than what we achieve and seek to be? Are people less than or greater than those around them by default? Is common hate for one another what controls society? Is this what society represents? Is this the similarity that will define people? If it is, at least people have something in common.

Should people hate their skin color because they are taught to hate the shade of it? Should people hate their gender because they are taught it is inferior or toxic? Should people hate their sexual orientation because it is wrong and not an acceptable identity, only an urge? Should people hate their faith because people pray to a different God, or do those who believe in science call it an illusion? Should I hate being an American because this Nation is the cause of much harm internally and externally? Should I hate my profession because some of my colleagues are bad?

As people try to create better versions of themselves, one that is more accepting of differences, they may realize that those differences do not respect them and will never accept them because they are taught to hate them. How do such foolish people armed with complete ignorance gain legitimacy to influence such a hateful arsenal? Is this what leaders wish to encourage, thoughts of inequality, self-hate, and inferiority? Should people hate themselves because they are told to do so?

These questions are inherently wrong and created from the minds of the innocent because those with hateful intent are trying to convince strangers of a truth that is neither accurate nor tolerant. Yet ignorance is promoted and given legitimacy by people who seem more concerned about preserving the status-quo and groupthink than the critical perspective. Should a group of highly educated, extremely enlightened, and independently overly qualified experts control the narrative because they make others fearful of dissent? Does creating your best self, depend on the approval of tyrants with platforms?

The truth of what it is to be human, the influences that control autonomy through fear may not allow a person to grow. It takes too much work individually to create a better version of oneself. Even trying will eventually make you hate everyone you have ever known and them hating you as well. Creating a better version of yourself will only make you alone in the world as no one else cares to remove their limits with you.

Ignorance is bliss, as understanding is lonesome. What becomes of your sanity if you understand what causes the issues but are powerless to stop the inevitable? Are people destined to become what they hate? Can they stop the big ugly beast within from eating them alive or prevent the eternal rot from the cancerous reality they all are a part of? What is the standard of being a person of faith? What is the standard of being an American? What is the measure of being a decent human being? Is it self-righteous to try to be better, wanting a better version of yourself, one you can be proud of? But, on the other hand, does any of that really matter?

Should people pursue a life of decency to be better? Is it only for the individual? Is this the lesson to beat insanity? Ignore the quest to be better, just to feel somewhat normal again? Do people care about others and their attempt to self-improve? Is it worth trying when people look down upon those who practice a life of virtue and integrity because they feel attacked, as attempts of goodness are offensive to their lack thereof? Being a better person will draw the attention of others, as representing the standard of decency will create a standoffish response that adds friction even in the most intimate of relationships.

We have standards, and we all know what these standards are, yet people are not willing to hold themselves to the same standard they hold others to. Do as I say, not as I do. To be honest, people are running around making decisions that have consequences that they cannot comprehend because they are too incompetent to do so. On the other hand, they may not care, which is even more worrisome.

All facts and decisions of logic must reconcile if they do not, how are people in positions of authority ok with their decisions? I have grown tired of people with influence and power fighting with one another, encouraging negative behavior from those they represent. I am so tired of people creating more issues in a world that is already plagued with so many.

Why are we not able to move forward, and what creates the inability to be better? We know what it is; it is us. We choose to be what we are, and we somehow believe that we need not be apologetic for our hurtful words and actions towards others. The means never justify the end, but we always manage to make an exception.

Somehow, we convinced ourselves to let dead people control those who are alive and allow their ignorance to influence the very structure we are a part of, which they had zero chance of understanding because the world has evolved progressively without them in it. At what point do we realize that the past is to blame because we are the cause and the root of all evil? How much more conflict must we create in the world, forcing us to remember why we do not need conflict and why we do not want it?

Alternatively, is conflict inevitable and a needed reminder of the pure evil humans are capable of? Do we get so accustomed to peace that we forget that conflict is real and is eventually needed to create peace once again? If people were graded objectively, we would fail. It is our selfishness that creates hate. It is our selfishness that creates conflict. And it will be our selfishness that will always destroy the good in others. That is what hate does. It removes the ability for personal growth and can forever inhibit those from ever wanting to try.

If the identity that people are trying to overcome is always in conflict with who they are, can they ever grow? Are they always limited by who they are? Is it even possible to grow and mature while the world around you chooses not to? Suppose a person is taught that the very thing preventing them from obtaining a better life is the differences between others and what that group represents. What is the purpose of caring as these falsities create societal conflict for which a cure does not exist?

If everything people are, and everything they represent is the root cause of the world's problems, and their existence prevents people who are different from having a great life, what is the purpose of living? Their existence, what they stand for, what they represent, is taught as a reminder to people as the reason, the direct cause, of what is creating hardships for them. Their very presence makes people sick and is blamed for all problems in the world. Why does that sound familiar?

Human civilizations have played this game over and over, have they not? What happens when the truth eventually becomes; their likeness is the only thing standing in the way of my happiness, and it must be removed? If people are taught the hardships in their lives are caused by a group of people or an idea, they will always have reservations about those individuals or things. They will eventually grow to hate what is perceived as their enemy even if evidence to the contrary is available.

If you treat your enemy as an enemy, they will always and forever remain your enemy. This cycle of hate leads to conflict, which leads to war, which leads to the extermination of what causes the conflict. All because people denied their counterparts the respect they deserved. Conflict cannot result in anything other than hate, as the understanding and repeated intolerance for differences will only reinforce the absurdities of logically flawed people.

People must view motivations of actions as a direct reflection of an individual instead of a generalized understanding used to associate blame with a group of people or an ideological belief. However, the world is never short on ignorant people enticing other ignorant people, each creating hate because an ignorant person has half the truth. Influential people willingly ignore the logic that can create calm. The decisions and poor choices selected instead create more deceit, only to further divide a people by grouping similarities into pockets of control.

And isn't that what politics represent—An attempt to collect power to minimize the effectiveness of people's perceived enemies and to maximize the influence within people's likeness to create more hate of differences? They want to control society because they represent a superior way. Is this what life has always been? The pursuit and eventual acquisition of power by those who are willing to bend the rules as they destroy those who are different from them.

The motivation for people's choices is always selfishness. It is not until our species recognizes this and makes decisions based solely on what is best for the common good that anything will matter. Maybe the common good is counterintuitive to self-preservation. We cannot kill ourselves by simply holding our breath. Maybe people are equally powerless from collectively growing as a species because they simply cannot fight their instincts. Survival requires the creation of hate due to selfishness by operating as designed.

One group or person extends kindness to another while the other group or person extends hate. The friction occurring is from our differences. It is caused by a false belief that people somehow owe something to one another, or they simply have a duty to be kind to one another. Maybe people's desire to be kind to differences hurts society's cohesive structure.

Is diversity what causes issues? Is that what is preventing togetherness and tolerance for others. To whom do we owe that standard, and how has that person or idea earned influence in our lives? Conflict is as natural to our species as the need to eat. Peace is simply the pause between consecutive conflicts. So, I guess what I am saying is, why try? To what end? What if happiness is obtained by simply ignoring our differences, and a failure to do so creates a hateful world riddled with conflict?

But, what if hate is happiness? It seems that those before us who we defined as the enemy or unscrupulous people were able to live an enjoyable life. Screaming and informing people that they are on the wrong side of history is a strange way to promote tolerance, is it not? Even more of a twist, how do they know what history has decided? But I digress.

Still, today those who should be nothing are usually well off because of the hate and division they create. Whether it is a politician using explosive rhetoric encouraging hate for differences, the KKK marching down the streets to protest their grievances, or an American who is given a platform by the media celebrating the murder of a police officer because he's had enough; including the Americans who are anti-American complaining about freedoms given by a nation as each of these people burn the American flag and scream death to America—these people seem to be happy.

I have long believed that given the chance, people will do the right thing; however, that may not be the case. A quick review of history will reveal quite the opposite. If a person was so inclined and decided to allow themselves to think deeply enough, they would be able to elicit a feeling of guilt and shame.

Guilt and shame for recognizing how people justify the mistreatment of those who are different. Disgust as others rape and enslave a people because they had the power to do so. Anger and rage for people who were murdered and robbed of their life simply for selfishness. Confusion, when their likeness is attacked, as those who are to blame for the atrocities are long since dead.

Is it fear that prevents the much-needed change from occurring? Is it self-preservation that prevents us from becoming more than the group we belong to? Is it the want to maintain the status quo to not disturb the group's cohesiveness we share? Maybe it is the fear of a lonely existence. The recognition that once a person can criticize themselves, they can criticize others like them. Doing this will create separation from likeness, making it so that people belong nowhere.

A universal truth does exist, and it exists outside whatever meaningless group people belong to. People seek conflict because they seek likeness, as this likeness is recognized and used as an incubator to create more hate. Our decisions, our purpose, are to create hate for the differences around us. This gives groups a reason to believe life would have been better if not and but for the existence of others.

A way to preserve and secure peace amongst similarities, hoping they can hate others instead of themselves. People can bury many hurtful truths about themselves and their group when they are called on to defend the ones they look like or those who think like them. They quickly acknowledge and dismiss the truth, all so they can justify their existence against the attack of others. They blame others and their differences for shortcomings. This mindset, this belief, all it can accomplish, all this can create is more hate; more ignorant people with ignorant beliefs, defending their ignorant existence.

This allows us not to have conflict with ourselves. The recognition of acceptance of others allows us to feel good and creates a group of people who will never grow because they can never recognize the decision, the choices, or the people they should hate; are themselves.

But the truth is too much at times for people to acknowledge. It is too much for people to recognize. It is a lot easier to accept the lesser version of whatever group they belong to rather than changing their selfish ways. Ignorance is easy as people do not need to take any further action. They, therefore, accept a make-believe reality that creates a simpler version of their lives. The longer people tell and repeat a lie, the more truth it contains.

It would seem to make logical sense that a society as advanced as what is represented modernly would be able to solve the world's problems rather easily and, in fact, achieve a resemblance of a utopian society. However, refusing to accept the need to change fundamentally as an individual will always prevent progress and the much-needed growth our species needs. This is moral bankruptcy.

Our pursuit of making a one-America has clouded the judgment of all people who have influence and created an echo chamber of cancerous decision-making. This posture has affected all aspects of human interaction contained in our society. Examples are plentiful, and a person need not look any further than the current state of this Nation.

Somehow ignorance and people who do not exhibit the minimum standard of decency have infiltrated the system posing as leaders. As they inflict their will on people and ignore the purpose of their position, they somehow amass excess wealth, creating a disconnect from those they represent, which equates to a more significant divide. The people put in positions of authority and trust cannot adequately represent those they must. If it is equity people seek, those they elect are incapable of grasping such a concept.

But they pat themselves on the back for doing an execrable job by creating a system that takes from those who work and gives to the ones who will not. People look the other way even though they know the system is riddled with corruption and abuse because it satisfies the vanity call to be famous, but more importantly, it yields votes to retain power. They call out others who do not wish to help those in need. They call them heartless and unite resistance against them and their differences. They scream as loudly as possible, calling these individuals enemies and enemies they will always remain. This behavior creates votes in a fraudulent system, only allowing the worst of us to wield power.

This is not to say people should limit growth by abstaining from pursuing a more equitable system. On the contrary, agreeing upon a controlling mechanism to create equity is a needed pursuit, but at what cost are people allowing personal convictions to manifest as irrefutable truths and forced rules for others to follow? This seems counterintuitive to the Constitution and the freedom of liberties that occur naturally. It is also at the detriment of others and to be honest the detriment of differences contained in a free society as a whole. As an American, I hate our status quo and have become rather upset at how things are.

The elected leaders, those few who can make a more equitable society, continue to divide people on purpose. Gaslighting all who are willing to consume the words of whatever half-truth they share. People allow leaders to remain in a position they should not hold. But the faithful continue to believe and support those in office by voting for the same hateful rhetoric. It is irrelevant where it comes from or the people it targets. They all represent the same incompetency that supports their America.

It is allowed because people's memories are tied to what is most recent or an incomplete picture only containing current events. This flawed perception, disconnected from what actually took place in the past, creates loyalty. They forget what the politicians in office did in the years prior or the legislative sessions of the past. Even the previous elections' antics have long since been forgotten. People believe "it will be different because it's a new election cycle," and their hopes are high.

Yet, their good intentions in voting for the status quo end up costing so much more. They fail to see a person's greatest weakness and fault; we are human. Everything we touch is subject to corruption and abuse, as the consequences to deter such action seem to be tolled as people continue to make excuses for those they love, those with who they share a likeness, or those they voted for.

As they justify the behavior of others who support them or look like them, the ones they love become a lesser version of themselves. People slowly abandon everything that makes it possible for us to tolerate each other's differences. The respect people once shared is replaced with an emotion, a very specific emotion. And this emotion is always directed at the source of the perceived threat.

This, in turn, creates a deeper divide amongst our differences. Especially from those who do not reap the benefits from those in power, as this lack of representation creates the continuation of hate against those who do have representation. Eventually, an ending occurs as those who are powerful seek to destroy those who are without because they believe the cause of the world's problems is in fact, those who are different.

And those differences are the only things in the way of the ability to maintain this control, have continued power, and create rules that benefit their similarities over those who look different or live different, allowing perception of enematic characteristics to creep in.

Differences create strength in one group and weakness in the other. It seems a solution to our problems can and will never be obtained because we choose not to actively seek it. Instead, we create emptiness and a void in our hearts as it takes too much mental work to view others as equals because someone we trusted told us not to.

"Those with differences are the enemy." These are the words of fools who divide instead of uniting. These are the words of sociopaths, who crave instability as long as their differences are in power. Those with influence said, "Anyone who disagrees with us is counterintuitive to America's purpose and the reason why the pursuit of a utopian society can never start." "These people are bad, and you must not trust them." "These people are the enemy." "These people are the enemy because we say they are the enemy, and if you do not agree with us, you are the enemy."

I hate living in a society that thinks like this. I hate living beside people who think like this. I hate having an opinion based on facts but perceived by others as intolerance. I hate that we created an alternate reality and chose this as what our new normal should represent. I have grown rather tired of people who are supposed to be the best of us but represent the worst of us in their failed attempt to lead our great Nation. Biden is not the solution, and Trump was never the answer. To make America great again, we have to build back better—together.

Those two statements are accurate, yet people get offended when I reference such a premise. People continue to allow bad or questionable behavior to be tolerated and the protection of the status quo to become justified. Since a part of them represents a part of us, we accept a lesser version of them. People allow and are ok with the inappropriate behavior, intolerance of differences, or hate their likeness represents.

I guess the secret to happiness is finding others who share your likeness. Most Americans fail to assimilate and are drawn to segregate themselves anyway. People crave acceptance as much as they need sustenance. If you are willing to be selfish enough to hate others, you will fit right in with whatever misguided people you are hoping to be a part of.

It's a continuous toxic cycle of behavior where an individual feels offended by another and casts doubt on whether those with competing views should even have a right to be offended even though offense is for children. The same process divides and creates conflict where conflict is not logical as both sides assume their opinion is superior, using the same recipe for cooking intolerance for their people.

What gives a person a right to cast judgment upon another. Where do they obtain such authority? And why do they feel as if they have the power to do so? What is more interesting to a person who tries to stay impartial, understands all viewpoints have limits and recognizes ideas are not absolute; who is right?

It is nothing more than a subjective understanding— who is right, who is wrong, and who should I support. Honestly, an objectively correct answer can never be achieved as the issue, the cause, what we all fail to understand, is the human element. With a touch of corruption, the truth divides as much as hate does.

It begs the question, should we as a human species choose sides? Should we draw lines and create enemies with one another for the sake of cohesion, as previously discussed? Are we incapable of letting individuals be themselves? People continue to hate the differences represented in society. To what end? For what purpose do we continue this practice?

Blacks, Whites, Hispanics, Asians, poor people, rich people, cops, liberals, conservatives, republicans, or democrats (not an exhaustive list) seem to attract hate for no other reason but belonging to the group. A people are not guilty of atrocities or behaviors directed towards others. It must be measured by personal accountability alone. These are individuals who committed the egregious act. Their actions do not represent their likeness, and they lack the authority to speak on behalf of a defined people. It is their actions alone; it is they who must face the consequences of such behavior.

People must not engage in the application of generalizations with such a broad-brush stroke. Great care must be taken to refrain from such unfair and divisive behavior. It is pure laziness and lack of respect for differences when people choose to believe half-truths internally while shutting down externally. It seems hate is truly what makes the individual happy. Although by not fitting the description of preferred likeness, this establishes the start of detrimental unity in a nation full of diversity.

Society and the people within seem to be more than happy to continue hating each other. Picking sides of correctness amongst the groups they belong to creates cohesiveness and purpose. But it serves only to exclude the key that can create inclusivity. This detrimental behavior removes a chance to extend one love through understanding and empathetic tolerance. A group's intolerance and lack of respect for differences create misunderstandings. This accomplishes nothing more than the furtherance of one-sided agenda-pushing divisiveness among people and the adoption of violence as an acceptable means of solving problems. Sadly, hate unites similarities against differences to usher in a destructive form of cohesion.

Hate is difficult and intricate problem humanity will always face. Mostly because people are afraid to hold others accountable for fear of being disliked, especially from the rise of social justice and the need to represent an acceptable level of tolerant or intolerant attractiveness within their group-identities. It is not that it is wrong to practice tolerance or stand for those voiceless.

However, the people who scream the loudest usually know the least and ignore thousands of issues within their likeness, focusing their full attention on casting stones at another group, hoping to inflict damage of a superficial kind. This allows the willing to push the divide deeper, destroying hope and the cohesive structure needed to maintain peace.

Hate, it is not easy to define and even more difficult to understand. The conundrum of hate is better explained by a need. It is a selfish desire and purposefully used to tragically dismiss[22] conflicting identities[23] while assuming a moral and ethical high ground. Hate is caused by irrational hijacking[24] by applying the appropriate level of subjective cruelty.[25]

---

[22] **Tragic Dismissal**- The anti-empathetic view that competing identities, beliefs, or experiences are irrelevant and are not worthy of respect, nor is their/its existence necessary

[23] **Antonymic Interest**- Positions opposite one another on the tolerance continuum in competition for legitimacy

[24] A form of deceptive discourse to create and maintain detrimental unity among the population of a people

[25] A choice motivated by intolerance allowing for a ranked placement with the purpose to create love or hate, support or opposition, and knowledge or ignorance

Hate may truly be the key to happiness for those seeking likeness instead of diversity, at the very least, maybe survival in a diverse world. But those who share similarities are usually more hateful to likeness than differences. It is easy to hate, especially when you are taught to hate yourself.

Hate is a vile systematic survival instinct in all people. It serves a very important purpose but only because people lack empathy and follow leaders who lack this divine creation. Hate binds people together. Hate destroys the innocent. Hate is what gives strength when people are without. Hate is a choice and a decision connected deeply to half-truths allowing people to justify their selfishness. It allows people to not have to hate themselves. I guess the truth is hate can bring you happiness, but it also can destroy you and what you hate—precisely the purpose.

Maybe people must discover the science of empathy before a step towards tolerance can begin. For sure it is time to start thinking a bit differently, at a rudimentary level even. Something simple, a thought process for all, may change intolerance. It could establish empathy, allowing differences to destroy hate, minimizing the societal consequences of diversity.[26] And it could allow us to grow as a species, to meet the absolute goal of civilization.

The best way to live a life tolerant of differences is a reciprocal act mutually agreed upon by the operating systems, thought process of competing viewpoints, or mathematical computations by the people in society—all through effective use of the critical perspective.

To promote peace, people must alter the way they think and balance the equation…

---

[26] Consequences from diversity occurring in society and are reflective of or caused by competing identities, thoughts, and/or beliefs.

# A Place for Your Thoughts:

# CHAPTER III

## *A Thought Process for All*

Amerika is a unique, diverse nation with varying lifestyles and belief systems. Not one can claim a superior right over another, nor should that be tolerated, and neither should it be an acceptable creative way to virtue represent.[27] Americans are free, and so too are our choices. Even if those choices do not meet our standard of decency, although each decision we make must not encroach on or violate another's right, all people can live a life of their own design because that is what "We the People" decided together. And every American must fight for this.

We are **Strong** when we are **United** and *weak* when we are *divided*. Logic must control our leaders and our people, not emotions. Divisions are caused by weak leadership and do nothing but allow the weakest of us to assume power or influence, forcing the innocent to follow, and permitting the weakest to destroy.

America and the freedoms extended by and through the Constitution must be represented adequately to prevent adverse consequences from occurring. Sustainability through individuality and togetherness is the catalyst of freedom represented by peace, protected by the strong. People must be willing to set aside our differences and think as differently as our population base if peace is to remain constant and freedom abundant.

Caution should be taken when tyrants permit governorship of self through entities. Limiting what influences autonomy is crucial to prevent fractures in society. This is especially true of a society containing the varying freedoms guaranteed in the People's Bill of Rights and what was later added to the Constitution.

---

[27] A way to imply how moral and ethically superior a person is by demonizing competing interests.

If tolerance is what people seek, then tolerance is what people should extend. Confrontations in society between groups of people are caused by a lack of empathy and a deficiency in the application of the critical perspective, as each side operates under the same irrational absolutism theory. Respect must be reciprocal, and when it is not, animosity is. Our judgments and understanding of the world around us are always based on logical interpretations of the emotional kind.

Situational awareness with logical inclusion but without emotion is a developed skill that takes decades to master. It still represents a probable failure rate tied to human experiences as our species is not machinelike, nor are we wired like a computer with redundancies to prevent such emotional influence. It is very difficult to experience life without emotion.

People tend not to make rational decisions when they are emotional—human beings are emotional and, therefore, irrational creatures. Therefore, it is not fair, nor is it appropriate, to assume or even force people to always behave in a logical emotionless posture, and it is detrimental to the human psyche when people are criticized harshly for its occurrence.

In general, considering emotional growth and growth as a whole is an everlasting process; people must seek understanding before casting judgment. In addition, removing ignorance is the same everlasting process, if pursued. But why would we not? Our hard drives, operating systems, and the computations tied within ourselves are written heavily in irrational emotional code. It is a calculation designed to fail due to an incomplete installation of information on the hard drive. Basically, human ignorance, executed with irrational emotion—harshly judged by history and those with stones to cast.

The issue is not the people's differences, but the flawed operating system uploaded when calculating a conclusion. Although flawed is subjective and only recognized by self-identity or whatever social constructs a person belongs to. Humans create and install what is necessary to survive in relation to the perception of their world around them. It is specifically for the individual making the decision and also specific to a time or place. It is for no one else or for nowhere else.

This is why people criticize past behaviors so easily and the reason why others would have done something differently. We are as different as the many alternatives that exist in decision-making and the myriad of possible consequences of such decisions.

The consequences all people suffer are a constant in society. These will occur no matter the time or where humanity exists as people are diverse, and diversity exists uninterrupted. However, America was built; differently, its people are required to be different, and it is these differences that allowed progress, growing pains, and peace represented by all our growth in the form of empathy, equality, and equity. But how can Americans continue this process? What steps will allow peace to prosper when substantial diversity is present?

As in anything in life, it is about asking the correct questions to elicit the correct answer. But the correct questions cannot be asked until the correct issue has been identified. Is there a better way to understand human behaviors? And more importantly, can people learn to be a better version of themselves, allowing the opportunity for others to do the same?

Have you ever been proven wrong or enlightened by a new piece of information never considered? Did you accept it? Or did you double down on the ignorance because your pride would not allow your identity and your truth to be altered? Sometimes these differing expressions conflict with your truth.

Maybe someone made you ponder an alternative thought or made you think a bit longer before allowing you to defend what you know to be true. This thought, what you are thinking, is insulting and contrary to your belief system. The notion of considering the alternative idea viable goes against everything you are, everything you know, and even makes you question what you knew to be true—the feeling of warmth consuming your body— am I wrong?

The immediate clammy hands followed by a dry mouth leaves you unable to address the sound argument or counterargument a person with a competing viewpoint just made. This new information was deposited in your cognitive hard drive and created what can be likened to a stampede in your mind. Your brain tries to digest the possibility of an inferior viewpoint making sense, being superior to, or just as logical as yours.

I am not describing your state when you answer a question wrongly or misinterpreting a question on an exam. Instead, I am referring to something so life-altering that it makes you question "your" understanding of everything you know, including your personal bias. It may have been like the discovery the planets are not flat or that they do not revolve around the earth.

Something substantial, so fundamentally concrete, you can finally open your eyes to see the truth. What it must have felt like for people to realize that the earth was not flat. To fall asleep one day and wake up to a new absolute. Accepting something new that was never considered, an argument destroying fanciful concepts of what should never be or more information of what was once not understood. It allows growth and the forward progress of our species. But it must be closely connected to a natural order, never altering what we believe we should because we can.

A change that conflicts with everything a person has understood to be true is a difficult but necessary process allowing what is irrefutable [externally] to control—tolerance, acceptance, peace. These terms carry significant meaning for a diverse society. Using these developed what was required to live a life filled with diversity. It also helped society finally understand—other people and their ideas, opinions, or lifestyles are not the enemies—but cohesiveness can be lost forever, altering tolerance, acceptance, and peace.

All people are guilty of small-minded narrow-focused thoughts and beliefs at some point in their life. Something so fundamentally connected to their identity that no other alternative can exist. As we age, we are influenced by the world around us, but our exposures limit our thought processes and what we know.

The minuscule understanding of "our" world contains only what we are aware of. This creates falsities and misunderstandings of what may be wrong, right, or the notion of an inferior lifestyle. These stereotypes later turn into prejudices and, if not altered, intolerance—eventually hate. And because I know what hate is, why it exists, and how it is formed, I know the ingredients to make such an indestructible tool.

It requires animosity, intolerance, and ignorance but also a formula that is interchangeable and easily understood:

**1)** Animosity is always allowed to grow when intolerance and ignorance control the hearts of the willing.

**2)** Intolerance is always allowed to grow when animosity and ignorance control the hearts of willing.

**3)** Ignorance is always allowed to grow when animosity and intolerance control the hearts of the willing.

54

It has the same outcome no matter the order of operation because it is simple to create, simple to believe, and its effects are simple to wield. With each occurrence, it becomes more and more intoxicating, satisfying the addiction of the user. And as the user abuses such a devastating drug, it becomes harder to get clean because the distortion of truth is too great to overcome. It infects, destroys, and removes our humanity, forever assigning animosity and intolerance to those we choose to hate because ignorance is easy. But the most crucial effect the hate produces; it allows those who are poisoned to be easily controlled, manipulated, and used by the leader of whatever group they belong to.

Arguments, disagreements, and conflicts result from the lack of civil discourse, the lack of will, and the inability to care for competing interests, all protected by ignorance to promote one identity over the other. It exists over competing views, occurring as a result of and from the lack of understanding or the lack of exposure; nothing more. People tend to focus on the bad, allowing it to encompass the entire identity.

It is an attack on diversity. These consequences stem from the removal of respect, not the existence of diversity. It is a sickness, a way to permit resentment, the ending of peace fostering the desire to hate. Each person allows this disease to slowly erode harmony, eventually destroying tolerance.

The human species comes in all varieties. Each diverse group and history are littered with evidence proving they can live in peace with all others. If people respected what is different, kindness would be extended and nurtured by those who have the power to do so. People only ever see what they are looking for because what is good or bad can be found in everything.

People choose sides well before valid arguments are made based on many different factors, but the most influential is self-identity with respect to what is known or understood as controlled by their group-identity. As an example:

### "Antonymic Interests"

It is either guns in America or not.
Religion in America or not.
Abortions in America or not.

Gay marriage in America or not.

Police accountability in America or not.

Systemic racism in America or not.

Transgender people's rights in America or not.

Republican/Democrat politicians in America or not.

Not one controlling argument in the realm of current opinion, politics, or policy allows for any of these competing views to coexist or be discussed further, either proving it invalid, valid or allowing its existence to live in peace. What people choose is based on their knowledge known to be accurate or their perception of an argument based on personal bias. This identity, this belief system, is an absolute that everyone must accept or reject regardless of personal views, removing the allowance of diversion representing free thought.

All people use the same flawed logic to establish and apply whatever absolutes competing sides use to create their selfish conclusion. All sides recognize one truth as correct yet use identical intolerant logic to dismiss any alternatives. Represented by virtue signaling, the need to possess ethical or moral high ground seeks division through intolerance represented by absolutistic viewpoints.

When applying for a morally or ethically superior position, the consequential truth created enables people, as an acceptable response, to dismiss all others as unimportant or inferior to their own. Competing views often fail to recognize both sides are equally wrong and flawed from an objective standpoint. It is the recipe to create hate, and these ingredients are interchangeable and indestructible, always remaining amongst diversity uniquely designed to promote ourselves over others.

What people believe to be a truth, their truth, is subjectively correct to their point of view, objectively correct to their identity group, but in reality, is absolutely wrong as a universal truth lacking any substance philosophically because all identities are shells. If one way of life is correct, all others are incorrect; however, if all are incorrect, then all are correct. Does this premise create issues in a society filled with diversity? Should people believe everything? If there exists zero truth, why do people follow the rules? What is the conclusion?

People's truths represent their identity for their identity only. It is the truth for them and is nothing more than a learned trait, thought, or lifestyle often gifted by the cognitive rules of growth[28] without the knowledge of the receiver, applied appropriately only in the company of likeness.

Their truth is a process of learning occurring at a young age as people's exposures are strictly limited to what their "parents" deem appropriate but continue later as an adult when their exposures are limited by what "they" deem appropriate. People assign value and worth to many things.

Because what is measured changes between people, the value assigned will have a subjective rank and varying levels of legitimacy. Since what has value possesses order, it demands numbers assigned to what is represented accurately reflecting a connection to a principle; this is reflective of the legitimacy ladder[29] and where people place value on what or who matters to them.

The cognitive rules of growth govern who we are, how we think, and our decisions on a daily basis. It is not until we realize this that we will be able to understand ourselves and those around us. These are mere observations that represent or alter our understanding of the world and the people around us. These stimulations highlight the motivations behind decision-making and influence people's cognitive processes in combination with our life experiences.

This allows the rejection or acceptance of proposed lifestyles or alternatives available to be chosen by an individual or group forming their/its identity level. A child who is brought up in a household with two homosexual parents will think entirely differently on the subject of sexual orientation than a child who is raised in a heterosexual household with parents who believe quite the opposite. Both represent exposures and truths created without the consent of the child yet consequential to society in every way, creating division and conflict beginning from the cradle.

The development we are subjected to by the cognitive rules of growth destroys what could be and create what can be. These rules govern all human interconnectivity and activity. From interpersonal communication to job satisfaction, even what box people select on election night. These rules influence our day-to-day life and are key to understanding tolerance

---

[28] All experiences and exposures that create self-identity and group identity
[29] A ranking of differences in society based on their importance to an individual.

and accepting differences. Unfortunately, sometimes these rules prevent growth and understanding.

People seldom practice a lifestyle different from one they were exposed to in their childhood or what was introduced to them by someone with influence, mainly because it makes them uncomfortable, or their beliefs are so ingrained in their identity that bias will not allow it. Changes or self-applied deviations from the growth process are rare, especially when exposure to differences is not present. Individuals may add small things in addition to or change something they believe their parents or others assumed was correct.

But wholesale changes are not something people do willingly without cognitive restructuring, especially as adults. Often most adults are relatively close in lifestyle choices to prior generations in the proximity of the growth process for exposures—parents to children or guardianship of the dependent. Children are more impressionable and can be convinced of many things without a verified objective persuasive authority. To children, a parent will always be correct until the child has convinced themselves of a new truth.

The same is true for some adults if the consumed information is used to reinforce a potential bias already engrained in their identity surrounded by their current viewpoints. A typical response, reflective of the growth process, is to agree with information closely related to viewpoints already owned. Especially when consumed from a subjective authoritative source currently trusted or mirrored to contain a similar likeness—family, friends, politicians, activists, media outlets.

Of course, finding examples of the consequences of groupthink and confirmation bias in the age of social media is relatively easy. People consume what is available, offering the least path of resistance. Who would have guessed imbeciles and floods have so much in common? Both mindlessly destroy anything in their way. Society has reached a critical mass from the instantaneous consumption of misinformation and the intentional dissemination of disinformation which has prevented quality civil discourse or stopped it altogether.

People will agree with any information circulated by likeness, encouraged through similarity, and referenced against a common threat. Half-truths continue to be digested and spread at an alarming rate. These developments serve zero purposes except to create additional hardships for differences to coexist while further dividing a people by likeness.

The friction caused in society, whether past, present, or future, is not the individual differences in groups. It is the need, the want, of whatever controlling group possesses power, influence, and the means to divide. These are consequences of diversity and are used to remove the legitimacy or existence of competing viewpoints altogether. Differences do not create problems in society; it is the endeavor to attain power that divides.

Because of this, civilizations and their innocent members are constantly experiencing the birth of intolerance and failed leadership of the so-called tolerant. People choose what or who to support while dismissing everything else and all others as unnecessary or irrelevant. It is nothing more than the intolerance of the tolerant, demonizing all who are different. Those who assume intellectual or moral superiority select what differences and identities are appropriate while dismissing those they find insulting ignoring decency by allowing hate to unite. A tragedy replayed in every civilization serving zero purposes.

When people face competing views, they should not judge harshly or perceive these differences as threats. Nor should people be overly critical of differences, individual choices, or lifestyles. Instead, a greater understanding of the motivations surrounding one's actions or opinions must be studied and considered, allowing dialogue to be abundant.

This is how a logical, peaceful society handles controversies and alternative thoughts. People are protected by America, regardless of the self a person chooses to be. Sometimes this is hard to understand in a world filled with villainous scrutiny[30], but we all belong.

The type of "self" individuals create is of no consequence if others agree or disagree. It is a choice of theirs and a form of expression unable to be bent by the will of those who try to force change. Influence creates self. Daily, people are literally exposed to thousands of different influinci. They pick and choose what to accept and what to reject based on many different cognitive responses. Mostly what they already know or have previously been exposed to.

---

[30] Demonizing differences to create detrimental unity

It is a choice but so much more. It is their identity; as such, it is reflective of their decisions and lifestyles, attaching a truth for the world to judge. People do things for a reason, even if the cause is strictly motivated by selfishness, and most of the time, it is. It is easy to overlook how difficult it is to accept others and their differences by failing to recognize the difficulty of evolving past our own limits. Or even change the smallest thing in life to create a beneficial outcome, such as a diet, when people fail to consider the cognitive rules of growth and the influinci engineering society's truths. Recognizing what influences a person and how successful this influence can be, allows truths to become more apparent.

Within limits, people are not always to blame for what they cannot control or change, nor are they entirely responsible for their world perceptions. Growth and the understanding of personal development take time and are constantly in conflict with the conditioning of others. Molding minds to fit whatever agenda is under consideration by those who control the media, the government, or the narrative in society is always the plan of such controlling arms in society. This type of control always interferes with peace.

The conditioning from outside forces creates hardships to personal growth, but it may also prove difficult for people to change simply because they do not feel the need to. It is tough to alter what people know to be true, and an essential requisite is a motivation at a personal level—admitting something is flawed internally.

A person must first recognize everything they are, everything they believe in, and what they know to be true; may all be wrong. Then they must commit themselves to relearn and reteaching all they know to be true. This process amounts to going to war with oneself. It is not easy to recognize that everything you believe in could be wrong or the possibility that everything you disagree with may be right. But, short of preventing criminal acts or attaching civil liability, why do people feel the need to control others or promote one belief over another? Opinions, lifestyles, and empowerment come easy to those who never sacrifice or compromise that of which they are a part of.

Is it disgust, anger, or hate that pushes people to ignore and dismiss what is different from them? Is it a defense mechanism for people to stand up and protect their identity when others fail to respect their truth or when critics attack their way of life? Does one identity enjoy the luxury of protection over another? If so, what greatness did society choose, over all others, that was worth protecting? Is there an arbitrary power that grants permission to exist? Should everything and anything always be tolerated? Is tolerance forced until the forced acceptance is unbearable?

People assume they are free, but what choices do people have control of, and do these choices advance an ideology unknown to the person choosing? Independent thought seldom exists among individuals anymore as they allow toxic influence from social engineering to overtake their problem-solving skills in deciding what is appropriate on their behalf. Is it a condition created through the influence of people and society, or is it the government deciding what others must accept without choice? But should people be manipulated to create the desired effect? If so, what desired effect is appropriate, acceptable, or advanced?

Difficulties in understanding one another outside our identities will forever exist. Therefore, we must figure out a way to counter the ease with which animosity develops when differences are expressing personal feelings on matters concerning our identities. The thought process we must adopt is relatively simple and will aid in our attempt to maintain peace.

It does not make others wrong or right to have different identities and beliefs, just circumstances out of our control that we have a connection to. People are born into a life and dealt cards not of their choosing but circumstance. I was no different; I was born an American to white American parents and a heterosexual male into a patriarchal family dynamic. This does not make me wrong or right, so true for others.

The connection we have to our people is what creates cohesion and our group identity. These connections develop into formed opinions and beliefs associated with an upbringing. People create a lifestyle reflective of their circumstances, shared values, and beliefs. Opinions influence more than the truth because subjectivity is a condition of freedom, and objectivity prevents dissension, effectively destroying autonomy. Opinions have affected positive change constructively through history, but these can also create a predisposition of intolerance through absolutism.

People's progress is limited due to their mortality and selfishness motivated by the facade of inner greatness. However, the feelings of what is appropriate and acceptable should be restricted to the lifetime of an individual who believes that such absolutes are correct because these are personal. Opinions are simply something that is usually best left with an individual and should pass with the person who created such a fantasy. Often it is so far disconnected from the truth and, consequently, a barrier to sustainable peace.

Allowing an opinion to reside in an individual only, and never a society, will promote cohesiveness. In short, things change over time from a collective of many focusing on a collaboration to discovering new truths, but a person's opinion limits such growth, and once the individual's life has ended, those absolutes should as well. As time passes, what was once understood as an absolute influenced heavily by a flawed opinion is no longer.

Progress is a process, and it is incredibly time-consuming. Ideas and beliefs passed from generation to generation eventually change throughout a time contained within a society. Society should never mirror an individual or a group when choosing the appropriate way to live a life, especially in America.

Evolution of the changes relative to society is always a dedication of work and oftentimes an outcome of generations of sacrifice representing the sought-after change. Progress is not only measured from an end, then a beginning, or a transition from not being anything to becoming something, but it also represents the process between once was and now is. It takes time and small incremental changes throughout generations to produce the desired effect. Society and people are no different. Because of this, what is in any lifetime should be celebrated at this very moment. This is the progress our people were unable to achieve in the past.

Obtaining the truth is a difficult pursuit. And the necessary change needed to comprehend such a divine creation proves to be a substantial burden on those seeking it. However, people must maintain vigilance and fight for the presence of dialogue, allowing the truth to be discovered. As long as a cognizant force remains to defend what is necessary, society will maintain a trajectory upward in its struggle to pursue the truth by progressing people to the end goal of sustainable peace.

The change required to obtain the truth comes at a high cost. It is also highly insulting as our beliefs are not kind to others. But eventually, progress occurs, creating a new truth, kindness, and acceptance. For some, it may not happen for generations within a family unit. Others are fortunate enough to generate changes by acquiring the truth in one lifetime. Unfortunately, these represent the limits of a people through the intolerance of an opinion based on irrational information.

Society must view intolerance as a problem that we can solve with empathy and the commitment to seek the truth through knowledge, allowing exposures to alter life for the better. To better understand what occurs when ignorance is present between differences, I created a continuum to aid in the visual understanding of subconscious prejudices and the implicit bias each person espouses.

These, often unknown behaviors, create tolerance, even acceptance, allowing peaceful coexistence. However, this bias can also destroy peace by means of either creating conflict or causing war and bringing about the end of a status quo. It is a means to encourage dialogue with each other and, more importantly, with yourself, preventing the zone of conflict from controlling. It is a conflict resolution tool to aid those willing to use it by discovering the causal factors creating conflict in society.

Throughout this book, most of my conclusions and beliefs are drawn or understood through this continuum. I try to remain steadfast in the zone of peace. This allows me to extend tolerance to the varying lifestyles I may come into contact with, even those I am unable to comprehend. Using this to develop a guide will address shortcomings of ignorance and hopefully highlight what people do not understand. Eventually, it will quickly become a cognitive reflex when viewing differences or attempting to understand competing interests.

The tolerance continuum's influence reflects a commitment to be factually accurate when all facets are necessary to make a conclusion. People who seek the truth are immediately drawn to the ***critical perspective***. And most likely, they engage in this problem-solving fact-finding process subconsciously.

It is something I now live by and try so often to practice. It does, at times, become hard to stay the course as differing and competing views do not extend the same courtesy. Or logically, I am sometimes unable to arrive at the same conclusion on different occasions, although my arguments are based on identical information. Nonetheless, I try to maintain this posture, often allowing logic to control instead of my emotions.

An understanding of the critical perspective is an understanding of a superior way to problem solve. It is a way in which a person can understand new or existing information by educating oneself enough to draw a **fair**, logical conclusion, inference, or self-expression concerning consumed knowledge by understanding the null hypothesis and why rejecting the alternative should be the focus as the null is undeservedly discredited just because disproving it was the target.

It is a procedural standard that allows people to prevent personal bias from consuming or influencing decisions. A control or failsafe represented as checks and balances of the personal kind. Something society's leaders should use more often when seeking accountability governing people and the differences within.

The critical perspective instructs people to look for the truth as understanding everything initiates the process culminating in knowing nothing. It offers peace to problem-solving utilizing accountability through knowledge. It also makes terrible conclusions or limits of an argument easier to spot. If a premise does not contain all the required information, then, although it may make sense, it may also be logically flawed and therefore false and untrue. This will mislead people into believing half-truths and allow such non-sense to continue to spread as misinformation and to, later on, be weaponized as disinformation. Before something is true, it must be proven not to be false.

This idea will solve the issues society faces which often create tension, verbal aggression, divisiveness, and at times violence. It highlights where an individual is in relation to knowledge, ignorance, and the level of tolerance extended for the person or idea in conflict. It also allows people to see their true selves, which can be ignorance of the bigot kind, ignorance of the imbecilic kind, or ignorance of the lacking kind.

A right or wrong interpretation of people's differences is the catalyst in society that creates the obstruction between competing views. People are different, and these differences are current, always present, and will continue to exist into the foreseeable future. The job of modern and future societies is to manage these differences as effectively as possible with appropriately designed formulas solving what emotions destroy.

Before the tolerance continuum is used correctly, a more fair and appropriate understanding of people must occur. People are limited by many things, but another person should never be a limiting agent. The most consequential form of limitation by another person is a dismissive posture towards what they deem to be inferior, morally wrong, or applying a falsity unto them as truth. Beliefs and lifestyles, right or wrong, are introduced and often the only way people live, view, or understand the world around them. It is not to be seen as anything other than a limit to overcome. But how can people address these issues or even identify their own limits?

There is truth in writing or self-expression. A way to solve issues and promote thoughts new or foreign to what is known. Self-expression can be a subjective view while creating but an objective view while consuming. It also has the power to create not only self-actualization by discovering truths but can also offer self-critical analysis by increasing self-awareness.

Amounting to fault recognition of a personal nature and growth based on discovery. Indeed, it may lend a hand to self-discovery and personal growth, but more importantly, it can highlight the truth that sometimes people hide from themselves.

They may also be surprised to learn how offensive or hateful some thoughts may very well be. In addition, while thinking more critically, it may develop into a process of personal growth as defending a position may change their mind or highlight weaknesses to assumed valid arguments.

Self-expression can be used to give clarity and extract a better understanding of the world around them or differences that they may see flaws in, especially never before seen flaws in themselves. When writing or recording thoughts and feelings on some form of media, people may be surprised to recognize the limits of their self-expression after reading what was written or listening to what was said objectively.

Think of any thought, opinion, or position that you feel strongly about. Write it down. Assumption of correctness is unnecessary. To be clear, that is always counterproductive. All positions have limits and most definitely weaknesses. Dialogue is created if the person can logically express their thoughts to others, and compromise or understanding is achievable. Do not waste your energy on deciding whether a given viewpoint is right or wrong; after all, these vary individually and are just a question of perspective.

Did you write in a way or express yourself in a manner that allows a competing view to coexist or have the legitimacy of importance, just as you are requesting? For example, is there a place where two or more competing thoughts can exist equally and free of unnecessary friction within your premise?

Do you allow alternatives to exist in your understanding of the world? Are your positions motivated by an extension of kindness to coexist while educating those who may have been misinformed? Or do you believe the world would be better off without those in conflict with your beliefs? Do people not deserve the opportunity to express their opinions when it is counter to your understanding of correctness?

Submitting to alternatives in kind allows reconciliation through the destruction of absolutes. If people are willing to recognize that they have limits by first assuming themselves wrong, it can be an enlightening experience. In so doing, they will be able to see something other than their truth.

This creates the beginning of the end for ignorance. Not because they are incorrect but because the process leads to factually accurate conclusions. For a truth to be absolute, it must be. If it is absolute, it must be factually accurate in all aspects, especially when considering an inverse conditional statement or the converse categorical or implicational statement.

If these do not align, it cannot be so. Using the critical perspective removes the want to be right for the sake of being right or being superior to someone and replaces it with the need to pursue truth only for the purpose of being factually accurate or respectfully accountable, allowing for more tolerant behaviors.

Applying problem-solving processes inclusive of logical reasoning or critical thinking may show a person to be an imbecile, and their position exists only to silence alternative competing thoughts, including differences, or extinguish these altogether. All of which are forms of hate or intolerance. When, or if, people are unable to grasp the concept of the critical perspective they will most likely fail to obtain the truth. An example of why the truth is important can be better explained with rudimentary mathematics.

Math is unique in science as only the factually accurate conclusion is accepted or permitted. Math is absolute and controlling because we know what is wrong because we know what is factually correct. Math is a finite rational system untouched by the bias of human emotion. Math reflects the critical perspective as all integers have defined values unable to carry different meanings or feelings from person to person or culture to culture. All agree on the system designed to maintain operational integrity, formulas to create, and consistency measured regardless of the process of truth-finding.

Math, to me, is peaceful. It allows the uninterrupted discovery of what needs to be known. I appreciate the ending it represents as no matter the problem; there is always a solution or a purpose for its existence. Even if the solution is not yet found or the purpose of the theory is not yet discovered.

It is always working to correct its own errors. But through time and a commitment, the logical foundation of math is second to none, always telling the truth because its purpose is to seek the truth. And the best part, people are free to apply the logic daily in a way that is non-evasive, non-offensive, and a benefit to society as a whole—value manipulation and wealth creation or generation arguments aside.

In addition, news agencies and even journalists are not imploring or demanding people to change the way numbers work/act for the sake of feelings and emotions as of yet anyhow. Although, a cumbersome alternative has since been introduced, creating more work for the same solution. But alternately, it still logically proves the point—a correct solution exists in multiple understandings and unique ways of problem-solving, even if efficiency is unimportant.

Not only can math explain the computational issues human beings face and the reason for friction and division, but it also references equality assigning value more appropriately to people because the Collatz conjecture was always about assigning value no matter the subjective placement of order. After all, all things reduced have a commonality equal to one.

Regardless of the value, no matter the number, all things can be reduced to being one; therefore, equal—including people. It only requires the perspective to see what is logically there, or at least accept an interpretation that allows this conclusion. It was never a math problem to solve but a sequence used to prove no matter the difference or value assigned through human constructs; people are objectively the same. Therefore, what is valued is objectively equal regardless of the subjectivity of worth.

If we look at people and their understanding of the world around them, we are better able to empathize and acknowledge their internal and external conflict in relation to their belief systems. Assigning numbers to beliefs creates a standard among groups who believe the same conclusion—our kind has value; our kind has worth. Tragically people never accept this because a flaw occurs long before we are able to prevent it.

All human beings are loaded with an operating system and a unique way to solve issues such as threat perception, determining right or wrong, and attractiveness, etc. Of course, not an exhaustive list, only an example. Human beings have scripts installed in their cognitive structures and use these processes to aid in daily activities, rationale understanding of influinci, or situational decision making.

For example, with respect to romantic relationships, a man and a woman can be represented by a specific number, let's say 3 for a man and 4 for a woman. When an individual sees those genders together, their brain recognizes the sum as 7, which is represented as correct in the operating system of the person observing the problem.

If the same person, much like a calculator or a computer, sees this problem, it will compute the correct answer based on what was loaded in the operating system as a correct prompt, always indicating the accurate solution. But if the person sees a man and a man together 3 + 3 = 6 or a woman and woman together 4 + 4 = 8, it will most likely flash as an error cognitively and not indicative of an accurate solution.

The example does not assume a right or wrong determination and an absolute answer. It is only illustrative of a person processing the information and can be recalculated to serve a subjective viewpoint of substituted values. However, a valueless understanding of behaviors or an equal expression of differences is also applicable.

Any answer a person elicits can be counterproductive to tolerance, assuming one single answer is correct. The application of an absolute will create friction if they view and accept that any computation is right or wrong, therefore inferior or superior to another as it is incorrect or correct subjectively but incorrect objectively when applying the combined logic of each competing truth. Recognizing all alternatives can be correct or incorrect allows an understanding of the computational issues people struggle with.

People are not the same. They do not act the same, live the same, or belong to the same subgroup, nor should society expect them to. Because of this difference, people use different calculations or thought processes when presented with a problem to solve. In addition, people evolve at different rates and therefore thought processes and applications of standards do as well.

Furthermore, recognizing a competing interest's growth from a child to an adolescent, and later an adult, or an idea in its infancy to a mature thought, objectively accepted truth is vital for two sides to move towards progressive unity resting in the zone of peace. Understanding this process will promote forgiveness and will allow a sliding scale to exist that can and most likely will be adjusted to compensate for changes within the variables as maturity and wisdom occur. These are always our limits.

Humans can only use the information available to them or knowledge previously gained before the person is exposed. These are the limits all people have. Only ever being able to use what they possessed when an incident occurs or when viewing differences. These are computation limits different generations have—more or less wisdom.

The more ignorant a person is, the less empathetic they are. And the opposite is also true. The more empathetic a person is, the less ignorant they are. As people are what they know, what they have observed, and what they choose to be, these limits are judged harshly. However, in addition to these limits, there are other considerations that must be weighed as well.

A fair estimation of their emotional intelligence must be attached during the experience as it is occurring or at the time understood, subjectively, when reviewed, objectively, allowing for people to be judged less harshly. Giving consideration to this discrepancy promotes forgiveness and encourages a high cohesive structure in society because the emotional maturity of a 16-year-old is quite different from the emotional maturity of a 40-year-old. This fosters growth, influencing objective truths, which in turn progresses society.

Just as individuals grow, learn, and mature, so too does society. The difference between the two is that a society's growth spans the entirety of the existence of the human species; it thus takes much longer for a society to reach maturity. The mistakes people made in the past are usually followed by the self-reproof, "What was I thinking?" This is exactly what an advanced society thinks as well, "What were we thinking?" or 'What were they thinking?" It happens because growth occurs, and the identity or thought process is no longer present—a greater truth has finally revealed itself.

What once was repugnant behavior is not typical anymore. Entities or those with power and influence cannot force change onto a free people when the proposed belief system directly conflicts with convictions possessed by those they wish to change. Over time those thoughts and ideas eventually leave society because an intellectual shift occurs among people. Misguided principles die with the people who believe them. Progressive offensiveness changes the norms and values of society. Outdated behavior and beliefs are viewed similarly wrong then as it is now by people who progressed in society.

People of history's past could not help themselves as they were in the process of growing; so too was society. Society had not yet created the necessary steps required to remove behaviors modern people see as repulsive, dehumanizing, or inequitable, nor were the people adequately equipped to solve the controversies presented.

Comparing a 10-year-old to a 20-year-old to a 30-year-old will always highlight limits. Crucial to growth are mistakes that they will no longer make. Comparing a 1000-year-old society to a 2000-year-old society to a 3000-year-old society will yield similar results. Growth is occurring; it is just recorded by different types of measurements by different types of standards reflective of different things measured. Individual lives are shorter and eventually end. Because of this, a complete understanding of progress is incomprehensible to some.

The life expectancy of societies and even the human species creates a more extended, more stable understanding of the progress achievable. Societies are considered to be long-lived because their lifespan encompasses that of many generations and the collective progress of billions of people over a time period that is hundreds and, in some cases, even thousands of years long. This includes current societies that have yet to end. Think of these periods as the decades of human growth in relation to the centuries or millenniums people influence each other in effecting societal change.

Those who lived in a past society of their normal would be devastated to see the modern normal that progressed without them in it. Not that it is a negative thing, but not being able to recognize your world is likely an extremely difficult experience subjectively.

Change is a hard thing to swallow over a 30-year time span; envision the change that occurs over centuries. Imagine King Tut or the Great

Genghis Khan living today. Still, some people's grandparents would not recognize the world if they were blessed with a day to discover and most likely would be uncomfortable. However, the existence or lifeline of the human species is longer, but its measurement will end, as does individual life. Just as each person will die, our species will meet the same end.

The time required to change people takes generations and may seem extreme to some. Especially to the ones, it is so obviously affecting. Whether it is viewed as oppressive, offensive, or unfair, the equitable extension of remedies[31] takes time. This is the same reason it takes time to change anything; convincing the majority of the truth is painstakingly difficult.

Each truth can change and be altered as the continuous cycle of what is known, tolerated, or forced works to fit in the timeline of this change with the people of the timeline who allow or prevent this change. What is objective is accepted or rejected, dependent on the level of division of people. Usually, objectivity rests on a reasonable person's standard.

Objective viewpoints are common when a controlling group has accepted a universal common understanding. This allows a subjective truth as an absolute in society—**their truth**—or as applied outside the control group in respect to a constant—**a truth**. An objective viewpoint recognized by society creates tolerance by accepting progress as the standard to be met. This is an absolute all people are willing or are forced to accept.

Progress is constantly occurring and constantly regulated but does it occur at a rate that is sustainable without constant conflict? Destroying a belief system or an ideological following is something that occurs with the death of all the people who believe it. Even still, what is recorded can always be sowed as a seed and grown to create the same destruction it accomplished in prior cycles.

Accepting a new absolute or tolerating what was never in conflict with people can create friction. But if people continue to work together, we can minimize these consequences or prevent these altogether and change anything. However, it takes time. Unfortunately, this is something all

---

[31] Allows for the cohesive structure in society to be positive and peaceful coexisting successful by creating equity for all.

people are running out of concerning the limits of time represented by human life. The change will occur through death, education, and the extension of tolerance as time moves forward. This is represented by societal life and the progression of maturity the human species collectively earns over time, establishing a new truth.

But again, that is also subjective to the groups applying the objective viewpoint. These acceptable standards vary in number, as do the groups people belong to. But eventually, a large enough dissent will create competing objective truths between the controlling arms in society, and these people decide subjectively what is correct or the truth in society. In addition, at times, competing interests create friction in the form of societal wedges[32] between each other causing unnecessary division. This requires an intervention to create a new truth creating an absolute by use of force, causing a reformation movement containing the people who disagree.

Americans are no different, and eventually, people will create new truths because generational growth, concerning evolution, requires a different path than that taken by our fathers. In theory, this should be progressively allowing a more appropriate and superior way to replace an old and outdated lifestyle believed to be inadequate, inefficient, or injurious to people. However, when the new truth attacks an old truth, one that people are unwilling to adjust to, the intervention takes place. It is preventable by compromising with diversity so peace may remain. This is the standard a free people must adopt.

And because this is the standard a free people must adopt; they must also figure out a complete way to address and balance interests. This can be done by using the tolerance continuum. It is important to recognize any espousal of preconceived notions or biases owned, hateful or not, when viewing the tolerance continuum. It is also essential to be honest because what is true is simply a condition of being factually accurate, allowing understanding and acceptance with oneself, which can be used to create the tolerance necessary to accept others. And this is the purpose of the continuum, to identify and promote internal growth by recognizing what

---

[32] Attaching enematic qualities to innocence strictly for the purpose of controlling, maintaining, or gaining power by division.

is causing friction or conflict in society. It is not about changing convictions, only honoring a commitment to respect others.

To understand what occurs when people perceive differences or what is in conflict with their existence, the process of the cognitive rules of growth must be categorized into two independent parts and separated as an equation but referenced as what affects the individual and what influences their actions.

The distinct method is grouped into two categorical parts. The first is internal and the second external. However, the formula dismisses the order of operation and combines the two parts by ignoring the categorical placement to solve what a person is processing properly. Basically, the order in which the interests are being calculated in a person's mind continues to fluctuate between internal and external until a decision has been made.

The external factors are Exposure to the interest and Knowledge of the Interest. The internal factors are Affects/Effects of CRG, Knowledge, Influinci, Computation Limits, Intelligence Level, Identity Factors and finally Judgment.

The effects of the cognitive rules of growth, the influinci consumed, the computation limits assigned to the person, the intelligence level of the individual, the knowledge of a competing interest, and also the exposure levels to the competing interest in combination create the formula used to judge differences accordingly when viewing the appropriateness of a competing interest.

This is also used to create sympathetic actualization and later the empathetic actualization needed to create acceptance, moving competing interest in the direction of the required cohesive structure necessary to develop and maintain peace. But consequently, it can also push the divide deeper by increasing apathy, stereotypical thoughts, and prejudices, leading to hate, which destroys cohesiveness with conflict or war.

Before people view and understand the tolerance continuum, they first must recognize a few cause-and-effect issues:

1. Superiority is reinforced by a belief in a false claim.
2. Tolerance can be created by personal accountability and a choice.
3. Ignorant misunderstandings drive divisiveness and intolerance.
4. The further on the continuum the competing interests are from one

another, the less knowledge possessed between the two, thereby decreasing mutual respect.

5.  The closer on the continuum the competing interests are, the more knowledge possessed between the two, thereby increasing mutual respect.

6.  Strong leadership lessens the divide.

7.  Weak leadership grows the divide.

8.  The level of tolerance between all competing interests controls the type of cohesive structure in society.

9.  The continuum is an ever-moving gyroscope, balancing thousands of competing interests until its orientation settles in the zone of peace or zone of conflict.

10. In either zone, the continuum settles; when this occurs, it is out of consequences to alliances being built or destroyed.

11. Incomplete, irrational, and nonsensical creations will prove to create tension as the belief in such falsities can never be shown to be true. This will always prevent competing interests from accepting one another.

12. The inability for competing interests to move closer means either intolerance is present, or an interest represented is simply a lie.

13. Unity or a reason for cohesiveness to exist will always draw competing interests closer.

14. Division or a reason for intolerance to exist will always push competing interests further.

15. The number associated with each emotion on the spatial behavior line indicates the type of unity present in society where the competing interests are and when the competing interests are present.

16. The type of unity in society indicates the position of the cardinal point always in continuous motion balancing interests in society, positioning itself in either the zone of peace or zone of conflict as one interest or combined to represent specific categories in parts or as a whole.

17. The higher the number of the sum in any category representing any interest of any competing groups, in parts or as a whole, the more truth is present, the more society agrees, and the more tolerant

diversity is.

18. The lower the number of the sum in any category representing any interest of any competing groups, in parts or as a whole, the less society agrees, the less truth is present, and the less tolerant diversity is.

19. The value of the emotional response plotted on the spatial behavior line can be placed in a formula to calculate how toxic  acompeting interest has become and is an indicator of the proximity and inclination of conflict or war.

20. Interests of which the controversies have resolved through acceptance can no longer impact the zone location nor affect the movement of the cardinal point; however, what was once resolved can quickly resurface, creating fresh disagreeance and renewed intolerance.

21. Tolerance is the only way to create acceptance and maintain or obtain peace amongst competing interests.

22. The human species can coexist, but it must come to terms with balancing interests to reach the Transcendent Summit of Harmonious Existence or submit themselves to a constant cycle of destruction.

Because of the limits of self-publishing, I could not include a version of the Tolerance Continuum inside the book. Instead, I created a website to allow readers to access these charts and graphs. Below is a QR code, and it will give you access to the Tolerance Continuum and other valuable graphs to better explain the process and how a person is limited by themselves and their environment.

I believe the tolerance continuum can prevent future conflict by quickly identifying previous limits and eliminating or minimizing the consequences of societal wedges before the truth is altered. It can also identify a past point of no return by associating the value of the position of the cardinal points into a measurable threat analysis calculation to determine 1) the causal sum indicating how likely specific events are to occur in the future, 2) what actions society must take to nurture peace or prevent conflict, and 3) at what point society created conflict by the actions taken when reviewing history—identifying these markers can teach the next generation how to live life appropriately with identities and interests, not of their own.

The more significant the difference between two interests, the more likely unrest and violence can occur, pushing the divide further and that much closer to war. It is also an indicator more work is necessary to prevent such a catastrophe. When this occurs, corrective action must be immediate and decisive to counter regressive behavior. Any deviation greater than four will start the collapse of peace by encouraging conflict.

Calculating the causal sum determines the position society rests within the cycle of destruction. This can be used to appropriately assign fault for specific deviancy that lowers the cohesive structure or allows society to record identifiable morality, which raises the cohesive structure. For this to accurately promote or prevent behavior, an agreed-upon truth must be present. If truth is absent from society, unity is also absent and division controlling. This is the last fault line before the point of no return becomes conflict encouragement[33].

When division is present, disparaging words are used to create the animosity necessary to promote violent acts and conflict. This is the justification for war because people talk themselves into destroying the representatives who lied and created the existential consequences.

To calculate the causal sum specific to an unresolved or ongoing issue in society, locate the cardinal point of each competing interest on the tolerance continuum. Each behavior location has an assigned value. The value is determinative of behaviors and is assigned accordingly: **Conflict**-0, **Hate**-1, **Prejudice/Stereotypes**-2, **Apathy**-3, **Acknowledgment**-4, **Understanding**-5, and **Acceptance**-6.

Each issue is worth twelve causal points and is weighted six per competing interest. For example: If A understands the competing interest of B within the issue, it is given the value of five. If B holds stereotypical beliefs or prejudice towards A within the issue, it is given the value of two.

These numbers are the epitomized attachment score and are added to indicate the causal sum. For example, five and two represent a causal sum of seven and are currently balanced as a cardinal point but can change based on the behaviors of each competing interest. Of course, actions and behaviors reflective of detrimental unity will lower the causal sum, while actions and behaviors reflective of cohesive unity will raise the causal sum. These create the trajectory of tolerance or trajectory of intolerance, leading to the trajectory of conflict, allowing the cardinal point to settle in the zone of peace or in the zone of conflict.

To determine society's location and trajectory, add all specific unresolved or ongoing issues in society. If the causal sum is lower than 50% of the available causal points and the willingness to extend respect to competing interests is no longer present, conflict is imminent and will eventually occur between the interests' creating hardships throughout society.

---

[33] The decision of the influential to consume the innocent destroying peace.

The higher the number, the higher the cohesive unity, and the lower the number, the lower the cohesive unity. The sum determines the type of unity present and can be used to plot the trajectory society is heading towards. The most vital indicator to establish the trajectory accurately is the presence or willingness from either interest to extend respect allowing tolerance. If this is absent, any location of the cardinal point on the continuum is in jeopardy, and so too is true of peace in society.

The continuum can be applied to individuals as well. The sum can be used to predict behavioral responses or to establish a desired change. For example, take everything that is controversial or your position on the many balancing interests society entertains and plot your judgment on the continuum. This allows the person to view exactly where they are and what they believe. It also can indicate if knowledge and exposure are the result of a high or low score and similarly will correlate to the behaviors shown towards the competing interests.

Conflict seems inevitable between competing interests, but each conflict's causal factors in the timeline when peace comes to an end are the same. Something allows the cycle of destruction to continue uninterrupted, and it must be identified.

Identifying the similarly assigned errors and ascribing them to the appropriate sources may allow future generations to limit the severity of the consequences or prevent the cycle from happening altogether. Dismissing history without understanding the purpose of what occurred and why it occurred is simply irresponsible. This information should never be dismissed as irrelevant or undesirable because it allows ignorant intolerance to control.

All interests in America must alter their current approach when representing or promoting their differences toward others. Instead of screaming and calling those who disagree with you the enemy, explain and be courteous in doing so. Representing ideas and beliefs is important but so is how people accomplish the much-needed discussion.

Creating peaceful dialogue while being a beacon of hope within an interest will elicit the change desired. This job and role are usually the responsibility of representatives from our areas; however, they have turned into the opposite of what is needed. Balancing interests is extremely vital, especially in America, as promoting one over the other or dismissing one for the other only pushes any divide deeper.

Historically, the adults or those represented by the age of majority have often failed to create a world of inclusion. A significant portion of the fault can be ascribed to what we know, what we are taught, and what we decide our truth is. Because of this, the subsequent generations have always dealt with what our fathers were unable to overcome.

We are born at a disadvantage to those in the future, and they will be born at an advantage. Where we struggle, they will succeed, and where we succeed they will never struggle. This will always be the case. Unless, of course, society somehow allows itself to regress. All we are, is what we were told, right or wrong. Altering our operating system is next to impossible. Even if a person is able to succeed, it takes very little to revert back to their original state because what we know is what we are always the most comfortable with. Treating each other with respect limits this backward movement.

This is the importance of teaching children right from wrong, kindness before cruelty, and tolerance in place of hate. Society must accomplish this not by forcing people to believe but by allowing them to understand and create a dialogue with that which is different. Not to change, not to destroy, not to indoctrinate, but to educate.

To learn the importance of empathy, equality, and equity. Not to promote, not to disparage, not to force, but to teach. To inspire individuality and togetherness so that we may live in harmony and sustain peace around the world. Acceptance is the end game needed to create coexistence amongst all people. The key to this—stop trying to control freedom and destroy the liquidity of hate.

After understanding what the tolerance continuum represents, how the cognitive rules of growth affect development, and what influinci people allow to have legitimacy in their life, I am still searching for the truth regarding many things with the use of all the tools at my disposal. Because people live and learn, fail, and succeed, discover the right way and the wrong way, it makes sense when friction between competing interests is present; the same growth process will occur at an individual level. What is unknown or what is being worked through takes time, leading to complicated and often tough questions.

This process can also produce controversial realizations as answers, and contemplating what the information suggests takes time. But people should not demonize others for still growing, nor should others be celebrated above those still seeking the truth. I would question what people know to be true in the first place. People seldom have the competency to be independent thinkers as they choose what is known, what is easier, or what creates the perception of being tolerant of the most logical forms of expression.

If a person believes something and has finally settled on an intellectual identity, this does not make them correct or superior; they have stopped looking for the truth, developing a taste for what they want to believe. But how much work and time did this process take, and are they considerate of others, or do they ignore the process when it is outside their likeness?

Do these one-sided beliefs represent intolerance and the decline of common decency? Has the peace contained within the tolerance continuum and the cycle of destruction run its course? Has the distance between differences entered the zone of conflict? Has the world entered a new chapter where war once again will be used to solve discrepancies because people have lost motivation to talk, as their distance has grown too great? Is that possible? Are we ever past the point of no return, or do we just crave conflict and give in to the blood lust just beneath the surface? I guess the answer is—it depends.

When I reference the many issues all people are a part of, no balance exists; therefore, compromise through understanding cannot occur. People are either of the group who believes one way, or they are the enemy. A tragic dismissal[34] creates neither a sympathetic actualization[35] nor an empathetic actualization[36], both of which are important for cohesive unity and creating beneficial progress for humanity as a whole.

Recognizing bias and lack of empathy for differences is extremely important to cohesiveness when a diverse society is present. No matter the topic or subject matter, when we view differences, we must see more than ourselves and surely protect those who are in need, especially when they honestly believe their likeness is unsafe or in danger of preventable harm. If we fail; we choose; if we fail, chaos ensues; if we fail, we all lose. We must succeed.

---

[34] An anti-empathetic view
[35] A sympathetic view of discovery identifying imbalances
[36] An empathetic view of discovery altering imbalances

Of course, this is contingent on people being more than self-critical. They also must be willing to engage in an expansive understanding different from what they know, allowing these differences to be treated as peers. As societies and human interactions become more expansive, it makes sense that exposure to differences or interconnectivity between these differences will be more frequent. In addition to the frequency with which people are exposed to new cultures or competing lifestyles, misunderstandings will also be more frequent as people carry biases and prejudices that are subconsciously projected to differences. These exposures and misunderstandings can result in conflict.

If societies are to be more successful, tolerance of all differences must be given the same respect requested. Respect cannot be given only to the beliefs of the influential, the many, or the elite. People must learn to be more comfortable with people, beliefs, and lifestyles different from their own. Even if people cannot agree with the lifestyle choices of others, all is not lost. People will always possess an identity insulting or unagreeable to others. The leaders of a free people must lead from the front to create cohesiveness through actions, as this should be the end game of all people in a diverse society.

Americans must learn to protect the unpopular from the popular by encouraging intellectually stimulating and often highly critical counterarguments. Some may very well be insulting but addressing these appropriately will allow discourse to do what it does. The willingness to engage in thoughtful self-reflection and critical analysis is vital to solving society's current issues. And it is also imperative to allow peace to prosper as we push our own limits, discovering what no nation has ever been able to obtain—greatness beyond generational periods.

This will bless all people with a chance to change, grow, and prosper by demanding that the best of us rise to influence the rest of us. This would once again create a standard worth pursuing, a people worth the freedoms offered by peace, and unity not only worth fighting for—but dying for.

Creating a more inclusive society regardless of differences is a heavy burden even for civilizations that share many commonalities. However, it is possible to create a template for success if people are committed to removing ignorance. Not by force but by the pursuit of knowledge; not by ignoring, but by the pursuit of engaging; not by dismissing, but by the pursuit of trying.

And as I plainly stated, what occurs when people perceive differences or what is in conflict with their existence—it's complicated. Society's diversity causes such friction. Recognizing how these issues affect, influence, and progress or regress society is crucial to understanding true tolerance and the power of acceptance. These differences must not be viewed as a negative but as alternatives existing in a free society allowing our species to focus on what truly matters and solve what threatens us all.

People will always have frictions between them, including those who are identical in every way. Therefore, to address the conflicts that are forever raging between competing interests, we must manage them more appropriately, allowing the discovery of common grounds through mutual understanding of such growth processes. Although people may not always agree, they can remain civil by acknowledging their existence or acknowledging that identity is not the controlling order of the world.

Life is complicated, it is messy, and at times unforgiving, but as long as people are committed to working on the problems in earnest, we can maintain a united front to defeat whatever friction presents itself as a threat to our way of life. Preventing the power of the dollar from influencing what is said and what is believed will be the greatest fight in the effort to remove this friction.

America, her people, and the world, for that matter have much to celebrate; yet true equity is a continued pursuit. Society's differences, the struggles for equality, equity, and the human element continue to pose a substantial threat to peace and the Rule of Law. It is the responsibility of all to aid in the pursuit of society's cohesive structure. Regardless of the differences present, viewing and understanding the continuum creates a more appropriate avenue for successful dialogue and personal understanding of such differences. It is a way to extend kindness by recognizing whether or not a person's location allows for such a necessity.

However, as with any successful outcome or hopeful pursuit, honesty, truth, and complete transparency must exist; but also, a recognition that whatever difference is present deserves legitimacy, at the very least, protection. The continuum and the thought process required to promote tolerance is not about wrong or right, superior or inferior. It is about acknowledgment and a projected path forward. It is about convincing a competing view to engage in dialogue by recognizing self-position for the sake of peaceful coexistence.

Life is not what you think it is. It is not a plan to retire at 40 with a million dollars in the bank. It is not a pursuit to buy a vacation home in addition to the place you already reside in. And it is certainly not bragging about the new materialistic garbage in your possession on your favorite media platform. It is simpler than that but so much more complicated. Our existence requires nothing more than survival. Our species craves surplus. We desire to have plenty even when it's not logical. However, as people accumulate, others suffer, as peace erodes, conflict emerges, as value is disconnected from worth; what is worthless destroys[37]. This occurs over generations and a climax can never be achieved because people die but what kills is always reborn-selfish, ignorant, and incompetent[38].

Humanity—a joke among the ecosystems. The most advanced limited species ever created continues to fail at the evolution type that enhances the cohesive structure required to possess foundational harmony. Our technology[39] advances yet our minds remain primitive and our desires selfish. This growth failure permits history to be repetitive, only advancing the means to create pampered, fragile offspring[40], grant longevity to what has expired[41], or conveniently kill what is undesirable[42]. This happens because people are not concerned with enriching the society they belong to, only enriching themselves while others go without or are removed for failing to comply.

I am not sure of anything anymore. But what I do know is we live a very privileged life, all of us, regardless of what we look like or where we come from. I am doing the best I can with the information available. This

---

[37] **Incremental destruction**- occurs as a result of those who benefited from the sacrifices others made and born with no cost to live in the privileged state better people created.

[38] **Toxic benefactors**- entitled people who are unable to comprehend what is necessary to keep what is and too selfish, ignorant, or incompetent to understand how it came to be.

[39] **Necessary Evolution**- science used to create what is needed to survive more efficiently.

[40] **Convenience Evolution**- science used to create an advantage to be pampered more efficiently.

[41] **Longevity evolution**- science used to create an advantage to extend life more efficiently.

[42] **Termination evolution**- science used to create an advantage to kill more efficiently.

is my first time being alive, and I think I am doing a mighty fine job because I strive to be a decent person outside my identity. I think most people do.

After all, we are a United people living in a country allowing peace to prosper because what is contained in 1 through 10 means we don't have to fight each other over the freedom to be the identities we are or choose to be as those wars have already been fought.

What will the future of society look like, say, in 100 years? What issues with respect to humanity will the leaders of tomorrow solve or create next? Most likely, the successes of the future will include things others alive today would be upset by. People who do not belong in that future will never know, nor should they. At what point does it not matter to know? Eventually, death will occur, and what progress and growth represent only matter to the living.

What society or form of governmental control will survive and create the next Rule of Law? The likelihood it will be reflective of what we know now is rather slim. But will it resemble America at all?

Americans are greater than their identity since it is our differences that unite...

# A Place for Your Thoughts:

# CHAPTER IV

## *Is Modern America Enough?*

I t may come as a shock and a painful realization to those who love this great Nation that I doubt the viability of its continued existence due to its current trajectory. The future seems uncertain when weighed against the backdrop of America and the many obstacles presently standing in the way of peace and causing division amongst her people. America can survive, but for that to happen, extensive changes must occur in political parties, governmental accountability, citizenry responsibility, addressing the cost of living, and repairing the educational system.

But is this the path forward? Are we always fighting with each other to evolve? And does this evolution hurt or help our species. Will it eventually destroy the societies we inhabit?

Each side lies and claims the other is an authoritarian type of governance rising to eliminate the other. And they are both right. But unfortunately, the leaders of the tribes involved spread half-truths, engage in tone-deaf obtuseness, and their commitment to conflate issues puts America right in the middle of another civil war. We must proceed with caution as our children are watching. They will grow up to believe this is the correct conflict resolution process. And it is not. There must be leaders present who can work together and commit to solving what ails us, together, united, as Americans.

But it seems each generation is ignorant of history and committed to removing dialogue because their side has no power or is upset at the type who do. People will forever fight, produce conflict, and disagree, but our leaders are assigned the task that teaches us how to conduct ourselves through each instance of the disputes occurring by leading from the front.

America's development into a mediocracy is, without question, the root cause of her problems. This tragic representation of inferior rule is not specific to any generation but instead highlighted in the divisiveness and faults of such a period in our history. Weakness rendering inferior rule exceptionally agreeable to those who cheer and protest its being into existence. And consequences are abundant when those who are not the strongest, most intelligent, or most qualified lead a powerful Nation. This toxicity is nothing more than incompetence which later creates division caused by allowing weakness to take the reins.

Is this just a temporary event in our timeline, or is America careening out of control towards danger? Have a free people met their breaking point with excessive diversity[43] within a people due to discrimination, bias, and intolerance? Is that an issue to consider when viewing the success or failure of a diverse society? And what is the corrective action? How do Americans continue to progress and create a modern society that accepts all regardless of group affiliation? The stability of America's foundation and the strength of her people have shown the ability to endure. Even after going through the harshest of divisions from past times, can we find a way to heal again? Will our people find a way? Will a leader emerge who unites us? What future will we choose, and by what actions will this occur. Will it be bloodshed forcing compliance or dialogue that encourages compromise?

Friction without resolution jeopardizes the integrity of our foundational beliefs. Corrosion is very destructive, and if it is allowed to continue, it will destroy all it comes into contact with. Prevention through participation by literate free people is a necessary deterrent for such a threat. People must be willing to be inclusive and reject the notion of exclusivity. Through and by the Constitution, all people are welcome, not just those included from a one-America point of view. However, each one must be protected collectively. Regardless of the group people belong to, they have the protection of America and should have the support of all Americans; however, they must participate in the system and prevent toxicity from spreading through constructive dialogue.

People live in a time of unknown truths and are overstimulated by influential selfishness. This does nothing positive for America and her people. It only adds to the tragedy of intolerance and hate. As long as people self-segregate, ignore accountability, and accept ignorance, society and those within will be unable to find common ground to move forward

---

[43] A critical level of diversity represented by intolerance for differences

in a direction needed to maintain peace. Do not continue to create lines and categorize each other by likeness.

In other instances, categories assist people in organizing, understanding, and aid in progress; however, this is not the case when people create, separate, and use defined lines against each other. As lines are continuously added, people create the polarization of what is right and wrong. If society continues to add lines, these societal wedges will alienate us from each other. Compassion, empathy, and respect will also be lost in the process.

When this occurs, tension will create friction, which will have existential consequences. It will later be accelerated through generational ignorance as the exponential rate of intolerance magnifies perceived threats between people in a diverse society, causing structural harm to the foundation of society. The more lines we add, the harder it is to see our likeness and further away from the solution we travel. If history has taught us anything, differences create revolutions; but they also create war, hell on earth.

Lines are fractures; thus, in society, as in bones; they create instability and jeopardize the integrity of our foundation. Without a fair consideration of consequences and a continuation of division, an ending will begin. We must heal and give significant consideration so we may blur these lines to recreate the only identity that serves appropriateness; American. Our people not only have a responsibility to each other through the Constitution but an obligation to protect the peace, preventing the cycle of destruction through war. Americans will prove competent if given the appropriate leaders to guide and govern through understanding, as this will prevent division. America has not only the tools but also the resources, rules, and a fantastic opportunity to build on the work of all our ancestors. The premise of America is inclusivity and protection for all through peace and through freedom. Regardless of why or what motivations led to the eventual formation of this great Nation, a thought existed:

"We hold these truths to be self-evident, that all men are created equal, that they are endowed by their Creator with certain unalienable Rights, that among these are Life, Liberty and the pursuit of Happiness."

This thought changed the landscape of inter-human relations in the world forever. It also led to greater equality, growth of tolerance, abolition of slavery, and the women's suffrage movement. It is represented by America's current fight for continued progress and also the world's fight. The first group created in this Nation were Americans. Closeness, shared efficacy, and common decency existed within the group. Built of patriots who recognized shortcomings in the status-quo and the intestinal fortitude to change it. They were countrymen, brethren; these men were not bound by intolerant regeneration; rather they were bound by the will to create a better way.

Yes, it did take evolution and revolutions to extend the understanding of freedom to others, but what started as a thought turned into a belief and something more significant than anyone could imagine. It motivated righteousness from those willing to continue to carry the banner making progress where it was lacking. The system is still correcting itself, improving, and evolving to match the needs of the people it represents.

Our system has improved vastly since the inception of personal liberties, and these changes are easily identifiable and measurable. And this is a banner America must continue to represent regardless of who agrees. It is not a way of silencing dissent but a way of caring for dissent, protecting those who do not agree, are not yet convinced, and those who will never conform—each with measurable benefits to society and the people its controlling arms serve.

Progressed societal self-image is a measurement used to recognize past limits as graded based on modern equity and moral growth standards. It represents the standard deviation of human evolution, mainly tolerance of human diversity in society over time. It indicates the many mistakes of the species' past, and the solutions used to solve such shortcomings, but more importantly, it shows the progress brave men and women were able to bring about.

Society, particularly American society, must continuously be committed to tolerance and inclusivity. It must reflect precisely the intent and purpose of the existence of freedoms extended to those protected.

However, with progress and grouping of diversity comes a dangerous precedent; grouped-isolationism. Yes, collectively, America should celebrate differences and encourage recognition for specific groups but not at the expense of alienating others. People should not ignore the consequential effects all ideologies can produce simply for acceptance. A single belief is not superior, nor is it an absolute people must accept.

A single group cannot claim superiority over another. Imbeciles or those with hateful tendencies believe such a premise, often encouraging and creating further division. America's strength comes from our ability to create through cohesiveness, not destroy through division.

Ignoring what makes America strong and failing to respect our diversity will allow the divisions to be transformed into threats. These threats will later be viewed as hostiles or enemy combatants. Disposing of which now becomes a priority for each side because the hate eventually consumes us.

Ignorance and lack of empathy can create hate which allows these divisions to sow hatred among differences. Human brains are wired to perceive threats as a means to survive. Creating enemies is often a reactive endeavor, yet intentional, usually justified because it is the end sought. The creation of enematic characteristics does not stop until the belief system that created the divisions is destroyed. It either dies from the force of war, the eventual death of those who believed a truth, or a generational belief that is no longer accepted because a responsible citizenry used the dialogue necessary to create compromise through a shared efficacy and the commitment for continued greatness.

What makes the progressive death of an inferior outdated belief system difficult to remove is the reinforcing and repopulation of a generational truth. The desire for hate is caused by accepting selfishness by those willing to assume a no-fault expressionism understanding of personal values. In short, "My way or the highway." It is intolerant regeneration through ignorance and a choice motivated by selfishness.

This occurs because members of society are not encouraged to create dialogue. In fact, most influential people discourage a mutually agreed-upon understanding concerning tolerance. Leaders very seldom create the opportunity for or suggest discourse. Instead, they usher in a defensive posture used to establish division by creating the perception of an immediate threat to the existence of those they represent.

It always has to be about them and their group over all others. Creating a platform by repeating the false narrative, "Those who do not agree with us are the enemy." Continuing to cite misinformation and using hyperbolic showmanship, those with influence exclaim, "They want nothing more than to remove your legitimacy by attacking your personal beliefs."

As each competing view grows more moronic, they distance themselves and those they represent further from the truth. Choosing to sow fear and growing hate creates the need for representation. The opposite is true as well. Sowing discourse creates tolerance by removing hate and destroying the need for representation.

An epiphany is born, "The problem is worth more than the solution." "Let us monetize this."

This is the secret recipe used by politicians and political hacks associated with the respective committees and organizations. These people and their associates disguise themselves as necessary. Still, they are nothing more than a mismanaged non-profit used to pay friends and family members outrageous amounts of money with little or minimal oversight. They influence education, children, legislation, and the acquisition of resources. Money is funneled to prepare for a potential conflict. This allows groups of the population to create literal armies of the ideological kind if it becomes necessary to create literal armies of the physical kind.

Our world is overpopulated by those who cannot see past their selfishness. And as the species continues to grow uncontrollable by the advancements in medical science, we are not allowing for the death of ideas and beliefs that should stay in a prior generation to allow for the cognitive growth of our species. Because people and their ideas evolve at a different rate, what may take one family a generation to do may take another five generations to accomplish. It burdens all people and is unnecessarily taxing on the system that contains our species—society.

We can never move on from making enemies as our cognitive processes limit our mental growth based on external factors such as the need for cohesion among similarities and hiding our own bad habits while focusing on the missteps of those who are different. Until the death of a generational truth destroys a belief or ideology, that thought process will continue to create friction in the society it belongs to, never allowing progress to occur properly.

That is the key element, as progress is always subjective—when one sees progress, another sees regression. What moral or ethical beliefs should win out, and who decides what the right side of history is before history decides such an unknown? What occurs is most likely conflict, and this conflict will determine not only the fate of the individuals of that timeline but also the society's status quo or shifts in the future. Better understood by our modern version of America and what progress those before us made.

However, this progress is not enough at times, and the dissenters with a voice must be heard. Even so, those dissenting must keep a standard for others to follow. Appropriateness of expressing concerns is vital, but so is the etiquette of listening to those concerns. The consequences of ignoring grievances and dismissing those seeking change can be devastating but are always preventable.

Demonstrations and protests which turn to violence have no place in this Country. Freedom of assembly is an assembly of peaceful people sharing a common cause. What's more bothersome is the allowance of it to continue. Americans must understand a liberal versus conservative and a democrat versus republican position is responsible for America's current divided state. It is possible for all sides to work together civilly to create positive change while retaining personal and often different convictions. It is a choice to treat others disrespectfully, but its prevalence is created and often encouraged by the leaders whom people choose to follow.

This choice, one that acknowledges others as unimportant and the inability to respect an opinion that may differ from your own, causes unnecessary tension. From this tension comes the polarization of what is considered right or wrong. The truth, right or wrong, is word association and perspective, nothing more. We must acknowledge this fact and view each other as more than being different, right or wrong. Americans must celebrate our differences, regard others as equals, and allow these differences to be an alternative way to live alternatively from what others may believe. All alternatives deserve respect, relevance, and recognition of their importance, even if those differences fail to align with your own. At the very least, respect others by ignoring those who are different as they are still people regardless of what you think of them.

A continued view that contradicts that statement is highly arrogant, irresponsible, and will do nothing more but continue to divide us. To be an American is to be a civil rights activist. To allow any discrimination to continue in our modern society is idiotic, childish, and is represented by civilization's most significant failures. All people deserve protection from discrimination or any form of violence. This is undeniable and should be easily agreed upon. For America to continue to evolve, her people must create a new type of American.

This new American must have the ability to think critically, possess the competency to examine all facts logically, and the intestinal fortitude to criticize those within their subgroup. The current status quo is not working. Our continued path is irresponsible, reckless, and counterproductive. Something needs to change; something must change.

America needs strong leadership and leaders reflective of such attributes. Great leaders will lead from the front and set a proper example. They will exhibit qualities that show compassion, empathy, and understanding. At the same time, they will stand for others and fight against all unjust isms. From this behavior comes a subconscious mimicking process. Enormous public exposure equals considerable public influence. If our leaders choose to lead in a manner represented by appropriateness, that is how people will conduct themselves.

However, if they act childish and inappropriate or foolish, what occurs are followers who do the same. This type of behavior is reflected in the breakdown of a civilized society happening all across our Nation and the world. We have leaders who promote this negative behavior, and it is not exclusive to just one side of the aisle or a particular industry/profession. With great power and influence comes great responsibility and accountability. America needs to find and seek moral error instead of placing moral blame. Associating error with individual responsibility instead of people's identities will create change.

As I believe in America's purest original purpose, I will protect any other alternative just as fiercely as if those who hate me threatened my existence and belief system. This is a call or battle cry if you will, to those who are also tired of the obstructionism, divisiveness, and all-around unnecessary behavior which prevents our society from achieving progress.

I am extremely sad and scared as the future of my people [humanity] is threatened. For the first time, I cannot see any light at the end of the tunnel. What has me more concerned is that; I am unable to see a tunnel anymore. I cannot even convince my own family of this, and the people I speak to about my concerns shut me off because they think of me as an idiot. I do not see any evidence to the contrary that leads me to believe it will get better.

But I suppose if any regular person can recognize failures in a complex system that allows people to live free and fully understands the appropriate way to treat a fellow human being, it should be easy for the rest of the world to follow suit.

I do not see this ending any other way unless we work together. If we fail to put our differences aside for peace and tolerance, we may effectively destroy the protections that keep us all safe. An informed citizenry must protect the Rule of Law at all costs, including holding those accountable who betray the faith and standards we as a people bestow in them.

At every level of accountability, it must be had. This is and must be non-negotiable. From the speeding ticket given by a police officer to the police officer abusing his power, and yes, even when dealing with incompetency in our government, such as Congress, including the White House, from corrupt actions, mental soundness, or partisan clowns. All levels of accountability must be present, or it is all for naught.

The accountability examples listed are by no means an exhaustive list, but they will do for their purpose. The consequences when lack of accountability occurs, it is evident and grow more precarious when starting at the bottom and working to the top. The consequences of failure or corruption get more severe as the examples of each betrayal become more dangerous.

People do not understand or seem to comprehend what happens when they allow civil unrest to be uncontrolled or divisiveness to grow unfettered. It soon can turn into civil war, forever altering society. The changes may not always be intended and may not all be positive. Those in denial of that statement lack the basic understanding of what tribalism will do to a free democratic nation. Nevertheless, the system in place works, it must be protected and nurtured, and sometimes a change in the status quo must occur to preserve the fragility of America.

America, what she represents, is the fairest system that exists. Why do people fear change when it is the type that can change society for the better? What have people become when our selfishness outweighs the benefit of helping others at little or no cost to ourselves? If this is what America's belief has mutated into, her people do not deserve any freedom. But I, for one, would like to leave my children and grandchildren something more than the ashes of the greatest country and society the world has ever seen. Is this not agreeable?

This is not an attack related explicitly to identities and does not represent any specific person, idea, or movement. It is from an architect's standpoint while viewing America as a machine to better understand the inner workings of the system and how people must protect what is so precious to us all. These are observations from a concerned citizen.

What do people want, a lawless, degraded, hypersensitive PC culture that arbitrarily removes standards of decency, allowing trash people and trash content to influence our youth? This belief destroys any representation of morality, character, and appropriateness by disconnecting children from their parents. It does nothing but attacks the morals or a standard of behavior by normalizing smut to sell cheap imitations of worth representing people who have zero value in society. This behavior and double standard are why modern society is unable to hold people accountable for individual actions.

If society fails to represent decency, then indecency will take control. People must be willing to protect a standard of morals that influences a people to maintain a level of acceptable morality, shaping progress, not urges, at all times. Technology has proven to be more of a curse than a blessing as it creates a consumption issue in the form of social engineering. It is accomplishing nothing more than normalizing an immoral world filled with people who do what they want because of empowerment and self-expression but also those interested in the price tag associated with vulgarity.

Garbage is what our people are becoming, trash is what they are representing, and a toxic world is what they are creating. When children can recite lyrics to WAP or sing songs that contain the phrase skeet skeet but cannot repeat the words to the Declaration of Independence or sing any part of the star-spangled banner, that is when a society of degradation occurs. Especially when patriotism and a love for a Nation that serves to protect is taught to be insulting.

Our Nation should always protect the freedom of expression, but the amount of influence people possess must be controlled. The species and what stimulates their mind is becoming less and less useful, as are the people who create the content people consume. Women are mad when men treat them like objects, but this is what they see them as on social media and in the entertainment world. Cops are targeted as enemies because this is what people are taught to see them as. Children consume pornographic images at a younger age because they are prevalently available, tolerated, and overwhelmingly accepted.

This free for all, everybody's opinion matters—is unimportant, and the vulgarity it represents threatens the very fabric of our Constitution, fundamental American values, and the ability for people to raise their children in a place that represents decency. Is that not the standard? To raise children who are decent human beings. Or are we slowly moving towards the crudeness of teaching our children to twerk in gym class? Is this what our leaders want. Are we abandoning the idea that we need people practicing couth, courteous behavior and strong men who practice chivalrous acts?

Or are manners unimportant, and have those who maintain these lost their worth to society?

We have to improve the system and make it better by making the people it represents better and improving them. Still, we must also protect the system by supporting each other, including safeguarding one another's freedom of expression, even when insulting. Society must balance interests in a system that creates more negativity than positivity. The consequences of perceiving religion as more offensive than a three-year-old twerking in Time Square while adults cheer her on are astronomical.

What is more alarming, people cannot escape this behavior as it is everywhere. A free people that protects indecorous behavior over decency will have just that; a free people who are indecorous. Is there a connection between normalizing behavior and the way people conduct themselves in society? Ignoring these consequences is a sickness.

As the current events show us, we have failed each other and are creating a tribalist culture based on acceptance through similarities and in the absence of decency. Our young Nation accepted slavery because it was considered to be normal. Women were inferior to men and included at times as their property because the behavior was normal due to common law. Same-race relationships were the standard because they were considered to be normal, and miscegenation violates the historical significance of "we tell you what is appropriate." Normalizing behaviors, interactions, and controlling the language serves to make what should be unacceptable acceptable. A tragic conclusion is approaching in modern America as people are as far disconnected from the intent of America as they are from decency and each other.

As a people, society must not give in to our animalistic urges, and we must prevent the want from separating us from each other. Our divisions are growing too rapidly without a chance to recover before the next one begins. This tragedy removes the ability to heal, correct, and move forward by bettering the system we are all a part of. Citizens may not be prepared for what comes next. When militias start to form to quell the unrest and to defend people's belief systems over the system that is already in place or against the threat of subjectivity, Americans are not what they should be. It may be the end of the current society, including the protections we all share.

In addition to creating lines between our differences and removing a standard of decency in behavior, people have made themselves weak and incapable of surviving as they sacrificed the knowledge and skillsets of gardening, hunting, fishing, and other practical, self-reliant necessities for unnecessaries. All for conveniences encouraging ignorance, being entertained, and ignoring what is essential to protecting peace through freedoms. And while people were lowering the standard of self-growth, morality, or ethicality, they decided to pursue individual materialism and extreme greed of a personal nature. They are doing nothing but destroying the notion of conservationism through moderation. Moreover, since the masses followed such a selfish endeavor, 1% of the world's population quietly amassed excess wealth and resources, exponentially making the wealth gap worse because the participation of the many made it almost impossible to stop a lifestyle the ignorant blindly pursued.

Instead of taking a pause to inquire into the system changing us, we quietly accepted that this was the way life was meant to be and we said thank you may I have another. May I have another $1000 cell phone? May I have another credit card to max out? May I have another unnecessary luxury in life that serves zero purposes but to distract and strip away our evolved values or the shared efficacy we gained over the last 250 years? These people, the powers that be, are accumulating and amassing enough wealth to prepare and protect themselves for the fallout.

We still have people making billions in this country as others around the world starve and are unsure what will become of them or their loved ones. And after we turn on ourselves, self-destruct, and destroy the precious life America offers us, they will wait it out, lie, and somehow convince you that they are the ones who are best fit to lead the world out of the very same circumstances/consequences that they created.

As I am writing this, our elected leaders make nearly $174,000 a year to legislate, represent and lead us away from demise and failure. At the current state of the Union, do you feel your money is being spent wisely? They support the rich, and the rich keep them. They do not help the poor, even those claiming to do so. Plainly visible in the lifestyles they lead. They may share the same zip code or districts like those in poverty and those families whose lives and communities are being destroyed, yet they do nothing for the neighborhood they claim to be from. They left, a part of them is there, but they no longer represent what they once did.

Great leaders have and are blessed with incredible foresight that most do not have the capacity to comprehend. The men who wrote the Constitution were able to understand what the limits were of self-governance and what would threaten it as well. Imagine knowing what would destroy America in the mid-1700s. It has the possibility to occur in the years following the bitterness of the Clinton impeachment, election issues of 2000, and the divisiveness that occurred as a result of current events up until the clown show of 2020's political embarrassment.

Thomas Jefferson doubted the viability of a self-governing people because it took participation, understanding, and unwavering support to protect what we cannot live without. Leaders must be present to unite, not divide. The American People are blessed by the sacrifices and incredible violence inflicted for change. Tragedy has always blessed the American People. Americans were given the greatest treasure in the history of human civilization. Yet, what have they done with it? People have almost squandered it and pissed it all away by failing to be involved in our democratic republic and respecting the differences this great Nation represents.

I am saddened, disgusted, and angry. I watched the Country I love slip into the worst political crisis ever because we decided that a standard of professionalism and accountability was unnecessary when leaders represent citizens at all levels of government. There is plenty of blame, and it is not a new issue. It has plagued our Nation for many years and many generations. People are all to blame. Yet, instead of trying to put out fires, they fanned them and doubled down on what is now the catalyst in this powder keg. And for what, to be right? Children are brought up to believe that one way of life is superior to another and in doing so created fractures that society may never recover from.

These words have always given me pause when I read them. I was never able to have a contextual understanding of precisely what it meant until recently. "A Democratic Republic for all, if you can keep it." I fear people may have lost what so many of us worked so hard to protect. America and her people are without a united vision of our future. Each tribe disagrees with what her identity should be. And each forgoes the standards of how to treat one another. When leaders disagree, they ignore compromise and instead substitute understanding and knowledge with a lack of respect and ignorance; only to throw more fuel on the fire of intolerance.

And all they were able to accomplish was the normalization of aggressive behavior that was viewed, consumed, and repeated by every ignorant person who could not grasp the consequences of what was occurring. What is worse is that garbage; what they created is passed down to their children and their children's children—generation after generation of intolerance for anyone who has an opinion different than yours.

In an attempt to protect people, our society spoiled an essential means of resolving conflicts. This behavior prevents people from moving toward peaceful coexistence. We abandoned understanding and compromise. We are effectively destroying the only acceptable form of conflict resolution that allows substantive change—dialogue. The societal conflict presently affecting our Nation has and always will occur among people. The only possible way to constructively solve it is by talking it out. Censoring one side will not aid in this process.

Somehow, people convinced themselves that a part of the Constitution contains the notion that they should be protected from being offended or sheltered from others who disagree with them. "They should not be able to think differently; force their compliance!" It is quite the opposite. Our system must protect the unpopular with the popular. That is what it means to be an American and allow true freedom. Being a part of and living in a society where people offend one another is what freedom looks like. But children are those who get offended, are they not?

"Whoever would overthrow the liberty of a nation must begin by subduing the freeness of speech."

Benjamin Franklin and the rest of our forefathers continued to give people directions to be successful and hints to destroy the country if they chose to do it. The actions of a few are failing our forefathers. They are failing to protect the Constitution, and they are failing each other. Not because people aren't capable or undeserving of the gift of freedom, but because for far too long, those who were elected and put in positions of trust; beat American's down, telling them they could not do it without them. All the while dismantling the architecture of America's protections to create a version of their America in their likeness. The greatest success of their cancerous views; was convincing a free citizenry they needed or wanted it, and it was the only way to move forward.

America may not possess enough of the people needed to correct the failures and continued destruction of this great Nation. And if she does possess those who have the competency and ability, people may be too selfish to change for the benefit of all people and the American way of life. The system is not broken; it is overwhelmed with incompetency issues caused by those appointed to protect it.

Do not misinterpret or take my position out of context; I am not trying to insult people. They all share in the blame, all sides, all views, all people. And it is reflected in their acceptance of being the worst versions of themselves. But the leaders who teach bad habits are encouraging this behavior. Do not follow weakness. I assure you I am that rare true patriot who believes in America more than I do in the people she represents and will protect it at all costs. And, if you are a true patriot or enjoy the American way of life, regardless of if you are an American or not, let us protect it together before we all come to regret not heeding the warnings gifted by history and those who came before us.

Humanity is in an exceedingly rare timeline of history, and together people can continue to improve the most incredible way to govern a society of free men and women. Americans are so very blessed as they have been given three of the greatest gifts in the history of human civilization. Most were born into this Nation without having to pay the cost or earn citizenship. They were given instructions on how to keep it. And thanks to history and the many mistakes made by societies before us, they know what not to do and what occurs when they fail to follow these instructions. It seems as if the choice is an easy one.

Please believe in something; whether this belief is a standard of decency from religion, America, the Rule of Law, the judicial system, the police officers and soldiers who protect our safety, your neighbor Tiffany up the street, Tommy down the block, or simply the great wisdom from those since past that is so often not given to the youth of this Nation. What you choose to believe in is irrelevant as all choices of decency, at the core, are pure, representing the best way to treat one another. It is not until these beliefs come in contact with human beings that problems start coming into existence. That is when people pervert it; that is when a belief system becomes flawed and weaponized with intent.

Let us not be judged by future generations as the "Ones who ruined it for the rest of us." If this is not something you are willing to do, I assure you, you do not belong here and do not deserve the result of a great many sacrifices those before us made, so we may share -EQUALLY- the protections this great Nation has to offer.

Yes, it will be a challenge, as should anything worth having. However, the difficulty of a task should and must never be a deterrent when visualizing a way to accomplish a task, no matter the problem or likelihood of success.

It is absurd that irrational thoughts can create the issues that innocent people are forced to live with. The kind that makes hate and rises to a dangerous level of hypocrisy used to consume people who are cognitively aware of it yet still lack the capacity and competency to prevent it or see the truth because it is inconvenient and maybe hurtful. The level and severity of the consequences of this immature behavior are astounding. That is why society is currently in an ideological divide and an etymological civil war.

The two-party political system represents just that, the two-party political system. But they are both representatives of the same bias that is leading the country to a violent end. It protects the status quo and will stop at nothing to extinguish anything that threatens it. That way of thinking is obsolete, and decency must replace partisanship at all costs. Not because they are wrong but because a better way exists. Leading in such a manner is an option, does work, but is not sustainable for peace.

People must understand the consequences of what is occurring. Once again—It is a cycle society continues to tread on, passing down hate to their children and their children's children. Generation after generation of intolerance towards anyone who has an opinion different than yours. This is unbecoming of what America represents. There is no longer a united vision of what America should be. Somehow, the standards of how to treat one another have been lost.

Better leaders who represent better ideas are needed because that is what is required of our system. Not necessarily new leaders, just a better version of the ones we have will work. America has accomplished what she has over the last 245 years because the system is flawless, and it allows for greatness to be created. But it does have its limits. Bad leaders are a part of these limits. It is sad and disheartening to learn our citizens get the politicians they deserve because WE, THE PEOPLE, hold power and control the attributes of those who lead us. Leaders are created from the imagination of all people and mimic what behaviors are preferred or what is perceived to be acceptable.

America is nothing without decency. People belong here no matter their race, religion, sexual orientation, gender, or birthplace. This place is meant to prevent persecution. It is a safe haven and must protect the weak, the oppressed, and the fearful. It saddens me to witness the amount of disrespect people show to one another. Please pay your dues and at least be respectful to one another. Be an American, stand up to defend her values.

There has never been a more critical time in America's history than right now. Failure to heed the advice of those before us will be catastrophic. The values of freedom and respect for our fellow Americans are of utmost importance to ensure our democratic republic survives any threat. Unfortunately, the two-party political system has intentionally divided us. When will the "American People" advocate for a leader who intentionally unites U.S.?

American Values are simple to define and can be put into four easily understood categories that transcend party lines and partisanship and will not offend any American. All citizens can support these necessities to protect the Constitution's framework. These are what must be protected at all costs—personal accountability, fiscal responsibility, national security, and the constitutionality of the actions of government officials.

Then and only then can people move forward advocating tolerance for all Americans. The only party that should matter is one of decency with patriotic principles. That is what Defending American Values means, and that is the standard of what America's Democratic Republic demands. Can modern America correct the divisiveness destroying American Values? What is occurring is not caused by the ones being led but by those leading.

America represents freedom; if you can't understand this premise, then you most likely should not live in a beautiful Nation that allows people to have independence. Before the freedoms we all enjoy are removed, a change must occur. Not in a legislative manner as writing laws grants citizens freedoms but as a way to extract power from the individual political parties and give it back to the people. Legislation's purpose is not to give people the power to oppress; it is to protect the individual from the powerful by extending autonomy to those deserving of such a privilege.

It always becomes easier for the next generation of people to do something that prior generations failed to address, support, or change. I am assigning fault and blame to those in the past, those in control, and those in the way. People cannot always understand the shortcomings of their methods; however, we are very much enlightened by the consequences of the past. If you do not want to change America for the better or are intentionally creating friction—you are part of the problem.

How can Americans work together to remove the lines politicians and their cronies created? These questions must be answered by each one of us if peace is to be protected and allowed to prosper with freedoms. Maintaining the original purpose of this great Nation by standing behind the promise of this Nation's founders will enable society to continue to grow. Americans must recognize the importance of individuality and togetherness, allowing people to protect our citizen's rights while also Defending American Values no matter the preference freely chosen.

Tolerance, decency, and a standard of accountability must be present...

# A Place for Your Thoughts:

# CHAPTER V

## *A Step Towards Tolerance*

Let us imagine that in the future, a majority exists in any other category that is absent in the modern understanding of what society represents. For example, ideas, thoughts, and the populous representation are now flipped; black Americans are now the majority; vegan and vegetarian are both the governing moral truth and most common diet; electric vehicles represent the fleet of consumers. The religion in America is no longer tied to Christianity, no longer respected, or religion has nearly been extinguished; the LGBTQ community is greater than the heterosexual persuasion; and same race relationships have been outlawed because interracial procreation is believed to end hate.

In addition, those who are against America and the Republic, which she stands for, have removed the freedom of expression, the ability to own a gun, and the free-market capitalism represents and replaced these with an alternative of their choosing.

Does empathy extend, or does it die? Do the oppressed now become the oppressor? Would they eliminate these differences because what is different refuses to conform and will never be, think, or look like the majority? If people had their way, would all others be forced to be like them? What kind of supremacy would that be, and would it be more acceptable? Is the current landscape any indication of the treatment that awaits a minority swap in any category? Finally, what type of governance would "We the People" be subjected to?

Is the lack of care and understanding removed because punishment must occur? Punishment for the ones in the past is impossible, so those who are the new minority must experience hate. It is now somehow represented by a premise of reciprocal intolerant equity applied with satisfaction by allowing those who are not like us to finally understand what it's like? The expression of, "how does it feel" or "how do you like it" seems to fit appropriately here. Two wrongs may make a right, especially when the system removed recourse.

Of course, what will occur is unknown, but what will society apply, hypocrisy and ignorance or ignorance and hypocrisy? Imposing punishment on those whose likeness represented the intolerant. It is scary to imagine a level of hate so high it can equal what is felt towards the Nazis—a type of disgust characterized by a feeling or desire to kill what is left of them. But they are trying.

Appropriately destroying everything they once represented because what they are, caused the problem—is the problem. What they believe in, love, look, pray, and eat like must be eliminated. A social engineering campaign over generations or a targeted purpose can accomplish this— Believe This, Be mad, Hate Them, Destroy Them. Highly effective and grossly ignorant, similar to what America's news agencies and media outlets have morphed into.

Control is effortless when the willing accept everything they are told to believe. Will there be those who fight for the new minority then? Are tolerance and the right to live a life of freedom only a gadget when people find agreeance with what the minority they support represents? Is this what occurs no matter the controlling truth or the minority protected? Is tolerance an illusion? Is it never extended to those perceived as an enemy, those we are told are the enemy, those we hate, or anyone that does not belong in our group identity? Does war start because tolerance has finally been extinguished and hate controlling?

Is this the cycle that our species is destined to repeat—the big ugly beast? Will conflict and war create the changes mentioned? Is the goal of those with influence represented by true tolerance? Are the leaders who represent the differences in America interested in coexisting, or are they strictly interested in eliminating competing views? And is this intolerant view, measured throughout history in the form of conflicts, always connected through the pursuit of power over people, animosity towards differences, and the extermination of competing interests?

Americans must be mindful of what occurs over generations of hate, and it will serve them well to fight for peace instead of encouraging conflict. Do not seek to blame those who are not mirrored perfectly. Likewise, do not hate those unlike you and those not representing your identity. Tolerating those who are different is the key to sustainable peace and prosperity for a Nation of diverse people who possess the freedom our people have.

There is a concept of a better American. A superior type of citizen. It is not represented by party lines, race, or religion, nor is it a reflection of history. It is based on actions and the possibility of a prosperous free tomorrow. An understanding that all people deserve protection in this great Nation. Not just the people who like you or think like you. Forcing people to pick sides based on likeness associated with location, religion, political party, race, gender, sexual orientation, or other identities will only accomplish one thing: force innocent people into these groups in the event a conflict occurs. A kill or be killed mentality forces people into an impossible decision destroying peace because they decided to.

People create conflict and will continue to create conflict. Where conflict exists, so must our way of managing these inevitable consequential emotional attachments more appropriately. Like how courts decide controversies, our law must be on decency and the judge—fair. It must be us and a way to protect each other from ourselves. Not to virtue stand about the level of tolerance we have but a greater understanding of empathy to prevent hate. Great care, consideration, and control must always follow to solve such societal issues. Competing interests, views, and ideological differences will always remain in America and in all societies.

It is without question when confrontation is present, both sides or all parties of an argument, disagreement, or conflict lack the competency to understand the premise of a competing thought entirely because they are missing something. It takes work, learning, and the empathetic will to address ideas or alternative positions a person has never before considered.

The internal beliefs of competing views cannot and are unable to pass to those who are not the creators of, consumers of, or believers of. These are only understood and comprehended by those who accept a truth. Human nature has always been about metamorphosis through convincing. What are you willing to accept, what are you willing to become, and finally, what version is created?

By gaining insight and understanding of the world around them or lack thereof, people create whatever version they are drawn to. Each person's construct develops a reasoned, subjective, justifiable mentality of selfishness. They are garnishing nothing more than applicability through likeness. A truth represented and reflective of identity. Understood and consumed by and through the willing.

The most important part of interacting with others who may be different or have competing viewpoints is to allow legitimacy by validating what they feel or accepting the emotions associated with the premise of their argument. Another critical step of understanding that alludes people when they engage in discussion for which they possess zero understanding—it is **I** who decides to be ignorant; It is **I** who creates the divide; it is **I** who decides to become intolerant; it is **I** who decides to hate.

A person will never fully be able to recognize the fact that part of the reason for such friction between differences is themselves. The inability to respect a person as your equal will always break down any society. These consequences will have catastrophic effects in the future. People who read history will try to understand past mistakes, but they always overlook what it was—hate. This hate is caused by a connection to any descriptors or identities a person acknowledges, belongs to, or looks like. This allows a competing group to quickly grab a superficial scope and fire intolerant rhetoric at people because they are too ignorant and too lazy to understand.

These are the reasons we are at odds as a species time and time again. We find fault in differences. Allow me to rephrase this; we look for fault in differences to strengthen our understanding of superiority. This tragic application promotes us and the identity we belong to above all others on the legitimacy-ladder of society. Finally, permission to hate. Each tribal leader gives our group-identity the authority to pick and choose what is acceptable based on what we think of others and ignore any other alternative—subjective cruelty.

The issue has and will always be us, people. And as we move forward, never fully understanding how ignorant we all are, we cannot be bothered to be considerate of those who are different. People fail to grasp what is different, so they choose to disparage, criticize, hate, and eventually wage war in the name of likeness or lack thereof.

What is more disturbing is the continued justification and arrogant belief that a person has been gifted with that God-like authority—arbitrarily making absolutes of the delusional kind. Selfishness makes their opinion or way of life the absolute and only alternative acceptable to the rest of the peasants.

Royalty is a term used to describe this type of perceived narcissism. They believe in their power through bloodlines, or a purity test based on irrelevancies. Somehow, they have been ordained and privileged to lead because their station in life or God will use him or her for a vessel to lead those who must be lead.

These false prophets believe people cannot understand the correct way to live morally and ethically because the population is too incompetent to live a life of their own design. So, they set in motion a way to control people through devices such as fear, overconsumption, and division of the populous. But why does this continue to occur, and are they correct? Should people be controlled, or can the ownership of genuine autonomy break this cycle?

Knowledge has power, but first, people must be willing to see what is right in front of them. The truth not only requires thinking deeply on many subjects but also a commitment to continuously do so. People gain a critical perspective by first destroying what they know is correct. Removing all close connections allows the truth to reveal itself. I live by this and seek truth without bias. I teach my son this as well.

People create their paths, and I chose a difficult one for not only me but him as well. I chose the way of being enlightened. Our conversations include many topics addressed throughout this book. His motto is "I do not wish to believe in anything for fear of not being enlightened." I chose to search for the truth, and so too my son. This occurred because people in our life taught us to do so. Although he has a difficult path, I believe he will stay true to the many lessons that speak of a better way. A step towards something better than either of us can imagine. Failure is not an option.

I do this so I may pursue an attempt to work out every issue I can imagine finding the cause of society's harm instead of only treating the symptom. Unfortunately, however, I am unable to obtain such a divine creation because I am stuck trying to understand and even solve the unsolvable, the human element.

Yes, society may have periods of peace throughout history, but they have always been fleeting and momentary. But it is easy to find the cause. Differences cause friction, people create hate, and leaders encourage conflict. Misguided incompetent leaders and those who engage in such harmful behaviors will always make an excuse to kill in the name of some misguided belief or banner they decide to follow.

It saddens me; I have concluded that peace between differences may never be able to be obtained. The realization that society is stuck in a perpetual cycle of destruction creates a mentality of why try, to what end, and maybe we all should quit. I am saddened because wisdom and understanding do not bring peace; it is quite the opposite. It is the final recognition that people may never fully achieve anything other than fighting with each other.

But what should people do with this understanding? Will our existence on this planet never know more than war? Should people quit or not care? Or must they fight harder and stand for righteousness? These questions are owned by people who can correct our trajectory or seal our fate. Will human intervention alter, or will complacency destroy?

What is required will be extremely difficult; however, all is not lost. The present can change the future with the knowledge of the past in combination with a new thought by attempting what once seemed impossible. Those who are committed to this should never be discouraged by the thought of past failures. Maybe they were doing it wrong?

This is exactly what a statesman understood. What the founding fathers discussed in secret and why they tortured themselves with mental gymnastics in an attempt to create a near perfect document with room for growth that would allow differences to live in peace.

They were interested in removing the concept of conflict resolution by means of war. Creating rules to govern through dialogue with understanding. A chance to allow and extend freedoms to people by controlling detrimental behaviors yet encouraging self-expression.

The idea of America and what it could represent to those who are different is a place of acceptance and genuine autonomy. There was a chance of peace, freedom, and protection from those who would harm the persecuted. It created a limit of power controlled by and through a people. But it also assembled uniqueness allowing the document to grow with the people it governed.

And if people with reckless tendencies are not careful, a conflict of astronomical magnitude can remove this failsafe. The system was designed to encourage tolerance. Our ability to live in peace can end at any moment. As our population grows, so too does the divide of our people and what America should represent subjectively creates unnecessary tension.

The internal fractures are caused by intolerance and the perception of entitled legislation defended by a ruling-partied nature. It is nothing more than modern tyrannical elites disguised as pigs in lipstick singing in an echo chamber filled with idiotic equals. These people sow nothing but hate for the masses—building wealth for themselves and those around them, ignoring those who voted for their campaign falsities.

Americans living in a free society must remember that intolerance leads to hate, which eventually becomes a conflict. Ignoring the symptoms and the cause will never change the outcome. A continued dismissal of the importance of others and lack of understanding of those differences does nothing but remove our likeness allowing the drums of war to beat again, getting closer and closer.

We are Americans. Our system was designed to remove hate. We must continue to seek and maintain the original purpose of our Constitution. Our very existence depends on it. Americans and their responsibility to each other, our way of life, and the willingness to defend our Constitution; is never over. Vigilance, resoluteness, and an unwavering commitment is required.

The Constitution is built to support one another and allow those with different thoughts, beliefs, and lifestyles to exist hand in hand, impervious to tyrannical overreach. Our system is built to keep overzealous imbeciles from doing harm to free people. This is what America represents, and its most significant role is to protect.

We must start the process again and heal our Nation. Our system can fix what is broken and mend the divide people seem so eager to create. But first, we must recognize all Americans have a different understanding of what America means to them and what they mean to America.

It is without question that those who had the chance to exude true tolerance by ending slavery when they fought for America failed miserably. The founding fathers created an illusion of tolerance by ignoring the truth. They allowed a contradictory statement to exist, all while encouraging the unethical, immoral, and un-American practice of slavery to continue—All Men are Created Equal.

The influential and those with power decided it was easier to concede to the south to defeat the British. Did they allow slavery to continue so we may defeat the red coats? Did they understand that they just created a Nation where all people are not created equal, and freedom was dependent solely on the gender and the skin a person has? What they did was wrong. Compromising with the devil only tolls what must be dealt with. It never disappears; it is paid for later by the innocent who would have never made such an agreement.

Did they understand that any attempt to create a new independent nation would fail without the southern states? Did the southern states unknowingly sign a document starting the process of their demise long before it was fully understood what would occur? Without the south and the birth of America, would slavery still exist?

Regardless of the excuse or the decision made, that was their—our— fatal flaw. Their inability to protect the powerless seems to echo throughout history uninterrupted. These were people, our people, and just like all errors in history made by those with power, we killed those we did not respect. Hate, ignorance, and dismissal of truths subjugated our people to a life sentence beneath those who owned superior perception.

But how hard is it to stop history from repeating, and would you be brave enough to do it? Do you possess the personal courage necessary to stand and fight knowing that your life is likely in danger? Or are you the person who simply complains, reaping the benefits of those who act? What must be changed takes strength, it takes sacrifice, and it takes a whole lot of what most people are without. This is why injustices, inequities, and inequalities take so long to correct.

Progress is of no consolation to those who were taken from their land, belittled, beaten, and raped. Slave ownership throughout the world created many things, but slavery in America began the end of such a demonic practice. Were the contents of America's Constitution, the people's document, always meant to transform society into a tolerant yet controversial place? Did it allow a minority thought to push boundaries and settle controversies between differences in a manner required to create civility among citizens?

Did they have the capacity to possess such foresight? Am I foolish to believe they had the ability to draft a document so pure they knew it would change the future? Is it possible what was created had the power to right any wrongs as long as the Nation possessed what was required? Are we to view the founding fathers as moronic and heartless for the acquiesce of behavior compared to **our** understanding of the America they just created?

Or do society's harshest graders lack contextual understanding from a time period that occurred without them? Do they deserve a pass for surviving a revolution that created freedoms that changed the world and allowed a free people to change the status quo anytime they saw fit? It is hard to imagine living in a world where slavery existed. A modern understanding of slavery is impossible to reconcile by a reasonable standard test of today's current population, societal norms, and our collective moral growth.

Make no concession that those who chose to be weak-minded and lacked the intestinal fortitude deserve criticism for the allowance and continued violent intolerance for a people. This old-world practice is disturbing and disgusting, to say the least. But are we not limited by our understanding of knowledge and societal norms contained within at the time of our decisions?

The current commitment to human rights and pursuit of equity makes the practice of slavery extremely difficult to imagine occurring today. Yet, as time marched forward, the call for a more equitable society did too. Eventually, through much sacrifice and on the back of courageous men and women, a change occurred in society; what was first a thought is now an undeniable truth. People changed what was necessary because they were able to change the truth.

Generational truths are what control what is accepted by the people who are frozen in time with their understanding of right or wrong. Is no generation without error and subject to intense scrutiny from those who apply a modern decency standard against past behaviors?

The reason for discussing our beginning, our truths, and our mistakes was to highlight that these limits existed and were changed by the system put in place by those who were committed to creating America. Not a selfish one-America, but an idea. An America which transcends every identity people needlessly cling to. This thought, what America could be, is a better way, a perfect place, a Nation containing a people who would fight for one another, defending those who are oppressed. That is America and what she must represent. But the people in any America where decency is lacking can permanently destroy it.

It seems all our species does is create conflict, grow, create more conflict, grow, create unnecessary conflict, change nothing, create more conflict, and wait. This cycle occurs because evolutionary progress will never end. It will never end because people are different; however, they will always represent their likeness. Eventually, they will decide to stand together united to fight whatever ideology is at odds with their existence.

The truth, and the sadness I am frequented by, represent my understanding of why people are the way they are. Why they will always go through the cycle of destruction and the rebuilding that has plagued civilizations since the beginning of free thought. I now know why there will always be wars in the future to fight. It is us. Our existence, what we are, is selfish. Our need to control, the want for power, and the desire for war always create the need for more.

But where I feel and am consumed by justifiable sadness, I have hope. Even though I believe I will see great tragedies in my lifetime, I am encouraged by the history of human evolution. I see those who are willing to fight the good fight, and I will stand with them. If America possessed the strength and courage to end slavery and aid in the destruction of Nazism, the future would seem tolerable. I have faith in the future and the people I have yet to know.

I am confident and hopeful our people will eventually figure it out. I am also a bit apprehensive at times, so I look to past leaders for strength and past battles as proof and what I found was a path forward is always available. Not that progress is easy, but when an idea is placed in those who seek a world that is fair by current generational standards, they can be successful.

We have the directions, and we must fight for and represent the change we believe is necessary. Another generational battle will occur where people must convince the masses of the truth only they can see. It is a form of equity applicable through progress and the good fight. Empathy brings out the best in us, achieving the change people are starving for. They can bring about the change needed in the timeline of human occupancy. This fight must occur, for the opposite is tyranny represented by absolutism or a one-America.

Those brave individuals who followed the strength of the past will succeed in their fight for tolerance—it will happen. Even though I can never be a part of that reality, it does bring me peace of mind to think of what progress lies ahead. There is a bit of sadness for the ones who suffered, are suffering, or will suffer as they will never know the progress or feel the amount of freedom and protection the Constitution was able to bring or will bring.

If people are listening, as an individual who pushes society's norms, your fight doesn't end with a life of being an activist standing for something. The next minority of free thinkers will pick up where you left off and find a solution to a generational problem a people were unable to solve. But you must influence those correctly so they may never have hate in their heart as this always allows the excuse to persecute those we decided deserved it.

The change is needed; that is what the fight brings—a brighter future. A necessary ending to create a necessary beginning. The necessary beginning to create the necessary ending.

The future is a bit fuzzy; not clear at all. But the system is in place, don't forget that. A good fight is always needed, representing tolerance or at least a step towards tolerance. But what is clear is the path. We have one; people have one; America has one.

This is the path forward, and it's through tolerance…

# A Place for Your Thoughts:

# CHAPTER VI

## *A Path Forward*

I am unaware of what it is to be black in America. I am unaware of what it means to be a woman in America. I am unaware of what it means to be any of the LGBTQ community members in America. I am, however, aware what it means to be different in America. Maybe that is the problem; we have too many different Americas, ignoring the many differing Americans.

The Nation forgot how to govern and respect those differences within their version of America. Even if we disagree or cannot understand one another, it should not mean we stop supporting Americans or each other. Instead, it means people work harder, committing themselves to understand what is necessary to move forward.

People work harder to create an inclusive society. People work harder to make America respectful. People work harder to make America what she was meant to be—a breath of fresh free air, protection for the persecuted, and an understanding of the need for participation. People work harder to be Americans. We must alter and change our perceptions of value to alter and change our trajectory of conflict.

Nothing has changed in our Country or interactions between her people. Even initially, Americans were fighting each other over the rules and what path our Nation should take, and—here we are again. The one constant that remains, the thing we cannot seem to escape as a people, is the continuous conflict consuming each generation. It is created by the need to be in control and the intolerance of differences while pursuing power.

However, it does and has created growth—our collective willingness to engage in conflict after conflict made what we have today. Our way of life is pretty close to being perfect. Some inequities need to be addressed and, at times, personal accountability problems, but we as a people are privileged to experience such a life. But we must stay the course and focus on shoring up our deficiencies. Doing this will allow citizens to create a better tomorrow for all people.

The United States has the potential to be flawless, and if operated as intended, with the correct leaders, it would create a system that people would unite around, promoting the cohesion necessary to ensure peace is abundant. But we are stuck with people who seem only interested in destroying one another. Never growing, never changing, always limited.

Thomas Jefferson doubted the viability of a self-governing people for many reasons, and most of those reasons are on display and visible today. Self-interests are destroying the greatest gift Americans share. Americans must defend against those who seek to harm our unity. People must challenge the weakness and incompetence in positions of influence. This would remove their ability to divide. And we must challenge the value that has since left worth.

We must not value worthless things and give value to equally worthless people. Unfortunately, Americans created a system that values and idolizes items or people that should not be associated with either. Toxicity and division occur when society gives power and influence to unworthy people. Society must highlight the absurdity of putting value where it should never be.

All people are better than this, yet somehow it seems they lack the competency to remove the cancer that causes their issues. What some call progress represents weakness. Of all the things our society could value, they chose being entertained as the most important. How can people continue to consume distractions that are designed to hide the cause [politicians] by promoting the disease [selfishness]?

Is it too far off to state most Americans value things that serve zero purposes in relation to surviving and providing for their families? They created a bunch of people and things that represent a refrigerator without electricity. What is more concerning is that when people finally realize what is happening, just how detrimental the influence of these fools is, it will be too late.

Being entertained can create a life complemented with joy. But when a life of entertainment is sought after and thought to be superior, people mimic what is created, ignoring what is cardinal. It has a place in society, but it is not vital and must remain a spice, never an ingredient. But when you monetize idiots, that is what people will be drawn to—fools with money. Seeking fame and fortune over what is necessary for the protection of America and what she represents will have devastating consequences. Fundamental literacy of Americans and participation must remain an important endeavor. However, people seek to be entertained by fanciful pleasures ignoring the cost because what's necessary is inconvenient or takes work to understand, something most Americans seem to be okay missing.

My suggestion to people at this current moment is to look back to how life was one hundred years ago and check your value concerning the skills needed and experience necessary to survive. Are you in possession of knowledge and/or skills that would allow you and your family to survive? Do not be that refrigerator, and do not allow those refrigerators to influence your life, especially your children.

We should never stop learning and teaching our children what is necessary to live, what is vital to survive, and what allows peace to prosper. We must work harder, seek to be indispensable, never give up on decency, always protect the society we live in and protect those who live in a community with us. Value these and allow your children access to role models with character. Ignore what we can live without because what we cannot, will destroy us all.

Thomas Jefferson said, "Those who expect to be both ignorant and free, expect what never was and never will be." This describes the lack of care a citizen of a free nation uses and a person who does not deserve the freedom offered and the protections extended. A system of self-governance requires all who are protected by the system to participate in the system. Citizens cannot simply dismiss, ignore, or choose not to accept this premise.

It seems to be an arduous, almost unattainable quest at times. However true that may be, it is needed more than people realize to prevent catastrophe. But those with the power through their own volution need to understand that America, what she represents, is the ability to create and the ability to maintain peace. Its purpose and design must be acknowledged and protected, no matter the cost.

Those willing to use expansive thoughts and fight for what is protection were able to create and improve on a system specifically designed to allow free people to live without the harmful interferences of self-prescribed tyrannical people or entities designed to enslave alternatives. But without participation, it represents the beginning of the end.

When did society's understanding of this leave a free people? At what point did Americans decide people are granted permission not to participate but still expect reciprocity of freedoms and the benefits of a Nation? Those unwilling to participate use all the privileges offered but never earn what they take. Who in their right mind allows citizens of a nation, a free nation, a nation that was built around the premise of "all must give, so all may have" to take leave from vigilance? Or was this only ever understood and given by the few?

I remain steadfast in my commitment to treat every day in America as the first because it is constantly under attack and forever must be defended like it was just created. America is failing because our form of governance does not permit its citizens to use blinders or become valueless. It does not protect without being protected. And it will surely not last if our understanding of this does not change.

In addition, Americans must learn to get along. We are not that different. A connection exists between participation and tolerance. There is no equality in our system because there is no participation in our system. A form of governance that requires its citizens to participate must have its citizens participate, not by voting but by creating a dialogue with others who want to live in peace and encouraging fellowship. This will alter detrimental behavior by promoting Americans to defend one another.

When we fail to extend respect to a people, animosity is created. When we choose to ignore the atrocities occurring to a people, hate is created. When we promote ourselves over others, extremism is created. All these creations of selfishness are constantly in the background of civilization. It is not until peaceful people feel these, practice these, and become these that society is in danger.

Is this the end of America? Has the desire to protect individuality, togetherness, and collective autonomy died from the refusal to nurture what is fair, just, and equitable in society? The lack of care for one another and the outright refusal to hold people accountable or make excuses for the actions of those who look like us, even the over commitment to allow feelings to control, can destroy us all.

Like a weed that strangles the crop necessary to sustain life, it consumes, constricts, and ultimately kills. A seed planted for sustenance requires nurturing to meet the desired outcome. So too is the requirement to have peace, freedom, and prosperity—these must be nurtured. It is an ongoing venture unless, of course, the desired outcome has already been met. It is irresponsible to believe our way of life will be maintained without nurture.

The past, the present, and the future can all die the same way, by the same threat caused by the same people. But this is what occurs due to peaceful ignorant people dismissing the need to evaluate, educate, and participate. Therefore, it very well could be the beginning of the end.

If we are not careful, the path paved by intolerance and ignorance will surely be the one traveled as it's easier than the rough and bumpy road of knowledge and enlightenment. One takes work; the other takes innocence, requiring nothing from the user and occurring through misplaced value, misplaced trust, and in people, all of which we elevate above what is decent that will never care because it is not in their nature to do so.

Pursuant to the Declaration of Independence, The Constitution of the United States of America, and the progress society has made, these create the duty as a United States citizen to support and defend everything represented, including differences from self-identity. This is a Nation of free thought, free expression, and free people. We must not create a triggered society offended by every nuance of diversity or encourage a pursuit in the attempt to find a reason to be offended.

Each competing interest must advocate for not only themselves but also others. This Nation was built on the premise of "freedom for all." Not one idea over the other. Not one political party over the other. Not one-America over the other. The past is essential as it gives us directions for the future. History is riddled with those who sought to control through intimidation, violence, a God's influence, or peaceful legislation disguised as tyranny designed to remove free will.

This type of behavior or the consequences existing from system failure is not new to a people. It is not just a modern problem society faces. It is in people just as much as the color of their eyes and will likely remain until our species is without eyes. America is no different than past civilizations. It is still vulnerable to the same threats, issues, and groupthink that has destroyed all people or societies in a timeline containing such consequences.

We must not let this poison continue to consume us or allow it to divide us further. A person's identity, beliefs, or understandings are not wrong. Those items must be balanced with the identity, beliefs, or understandings of others. Selfishness and assumed righteousness will do nothing but point blame and assign fault. It is the responsibility of all Americans to Defend American Values, especially those who have the privilege to represent the American people. This Nation does not only serve a one-sided "your" America. It serves an all-sided "our" America. A message from Chapter III seems appropriate here:

Recognizing bias and lack of empathy for differences is extremely important to cohesiveness when a diverse society is present. No matter the topic or subject matter, when we view differences, we must see more than ourselves and surely protect those in need, especially when they honestly believe their likeness is unsafe or in danger from preventable harm. If we fail; we choose, if we fail, chaos ensues; if we fail, we all lose. We must succeed.

You can never understand what you do not know. With this comes the realization that exposures limit our understanding. If people are not exposed to differences, understanding, and empathy cannot occur. This determines what people can solve or become by introducing new and unnecessary problems. An expression of the need for respect is not one way. Craving legitimacy while dishing out accusations of illegitimacy only deepens a divide. Society is left with inequity as an extension of animosity from one side to the other.

How can people encourage each other to be themselves but also accept the differences of others, even when those differences are at odds with a chosen lifestyle? What must be done to prevent the collapse of society due to the divisions growing among people? Can it be stopped? Encouraging others to be themselves aids in the creation of a tolerant, cohesive society. But some people are not yet ready to accept the ideas and beliefs of others, and that is okay too. If a hostile environment is not created or intentional discrimination legislated, what is wrong with people not agreeing with a lifestyle?

It is not your place to force people to change because you feel they are wrong for not accepting you. It is wrong for them but not you; it is wrong for you but not them. A continued conflict based on the premise that everyone must believe the way you do or live the way you do is equally wrong. Regardless of personal convictions, maintaining balance is crucial to peace. And differing thoughts that pose challenging questions should never be attacked because the questions hurt your feelings.

Recognizing how these issues affect, influence, and progress or regress society is crucial to understanding true tolerance and the power of acceptance. Society's diversity causes such friction. These differences must not be viewed as a negative but as alternatives existing in a free society allowing our species to focus on what truly matters and solve what threatens us all.

It is odd that the American population found peace ten, twenty, or thirty years ago, yet somehow it disappeared and is no longer achievable for the Nation in 2020 and beyond. What changed? Why the change? Or is this the constant? What force pushes the unnecessary change from peace to conflict and eventually war? What happens when a war occurs?

A place will remain, but it will not be America, and the destruction of our institutions will cause this place to be filled with a type of horror most cannot imagine. All people will be devoured by greed, selfishness, and the attempt to create correctness through likeness. This will encourage detrimental unity instead of promoting cohesive unity.

Americans must understand the consequences of short-sighted emotional behavior of the selfish kind. They must not become blinded and seek knee-jerk reactions when a decision does not turn out in their favor, regardless of political affiliation. Laws must be changed and influenced by people, never entities. Legislation of a free people must continue as long as it does not offend the Constitution and Judicial review.

Those are the avenues for redress, reconciliation, and relief in a system designed with internal fail safes. Not economic prowess of a selfish kind to create virtue signals in an attempt to inflate valuation or promote superiority. This will only lead to identity businesses and the demise of a free market in a capitalistic economy supported by a people's Constitution. The consequences of allowing businesses to subvert our governmental legislation process and hijack the fragility of our economic system by leveraging their strength against the will of the people are highly ill-advised.

When CEOs flex their economic might, people will choose sides, furthering an already consequential divide that will do nothing more than create additional internal conflict. Just like the result of the colonies introducing our Declaration of Independence after the revolution, the influences of the powerful and the wealthy create unnecessary tension, friction, and eventual conflict between the poor, who are always willing to die for whatever misguided belief is introduced and conditioned on them as an absolute.

Aligning its dollars with its values is another line drawn to create conflict. It amounts to an alternative governing system within the three branches already established with possession of assumed power and legitimacy. This occurs with states, too, as the inconsideration of federalism is lost or never really understood. The demand of respect for their way of life but not a shred of respect for others. Entities cannot create such a volatile process. It will do nothing but fracture and destroy—for that is the final step in creating a one-America. The recognition that people do not need those differences in their society will start the process of moving forward without those differences in their society.

The government's protection of arms is not going to support one side over the other. It will indeed split into the tribalistic tendencies and factions supported by the already underway division and witnessed behaviors of businesses around the Country and pockets of partisan or ideological unrest.

Of course, that was the result and eventual process in America's revolution. But one difference, one fatal flaw between a not yet formed America and the one we are accustomed to now, is that the commonality of historical progress is shared. There is interconnectivity within the borders sharing freedoms and a way of life protected under the Rule of Law and a single constitution.

The issue is magnified as the perceived enemies are among us. The problem is not extremism; of course, it is on full display and currently active, but the threat, the genuine concern, is a divided hyper-stimulated entire populous, not a fringe ideological movement containing insignificant numbers. Our citizens will be identified as combatants and enemies of the state by whatever one-America is chosen based on likeness, and it seems as if it has already begun.

That truly is the fatal flaw. Assuming America will always stand without participating in the duties required. Forgetting and dismissing what is required as a U.S. Citizen has caused this. Forgoing the use of dialogue for competing views and the much-needed respect for differences started the collapse. We are failing in the duty to extend decency to fellow Americans. And the leaders are failing by ignoring the responsibility of setting examples worthy of this decency.

But it is a common theme for weak leadership and those they represent to entice each other with toxic tirades. Doing nothing to promote cohesion but adding unnecessary fractures creates more division in an already divided populous. They are seeking only to push free people to the breaking point intentionally. Defending likeness over justice. They are removing decorum to create motivation and anger within their constituents.

And in the end, it is nothing more than a result of drawing poor conclusions based on a fraction of information to strengthen one's position and motivate those who vote with ignorance. All in selfish pursuits are failing to use the critical perspective to the detriment of America and the people she represents, being unapologetic as people engage in legislative gymnastics to prevent or inflict outcomes not accepted by the majority of Americans yet easily identified by irresponsible party lines.

Partisan influencers and partisan representatives create unnecessary tension by seeking total control. Each party or political force subverts the rules to achieve one-sided legislative success to obtain a one-America-themed outcome benefiting likeness instead of a free people.

Convincing themselves that they are the correct party, the right identity to lead America. They are the keepers of the Constitution. They will protect America from the plight of illogical, intolerant extremism threatening their democracy from the enemy contained on the left or right opposite of where they stand. What occurred in the past as war in conflict resolution will always happen when an internal ideological difference reaches a breaking point; innocent people will be forced to choose a side. The wrath of war and selfishness will swallow all it encounters.

Who and what is right? The answer to these questions is evident and racist, bigoted and tolerant, hateful and accepting, dependent solely on the identity of the people answering the call to fight for what is entirely objectively correctly incorrect and subjectively much, much worse. But what is disgusting—the answers to these questions will not be known until a cataclysmic conclusion occurs.

If I had to choose the people to fight for, many Americans would not make the cut. Not because of their identities, I can accept many alternatives. But because, deep down, their character, principles, and what they represent are simply selfishness disguised as some patriotic duty promoting what they feel is the right way to live or a social justice movement that is collapsing our social integrity. Dangerous and perilous times have risen once again to challenge the peace fought for by our fathers as they ignore the accountability process at our disposal.

The thoughts that consume my mind are a need to understand and a want to know the future. It is a hard pill to swallow that both take time, and eventually, the future arrives, and it does so with a bit more understanding. Although that is no consolation to those who seek immediate relief from the toxicity promoted all around, it will have to do for now so I may possess a shred of peace. But not knowing, especially when a person is in constant despair of the many possibilities running through his mind, is tortuous and exhausting.

I want answers to questions that may not be available, will never be known, or are unfathomable to my small insignificant mind. If these answers do exist, they can only come from people who are not available. It is not because their presence is unreachable or unattainable, but their being does not exist.

At times I feel alone in my anger towards those who defend and protect the status quo, alone in my disgust with the reality inflicting harm to my countrymen. It seems as if I am alone with being fed up with half-truths decreed as irrefutable evidence supporting absolutism. Are people okay with living a life filled with imbeciles thinking and acting in an unbecoming way of the influence that has fallen upon their laps?

I am unable to depend on any news source. I am unable to follow any politicians. And I am unable to find the truth. One thing is for certain if my thoughts and what I believe in or represent are becoming censored; if my dissent is made to be the enemy; if I lost the ability to express myself in the ways I have done so in this book—why do you imagine I still swear allegiance to the flag and to the people this Country represents?

Because I believe in truth, peace, and what this Nation represents, I will stand, fight, and defend the freedom we all share so your children will never have to kill each other in this land ever again. I will die for my convictions to prevent the demise of what I know our people will bring upon the innocent. But there are many obstacles, and what prevents change, or a different path forward will gladly eliminate what threatens the status quo. Where do we start? It may be time to pick the side of America over partisanship by purging the current politicians from our system. These people cannot change what is necessary because they are connected to the cause. A change must occur; it is time to look to ourselves.

I have lost respect for the Legislative Branch and the Executive Branch. I imagine the Judicial Branch will soon be a part of my angst as the constant inability to stay neutral allows its actors to destroy what justice is. They seem to be overcome by a desire to ignore accountability disconnected from the words these institutions are bound by. What is highly disappointing is when the political activist Judges become social justice warriors by virtue standing. They bypass the legislative process altogether. All branches are doing exactly what is necessary to destroy our system's core command.

Creating a deeper divide, pushing the U.S. population to dislike each other even more. Throwing gasoline on the intolerant flames and fanned by those in favor of one party over the other. Each is seeking the one-America that benefits their kind the most. This leads to nothing more than lines drawn in preparation for conflict. Each side assumes that the other will of course, receive the protection of the military in the event another civil war occurs.

If that is the case, then these people are my enemies. They should also be the enemies of all Americans who seek justice, accountability, and peace. I find it highly probable I will be the target of pushback, anger, and eventually violence because people will misunderstand my intent or will try to stop me. Why? Am I a problem because I don't identify with the left or the right, the black or the white; because I see the good before the bad, the positive before the negative? What is logical is losing. What is destructive is winning.

Do I stand up for myself and become as vocally obnoxious as those who are sowing more chaos are doing? They only fuel what I know is coming. Do I draw the line as they did, they are currently doing, and will continue to do just to make a point? Am I allowed to fight with every breath for what I believe in? Or would it have been better for my kind to have never existed because a group of people wishes to move society into a place where my existence is no longer necessary and overtly insulting? I am undoubtedly unmanageable or uncontrollable by any definition of the words. The ability to "be" is lost because what we can "be" is no longer our choice.

An attempt to recreate the population of America is occurring once again. It does not register as a necessary evil for me. But, predictably, it is yet again dangerously approaching that point, pitting private citizens against each other.

Some things are indeed worth fighting for. Lives are disposable to create a better future for generations to come. But all that is visible is tyrannical overreach ignoring the premise of defending one another or Country over party. The leadership in past and present of this Country has been abysmal for advocating togetherness. When graded against the purpose and minimal understanding of the Declaration in combination with the Constitution, they all fail miserably to encourage cohesion. Misguided use of political parties and lack of bipartisanship created weak leaders.

Fraudulently in their representation of patriotic endeavors, do they sit high up on their platform, sowing cynical and hyperbolic rhetoric. Encouraging violence, encouraging unrest, and publicly making a mockery out of civil discourse. These leaders dangerously approach treason but for the normality of a circus created and tolerated by American voters. Shame on us all. It should sicken even the least patriotic person to think Americans are required to be represented by incompetent sociopaths of the selfish kind.

If America wants progress, cohesion, and a resemblance of professional representation, the strongest, most capable of our people must serve. Those who pursue civic duty, not a paycheck that triples the median income of America's people. A career it should not be; a duty to one's Country it must be. It is not a job but a calling. Like all things in life, a transfer of some form of currency marks the end of that transaction. In the case of politicians, their currency is votes. Our people complain, continue to criticize, yet give these people exactly what they want—their blessing every election day. Those who represent America do so and maintain power simply by doing what Americans tolerate. Stop tolerating it. We should all be tired of the way things have been.

In a different world, a much different place, those who are the weakest of us would not serve in positions of importance with incompetent, self-serving tendencies. It would not be tolerated for this long if not for the ruse of the Rule of Law used to maintain their protection and inferiority in the halls of Congress or other institutions responsible for the decline of America. The ease of life and conveniences in America have been used to distract from their incompetency.

Who among us would die for such a cohort of misfits? Are those who represent us worth fighting for, worth dying for, worth representing such a document such as the Declaration of Independence or America's Constitution. Are these imposters worth the fractures they create and the deaths they have caused or will cause?

Only those reviewing history may answer without participation bias. Only those who are on the winning side can measure correctness. But applying a standard of what a statesman was and the requirement of true leadership from history's past, short do they measure as they are found lacking. Cowering would they be if they had to stand and Defend American Values instead of sending young men and women to do the bidding of the weak.

Not all are deserving of such criticism, but if you serve in those seats, considering the history of what authentic leadership looks like, you will rank among the weakest. And if you are one of the strong ones, your complicity in allowing unworthy representation to hold power has not gone unnoticed. Do not take America to where she should never be destined to go. Fight to protect unity. Do not fight to create division. History and those who hold your kind responsible will hopefully punish harshly. Those who practice lack of care must be met with a lack of respect.

Those positions of leadership, the purpose of those seats, and what it represents must contain the best of us, the strongest of us, the most competent of us. Not just the ones who possess the means to or networking for such an endeavor. Serve honorably by representing one common interest—unity. Leadership is not a career, a job, or a paycheck. Nor is it an avenue to be traveled only to secure the necessary requisites in anticipation of the next seat of hierarchy.

Certain leadership qualities must be present to create substantial sustainable change and contain those who are willing to stand to support it. A people created by progress must remain devoted to improvement. Americans must look for new leadership to survive the landscape of ever-evolving diversity. Not those who wish to crush it or ignore the causal factors that plague and threaten America. It is nothing more than repulsive acquiesce of such ignorant interpretation, misunderstanding the requirements of a free people. Our people have lost something, and they cannot even see it.

Let this be a warning, America's society has chosen a life of entertainment over necessity. Her citizens decided a skill of a children's game, voice-over substance, and dishonesty through corruption dawning a mask behind the shadow of a curtain is worth more than the literacy of survival of a free nation. It may seem unnecessary in a world full of conveniences, but be forewarned, the lack of strength in leadership has removed the importance of and instead surrendered to the jesters of modern times. Substance these fools lack as they make people weak and enslave the minds of a necessary deterrent. Weakness is what remains. So true and is the descriptor of those who substituted education for a life of enjoyment.

All who practice triumphing in the unnecessary expression of self, have removed the ability to survive on their own, weakening the resolve of the literacy required to live within a self-governing border of freedom. As a result, a majority have now enjoyed the freedom this great Nation has to offer without suffering the cost.

It now becomes true in the belief that freedom is not free. What remains is a debt not contingent on denial, but a requirement of understanding represented by sacrifice. Free people must pay for this. A dismissal of responsibility is now represented in all aspects of the American life.

Its leadership, those who influence, business owners, and most regrettably, its people have cheapened America's necessity of participation. This burden is real, but its importance has now been removed by the selfish endeavors of those lacking the comprehension necessary for its survival. A majority lacks what the minority represents.

**All** must stand, **All** must fight, and **All** must be willing to defend those who are protected by the American way of life. Do not defend the recklessness of cowards who cannot comprehend the consequences of their actions.

If we are not careful, democracy is over. The United States of America will fail. And when it dies, what replaces it will no longer resemble our Nation. Each side will blame the other. Because separate truths exist, separate nations will also exist. Except whatever behavior caused the destruction when applying accountability will never be included in the newly minted nation and will likely be legislated against.

A nation without guns, liberals, transgenders, religion, conservatives, dissent, fairness, equity, justice, and empathy. No safe place where differences can exist. What will happen, what will be created, are two separate nations devoid of freedom.

I am still unsure why this is occurring. Is it because people are too incompetent, selfish, or ignorant? Or is it because they are not invested? I do not understand what it is, and I cannot understand why people are letting it happen—it is destroying me. It consumes my existence throughout the day and plagues my sleep at night. I am haunted by the words left by people in the past to remind the future of impending perils and those who will be responsible for such destruction. I guess we never think of ourselves as one of those people. We never believe we can be what we are, good or bad. But there are way too many of them. It is upon us.

Maybe that is what it is. When the majority of people become less intelligent, society starts to crumble. I do not mean educated. I am talking about free-thinking, pondering, and the ability to see what others do not. Not a school that targets specific instruction and requires those who attend to become dependent on others to tell them what to learn or what to believe; this is nothing more than control through propaganda. What do you know for yourself? What parts of you are you because of you?

Being informed, intelligent, and enlightened is a process that destroys and rebuilds with no direction because that would limit the growth needed to have autonomy. This freedom is the ability to see through lies or question those in power. It is dangerous to the status quo and the reason why weak leaders keep their people dependent on falsities, convenience, and entertainment. Because if people ever realize their potential and can teach themselves, a shift will occur, correcting the errors caused by weakness. There is an objective standard, and we must pursue it.

Defend righteousness, not the distortion of the Rule of Law, or the blood lust of partisan corruption. Defend our way of life with the power granted through America's Declaration of Independence. Only free people can do this. This is the most crucial piece of the puzzle and the only document exercising authority over my allegiance. The accountability of governmental actions and the strict adherence to the Constitution are required to sustain our way of life and to limit its power over us.

The Declaration of Independence of the United States of America cannot be altered to benefit partisanship. Its words are unchangeable, irrefutable, and a warning to those who wish to ignore unity through patriotism and peace through freedoms. Do not substitute these words contained in that document for the selfish pursuit of a one-America.

The absolute statements and their meaning are not open for interpretation. It is ill-advised. Doing so will result in nothing more than death and destruction. Those willing to ignore the required cost to live in this great Nation are not worthy of her or the freedoms she offers. Your arrogance is insulting, and your ignorance is its equal.

Participation is not discretionary. A free people must demand it but also defend it—all Americans. Our Nation must always refuse to accept the corruption and detriment offered by the weak. The manipulation of the judicial branch, legislative branch, and executive branch to change, alter, or destroy the Constitution by partisan lines will result in the pushback of a violent nature.

All Americans are required to live a life in consideration and out of respect for their fellow countrymen. Diversity of identity and thoughts are the reason modern society has come this far. Do not seek to silence conflicting thoughts or competing interests. Stay true to America's pure purpose so people can achieve progress together peacefully despite our differences.

It is not a coincidence that the word path is contained in empathy, representing a way forward for all—a way to create unity and represent all instead of the few. The Nation and her people must heal. All must create intimacy through cohesion, allowing for a shared efficacy to unite once again. This is the only way forward; it must be the way. Compassion, empathy, and unity through accountability will strengthen our desire to defend one another.

Everything in life evolves, and it must if it is to survive. People, more often than not, are the direct cause of such evolution (societal evolution) and have a great influence on the direction society takes. At times it is not progress but regression. Evolution is a change. Not representative of good or bad just a change. Where is our Nation heading?

History is full of people, and leaders who decided to maintain the status quo or regress in hopes of achieving some selfish benchmark in their own glory. This is occurring again. As people get further divided, a need to create a place where likeness can be protected is born. It happens when differences have numbers and whatever belief has legitimacy. It happens when a system fails to operate as designed. It occurs when people decide to quit.

Often, I seem to be surrounded by an uncontrollable urge to quit. To run away, leave everything behind, and seek refuge from impending doom. I feel like I am drowning, being consumed by something and suffocated. It is everywhere. As I turn on the television or read the news, I get physically ill. Something terrible is coming. A fog or mist, something I cannot describe, but it is thick and consumes without remorse or irrespective of differences. All I know is it constricts life by removing the condition that can stop it.

America is well on her way to becoming a shell of her former self as identities are trying to create separate nations within the walls of a single entity. I fear what others do not see. The divisiveness consuming the world has only one purpose, one design, only one command of execution— to destroy. I see what others cannot. I feel it approaching. It is nearing a point that will consume as that is its purpose if not controlled by prevention, and the process will work as intended. Society will be powerless and unable to stop this threat because completion is its controlling order of operation, and the formula will always produce the same consequential answer.

I am unable to stop it or warn people of the impending doom. Even talking to people in public gives me an overwhelming feeling that something is horribly wrong. But it is real. The evidence I offer so people may see the path they are on is represented in history books or societies that no longer exist. The cycle is on its last step before the reset occurs, before war consumes the innocent, before the foolish and weak force the willing and dangerous to the point of no return.

It will most likely occur during an election cycle, represented by a people losing or gaining representation or some other determinative outcome that is gifting power to the eager. Not that the specific outcome is detrimental on its own, but when leaders forget they must represent all people, leaders will be reminded they must represent all people. Those who feel their interests are not cared for will explode, turning our street corners into a war zone consuming everyone. These people will be dangerous; what they seek will be the destruction and elimination of their target.

This will not be by trespassers who stormed the gates walking around documenting their arrival but by those whose intent is to kill, removing everything in their way. The strong will be powerless to stop it because they will be forced to pick a side. The weak will be unable to survive because the strong were forced to choose a side. Not a choice made on their own volition but one that represented by no choice. That is why the founding fathers understood participation was necessary because they saw it happen. They knew peaceful men were the most dangerous and the ones in the best position to prevent such an atrocity.

Everything they wrote was done so with emotions. Their words represented firsthand accounts of atrocities and firsthand knowledge of a way to prevent these atrocities. That is why fools should never represent America, the Constitution, or a free people—they are unworthy. They are unable to feel the history with emotion. They lack empathy and are only interested in changing what they are unable to comprehend because they lack competency.

The process has begun. It happens because respect is removed, hate is controlling, and those with influence lead with the intent to destroy. It is line crossed or a line created but eventually, people grow tired of being called the problem or living a life of someone else's design. Destruction is the only means represented by an ending of choice. Humanity is at the most critical liminal stage ever, and it was created by nothing more than selfishness.

The places I sought comfort in are no longer available. Who should I become? What is right? What is wrong? Where are my leaders? I cannot breathe because I feel alone. I cannot see what is true any longer. But one thing I do know, my ability to touch the bottom is slipping. I am losing my foothold, and it feels as if I am starting to drown.

I am out of my depth...

# A Place for Your Thoughts:

# CHAPTER VII

## *Out of My Depth*

I am not a great man. Although I don't think I am a bad man. I am capable of great things and horrible things, and I have done both. What makes me different is my honesty and willingness to hold myself to a standard. My honesty about who I am, what I am, and what I've done weighed against a standard is what I consider personal accountability. It allows me to grow and gives me the strength to prevent a cycle of detrimental behavior.

I've hurt people, innocent people. People that didn't deserve it. But I also hurt terrible people—those who definitely deserved it. I've watched the worst of me firsthand. I have highlights playing in my head on a continuous reel, always reminding me of the many failures of my existence and the limits my character had to overcome. I cannot escape my past and will never run from it. Of course, I expect to be held accountable for what I have done, but I also expect forgiveness, understanding, and kindness when I show remorse.

I know what I have done and see the people I've hurt. I am aware of what is wrong because I know what is right. Unfortunately, it seems those among us have lost the ability to self-reflect, removing critical analysis of one's actions to create a better version of themselves. People are wrong when they fail to recognize just how short-sighted, sided, and narrow-minded they may be. How can people correct deficiencies if self-analysis or being self-critical is not done? People are stuck in a generational life cycle that cannot be solved because those who need to change are afraid to be honest about who they actually are.

Their story and their life cannot be shared. Not because the story is unworthy of an audience. The truth, human beings as a species only forgive likeness allowing similarly identical idiots to make mistakes, not those who are different. People cannot grow from what they are unless they are allowed to grow. The fault must be first identified and recognized as such.

People must also be exposed to correct behavior to limit incorrect behavior—a standard to aspire to. Not to be beaten and publicly shamed as a self-celebration of virtue for your kind. But permitted and allowed to be put on a more appropriate path. People must seek justice, not retribution. Atonement that encourages growth and forgives the trespasses of the guilty. Education for evolution.

Have you never made a mistake? Do you believe every action in your life was just and free of fault or above reproach? Unfortunately, people make mistakes and decisions that harm someone innocent often occur because of what is unknown. But, of course, most ignorance is limited to youth and adolescent years; however, being heavily influenced or exposed to such toxic behavior usually reinforces it and creates longevity for it. And lack of exposure to differences always establishes incorrect prejudices and assumptions.

However, it seems people who live in glass houses want to destroy instead of growing. What is more troublesome, and problematic is that it seems people want to remain at that residence indefinitely while working at a quarry.

I never sought forgiveness for my past beliefs. Although I carry a large amount of emotional regret for my past mistakes, I do not think forgiveness is necessary. For one, I am not that child anymore, nor do I bear any resemblance to that person. Secondly, short of the pain, I caused, people only know things are wrong when they learn them. Growth and separation from ignorance is a process. Exposure to knowledge increases the efficacy of the human element.

Some people take longer than others to grow. What is not understood may be hard to identify with, or it may prove challenging to establish an appreciation for—alluding to the entity who would benefit. But I have learned and continue to discover new ways to appreciate whatever difference I am not a part of.

That is progress and the reason for my sincerity. We all fight demons on the path to righteousness. The job of those who are perfect is not to judge but to encourage the creation of the much need company as I am sure it is lonely up there. Leadership creates maturity, and maturity begins leadership which in turn promotes empathy.

As a soldier, I needed extra attention and structure, to say the least. But I wasn't a bad soldier. I was quite good at my job, always stayed in top physical condition, and competent in any weapon system I was fortunate enough to get my hands on, and I tried to live by the core values representing my Country the best I could.

But I was young and hell-bent on making my life more complicated than it had to be. Mistakes were plentiful, as was the pain inflicted or received. I did, however, respond well to strong leadership, and eventually even craved it. I also valued the competency of those responsible for my growth as a soldier, as a man, and as a person.

I still call on the advice of those who taught me what leadership is, as they represent the importance of such a necessity. I never made it easy, but I was shown why it was crucial to maintain professionalism each time. I also learned the importance of restructuring behaviors to form better compliance with examples and the power of forgiveness.

My experience in the military showed me precisely what great leaders can do and what great leadership looks like. Leaders are essential as they inspire people to represent a standard, and their presence allows individuals to get the best out of themselves. Knowing this, I pursued these attributes and likeness while looking for new leaders to follow after my exit from the military.

Although, as a Veteran, at times and more often than not, I feel like society has no place for me. This feeling follows me most places I go, and it is represented by the lack of structure or arbitrary accountability that civilian life represents. Freedoms create a smorgasbord of free for all behavior that insults most but is allowed because true freedom is just that, insulting.

But this behavior is only allowed because people accept it and tolerate it. The moment it is created into a substance of disgust, it becomes easily preventable and less likely acceptable. Bad incompetent leaders are easy to recognize as their existence; their only purpose is to create friction and emotional rage instead of cohesiveness and logical understanding.

How can our leaders and others act in such a way that is unbecoming of what it means to be a decent person? Is it possible that they cannot see their behavior for what it is? Do those who follow irrational, ignorant, and selfish leaders understand that the behavior represented by their character is unacceptable? Or is it that they are aware but do not care? Being unapologetic is an excuse people have when their emotional maturity is less than their logical maturity. Regardless of what happened or what occurred, a standard of decency should always govern behaviors tolerated in society.

I cannot understand how people cannot see the detrimental behavior society has been overrunning with. How can they witness such a disgusting display of incompetency and not be appalled by people in positions of authority, influence, and power acting in such a manner unbecoming of the civility needed to govern a free people? I am saddened while watching the steady decline of my society and its people over the last 30 years, including the extreme rot occurring in the last decade. I remember everything I was exposed to, every behavior, every action, and every person who sat in a position of leadership not worthy of such a privilege. It is frightening to think about what comes next.

What and who have we become? America and her people have created multiple realities within the borders of our great Nation. How can people in our Country be fearful of not knowing where their next meal will come from? It is especially absurd that this occurs as athletes, entertainers, business owners, and politicians possess a wealth of astronomical proportions represented by a materialistic fortune they do not need, nor are they worth.

The poor versus the rich. The haves versus the have-nots. Republican versus democrat. Americans are allowing leaders to assemble us into groups that may very well lead to the collapse of our way of life by promoting ignorance versus truth, skepticism versus science, and selfishness versus selflessness. The society we have come to know, and love is slowly being destroyed by our inability to work together and by those we elect. Incompetency has infiltrated the system that was meant to protect our best interests, and it will destroy us all.

We are in the beginning stages of the worst crisis in the history of the United States, and the world for that matter. Yet the majority are acting in a reactive short-sighted manner by encouraging ignorance and promoting destruction. Our greatest strength is our people, and how do we respond? Americans choose selfishness and defiance for and against those who are different or those we do not like. People are somehow willfully against actions and progress that will benefit all of humanity and the very survival of our species. Why are people choosing to ignore all warning signs leading to the possible collapse of our way of life?

People know and are aware of what competent leadership looks like. Americans know what type of leader they must follow. I always offer my understanding of leadership in the form of a test that any and all are free to use. When you are looking for those worthy of your loyalty:

—read the following then close your eyes; imagine and create the leader you would follow:

> This person is a figure you would die for because they represent something worth protecting. A person who unites instead of divides. Someone with compassion who has the ability to not only recognize hardships and atrocities but also empathize with the struggles of those they represent. This individual represents a standard of decency that is sought after because parents teach their children that the character of that person is what you should grow up to embody.
>
> A person deserving of influence. No matter the family home visited, they are a person who is welcome to sit down at the table for a meal. Not only to share in the culture but also the love extended and represented by those at the table. A leader whose death would make the world cry as the people would recognize what was lost.
>
> A leader whose absence from the world is noticed. And the toll paid is felt throughout the land regardless of the identity, views, or beliefs held by the particular person overcome with sadness because the leader we lost was always willing to die for you, no matter the identity.

This is the standard of leadership I see when I close my eyes and the person I would follow. Not perfection but the epitome of. When I open my eyes, I do not see anyone relatively close to what was described. I don't, not even in the slightest, and that angers me greatly. So, I decided to do something about it.

I could not allow and still am unable to let myself stand by and do nothing while selfishness destroys my Country. The Country I love. The place where freedoms are celebrated. I may not be that leader because my existence and life choices are not perfect. I may lack all the money and pedigree needed to look like an imposter, as they do. It may not be me, but

I sure as hell know—it is not them. And I will not follow a person I do not respect, especially one devoid of empathy for others.

After recognizing that America and her people were being led astray by those who do not deserve the honor nor the privilege of representing a free-thinking society, I decided to start a campaign to become a congressman. Even though I knew the chances of winning were absolutely weighed against me, I believed in myself.

I honestly believed I had a real opportunity to compete as a congressional candidate to create an alternative to the partisanship that continues to divide. Who wouldn't vote for a free-thinking independent candidate not controlled by any party or outside influences?

In addition, I wouldn't be able to live with myself if I did nothing while I watched people attack and destroy America, my people, my family, and my home. I was willing to try something, anything to help; America was [is] failing.

It makes me cry to think of what our people are turning themselves into and the amount of destruction that this behavior is causing. This is an America that does not represent what she should because→ the people do not represent what they should because→ the leaders do not represent what they should. These integral pieces work together to produce the desired effect.

And so, Cosner for Congress was born. I first wrote a declaration letter to my family and friends for two reasons. One, in an attempt to explain my feelings so I did not seem foolish to them for taking on such a significant endeavor or have them believe I was operating under illusions of grandeur. Secondly, in hopes I would be able to generate a movement— for lack of a better word. These were the first words I created from my mind in hopes people would believe in me and what America should stand for.

It read:

> I would first like to thank you for being the person you are. When our paths crossed, it created a very important change in me. A change that can only be described as life altering. I am about to start the next phase of my life. A path that I believe I

was built for. A journey allowing me to use the gifts God gave me in addition to the influential change you had upon me.

Thank you, I love you, and I am forever grateful. I am truly a better man for it. I must Defend American Values. At all costs including and up to my life. I swore this oath as a soldier, and I am not willing to part with the standard I hold myself to and the meaning of such an oath. I am not afraid of failure because I know I will not.

America must have leaders present to protect everything she holds so dear to her heart, our freedoms. America's freedoms, our way of life cost something. This cost is non-negotiable, and it is past due. While the few continue to do the heavy lifting, every American must participate and give what is owed. At a bare minimum, we must hold people accountable to a standard. This standard is what is necessary and required so we can learn to live together.

What we all must possess is an agreed upon common decency for people. Somehow, we lost that in our daily interactions with one another. The standard of what America requires from her people is eroding and being replaced with rot, cancer, and discontent for the Rule of Law.

This behavior is being justified by those who are doing it with flawed logic and later defended by people in positions of authority. Americans are somehow rationalizing this vile behavior as acceptable, by the continued enabling of these actions and words.

As this continues to occur, a new normal from these selfish acts are created and later repeated, but often much worse. As this vicious cycle continues unimpeded, we lose a piece our American Values and ourselves. Please do not mistake this letter as me being self-righteous or believing I am any more capable than others are.

I am fully aware I am not superior to anyone. I assure you; I have zero delusions of that. I recognize how unworthy I am for such a role. However, I do not see anyone else doing it. At this current moment, I believe myself to be a more qualified candidate compared to most politicians leading the United States in 2020. It begs the question, if I believe myself to be unworthy of such a role, how have they convinced people they are?

Are we so foolish to believe that our elected leaders should have different attributes in different geographical locations in our system? How are Americans so easily convinced to vote for such horrible leaders? I know this is not the best we can do. If you are reading this letter, I believe you are superior to those we have in elected office at this moment. Not because you are a better person but because you hold people to a standard.

More importantly, you held me to a standard in some capacity, at some time, in my life. That makes you better. If we want better, we must be better, but at the same time demand better from one another and ourselves. Tomorrow we all should be better than we are today.

Whatever standard people use to create a better version of themselves is irrelevant. My standard, what I use, I get from my religion, America's Rule of Law, and my family. Those things and the individuals reading this letter created the man who wants to be bring change this Nation so desperately needs.

There is no greater time than now. A threat is growing in our society, and we must destroy it before it causes irreparable harm. Our Nation will do this as we always have; leaders will identify the issue, they will find a solution, and we will execute the plan united, as Americans.

If you believe in me and believe in America's way of life then stand with me as patriots before I have to stand against my fellow Americans labeling them traitors. My military training gave me the ability to deal with anything and overcome everything. People are not nor can they be defined by their current situation. They are however, limited by it.

Our Nation must stand strong, firm, and resolute while we fight our generation's greatest threat. America is an idea and this idea, protects people. Our freedoms represent this protection but not in the form of individuals doing what they want, but by protecting each other from aggression and hostility.

To fulfill this idea America had to create absolutes in our society. Allowing freemen and freewomen the opportunity to live with one another regardless of our differences. And this absolute I reference is America's Rule of Law. This must be our standard, and the only standard America shall operate under.

Like any construct of man, the Rule of Law must operate as intended within the parameters it was designed to do so. Accountability must be had, and it must be protected at all costs. For if we ever lose the respect for the Rule of Law, we lose legitimacy in our identity; forever altering history in a negative way.

This letter represents a commitment from me to you. You knew the man I was prior to turning into the man I am. You still respected me, believed in me, and remained my friend or mentor even though I am most likely unworthy because I am a flawed man. Thank you to all my friends and family but also to my friends who are family.

This letter represents a thank you. Thank you for being in my life as a role model, educator, or mentor. One day I hope to earn the privilege of calling you, "friend" - if I have not already done so. Do not be afraid of continuing to teach me. I seek the truth and will never be offended.

I will always be willing to accept factual information as I make decisions based on the best interest to protect the American people I represent. The fact I have people in my life I hold in high regard who are willing to criticize me informs me of two things. One, you respect me enough to pay attention to my limits or faults and two; you care enough to let me know.

It gives me hope that one day you will consider me an equal and I will have the opportunity to call you by your first name and friend. Until then, I will treat you with the same respect that I did when we first met. I will refer to you and keep you in the same capacity when you influenced me to be a better man, a better person, and a better American.

I will extend to you this professional courtesy; I will show you the same level of respect you earned before we met. This kindness represents how much you mean to me but also the level of respect I have for you.

The fact you are holding this letter is a recognition by me that you played an important part in my life. I thank God and recognize everyday how truly blessed I really am. In addition, I will always seek guidance from you if you are willing to give it. I will always do what is necessary to protect our way of life and the American people. Americans are blessed to share these ideals with one another in a society that allows them to do so.

My entire life, my family's entire life, has revolved around protecting this Country. My family sacrificed for America, shed blood for America, and perished protecting America. I will continue to serve this Country in any capacity that I am able to do so.

The biggest concern to me as of this moment, I cannot do is this alone. I need you and your support to be able to accomplish the task laid before me. I am running for a seat as representative of the 1st Congressional District of West Virginia in the United States Congress.

I will use this platform to inspire change as a leader; by showing the American people, it is ok to demand better from a leader and require core values and principles. A good leader, one who is willing to stand up for what is right no matter the cost or the difficulty of the task.

Good leaders will always bring out the best in all of us. They inspire individuals to be better. Bad leaders bring out America's reality in 2020 representing the cycle of rot and decay over the last few decades. I need you to convince other people that I am worthy of such a role. I need your influence to help realize the goal of uniting a people and protecting America's Rule of Law.

I must convince the American People that I know them and have the competency to represent them better than any candidate or politician currently in office. Not because I am trying to represent all Americans, but because voters must believe, they have a choice when deciding what type of leader represents them.

Voters must believe they have the power to create a fantastic future when given the opportunity to choose such a person. When I succeed, Americans will finally have a standard of what a leader should look like. Voters will hold candidates to a standard they long since have forgotten. They will force candidates to be leaders and role models instead of people who divide to gain power.

The American people must remember what representing decency can do for the betterment of a society. I concede and recognize we have great leaders among us, but we pass legislation by party lines, appoint judges by party lines, and hate one another by party lines. Am I the only who understands the limits of these actions and the consequences as such?

Our differences should be our strength. We must use these to lead together. When judges are appointed or legislation is passed it should be done by and for a very unique reason: We, as Americans, all agree it is in the best interest of our people and the future of our great Nation; not because people who think like us have the ability to force change on people who do not think like us.

Forcing tribalistic behaviors in the halls of Congress is very dangerous precedent to set and a type of behavior I will not allow. Let us stop this foolishness and remove the ability for imbeciles to lead us. Our system is designed to be better free from corruption. To revitalize such a belief we must be disciplined, focused, professional, and creative.

We must not fall prey to choosing feelings over facts nor should we falter when we must hold people accountable, no matter how inconvenient or uncomfortable. The truth must always control our Democratic Republic and we must continue to stay vigilant promoting tolerance, insightful thoughts, and possess the discipline to use a critical perspective when forming an opinion or making decisions.

As this is no easy task, I wholeheartedly believe it is something we can accomplish and something we should always pursue—A better America. America is not and never will be frozen in time. The American Flag, the National Anthem, America's Constitution, and the commitment by Americans represent what America could be and what it probably should be.

Promoting the truth and encouraging voters to share the truth above all else, especially through their own bias, is key in this venture. I sent this letter to over a thousand people who are important to me, and not one of you are exactly alike or share the same beliefs.

Yet, somehow, I would give anything in my possession to you, if needed, and would not hesitate to die to protect you. NO QUESTIONS ASKED. Why is that? Why are others not following this template? As Benjamin Franklin said, "Either write something worth reading or do something worth writing about."

I want to do both. I am not motivated by selfishness I am however motivated out of need and a sense of responsibility because it must be done. It is my responsibility to act as an American, a man, a soldier, a veteran, and a Christian.

I am not motivated to be famous; I am not motivated to be important; I only want to do what is right. My convictions, my beliefs, and my principles are under attack. Everything that makes me the man I am today is threatened by a dangerous ideology

~ ignorance ~.

I will seek to destroy this plague and show others how to remove this sickness from their life. I will introduce knowledge and the truth as an antidote so America may solve the partisan issues that continue to put American lives at risk. All of you are very special to me because you added substance to my life.

Each one of you have differing backgrounds, but each one of you opened my heart and mind to unique or wonderful things. Each one of you had the ability to influence me in my life. By doing so, you made my life have purpose. This purpose allowed me to grow into the Leader I am today.

An individual's success, a group's success, or an entities' success is only limited by their thoughts and by their actions. All successful ventures start out small, but they all have one thing in common, a belief in their legitimacy. All things require hard work and time. In time, days will turn to months and then years. What I believe America is shall be realized and that goal accomplished in time.

Please believe in me as I believe in you. I will work tirelessly to promote the betterment of all people at any level I have influence to do so. My commitment will not waiver, my determination will not falter, and my PATRIOTISM- infectious.

This is my declaration letter to my family, friends, and people who influenced me to be a better man. My entire life I have been transparent, at times probably too much. Nevertheless, I know this is one of my strengths.

I give you my word that everything I do, will be in the best interest of America. Those actions will always be done selflessly without bias.

God Bless America!
Shawn Paul Cosner
Candidate West Virginia, CD1


Shortly after I sent the letter, I assumed people would agree, at least offer support emotionally, but to my surprise, very few people even responded. Again, these were my close friends and family, or so I thought. I expected them to react the way I would have responded if a letter came from one of them asking for help if they were planning such a challenging endeavor. Because I knew it would require everything they had, I would have given them anything I had.

It could have maybe been that they do not recognize the threat yet. Not recognizing the dangers of unruly mobs definitely caused issues in the past, so most likely, that is it. That is what I decided on, knowing full well I am wrong. But the reality is/was I am perceived as a nobody. I do not come from money; I am not well known, nor was I groomed for any type of political seat. People most likely do not think Shawn Cosner is synonymous with success, achievement, or intelligence. Maybe they didn't take the time to read it or found what I sent unimportant.

But if a person is not willing to read the words, they are equally unworthy of the words. So, most likely, the letter was dismissed and never read. Whatever it was, I started to doubt myself. If I am unable to convince my own people [Friends and Family] to support me, how will I convince strangers [voters] to support me?

I tried to brush it off, and for the most part, I did as I was on a mission. I was focused and ready to make real changes. I was ready to set an example of what I believed the Country was missing. After I developed my logo and slogans, I had to publicly declare. And much like Ralphie writing his wish list in A Christmas Story, I too, had great expectations of what was to occur. So, I publicly declared on Facebook with a unique post.

It read:

I started this as a reply to a comment on one of my photos. I chose instead to share it as a post. She said we are missing class as Americans; in the context of a letter President Bush left for President Clinton.

She was absolutely correct. We are missing class, but I wanted to explain it in my own words, why I believe it is so much more.

It is so much bigger than class. What we are missing; embodies everything America was, is, and can be. Half or more of our population are unworthy to live in this great Nation and we know it. Giving nothing but taking everything.

We failed, when we refused to hold people accountable. We failed each other and the Rule of Law. I am apologizing for those who will not apologize for themselves. I am sorry. I am sorry your children must witness the destruction of the greatest Nation our species ever created. We failed; and the cost will be too high.

This is not a game nor is it a joke. What comes next is the consequences of generational failures and lack of accountability. Shame on all of us. We do not deserve this wonderful freedom. It sickens me to say this, as I love this place more than life itself.

This place gives me the ability to walk down the sidewalk holding hands with a black woman who I am madly in love with. The ability to do this, free from the fear of violence. That freedom has now been threatened. The ability for me to raise my biracial children in this Country does not exist anymore.

The continued sharing of half-truths and false words are destroying our ability to live free. You have taken something so special to me, so special to someone I love so deeply. You are the reason why my family cannot be free. I have never done anything to you. I tried to live a good life; I tried my hardest. You ruined it.

We have worthless citizens; that is America's problem. I bet less than 10% of our population knows what is contained in the Declaration of Independence. I would even wager lawyers and law students somehow went through the J.D. program and intentionally skipped the only thing that really matters.

Without those words and the Soldiers who died creating this Country or the brave men and women who protect the laws, we would not have athletes to kneel at the National Anthem. Why choose to disrespect the one thing that is meant to bind us together, forever?

Most in this Country probably do not know what the Declaration of Independence is let alone the duties and responsibilities of a citizen who claims the protections contained in the Bill of Rights.

Somehow, we let people convince us that they should not be held to a standard and it is America who owes them something. It must be nice to wake up and breathe this free air and never come anywhere close to paying their portion of what is required.

What happens when those who continue to bleed, pay, sacrifice, and die; grow tired of those who lack the knowledge or basic understanding of what is required to live here? Is that not unjust enrichment? To keep something and to be enriched by the expense of another.

What does the Supreme Court say about that? What do you suppose the 9 supreme beings in black robes are going to tell us about equitable administration of the law or how to fight a civil war?

Justice David Davis noted that the Constitution was not suspended in time of emergency and wrote that it was "a law for rulers and people, equally in time of war and peace." But, what if no one respects the Rule of Law anymore? What if the legitimacy has been erased in the eyes of the only ones willing to die to defend it?

You see when you hold athletes, entertainers, and other individuals who have zero value over those who are willing to die to create value; a fracture is created. This fracture, if not healed, will create the biggest conflict America has ever known and one most likely we will not be able to recover from.

If you cannot see that it is wrong to kill someone for any reason, I hate you. I hate what you stand for. I hate what you are. You are my enemy, and I will treat you as a traitor. I assure you that is far more than you deserve.

If you want to promote one race over the other, I hate you. I hate what you stand for. You are my enemy, and I will treat you as a traitor. I assure you that is far more than you deserve.

If you believe you are superior simply because you were born with an identity, I hate you. I hate what you stand for. You are my enemy, and I will treat you as a traitor. I assure you that is far more than you deserve.

If you think its ok to chant outside a hospital, "let them die", I hate you. I hate what you stand for. You are my enemy, and I will treat you as a traitor. I assure you that is far more than you deserve.

If this post offends you, I hate you. I hate what you stand for. You are my enemy, and I will treat you as a traitor. I assure you that is far more than you deserve.

As a Christian man, I should not hate but I am a soldier and at times soldiers must do what is necessary to defend a way of life when it is threatened. Because only a few stand, I will fill my heart with hate and betray the promise I made to the Lord. That is something I said I would never do again.

This will be my cross to bear. I hate you. I hate what you stand for. You are my enemy, and I will treat you as a traitor. I assure you that is far more than you deserve.

You took something very special from me, **my happiness**. All of you who are creating this, shame on you. What is wrong with you? Have you no decency in you? Are you not ashamed for your children to see you or what your parents will think?

This will not end peacefully, if we do not try. Please let us try to work together. Put aside your partisan games and half-truth biasness. Can the remaining adults who are in leadership roles or positions of authority please take a stand? Hold one another up and make us better.

If this behavior continues, I will stop at nothing to destroy those who wish to do harm to this Country and our way of life. The Rule of Law must be protected at all costs. Because you are not going like what happens when the men I know are without a moral compass.

I am publicly declaring my candidacy for United States Congress. This November I will be on the ballot as a write-in candidate for the 1st Congressional District of West Virginia. We can do better, We the People deserve better, We must Defend American Values.

In all of my words, I still believe she was correct, class we are missing, but more importantly, where are all the Americans?

After I publicly declared, I also submitted press releases to all news outlets in my congressional district and a few national ones. Unfortunately, to my knowledge, only two organizations printed or ran the story.

It read:

[FOR IMMEDIATE RELEASE]
Contact:
Jennifer Cosner
Campaign Manager
jennifer@cosnerforcongress.com

Shawn Cosner write-in Candidate For 1st Congressional District of West Virginia

Bruceton Mills, WV- Shawn Cosner is announcing his candidacy for United States Congress as a write-in candidate for West Virginia's 1st Congressional District.

With an unwavering commitment to his Country and the Rule of Law, his military service and educational pursuits will serve West Virginia's 1st Congressional District well. His love for West Virginia is as deep as his connection to her. His family has always answered the call to service, putting duty, community, and Country above all else—from West Virginia Coal Miners, West Virginia teachers to West Virginia Soldiers and everything between; his life was never short of fantastic West Virginia role models.

Because Cosner understands the needs of local citizens, and what he must do to protect their interest, his motivation will always be to his home and to her people.

Candidate Shawn Cosner sees the current state of affairs in America as motivations to run for office.

According to Cosner "Voters must demand a new standard of leadership" He adds, "I am not passing blame nor am I criticizing those in office; however, we can do better." He questions why others fail to understand, "We are West Virginians, we're not a political party we are mountaineers. West Virginia, like America, is a place you can be free."

Candidate Cosner has also spoken out on the need to protect the Rule of Law and hold those accountable when it is required.

More information about Cosner and his campaign can be found on his website, cosnerforcongress.com. This site includes biographical information about the Candidate, as well as his position on many of the important issues not only affecting West Virginia but also the Nation as a whole.

After the continued rejections to publish my press release, I completed a Ballotpedia response questionnaire available online free from local persuasion to print or not to print. This was a chance for me to get exposure without any editors' permission. In hopes I would create a bit more legitimacy, I answered every question with an appropriate response. Unfortunately, at times I ran out of allotted characters.

It read:

Tell us about yourself.

I am a West Virginian with deep roots in the state, a Veteran, a patriot, and a human rights activist. I helped organize and run a non-profit organization that contributed to the betterment of the youth in my community. I hold a bachelor's degree from WVU, attended Graduate School at ETSU and have a Juris Doctor from Appalachian School of Law. I am a licensed contractor and was able to secure nearly $8 million dollars' worth of contracts through the Service-Disabled Veteran Owned Small Business set-aside program. My greatest accomplishment and my guiding light is my son, Owen Carter Cosner.

Please list below 3 key messages of your campaign. What are the main points you want voters to remember about your goals for your time in office?

We can do better. Our society created norms that encourages disrespectful treatment of one another. We have removed the ability to have constructive dialogue. By doing so, two competing points now rapidly accelerate into an argumentative fight or violence. America must have citizens who are willing to engage and participate in thoughtful, respectful, and constructive discussion. We are Americans, our differences are our strength not our weakness. Our system, what it means, extends protections to those who would normally be without, so they may have a voice. Those are American Values and something we must encourage every American to do. We must encourage respect for one another. To accomplish this, we need to hold our fellow Americans accountable to a standard.

We the People deserve better. The standard we hold ourselves to will be the standard our elected leaders hold themselves too as well. America, what she stands for, is a beacon of light for the rest of the world. The standard of governance, the standard of freedom, and the standard of accountability. America's freedoms were created and are protected by brave men and women who transcend gender roles, race, religion, sexual orientation, or any other descriptor used to categorize people. Let us honor their sacrifice and the hardships those before us endured by holding those in office to a standard; one of decency and mutual respect.

We must Defend American Values. Freedoms of the Constitution are the only way we can live with each other; Freedoms of the Constitution are rules that allow people with differences to coexist; Freedoms of the Constitution gives us the blueprint to live in harmony. If at any time the freedoms of the Constitution are threatened, peace can never be obtained. More importantly, failure to defend these freedoms and values will start the destruction of a system that offers so many protections for those who need them.

What areas of public policy are you personally passionate about?

Currently, the only public policy I am concerned about is decency. We have let behavior that is unbecoming of public servants infiltrate our system. Our system is designed to allow for open discussion on the floor and dialogue so we may move forward with legislation that benefits all Americans not just one group or political party. It is time for the American people to remind those in power how the system was designed and how Congress should operate. Items that I will work tirelessly to make better are—A national Covid-19 Response, Protection of the Constitution from Political Party Attacks, Personal Accountability of Government Actors, Fiscal Responsibility, National Security, Coal Advocacy, West Virginia Small Businesses, West Virginia Economy, Veteran Advocacy, Education K-12, Education Post-Secondary, Criminal Justice Reform, Consumer Protection, Wealth Creation for West Virginia Families, Youth Advocacy, Single Parent Advocacy, Opioid Reform Including Access and Addiction Prevention or Addiction Treatment, Voters Advocacy and Protection, Health Care Access, Duties and Responsibilities of a Citizen—And, any other public policy issues that arise during my term regardless if it is an election year.

Who do you look up to? Whose example would you like to follow, and why?

My father, for the man he is, everything he taught me, and everything he will continue to teach me. I cannot say enough about the man he is. He has given me many things but the most important, is my capacity to care for others and to stand up for those who are voiceless. This guides me and will eventually put me where I belong. Thank you, dad, as you are my best friend, my world, and probably the only other person who can ever truly understand who I am. I am a direct reflection of my father if you doubt this; try to disagree with either of us.

My mother, for being all she could be and doing PT in ARMY boots as she was 8 months pregnant. What a strong, capable, and empowered woman. I am lucky to have such an angel in my life. How'd ya do it ma? My dad is extremely lucky, as he is harder to deal with than me and she had to deal with us both... She was able to keep our family together and show us love at times when we were undeserving of. She blessed my father with three children. We never had much yet we had everything we needed and what we needed was each other.

154

Every night we had dinner at the table as a family and that made us the richest family in Pisgah.

Finally, a woman who is a product of all those who hold special places in my heart, my sister. She is the only person who believes in me no matter the situation. If I had a dream or goal she would never question it. She would say what can I do to help. We were cut from the same stone, and everyone needs a rock like her. She has been pushing me to be a better person ever since I could remember. In doing so she was one who would not shy away from her criticism with me. If I was deserving a butt kicking so be it. If I was deserving of a congratulatory hug, it also would come in the form of a butt kicking.

My brother is an American Hero. When I think of him, I cry. I cry because I am so very proud of him. I will never be as much of a man as he is. So much more but I ran out of my allotted characters

Is there a book, essay, film, or something else you would recommend to someone who wants to understand your political philosophy?

The Patriot

What characteristics or principles are most important for an elected official?

Throughout history humankind looks for guidance, clarity, and reassurance from those who are in position of influence in hopes these few will aid in the eventual end to whatever clear and present danger society faces. These individuals are not many. All, "true", leaders make decisions not for the ease of implementing them or how the choices are perceived by others but for the benefit of many, even in the face of not maintaining the status quo. Competent leaders perceive threats and have an innate ability to foresee the path needed to guide those who they represent. The task to lead comes with varying levels of difficulty. The majority of most leaders very seldom face a crisis outside the normal parameters of society and are never tested. This creates a danger to those they lead. When this danger involves human life, the threat is magnified and the urgency to find great leaders becomes the utmost of importance. Our elected leaders must legislate, represent, and lead us away from demise and failure. Thomas Jefferson doubted the viability of a self-governing people because it took participation, understanding, and the unwavering support to protect what we cannot live without. Leaders must be present to unite not divide. Growth is the recognition of noticing what you are doing is wrong or incorrect. Maturity exists when one has the ability, competency, and unwavering commitment to change. America needs more mature leaders so she can create more mature citizens.

What characteristics or principles are the most important?

I believe Loyalty, Duty, Respect, Selfless Service, Honor, Integrity, Personal Courage. Those are attributes of a leader and the bare minimum that is required to hold any seat in public office.

What qualities do you possess that you believe would make you a successful officeholder?

Good leaders will always bring out the best in all of us. They inspire individuals to be better. Bad leaders bring out America's reality in 2020 representing the cycle of rot and decay over the last few decades. I am not blaming anyone; all I am saying is we can do better. My commitment to die for this beautiful Nation is a quality that will make me successful as an office holder and one I believe is necessary to represent people at any level of government. I will do whatever it takes to protect the Constitution and protect the interests of Americans especially West Virginians in the 1st Congressional District. I swore this oath as a soldier. My family members and friends swore the same oath and because of that oath they paid the ultimate sacrifice. This is a belief I will carry with me to Congress. I have always been willing to do more for others even to my detriment. I am not afraid to stand for what is right and will always Defend American Values.

What do you believe are the core responsibilities for someone elected to this office?

There are many. An important one is defending the Rule of Law. We must lead from the front. Always focus on being the change and setting the standard so others will be willing to follow you by example. I wish to encourage and usher in a new generation of leadership with standards we all hold ourselves to. When these expectations or standards are violated, sanctions must be in place to hold those to account. This is what I stand for and this is what should be the standard. We all must demand more and better from our leaders. There exists no greater time than now. Growth is the recognition of noticing what you are doing is wrong or incorrect. Maturity exists when one has the ability, competency, and unwavering commitment to change. America needs more mature leaders so she can create more mature citizens. I will use this office and platform to inspire change. Voters must understand it is okay to demand better from a leader, require core values and principles. A good leader, one who is willing to stand up for what is right no matter the cost or the difficulty of the task. Good leaders will always bring out the best in all of us. They inspire individuals to be better. Bad leaders bring out America's reality in 2020 representing the cycle of rot and decay over the last few decades. I am not blaming anyone; all I am saying is we can do better. My commitment to die for this beautiful Nation is a quality that most in Congress are without. I will do whatever it takes to protect the Constitution and protect the interests of Americans especially West Virginians in the 1st Congressional District. I have always been willing to do more for others even to my detriment. I am not afraid to stand for what is right and will always Defend American Values. My life has been filled with many struggles as is the case for most people. I have never went without. I may have not had everything I wanted but I had everything I needed. I have been blessed.

What legacy would you like to leave?

One of decency and compassion. Strength and understanding. A fearless leader, one who will stand in the face of adversity for what is just, right, and required. Leaders should never waiver in their commitment to America's Constitution or her people when representing citizens at any level.

What is the first historical event that happened in your lifetime that you remember? How old were you at the time?

Three historical events come to mind, 1) the Berlin wall coming down, 2) Pan Am flight 103, and 3) watching the United

States Army's Patriot Missile system defend American heroes like my Uncle Charlie Royce and Uncle Mark Royce in Desert Storm.

What was your very first job? How long did you have it?

I worked for CEC and March-Westin in Morgantown, doing small tasks and learning from my father. This was my first job in the summer of 1998. My first permanent job was Burger King in Cheat Lake.

What is your favorite book? Why?

Anything that can teach me something. I avoided reading at all costs growing up, but my father always read, and I never understood why. It was so boring to me. I wanted to be in the woods on my family's property or playing baseball. My father always handed out life lessons as most of my family members still do. One of these gifts of wisdom was, read a book. And, I have yet to read one for pleasure, but for learning; I will read as much as I can as I believe ignorance is a lie and something we must prevent people from catching.

If you could be any fictional character, who would you want to be?

Iron Man

What was the last song that got stuck in your head?

I have two: 1) Tyler Childers- Nose to the Grindstone 2) Uncle Lucius- Keep the Wolves at Bay

What is something that has been a struggle in your life?

My life has been filled with many struggles as is the case for most people. I have never went without. I may have not had everything I wanted but I had everything I needed. Struggles are connected to our lives as much as our success. I learned to be a successful failure and that is what I teach my son. I also believe that we should never let hardships define us. We are not our past, but we are limited by it. Perseverance and a belief in oneself allow a person to overcome struggles; no matter the size. Keep

158

representing yourself as you see yourself and one day others will see that self as well.

What qualities does the U.S. House of Representatives possess that makes it unique as an institution?

It is unique for the same reason the U.S. Senate and U.S. Presidency is; representation. That is what American Politics has always been about and why our Deceleration of Independence is so powerful. Representation is key when governing a people as those who feel they are without representation create revolutions. What makes the house extremely important and unique is its members. It is the only part of our government that represents the American people adequately. The House is vested with certain powers and because of this, it must always remain impartial as it seeks the critical perspective. The House has the ability to initiate impeachment proceedings against the President of the United States of America. This is a very powerful and important tool to maintain a standard in the White House. However, people use systems to leverage personal interest. People should not be able to abuse a system that was designed and built to protect. Impeachment proceedings are very important and when the votes are aligned with parties instead of representing the Rule of Law, the House loses a piece of itself. This is why our system, especially the House, must continue to have legitimacy and appropriate people elected. For if we ever lose the Rule of Law we will lose ourselves. The integrity of the system must be absolute so the belief in the system remains resolute. I am unsure what the U.S. House of Representatives represent in 2020 as an institution.

Do you believe that it's beneficial for representatives to have previous experience in government or politics?

Fantastic question. My answer, unequivocally, is no. If previous experience in government or politics is any indication of how well a person will perform, then our reality in 2020 removes all doubt that experience is not as valuable as people believe. Rather it is only part of what makes a representative successful. Experience occurs as progression does. If those in power aspire to be better today than yesterday and better tomorrow than today, that may be the most beneficial quality as experience can develop from there.

What do you perceive to be the United States' greatest challenges as a nation over the next decade?

We the People are destroying ourselves. We are substituting ignorance for knowledge. We must not defund the police, how absurd of statement is that. The Rule of Law must be protected at all costs. All laws, policies, and guidelines are created and grow from necessity. Law is arguably the single most important invention in human existence. From law we are able to interact and operate in day-to-day situations with fellow humankind. It sets limits, restrictions, and enforces sanctions when the former is violated. In short, law exists to govern conduct. As societies evolve, laws need to do the same. In our modern society, laws not only govern individuals, but they also govern and protect entities. These include but are not limited to, governments, businesses, organizations, animals, the environment and any other institution or entity that may interact with humankind. Through evolution of human civilization, laws must continue and extend protection to other living and breathing entities. By doing so, it allows peaceful common ground to be accomplished. To me, law is a way to control vigilante justice by controlling the outcome when those trespass against us. It is a reflection of religion, not always, and an extension of the society's norms of which it represents. It is not reserved for any but can be applied to all. It is not absolute, as it is a fictitious attempt by man to control others. It is only allowed to survive by those who welcome control over chaos, for if it fails, the society and order it represents will also fail. The next decade will bring many challenges, but they are easily solvable if we work together with the commitment to succeed and actions that are the selfless rather than selfish. But, if we allow our Rule of Law to mean nothing, everything loses value, including human life.

If you are not a current representative, are there certain committees that you would want to be a part of?

Anything the American People and West Virginia's 1st Congressional District has confidence in me to do.

Do you believe that two years is the right term length for representatives?

I have zero preference for term limits. If an individual is good at their job, they should stay as long they are able. At least with politicians you can vote them out. Other seats and positions have the ability to stay too long and at times place themselves above American Values.

What are your thoughts on term limits?

No preference. Competency is key in any position.

Is there a particular representative, past or present, whom you want to model yourself after?

No

Both sitting representatives and candidates for office hear many personal stories from the residents of their district. Is there a story that you've heard that you found particularly touching, memorable, or impactful?

Yes. A young gentleman is facing prosecution for killing a wild animal with charges that may not belong. This highlights the need for continued oversight at every level of government. It seems as if the prosecution office may have a problem with discretion and everyone involved should be investigated and removed from their positions if they are found to be corrupt or failed the abuse of discretion standard because of incompetency. The Rule of Law must not bend to those who yield its power. It must be protected from abuse of discretion and especially corruption. For if we ever lose legitimacy in our public offices, the Deceleration of Independence and what it represents must be studied. We must not ignore our past and why America created a standard to govern. Just as the government holds the people accountable the people must hold the government accountable.

Ballotpedia is not only a fantastic place to learn about declared candidates, but I found it also was a place that has a plethora of fantastic, often vital, information citizens can use to learn quite a lot about our system of governance. In addition, Ballotpedia also had a video questionnaire for candidates, Which I also completed. It was encouraging to me to see progress being made.

The West Virginia Times reached out to me when the organization was doing their voter's guide for the 2020 election. I felt this was the greatest opportunity for me to get exposure so voters would know I was a candidate. It also gave me a chance to see what the other candidates of CD1 were thinking.

It read:

Why should Voters choose you for this political office?

My political philosophy is personal accountability, national security, and fiscal responsibility all executed in respect to and in protection of the Constitution. The Constitution is the governing document of this Nation not its politicians.

My employment history, my military experience, and non-partisan views make me a unique candidate. A candidate, that I believe, the 1st District has never had the chance to vote for on Election Day.

It is my hope, as voters find out more about my family's connection to West Virginia and how we have always answered the call to service; a sense of confidence will allow them to cast a vote for me.

Voters should choose a candidate only if the individual was able to earn their vote by convincing them they should have the privilege to represent them. I know how hard it is for a candidate to convince me they are worthy of my vote.

I expect the same level of scrutiny from those in the 1st Congressional District. It is an honor to have an individual vote for you and I would expect nothing less. Voters can feel confident in voting for me, as I will work tirelessly to represent them and their interests.

I believe Congressman McKinley is a fine representative and Candidate Natalie Cline would be a great advocate for West Virginia as they both have West Virginian's best interest at heart. However, I believe, as countless other Americans believe, our two-party political system is a contributing factor of our issues as a Nation.

I am not saying our elected leaders or candidates are wrong nor am I attacking them. We must do a better job of working together before that is no longer an option. We must lead by example and stand for more than just party lines.

What is your position on law enforcement reform and the use of police restraints that limit an individual's airflow while in custody?

I am in favor of any reform that allows our police officers to successfully execute their job and helps strengthen their confidence in the public eye. These brave men and women are the ones who risk their lives everyday so we may enjoy our freedoms and the Rule of Law.

As a private citizen, I encourage other private citizens to gain the critical perspective before rendering a verdict on police policies. Does every situation require a restraint limiting airflow? No. Do situations arise where police officers must use a particular restraint based on a split-second threat analysis? Absolutely.

We cannot generalize or make assumptions when we have enough facts to get to the truth. The Rule of Law must be protected. There are standards for every private citizen and standards for employment activities.

Rioting, violence, destruction of property, and civil unrest is not a form of protected assembly under the 1st Amendment. Verbal and physical assault or taking a life of a private citizen by a police officer is not acceptable under the 4th Amendment.

If you are a protester, protest. If you are a police officer, be a police officer. However, once you cross that line you are neither a protester nor a police officer and accountability must be had. I am not anti-cop, anti-any race, anti-Rule of Law. I am however anti-ignorant. Do not let your bias blind you to the truth of what is right and just.

I am not a police officer, so I do not have the knowledge or experience to aid in the process of police reform or what is required to accomplish such a difficult and complicated task. Nor would I be so arrogant and force my will on the profession, but we can all agree on what should be appropriate and inappropriate.

How will you stand up against all forms of discrimination based on sex, race, gender, ethnicity during your term in office, if elected?

Our Constitution speaks directly to these issues. Not only do the protections exist in the form of guidance from the Constitution as the supreme law of the land, each State, County, Municipality, and employer most likely have very similar language protecting against any form of discrimination.

To answer the question; hold people accountable. If an individual violates the law or a policy then the proper authorities, controlling or governing body must follow the proper procedures to resolve the egregious behavior in question.

We have laws and policies at every level to give relief for the victims and punishment for the accused. The American people must understand that we should not substitute an accusation or charges for guilt and offend America's Due Process Rights guaranteed under the 4th Amendment.

The system currently in place prevents McCarthyism and must remain above personal attacks on character. The Supreme Court confirmation hearings were utterly disgusting and are an example of this behavior. I am not dismissing anyone's claim as a victim, but a court of law is the place for truth, not grandstanding for political motives.

New York Times v. Sullivan set very bad precedent and allows people to say whatever they want towards public figures as if they surrender the protections in our law because of the profession they choose.

Absent a showing of actual malice—that is with knowledge that the statement is false or with reckless disregard of whether it is false or not—by clear and convincing evidence, a public figure cannot recover under a defamation claim.

America's standard must remain one of decency, respect, and the commitment to find the truth not a truth. In any situation including or any form of discrimination; I will always stand against it as should all Americans.

As the COVID-19 pandemic continues, what steps would you take, if elected, to safeguard the people of Marion County?

Any decision made will always be in the best interest of the people I represent. As new information regarding COVID-19 is updated, the task of all governmental agencies is to safeguard all people and help mitigate the consequences of such actions.

This virus is dangerous and a serious threat to West Virginia and our Nation. What makes this virus unique is how it spreads and creates a false sense of security as the delay in symptoms allows it to spread with ease.

The danger of the virus itself is apparent to those who belong to the high-risk categories. However, it is a new virus, and we still are unaware of the complications it can or will cause later for those who contract it.

Most who test positive can and will recover with little or no symptoms. We have a responsibility to those who are in the high-risk category. Our actions and inactions have consequences beyond ourselves.

The most dangerous aspect of this world pandemic is lack of truth and clarity. People have weaponized ignorance and for those who are seeking answers, they are without. The truth exists outside of people's bias or political party.

My concern and greatest fear for West Virginia is the economic consequences that will occur if we are unable to work together. West Virginia, no matter the County or Congressional District, must make decisions with the facts available to its leaders at the time the decision is made.

Testing is key. West Virginia must know where this virus is and isolate those who are infectious. We must be comfortable with being uncomfortable for the greater good. It is reckless and irresponsible to bring people together without knowing who has the virus.

This started with one person in China and forever changed the landscape of the world.

I felt honored to have a newspaper reach out to me, of course it was only after I submitted a press-release that they knew or even cared that I was a candidate in the upcoming 2020 election. And after sending multiple emails acknowledging my candidacy and the declaration available at West Virginia Secretary of State's office, not one other organization put me in their voter's guide.

The Dominion Post flat out ignored my candidacy and printed a voter's guide without me in it. Even though I reached out multiple times, including phone calls, they ignored me and any correspondence I sent. However, that was par for the course and heartbreaking to say the least.

I recognized I was running out of time and running out of money. I was taken aback and quite insulted regarding the amount of people who failed to support me or my campaign. Not that my friends and family were required to help but it was clearly an error on my part. I included those people as they were a vital part when I was planning my campaign. I was counting on those who knew me to stand with me and help me as much as they could or at least recognize I was in need of their help.

I guess I just assumed those people who I gave my time and effort to would be more than happy to contribute in a reciprocal way. That is what I would have done. It would have been without question if someone I knew in my life needed aid, I would have been right there. Many times, and often in my life, I have stepped up, been there for others, yet they were nowhere to be found.

Maybe they were unaware or maybe they were busy. I try to give people the benefit of the doubt because I believe people are inherently good. Believing this I sent a message to all my friends asking for support in any capacity I could receive it.

It read:

In case you were unaware, I am a write-in candidate for West Virginia's 1st Congressional District.

I do not have the backing or support of the DNC or RNC. I do not have access to PACs or Super PACs. I am with without the normal endorsements of influential people or entities.

I created my campaign, and everything associated with it by myself with little or no help. I worked hard to get where I am today and will continue to work hard as long as I am able.

Although I am without all the money and the benefit of powerful special interests' groups, I believe I am competitive and have a good chance to win on Election Day.

I have not asked anyone for support with campaign contributions nor have I asked people do much for me.

This is the home stretch, and I am asking for your help with contributions and anything else you are able to do for me.

I need to push hard the next couple of weeks, and I need your help. I have done everything I can on my own up to this point.

Below is my campaign website, my merchandise website, my contribution website and my Ballotpedia page.

This is everything I am and everything I stand for. Please do what you can. Share, read, or contribute to assist me in my

Congressional run. I am a leader who is not bound by anything other than what is contained in the Constitution and respect for my fellow Americans.

Even if you do not agree with me on all points, help me Defend American Values. At least you will have a leader who will always respect you and defend your freedoms as fiercely as I defend my own.

I don't speak from ignorance because people are imbeciles when they do this. If you say something untrue, you are a liar and those are the worst and, in my opinion, serve zero purpose in a society that values truth. Well used to...


I was determined and believed success would be mine. But, also, much like Ralphie in A Christmas Story, my expectations failed miserably. It was to work like a charm, but unfortunately, my aspirations to become a legitimate candidate never really materialized. It was very disappointing and, honestly, quite embarrassing for me that I was unable to generate a small amount of momentum. Not even enough to act as a springboard for the 2022 midterms—which was always the purpose.

I was able to raise just under $1,500 in campaign contributions from 14 people and was extremely honored to have 58 people vote for me. That's it. I gave everything I had and devoted the best of who I was and all I was able to do, all that I created was a void in my heart. I had a mental breakdown because I could not understand where I went wrong and what I could have done to increase my efficiency.

To be honest, my greatest strength was my connection to people and their connection to me. But it proved to be my greatest weakness. I was unable to generate enthusiasm from my own people, and consequently, they were a big part of my plan, which my abysmal performance during my campaign and the results on election night show. And it hurt more than I can explain. I do not have words to describe how it made me feel inside.

Am I deterred from the challenge of standing for what I know is right? Or becoming someone with influence who can bring about the change needed to maintain peace in society? No. Not even in the slightest. That is not to say I was not hurt or saddened by the ineffective attempt to become a representative. It is often hard to accept the truth, but the truth should never insult as that is not the purpose. How success is achieved is by figuring out how to push yourself further and harder than anyone you have ever met. This is what people must do to become the best version of themselves.

However, quite often and being the controlling demon my entire life, the imposter syndrome creates an internal conflict letting doubt creep in as it attacks my self-worth. Although I learned years ago, my struggles or failures have been more valuable than my successes, it is still no consolation to failure. So, I will eventually decide what path will best suit me and my aspirations to bring about change and plan accordingly. Whether in politics or the private sector, leaders who stand for decency are always needed. Influence and change can occur from many different places, not just as an elected leader.

My devotion to this Country, what America is in my mind—is described in the letter I sent my family and friends, the Facebook post, my press release, Ballotpedia questions, and this book. I cannot express what America is and what she means to me any better than this, nor am I able to implore people more sincerely to argue with kindness, fight with love, and coexist with understanding.

And because I am against a pursuit of a one-America and do not believe in the two-party political system or its inner workings and its proponents, I will never submit to the status quo or its protection. It delays progress and will create a tribalistic nation. One that builds alliances to defeat one another. When we are no longer guided by the documents created to maintain peace, we are no longer worthy of the words it represents as a people.

Society keeps looking for answers from those before us, which is short-sighted as their understanding, experience, and knowledge of reality are frozen in time because their thoughts reflect a reality that has long since passed, and a future was born without them in it. Therefore, every modern society needs generational leaders and philosophical thinkers who adequately reflect competency and represent the current state of affairs. Anything less allows us to fall victim to the same trespasses and transgressions of those before us. Never solving, never reimagining, and never progressing.

We must lead and think in a modern world with modern solutions. Traditionalists and protectors of the status quo have often left society to pick up the pieces long after they are gone. Laws, ideas, and beliefs must reflect laws, ideas, and beliefs for the generation these systems of control represent. Society can never be governed by the past as that is a belief that will only serve to enslave and inhibit the solutions for tomorrow.

The opportunity to lead a free people is the most incredible honor bestowed on a person. Especially one who believes in the importance of participation and mutual respect in relation to the understanding of what America represents. It is not lost on me the difficulty people face when pursuing a path of leadership in the political realm or an attempt to lead those who are represented by the few.

But suppose all Americans would start conversations with each other about what we need to do to make America better. In that case, we can solve the problems we agree on and begin the tolerance process on those we do not agree on because our identities are never the issue.

I and my want to lead is not for a selfish endeavor, nor do I seek power for the sake of ego. I want to change the world for the better because that is the standard of human existence in relation to the responsibility and gift of life. I have been told my entire life I would not be able to accomplish what I envision in my mind. Although my success has never been contingent on whether or not someone believed in me, these people create roadblocks preventing substantive change. It also is a shame when people speak from ignorance and pass bad advice as a piece of philosophical treasure.

I read this recently and it seems as if people are committed to letting things collapse around them:

If you know someone that uses the phrase "it is what it is", they are dangerous. Because they no longer allow things that are outside their control to affect them. They have mastered the art of acceptance.

This is always said by people who enjoy the benefits of someone else's success and determination to never accept the status quo by striving to always say "it is what it is" because "I allow it to be." Change never occurs by acceptance. It is only possible by never accepting anything especially what is out of your control. If it bothers you, that is the motivation needed to change what must be. The only thing missing is discipline and the ability to ignore those who say, "it is what it is."

Those people will never have books written about them, nor can they inspire the will to fight for the impossible and can never change the world because they accept what should never be. All things are possible, including accepting you have to believe the premise "it is what it is" as a way of life. But when you finally decide to accept everything, stay out of my way because I do not want to live in your world. And that should be relatively easy for you to accept.

Change is needed, and everyone must acknowledge it. However, people must never unwillingly accept things others are forcing them to believe. Do not fear standing against people who call you an enemy, especially those at odds with the truth. Do not sit idly believing "it is what it is" while people suffer needlessly simply to have personal peace—how selfish of you. There are three things in life that give differences a chance to prosper together or die apart, and it will take work to promote these especially when people are more than happy to accept what they cannot change.

The first is spirituality. It can be influenced by religion or not, but it is a strong belief people must represent decency and something greater than themselves through a connection with people and the environment. Being correct is not exclusive to either one denomination over another, nor is it a specific brand of faith that matters. The second is a strong constitution. A law connected to a human experience of life. A way for accountability to control and a standard or code of conduct to exist. This must represent people, not faith, not Gods. The third and final part is an appropriate economic model representing both a sense of spirituality and a strong constitution. These demand equity, as do the people in whatever economic model they are a part of.

These are necessary to the survival of a free people. I am certain if our people cannot find common ground, if Americans are not able to push one another allowing for a better version of ourselves, if they are unable to create cohesiveness through compromise—it may be time to divide the nation peacefully before a war destroys peace around the world. Although I am unsure how this would work, the alternatives seem rather difficult on one side and extremely dangerous on the other. I do know one thing; I know exactly what happens if we maintain our current trajectory, and that decision will end America as we know it. Even though I think some people believe this is an alternative and they would enjoy the destruction of what is known by a recreation of something in their likeness, we must stop it from occurring. These people are fools, and the only truth they believe is an absolute someone convinced them of due to and caused by hate.

But in the event I am unable to change what is broken or be a leader in my generation, what follows is my understanding of how we can make America work better. These do not represent an exhaustive list, nor is what I am proposing absolutely correct. These are alternatives to what we know because what we have is not working in the people's best interest. But these represent what I believe are the most critical and necessary as we are at a breaking point in our Nation. I believe this can bring about the maximum amount of change in the minimum amount of time. America, her people, must create unity. They must fight for it, and they must commit to it.

What absolutes are you holding onto preventing the truth from saving us all???

# A Place for Your Thoughts:

# CHAPTER VIII

## *Critical and Necessary*

### Absolutes

When applying the subjective taste of purity, to believe these from a personal view is to assume your life and your beliefs are superior to all others. People should not convince themselves of this or any absolutes relative to social identities, nor should they pursue pleasure in doing so. Death and destruction are the results of such a premise in society's past and present, and this outcome is what awaits those who are foolish enough to try in the future.

Disparaging one another to defend oneself creates an imbalance in a society that is without a need to possess such a device. Absolute beliefs will absolutely consume and absolutely destroy. The consequences may not occur in your lifetime but those who are forced to come after must always resolve and suffer through the shortcomings of a selfish nature created by the intent of foolish order.

With that being said, all but one absolute exists. It is not a product of human touch, and people do not control its existence. The only absolute is a natural order existing outside our species' control or laws regardless of people's feelings. It exists with or without the presence of our species, and its preference is selfish.

Advancements in technology are altering these absolutes through scientific experimentation and emotional human intervention disguised as expansive thought. Operating outside of the parameters of what occurs naturally in nature, absent of human existence, will create a rift between people who do not want to be forced to believe something that conflicts with their way of life.

It will also destroy the progress of peace in society, question the efficacy of science, and form religious opposition against meddling in affairs humans do not have the authority to exercise or submit to. These are all invitations to a revolution through conflict or subjugation by force of war. Ignore the trend to have relevance in a society that values utterly worthless items, ideas, and people.

The natural order of things cannot be manipulated past recognition. In doing so, war will be the only absolute ever maintained. This is the exact cause of America's waste and the slow tragic ending approaching. Even though people cannot establish absolutes, they must be able to instill order. These control mechanisms maintain peace, justice, and legislated agreed-upon rules for people to follow, encouraging cohesion. When the Rule of Law of a nation is ignored the legitimacy of the nation is jeopardized and destruction always follows.

# Rule of Law

To maintain a true understanding of these control mechanisms, worth must match value, what is just must match accountability, and liability must match ownership. It is simply the fight to protect the innocent. And it has raged since the first taste of a transgression caused by lack of care. Religions fight the same enemy but are unsuccessful because they are divided, so too is true of those governed.

Each separating selfish purpose from true meaning to allow the growth of sin and steady decline of what can be defined as righteousness—the battle against evil and those who are devoid of care.

All laws, policies, and guidelines are created and grow from necessity. Law is arguably the single most important invention in human existence. From law, we can interact and operate in day-to-day situations with people. It sets limits, restrictions, and enforces sanctions when a standard is violated.

In short, the law exists to govern conduct. As societies evolve, laws need to do the same. In our modern society, laws not only govern individuals but also govern and protect entities. Through the evolution of human civilization, laws must continue and extend protection to other living and breathing entities. Doing so allows peaceful common ground to be accomplished by balancing competing interests.

Law is complicated, as is the application in practice, but consistency must be absolute; if it is not, unrest will be. Law, what exactly does that mean? Many influential thinkers have tried to define this term in its entirety. Of course, the definition accepted or legitimacy in what is described represents power and influence as the ability to control is contingent on both.

To me, law is a way to regulate vigilante justice by controlling the outcome when those trespass against us. It is a reflection of religion, not always, and an extension of the society's norms which it represents. It is not reserved for any but can be applied to all. It is not absolute, as it is a fictitious attempt by man to control others and the chaos of selfishness. It is only allowed to survive by those who welcome control over chaos, for if it fails, the society and order it represents will also fail. It is many things, but necessary being the most significant.

Understanding the term law, in its entirety, allows further understanding of the process of making law and the maintenance required to keep the law. Philosophers and people who see the need for intervention influence the way laws are created and how they operate. This thinking allows laws to be considered either just or unjust, fair or unfair, and how these should be applied to everyone in society, regardless of their position.

Philosophy is a term used to describe critical thinking and logical reasoning. All people can be philosophers and can recognize a need, not just the famous ones. I imagine our parents, grandparents, or even siblings have given us some of the best advice ever; all without a book deal or their words being taught at a university. Philosophy is an examination of obvious observations surrounding life's expectations within a civilized society; a way to develop a personal outlook. These common knowledge thoughts naturally occur with or without influence. But all are represented by an individual's capacity to understand more.

Perspective observations occur naturally, as does the conception of wanting fairness among each other. For example, two toddlers playing in a room will acknowledge when the opposite violates their expectations. In doing so, one will leave the room to seek the authority of an adult, in this case, a 20-year-old mother. She provides the necessary guidance to solve this violation and satisfies the child's need for fairness.

Where does this urge to seek authority come from, and why does it matter? Does it come from a person's self-awareness and consciousness?

Is it contained in all of us, yet some choose to ignore it? Wherever it comes from, it allows people to understand when unfair treatment occurs or when someone has violated an individual's expectations. This understanding creates the need for justice. Law reflects a necessity of our species.

To keep order and to allow assurance of one's expectations in society, the Rule of Law must exist. It must be applied on-demand with care and understanding. It cannot be applied arbitrarily. It must be consistent, protected, and respected by a process that must remain transparent. It must be uninterrupted as is the case for lightning when it crashes to the earth, as they both possess such great power. Thomas Hobbes and John Locke understood observations of what is being by the control and guidance of human touch. Without operating parameters, chaos would ensue.

But the role of law and its relationship to justice is an extremely critical aspect in continuing a civilized society and protecting human life. For any society to continue and successfully operate, a form of an absolute needs to be present. Everything in life is fiction and nothing more than a word association and acceptance; however, because humankind has always created what was previously nothingness, it must contain control mechanisms. Certain limited internal absolutes must be present for its creation to exist and operate. If these were to fail, their creation would collapse on itself and cease to exist. These variables must be constant, regardless of the idea, identity, or entity. In this example, justice and law take center stage.

Again, laws only exist out of and from necessity. It is very rare to have the foresight to predict what laws are needed until an occurrence of said necessity is present. Who would have imagined that taking a human life would need to be written as a restricted act in law to be understood? Not only is that in an instauration of man's law but it can be found in centuries-old documents telling people it is not ok from a religious standpoint from prophets reciting God's commands. Nevertheless, here we are continuing to murder. The law is in place to create balance when harm occurs. This example speaks volumes about what justice is and how important it is to hold people accountable when people violate society's laws, especially murder.

This represents the implied absolutes that must be present to keep the Rule of Law from collapsing. Keeping the Rule of Law allows society to seek justice by punishing those who offend norms, allowing a sanction to be applied against them. Exploitation and the perverseness of things by a human element have continued to be a constant in human history. External and internal influences control the criminal justice system, any law, whether by statute or common law. These influences can prevent unjustness from occurring and have the same power to inflict these unjust acts. Due process is an essential part of our laws being just and fair.

This is a crucial part of justice within the law. Law must remain just. Just is the punishment of those who intend to take advantage of a system built to be fair. Law must remain fair. Fair is the application of justness to all regardless of job, identity, or money. By handing down judgment, the creation of competency, efficacy, and trust will start among individuals within the society. It also gives individuals expectations when dealing with the federal, state, or local court system.

As a value system is formed, so are the arguments for and against it. If the Rule of Law ceased to possess legitimacy, society would fail. Total anarchy would be present, and the law understood by people would be of little or no concern for survival. On the other hand, if submission by force is used to maintain control without a choice, maximum efficiency is present, as is tyranny. The United States government will not represent what it is meant to stand for, and our Constitution would be worthless.

If all things with human touch are subject to abuse or perversion, how can we assume that the ones who hold power will function within the bounds of what is just, legal, or fair? What happens when actors in the system use discretion to set a precedent by personal preference and change the law by doing so? What's more troublesome is this can create rights, remove rights, and abuse discretionary authority to generate an outcome supported by their political allies. And the ability to set a precedent with judicial review becomes a force of political corruption. Are we left to assume or hope that each follows the correct course of action when operating on behalf of the government by representing the best interest of America and her people?

Justice is not only reserved for the government, but it also needs to be present for the law-abiding citizens who may have had their rights removed or infringed upon by the said government or its actors. Man's laws will become unimportant when individuals feel their government fails to represent their best interests. And this will start the fraction of violent dissent used to destroy the status quo and replace what is broken with what is preferred.

Society must produce greater consistency in the justice system and in our Rule of Law. Developing any accountability system is vital to prevent abuse of power and perverseness. It's hard to respect and take the rules, laws, and guidelines serious if those who enforce them remove their and its legitimacy due to corruption. Judges tasked with the responsibility to ensure a law is constitutional must maintain decorum for law. Their decisions must not be influenced by a conviction related to self-identity or the political party that contributed to purchasing their chair or their black robe.

The impact judicial review makes is far reaching and is an integral part of the checks and balances system in our judicial system. It has led to equal rights, individual rights, and employee rights. However, it must be limited to prevent activist judges from pushing their own bias and influence outside of what it means to review constitutionality. Great accountability must be taken to ensure abuse of power is far and few between and occurs as infrequently as possible. The human touch always carries with it the possibility of abuse, but it also brings with it the possibility of progress and greatness.

The court's ability to enforce its judgments or the effectiveness of the policing force in any jurisdiction depends on its credibility and on America's cultural understanding of respecting the Rule of Law. If the Rule of Law starts to lose its legitimacy, its power within our society will also be lost. The court's judgments and police officers' authority will have less influence, becoming less effective, allowing mayhem to control. When the credibility of these controlling forces goes away, or if Americans stop respecting the Rule of Law, the court's judgments will have less force, police will lose their support, and an attack on our institution will occur as is being witnessed currently.

The Rule of Law can never be politicized or weaponized. All decisions in this Country are based on some sort of political bias, and it must be removed. This is a limit and flaw I find in all of America's political systems. For example, our Supreme Court Justices all vote and make party-line decisions; very seldom do they or have they altered this behavior. But this is in our nature and may prove too difficult to remove.

Even our process to elect these Justices is made into a circus event. Our elected leaders cast logic and critical thinking aside, making the process a grandstanding event for their voter bloc or a social media smorgasbord of views, likes, and shares feeding the addiction of self-importance by the self-important. The process of electing the most capable candidate to arguably the most powerful position in our Federal Government must be done absent of unnecessary rhetoric, hyperbole, or grandstanding by those who win popularity contests to grab fame, fortune, or other selfish desires. It should also demand a supermajority for such an appointment to a bedrock institution. If those who have the authority to hire these servants cannot agree, compromise is likely absent, and the choice benefits only the taste of subjectivity through power.

The Rule of Law must be respected, protected, and enforced appropriately, free of bias or any behavior that can undermine the legitimacy of its existence through lack of accountability, including the influence to weaponize resources against political foes and, more importantly, private citizens. It must remain without corruption representing a constant of morality and fairness defined by American Values.

# American Values

What are American Values? These are not defined by a subjective understanding or an objective understanding. These are all-encompassing with only one restriction—the freedom to live life to a device of one's choosing as long as this endeavor does not infringe on the rights of others with direct consequences to the innocent. American Values allow each of us to live a life we choose to live. Not a life that someone chooses for us. A free life from persecution allows our children to grow up in a world where they can be free thinkers, achieve greatness, and create a better world if they so choose.

Americans must and need to remove the notion of being offended. Actual harm is different than being offended. Once an individual violates a protected right of another, that is where the line is crossed, and accountability must be had. But those held accountable must have the ability to move beyond their mistakes, allowing growth and further integration back into our society. We learn from our mistakes and create a better version because of those mistakes. People are not direct reflections of their respective pasts, and we must allow forgiveness to create better versions of ourselves.

With understanding and forgiveness, we allow those who made mistakes to belong in our society once again. When Americans create an environment conducive to growth, our people can accomplish great things and use whatever privilege possessed to make a fair but just society. Our strength, power, and beginning have always been about protecting our differences through freedom, and it is high time Americans start remembering that. We must not allow our differences to divide and destroy. Instead, we must unite and enjoy this beautiful Nation together, allowing American Values to flow free.

The direct result of peace through freedoms cannot be understated. It is an integral part of what American Values represent, and these must not be taken lightly:

> Freedoms of the Constitution are the only way we can live with each other; Freedoms of the Constitution are rules that allow people with differences to coexist; Freedoms of the Constitution give us the blueprint to live in harmony.

> If at any time the freedoms of the Constitution are threatened, Peace can never be obtained.

The enemy of freedom has and always will be a government [an illusion of power through authority people create and people submit to] trying to inflict its will on a people. Therefore, all Americans should be against any group of people who try to take the freedoms of others on behalf of a ruling party in the name of a misguided partisan principle. That is what Don't Tread on Me means.

Let us unite and stand with one another so we may Defend American Values together. By doing this, we can ensure that every American has the freedom to choose the life they want to live and one that is important to them, whatever that may be. Humanity must remove irrational emotional logic associated with and represented by identity.

Those feelings are dangerous and only serve to destroy unity and peace. Do not defend likeness over intent and fault. As if guilt by association somehow is a direct attack on self and provides an avenue to rally against the actual victim. The world's truths are slowly being distorted by a reality unrelated to the necessary understanding of available information. The taste of insanity and the intoxication from the addition will destroy our society.

It is absurd to cloud others from the truth and shield those who must be held accountable. At a certain point, people must make a change to stop detrimental behavior and forgo the idea of believing somehow, "it is not my problem," ignoring it and passing it on to the next generation to deal with. Nothing changes if others are continuously and willing to remove or defer responsibility and accountability.

When the citizens of this Nation defend American Values, it allows the world to live in peace surrounded by decency. Unfortunately, those who wish to harm will continue to attempt to do so. Its occurrence is unavoidable yet can be mitigated. It is not controlling in our species until a decision is made by the inhabitants of a civilization to dismiss righteousness, ignore responsibility, and accept intolerance.

Do not discourage others because their politics and opinion do not align with yours, as their experiences in America are most likely different from yours as well. Somehow Americans have misplaced their understanding of self-expression and free thought. People must have the freedom to think differently, or all that exists are echo chambers resulting in groupthink. We are better than this. No matter the result, our issues are not going away. Americans and their differences will not magically disappear after an election. The status-quo does not offer solutions, only more division.

Do not let our issues grow and create a further divide. Our Nation and her people are going in the opposite direction of progress. The media, social media, and those with influence are dividing us recklessly, irresponsibly, and purposefully. Do not mimic their behavior. Even though it may seem more difficult now than ever, we must strive to see eye to eye and strike a balance allowing our system to work. The days coming are why people must be more considerate and understand one another.

America and the Freedoms she offers are fragile, and we all have a responsibility to look after these with great care.

We cannot assume that our way of life will always be here, and those with power will do the right thing to keep it. If history is any indication of power, then power has destroyed many a civilization. So my suggestion to all voters and those who reside in this beautiful Nation; read the Declaration of Independence. Please read it with emotion. With the same feeling that our founding fathers must have experienced when it was written—because it was necessary.

After reading and understanding how important that document really is, ask yourself, "What have I done to help protect my fellow Americans and their way of life?" America and her people must move forward with a plan to meet a benchmark of cohesiveness for the varying level of differences in society. This can be accomplished by educating children from a young age to perceive differences in a non-threatening manner and develop the cognitive reflex to pursue understanding through knowledge of the unknown.

What do you do to Defend American Values? America owes you nothing, but you owe America everything. I do not want to share a country with people who disagree with this. It takes togetherness, cohesion, and an empathetic will to create an extraordinary existence.

I believe fairness is—allowing people to keep what they worked hard for, but at the same time creating opportunities so others can achieve. People are not created equal, but given an opportunity, their actions could be. Because of this, we must reward and protect those who are willing to go the extra mile to achieve success, not reward the unwillingness to achieve success. That is what a fair society would look like. If we want a better America, we must create better Americans.

Do not be afraid to stand up for what is righteous. Do not be afraid to protect the Rule of Law. Do not be frightened to Defend American Values. Do not be scared to share things worth sharing or words worth reading. We, as a People, are willing to share irrelevant information via social media and get overly excited about grown men playing a children's game but will not hold each other accountable to the responsibility of a citizen; shame on us.

Everything that is happening, everything that is, is our fault—shame on us for knowing more about WAP than we do our Declaration of

Independence. My Country is dying because of worthless people. . . America is nothing without decency. You belong here no matter your race, religion, sexual orientation, gender, or birthplace as long as you can accept your role as a responsible citizen and take it seriously. My family, friends and I are willing to die to prove that to you. Unfortunately, some have. If you cannot be the best version of yourself, you do not belong in this Country. It saddens me the amount of disrespect people are showing to one another and to this beautiful Nation I swore my allegiance to.

People dislike each other because people create problems. The more issues created from controversial topics, the less likely people will tolerate those identities. Not because they hate them or the topics are not worthy of discussion. People generally do not want to be around those who create problems or force dialogue that is neither wanted nor needed. People will start refusing to work with one another, be around one another, or respect one another. It will push people into tribes, and violence will surely follow.

Please pay your share and be respectful to one another at a minimum. Be an American. Stand up to defend her values. There has never been a more important time in America's history than right now. Failure to heed the advice of those before us will be catastrophic. Accountability where required, tolerance where needed, and consideration given to those who understand the premise. **We** must stand, **We** must fight, **We** must defend **American Values**. Although to protect these, people must practice dialogue, not deceptive discourse.

# Deceptive Discourse

Freedom and the system built to permit such an elusive idea requires those who benefit from it, to nurture, guide, and grow her people. It demands deference to logical inferences and tolerant endeavors. America is synonymous with many different terms, but the most important is discourse. The opportunity to participate and the importance of citizens engaging in this process cannot be understated. This process allows for peaceful interactions, coexistence, and a peaceful method to transfer power. Those who are angry cannot ignore it, it cannot be circumvented, and the methods of control cannot be removed. Its power should never be stolen, nor should the legitimacy of its existence be attacked because the system worked or its result was not one of personal preference.

Especially by those who assume that everything they are, everything they believe in, is a product of superior thought. It is easy to convince people of your superiority when you are speaking directly to the likeness of a superior race, superior gender, superior political party, or whatever complex your group does not feel the need to apologize for. It is unwise, it is counterproductive, and it is most certainly divisive. Whatever it is, it is not the discourse America needs, nor is it representative of American Values.

A lie cannot be made into truth until it is repeated and consumed by those misinformed by actuality. A state of mental numbness and cognitive laziness has infected the masses, believing anything those with influence tell them to believe, even to their detriment. A leader does not encourage rioting or childlike temper tantrums when a system built to decide the will of a people—decided. Neither do they act in a manner that is unbecoming of what honor and integrity represent. Incompetency at any level is a tragedy, whether it is from mental soundness, cognitive decline, or character flaws; these should never be tolerated.

For every action there is an opposite and equal reaction—this is true with everything, especially people. But in the realm of decision making, it is more of an acceptance relating to justifiable responses because each person has convinced themselves the behavior is warranted and agreeable among the weakness leading and the weakness following. There is a standard of what is appropriate and inappropriate. What is occurring is outside the realm of proper; even children have recognized the sickness befalling the adult population.

Not only are the norms of intolerance and unprofessionalism becoming accepted, but a new way to create rules and knowledge has infiltrated those with educated influence and those who legislate in Congress. Regardless of the acceptance, without the required discourse to counter what may or may not be true and what may or may not be needed as a law, those who are more intelligent decided to change what the truth represents, changing the way the truth is decided.

What is understood or accepted is not arbitrarily decided by self-appointed oligarchs, nor is it equitable to believe people are too ignorant to recognize what is true or untrue. Communistic tendencies are wreaking chaos among free people. Whatever word or term is used to describe America's new reality is irrelevant because it is wrong and highly destructive.

Creation and dialogue are no longer called discourse. It is called the awokening. People, perceived intellectuals, and those with influence are requiring a connection of our sense of disbelief to convince the world of their truths. In a sense of misinterpreting causation with correlation, by ignoring inconvenient truths, and later accepting falsities, the leaders of the woke-cult incorrectly yet successfully apply facts while associating blame, ignore accountability when needed, and believe half-truths to create legitimacy. All, so their positions are advantageous to their ideas or beliefs, many of these are not only untrue but incendiary to society.

A period of the auhwokening is upon us. Outwokening one another with absurdities and using their exceptional privilege. Disguised as intellectual superiority, caught in a fanciful version of expansive thought, these self-prescribed leaders not only attempt to influence public opinion but also attack political influence to misrepresent reality to benefit a kind, one kind, their kind. Despotism because what they know to be true is the only viable alternative.

Somehow, they were also granted access to the dictionary. In a weird set of circumstances, these tech savvy and organized elites quietly and covertly distort reality to their will. Arbitrarily controlling not only whatever subjective new words or knowledge should be accessible to the world, but also changing words to strengthen their argument and solidify the truth in their likeness to alter the future to benefit their likeness alone. Participating in truth assassination[44] similarly as those before them erased history to benefit their likeness.

These are the controls to establish obedience and pursued for that purpose. Not allowing for a deviation from thought yet demanding a self-imposed reckoning disconnected from discourse or alternate beliefs is used to create enemies and a necessity for representation to unite against a common enemy. If a discussion is what is wanted, discuss. If civil discourse is what is desired, then create civil discourse. Making enemies is relatively easy when specific intent is used to accomplish such a goal. When

---

[44] Altering the truth for personal gain.

partisanship and dialogue are disguised as a necessary tool to prevent the collapse of the Nation, division is the result because the plan went accordingly.

The danger is not one of a statement's subjectively viewed accuracy or inaccuracy. It is not the arguments or positions people hold that create friction. Instead, the issue, the condition of destruction, these ideas are tragically accepted and consumed without consideration of alternate theories or competing thoughts. Later those who do not accept what is being offered are the enemies and why America is failing.

A one-America represents a total bar of civilized debate where one side removes the ability to counter an argument or theory by means of destroying discussion. The possibility of conflict is now upon us. An earned privilege of influence does not include the ability to silence critics, nor does it allow you to maintain correctness without being challenged. People's thoughts and opinions, beliefs and convictions, knowledge created, and knowledge submitted; should not be viewed as accurate, superior, or absolute only because they originate from those in a position of authority.

It must be vetted by peers as everything else is and should be, and it must be able to be accepted or rejected as such. Power and influence do not equal intelligence. Neither does an Ivy League education nor the ability to memorize someone else's thoughts. However, it seems those who have control over knowledge would like people to walk around on a flat earth while the universe revolves around them.

Am I your enemy because I disagree with you? Are you willing to create conflict because your theory is different from mine? Do you associate my likeness with cancer and the cause of all your problems? Am I to blame for the atrocities that occurred before my conception?

This you ignore and assign punishment based on feelings. You are misguided in your attempt to request penance from the innocent. Manumission out of egalitarian principles occurred long before the civil war because kindness is not specific to time or a race, and neither is the absence of such a thought. All people represent all variations of human conduct. Good exists in the people you trash and accuse of creating hardships they had no part in. Do not alter truth or define a person you have zero knowledge of. It is irrational to believe that the worst of people should be the rule and not the exception.

A victim you are not. A tragedy you have never faced. Your blame is misdirected as your logic cannot stand on its own. Its foundation is of weakness and tied to fallacy. So too, is your understanding of reality. It is consumed by your ignorance and a need to fulfill a selfish desire while turning friends into foes.

People stand for what is right. People stand for what is just. People stand for your cause. Stay strong and stand with them. Let us unite as a people to inflict equity for the many against the glutton of a few. We can change the improprieties within the power structure. Our strength is together, not apart. **United we stand** | *divided we fall.* The means do not justify your end, but your end is justified by your means. A level of being offended should not be weighed by your level of acceptance. Unless, of course, we are encouraging a double standard. Is my existence, and are my feelings offensive to you?

Of course, the level of offense taken should be weighed against how intelligent and logical the person offended is by considering the trigger that created the emotion. Most things that are understood to be offensive are considered as such in light of a reasonable person's standard. That is the standard that guides our law and should objectively guide moral outrage in public opinion. So, if intelligent people who have a decent resume can find flaws in the inappropriate level of moral outrage considered and given to a triggered, hypersensitive, and destructive cultural movement, why do we listen to ignorance?

This is what happens when the less intelligent lead and create a standard of decency applicable only through identity. Tragedy is relative to the association as the association is relative to tragedy. Do not claim outrage and harm outside your experience. Wisdom is the standard. Not a book read, experience heard, or a likeness of.

A pursuit of dividing will have the intended consequences but not the result sought. Do not seek an emotional campaign without rational dialogue. People understand. They are willing to engage in appropriate measures to prevent and attempt to atone for legitimate past grievances.

Do not pursue frivolous accusations of an emotional kind. A decision of penance is not subject to your authority. This you do not possess and are unauthorized to do so. Pursue forgiveness, absolution, and peace before anger, hate, and conflict. Those who committed harm were wrong, hideous, and are in hell for the evil atrocities perpetrated against our fellow human beings. However, they are not present, and neither do they represent a current controlling likeness nor should their earned animosity or guilt be assigned to those who are not responsible.

Patriots stood against the affliction of will from the powerful. They fought back and changed the world. So allow us to once again stand for a cause to eliminate the unnecessary from our existence. A choice of righteousness is a choice of peace, survival, and coexistence.

America is growing, as are her people. Do not force regression on the many for the actions of the few. Enematic characteristics are not a threat unless their likeness is forced to be. It is time to end the sins of our fathers who forced the unspeakable upon the innocent. This is the first time America had to address these issues, and the first-time current people were given a chance to remedy what occurred. Allow the opportunity for success. Remember burning the system down results in a charred reality and a place where the diversity of aesthetics may not find shelter.

Pushing a theory that is not recognized nor accepted by a people will create conflict where it is not necessary nor warranted. If you are as smart as you think you are, you will not pursue such divisive rhetoric. If you are not careful, your call for forced consideration will not be met with understanding or acceptance but by rebellion. Tread carefully as people's tolerance for one another is slowly disappearing. A standard of decency exists, and it is outside the accusations of being a democrat or republican, liberal or conservative, white or black, Christian or Muslim, heterosexual or queer. America is approaching an extremely volatile point in the history of our society and our species. An increasingly ever-important revelation is about to occur. The next few years will influence the next 300.

If Americans do not rise and stand together, what will be accomplished is not understanding. It will not create an empathetic will. It will represent the same ending from the same failures created by the same leaders. People will listen and create the necessary change, but our people need a different type of leader. Humanity has been doing it long before America was formed. We all must tread respectfully and force the change our species is destined to create. Inform do not demand, enlighten do not persecute, convince do not force. These are the foundational structures required for discourse. Respect is given to those who respect. Americans need to unite regardless of our differences.

Failure to heed just the smallest amount of understanding will seal our fate. And human tragedy continues in the form of generational mistakes unknown by future generations but felt by those who are simply trying to live in peace with those around them. Broken things must always be fixed; however, we are not enemies, and destroying the land that I love will not lead to a place worth living in.

I recognize the argument; I understand the premise; however, I reject the conclusion. We agree in principle, but caution should control the next subject and the path chosen.

# Race

I am reluctantly wading into this argument, but if Americans do not address this, everything we worked for, all the sacrifices those before us made, the progress we enjoy today will be all for naught. Nothing will survive if we do not come to terms with the past, the progress made, and the progress yet to be made. Our system is dangerously close to a reset, and if the course is not altered, war will be the only truth this continent understands. This will be the location of yet another civil war or WW III, dividing and altering the power dynamic of the world to support what our likeness represents the most or the side that offers a need over decency.

All because skin tones want to insult, find offense, or fabricate issues resulting from a simple misunderstanding altering the contextual origin out of selfishness and the need to justify unruly behavior. I have much more to add, yet I chose to omit these additions because I am not trying to gaslight people or justify the way I think over anyone else. Forward progress is necessary, and we are heading in the wrong direction. Our cohesiveness will prove vital to altering what has begun and changing what we must.

The correct argument will always be a people argument because it is behavioral. Issues plaguing society are not caused by white people, black people, brown people, or any other people. The fault and responsibility rest with individuals who are white, black, brown, or any other people who have the power to cause these issues. But it is the individual(s) who must be held accountable, not the entire group identity they belong to. If

Americans fail to realize this, our future will remain in jeopardy, always repeating the cycle of destruction society seems eager to complete.

These errors are being rewritten in another form but will have the same consequences for innocent people. Most people are unaware of what others are fighting for because affliction is lost on those who never feel the suffering borne by strangers. Their lives are equally different, and their experiences of America are as well, allowing the separation of humanity to occur. People must be mindful of one another and appreciate the struggles that each one of us may be blessed never to experience.

Is this what occurs because people have decided to create chaos by seeking emotional assertions influenced by half-truths instead of promoting balance through participation and understanding to seek— what is? The most controversial and consequential identity America has ever created is upon us—Race in America.

I'm not sure what the correct level of blackness or whiteness I should consider is. What should be the truth? Each brand of our species wants something more or less to control. More black, less white—more white, less black. Why does it have to be either? Why can't it be truth regardless of the splash of pigment painting our skin? Are our races now stuck in a perpetual fight until payback is committed or slavery is a thing again?

When I reference the racial divide, no balance exists; therefore, compromise through understanding cannot occur. People are either of the group who believes one way, or they are the enemy. A tragic dismissal creates neither a sympathetic actualization nor an empathetic actualization, both of which are important for cohesive unity and creating beneficial progress for humanity as a whole.

It instead forms a vacuum of intolerant regeneration, expressing anger for all who may form a separate opinion all their own. This does nothing but create an opposite and equal movement permitting each group to swallow the innocent as they demand loyalty to each misguided pursuit of absolutism through identity.

What follows describes the issues I see as a white male in America. I am completely broken inside, utterly lost. My soul hurts because of the people I love and the fantastic relationships we share. This reality is not easy, nor is this a pleasant feeling for people like me who love the way we do and carry a sizeable empathetic heart, always wearing our emotions on our sleeves.

This is me thinking out loud so others understand the problems we face take work and a large amount of thought to resolve what must be settled. This is what I am working out in my head and the answers I am without. These questions do not make me a bad man, nor am I wrong for asking or sharing my perception of errors. Instead, this represents the friction and societal wedges that continue to push my identity away from others, including the ones I once cared for. So, here are the thoughts I am working through to solve society's most volatile crisis—Race in America.

The question is never, am I "wrong" or "right," as I am not petitioning a people to accept my thoughts as gospel or an absolute that makes the demand on people to forcefully accept my assertions. Instead, it is more of a plea from my conscience that a black and white application is consequential when viewed on the tolerance continuum and even more so in actuality between these competing interests. Especially when we all miss the point, we are all human.

What is interesting to me is the continuous surety I see in all people around me. It is strikingly odd to witness the over confidant arrogance that they own—knowing they are right. It is without question their truth is undeniable, and it must be your truth as well. And it all stems from what people value. Respect and tolerance directly reflect the placement they assign others in relation to their own position in life. People are either above or below, and this is solely based on identity or the diversity a person represents.

I try to remain consistent in my approach when viewing people or actions. Would I befriend a person given their character? Would I follow that person as a leader? Are they an adequate leader? Would I be disappointed if my children or parents were responsible for the behavior in question? What does their character represent? And finally, how would I feel if I were in their shoes. If our identities were the same, would my perspective be similar?

Do I find agreement with what is being done, how it's being done, and why it's being done? How much is enough, and how much am I ready to lose? And finally, do I condone such behavior? These questions define me as a person and define what I believe in. It also keeps me relatively balanced.

It is not a crime, nor is it wrong to be who you are and believe in empowering others who look like you or think like you. But don't forget others, unlike you need to be empowered as well. It is a balancing act a diverse society must commit to. But really, how difficult is it to treat people with respect, hold people accountable, and give credit where credit is due?

The proposed trajectory Americans are heading in is the direct result of our inability "collectively" and refusal "individually" to listen to one another. Of course, the presence of weakness in leadership creates an echo chamber of allowance for detrimental and toxic behavior; however, people must recognize those imposters ignoring them as much as possible.

But people continue to dismiss people's concerns, those not of their likeness, and ignore what they say because some moronic instigator gave them permission to do just that. To the point where what remains the cause of America's decline is ignoring what each side has to say. Each group requires only legitimacy, equality, and recognition of being important. The want and need to be represented fairly while also being heard seems to be missing.

Who is to blame for the race issues in America? I do not blame black people for the division and divisiveness present. Although the instigation and rhetoric used are seldom constructive, I see a group of people fed up with "individual" instances of discrimination and lack of accountability justice seems to provide or lack of respect society seems to extend. I imagine it becomes exhausting at times.

I blame past white people who oppressed and decided to ignore what should have never been ignored. These atrocities occurred to human beings throughout our Nation's history. No, it is not black people I blame. The blatant inequities and injustices represented by the lack of equality were the cause, and it just so happened white people were in charge. It is a burden that falls unto those with power.

And this burden, specifically regarding race in America and the introduction of America as an idea, has always rested with white people, as the power dynamic has always rested with them as well. With power and influence comes great responsibility and care, especially when this power can oppress.

Those who had power in the past decided what rules were applicable to people based simply on the flavor upon a person's skin. What's more, examples of this are not that distant from the present. That seems to be a legitimate concern, and the accountability for certain atrocities has been what, to treat people equally? The guilty have lived side by side with the innocent because people fear and avoid the act of holding themselves and others accountable.

But it is the historical significance that adds the volatile exponential effect. Remember, the representation of power is simply the ability to disrupt the status quo. If you cannot do it, you do not have it. And what peace represents is just the commitment to not use it. So how can we convince people peace is a better way than conflict?

What is occurring is the self-realization of power or equality. I imagine if the black population in America had this much power in the 1700's things would likely have been a little different. I can assume that this would be the case for any oppressed people in any time period. At what point do society and those possessing power listen to those without?

Even though I understand and try to be empathetic as possible, black and white people are both wrong for omitting history in their positions when antagonizing each other. They are both wrong for promoting themselves by ignoring others. And they are both wrong for allowing their bickering to careen our Nation off a cliff.

It is wrong to forget the progress children of the oppressors have made. This cannot be ignored, and the difficulty of such an endeavor must be acknowledged. This is a generational change occurring over hundreds of years, successfully altering people's lives for the better. Still, sadly it takes time and consumes innocent lives as well. The question is always, how much progress is enough? I guess the future generations will tell us that. But I imagine it is never enough, for the sins of our fathers are invisible to those with life.

Trying to ignore hundreds of years of oppression that has consumed the lives of the innocent is a consequential oversight stuck on repeat. America has one group of people screaming, "it isn't enough," and the other group shouting, "we're trying." But both are ignoring what the other is saying. My fear, what has me concerned, eventually, people will stop caring and become tone-deaf, blinded by hatred allowing rhetoric to grow into violence.

Words into actions because each group is too selfish to care for anything other than themselves and their unimportant identities. Why? What is the constant necessity of war? Is it the older generation gaslighting the younger generation because they were too scared to do it themselves? It seems if peace exists by choice, then it also expires by choice. Whatever it is, Americans have a difficult road ahead. But more importantly, what will the youth of our Nation decide to do?

America must come to terms with race issues in this country. Our system of governance and its people cannot survive a strict black and white application of understanding associated with our differences stemming from our history. We must create understanding without demonizing one another.

In addition, it is time for people to start acting like adults and speak to past and present truths. Being offended is something children complain of. It is well past high time to grow up. If people are unable to approach what divides us with maturity, they will lack the humility to prevent what will destroy us. Truth is an extremely vulgar necessary tool. Without it, bad decisions are constantly destroying society simply out of a desire to ignore what is hurtful, unkind, or shameful. It may be the answer to fostering understanding.

The truth is undoubtedly required to have the shared efficacy necessary to ensure our continued existence. From this point on, my words may sting, but this sting is simply due to the consequences of human interaction and a constant need for representation or validation. Or, in other words, a selfish want by the acts and beliefs of the ignorant. These are nothing more than conversation starters to develop the dialogue to solve or confront our friction.

Without question, the beginning, the founding, and the birth of this democratic republic is tarnished with an irrevocable stain. America's coming-out party could have put the world on notice that a monarchy rule and the mercantilism slavery destroying the innocent, has zero place in a modern society where citizens govern themselves. But instead, those with power folded and failed the persecuted they were selected to protect by ignoring their own words and arbitrarily applying what they believed was unnecessary to change.

People who are graded by those who follow will always fail the standard of accountability enforced by the morality clause adopted by the controlling norms in the current society. People must come to terms with difficult truths. History and those who have since passed have not been kind to differences in this country. Acceptance of this is vital and extremely important to maintain truth and peace.

It is equally important to accept and realize it is not where this Nation has been but where she is headed that matters, regardless of how you subjectively see things. This Nation, other nations, and the world are no longer controlled by an inferior, inexcusable, unacceptable system of slavery. We must not forget that, not by ignoring the truth but by acknowledging progress and what remains to be done.

The change required to form a more equitable society takes times. Unfortunately, many mistakes and short-sighted beliefs must first be recognized before this can occur. This is not an excuse, nor am I justifying behavior or offering a lack of accountability argument. Instead, it is a dangerous reality, and a difficult realization people must be willing to engage in and recognize.

Five hundred years of persecution, discrimination, and abuse contains 500 years of anger, resentment, and hate, but it also includes 500 years of growth, survival, and a people worthy of celebration. What happened to a people and continuously seems to repeat, represents "their" experience of America, and it is incredibly short-sighted to dismiss those feelings as irrelevant.

Our job, society's role, is to ensure our people no longer face our past hardships. Therefore, change must occur, and a commitment to protect people (human beings) from any discriminatory practices must be present. However, this change that must occur should not destroy the system that we are all a part of or push us to treat one another as an enemy. To achieve a peaceful equilibrium between free people, we must do this by working together.

Those atrocities were performed and practiced by people who are no longer alive by a system that is no longer in existence. It represents the standard of what was, what isn't, and what should never be. The commitment to change the status quo takes centuries. These people were doing what the world was doing, and that is all anyone ever does. It does not excuse their behavior when applying people's evolved ethics and morals, but it explains their limits.

What motivations or reasons for such actions justify the decisions those before us made? How can we sit idly allowing atrocities and the unspeakable to be done to those who are without power? At what point do people stand, shout "enough is enough," and stand up for righteousness? A vital piece of the puzzle is represented by a willing Nation and a people who are not only committed, but able to accomplish progress because the system allows it.

The founding fathers and those who could change the acquiesce of slavery failed. They were continuing a historical norm of traditionalism and protecting the status quo. The first opportunity for equity was lost on great thinkers. Not only for slaves but also for women. They were unable to rise to the occasion for many unacceptable reasons but eventually, progress and the much-needed change occurred. It is not lost on my soul, heart, and understanding of those affected by such atrocities.

As the toll is arguably unfathomable to those who are present today, any half conscience, informed, aware person who has the slightest shred of empathy and intelligence knows slavery is wrong and recognizes it as such. Those who participated in such an inhumanly gross unjust practice represented the worst of humanity. But the system at that time, the people at that time, and the world allowed it. Right, wrong, indifferent it is no more, as are they.

Both the black and white communities (others as well) must find a way to heal, and it must be separate from our legislative process or influence from politicians as they do nothing but deepen the divide. No matter the concessions or progress, it will never be enough. Politicians create division on purpose. It will always be an issue to generate votes and, more importantly—money to feed their political committees.

The government and those associated with it cannot solve the race issue in this country or world and never could. These solutions are handled best by society outside the corruption of government, but with the protection of the government and influenced by modern ideas and representative of the people currently living in society. Forcing people to believe something without convincing them is contrary to progress, destined to fail, and will allow history to repeat.

When change comes from people, it has a more profound, more powerful message. To accomplish this necessary change, uncomfortable truths must be discussed and accepted by both sides. It seems futile to try and incorporate all racial issues into one sub-chapter, especially given the rich history of such inequalities, but the purpose is not to inform. Perceptions, perspective, and persuasion are pillars of progress. If people are able to think differently, solutions become more apparent.

What purpose does it serve to deny or justify any type of discrimination past or present? It is equally asinine to hide the truth in an attempt to lessen the severity, depict a group of people or represent them as they are better than they were, or justify actions because "that's just how it was." White people must understand and somehow remove their likeness and disassociate themselves from the injustices black people in this country have experienced before America, since its inception, and continue experiencing in the modern version of this country.

It is not necessary to defend your whiteness, your blackness, or any other identity. Ignore all who wish to create division and seek unity even though it may seem hard at times, given the lack of tolerance from people and a push to increase detrimental unity through selective creation. Stand and defend the truth with a current understanding of what equality means in this Country, by what it is represented by and what it must stand for.

Victims are unique as they are represented by an action in the past, not one of speculative conjecture. In the event people have been living under a rock for thousands of years, people, in general, have not been too kind to differences. All races or people are guilty, equally wrong, and are represented in a continuous cycle of hate passing through generations.

But from the standpoint of grading people when controlling documents were in place most recently, white people have truly inhibited progress against a people. It is irrefutable that history is filled with people who encouraged discriminatory practices and possessed racist tendencies. This is especially true when the intolerance manifests in the form of governmental control. Not current white people but whites from the past were not over-friendly to black Americans in this country. However, still today, white Americans and black Americans each carry animosity towards one another because of what occurred.

Good people did step up, but that does not erase fault or atrocities, nor does it allow blame to be directed and applied to the innocent. Things changed, and although the resentment is still measurable, it is not because a group is less than others or a race is superior; it exists because generally, people do not like each other.

Black people must not blame the current population for the past atrocities. The responsibility and association cannot be forced upon people who are not liable for what they did not do. Likeness is not evidence of liability, nor is commonality. Simply put, these people are not those people.

White people must come to terms with the adversity that black people in this country have faced and continue to face in some situations and circumstances.

There have never been laws in the United States of America that read—Black children cannot be in a household with white parents (although these are connected), whites cannot marry blacks (although these are connected), blacks cannot teach whites to read, whites cannot vote, whites cannot own property—but quite the opposite is true for the black community. These were laws written by legislators and even protected by judges in America. For heaven's sake, there was a war that killed 750,000 to free a people to apply an understanding that they cannot be owned. And who could have imagined that people would find the end of slavery insulting?

These beliefs were sought, discussed, and designed intentionally to create a second-class citizen—a second-class human—represented at an unjust beginning by a three-fifths compromise: taxes, representation, and property implications were considered, and no one spoke kindly regarding the human beings involved. Should enslaved people be counted as property or as constituents for representation in Congress? If so, how much of a person? They lacked freedom, liberty, and the ability to pursue happiness. These specific citizens represented power, liability, and a bargaining chip for the north and the south to barter with. These atrocities and discriminatory practices based on skin color are not fictional. These are not made up; it was normal and discussed at the dinner table. A compromise always falls short of what is considered fair. It is simply those "with" giving a little to those "without" not to upset the power dynamic too much.

In any event, these were truths, regardless of how or why this was the reality innocent people faced. Imagine living that life. Imagine teaching your children to look away as speaking to a white person while making eye contact is disrespectful. The people involved in history's past were unnecessarily cruel to other human beings simply because they possessed a different shade of skin color and the power to inflict their will upon them.

Nothing more, nothing less. This was the truth. This is what black Americans are asking, "Hey, white people historically, not you specifically as individuals, but your kind, those with the power before you, did not like us. If we aren't careful, you may very well target us too."

I imagine they are asking, what side you are on? Are you from the camp that believes the south will rise again, or are you from the camp of equality matters, willing to fulfill a promise of a more just nation? There exists zero in between. You are either supportive of racist tendencies or not. Black Americans must stop following imbeciles. White Americans must stop following imbeciles. If people only follow those who are worthy, worthiness is what people will represent, and decency is what will lead.

And to be quite honest, what kind of person is okay with destroying the understanding that all people are created equal? "All people are capable of great things and are deserving of the opportunity to prove this and are entitled to the full protections under the Constitution of the United States of America." Who could disagree? Why would you possibly want to? What is happening to our Nation and the world, for that matter? Regression, resentment, and rudeness have consumed our ability to reach one another, destroying peace by preventing growth.

The year 2020 was a very enlightening year. I learned much about our species; most of it was the prevalence of selfishness. It gave us a greater understanding of people and what they truly represented. Actions do, without a doubt, speak more loudly than words. These actions, what were on display, most of it was selfishness. Most of it was because of selfishness and the desire to be. I watched the world choose not to solve problems together. But more importantly, it represented something; it felt different.

It highlighted every bad part of our species in one year. It showed us how society could be destroyed either economically, biologically, or even through chaos represented by the lack of accountability. Understanding this, I wrote a piece about Black Lives Matter. I wrote what I believed caused some of it. I wrote because that is what I do. I wrote even though many people would never read my words. I wrote because I had something that needed to be said. I wrote because I was motivated.

That is what 2020 represented: the motivation to vote, the motivation to save, and the motivation to do. Whether or not what people did was right or wrong is irrelevant. Because something motivated people. This is the same reason I spent the last two years of my life trying to understand and maybe change things for the better; I was motivated. I was motivated to support black lives. Not the movement but the people. Not an opinion, but a want to get involved and try to help, try to change, and try to explain. But more importantly, I was motivated to represent the best of my people, my race, and my existence. I was motivated to find the truth. And this is what I wrote.

It read:

> I would never imagine that American's factual statements can be considered an insult. Not only do these harmless factual sentences offend but repeating dictionary approved, factual, non-opinion words can be perceived as an act of aggression that could lead to violence. How is that possible?
>
> I am not speaking of/to or showing support for the organization. I am however, making a factual statement that describes an absolute truth. Black Lives do MATTER. And, if that bothers you, come see me. Please direct me to evidence showing that this is not true.
>
> We should not defend any violence, anger, hate, nor discontent against one another; no matter how people can rationally justify it in their own mind. This behavior is shameful, un-American, and dangerously close to treason.
>
> Black lives matter
>
> All lives matter
>
> Police lives matter
>
> Donald Trump is your president.
>
> Those four sentences are all absolutely true, yet those words cause so many people to be uncomfortable and in the right situation can cause violence. How can a word be loaded into a person's mouth and directed at another but create the illusion that a victim was shot with a gun like a bullet penetrated their body?
>
> Have you not heard sticks and stones before? Americans must be comfortable with the uncomfortable. People must learn to work out their differences so we may learn to live together. The hypersensitivity consuming our people is the worse type of virus our species has ever spread.
>
> Freedoms of the Constitution are the only way we can live with each other; Freedoms of the Constitution are rules that allow people with differences to coexist; Freedoms of the Constitution give us the blueprint to live in harmony. If at any time the freedoms of the Constitution are threatened; Peace can never be obtained.
>
> I am saddened by the behavior of a broken system and the continued defense of the indefensible. It sickens me that in 2020

we must have this conversation with grown adults. In what reality is it okay for a person abuse another? In what reality is rioting protesting? In what reality is it okay for a person to take the life of a defenseless human being?

Uncomfortable truths lead to uncomfortable questions, which must elicit uncomfortable answers. If race, politics, sexual orientation, and religion all are topics that make you uncomfortable, imagine what it's like to have a knee pressed against the back of your neck as you beg for your life. Try explaining to your family your business, the sole way your family eats, was burnt to the ground by peaceful protesters. Imagine living in a world containing people who are destroying with intent.

This moment was meant to happen. Not the continued acts of violence and the tolerance of hatred, but what will come from it. This is a perfect storm. This is what revolutions are born from and what movies are written about. This could very well have been another round of injustices acknowledged and quickly dismissed by the powers that be.

However, many hardworking Americans are out of work and upset at the status quo, and rightfully so. We must focus on healing America and respecting everyone. We will make tomorrow better. Everything fell in place at the right moment at the right time.

These events will be studied and analyzed for years by politicians, sociologists, psychologists, and anyone one willing to address what we were never allowed to discuss in public. This will be taught in our children's history books and future generations will question the competency of our leaders in the timeline of the last 150 years.

They will not be able to comprehend why people treated each other this way, especially in the land of the free. We are witnessing history and it is about damn time. Do not run from it, do not hide from it, do not try to stop it. For this, is how change is achieved.

These words are not a blanket statement and not every person is deserving of this criticism. But those who are upset at my words, may need to take a good long look in the mirror and ask yourself, ["Do I defend the indefensible, "Is my bias clouding my judgement?", Do I contribute to the problem?"].

What is more perplexing to me, is the fact some of these atrocities are committed by government actors and people who know better. It is much deeper than the abuse of power we witness on television and social media. The very system that is built to protect the innocent; strives to protect the guilty.

It is a systematic failure that prevents society from holding those individuals accountable for their actions and inactions. Because of this, it continues to be a generational lapse of judgement, allowing the same system to wash, rinse, and repeat without failure exactly the way it was designed.

It is ingrained in the fabric of our society and in our daily routines. We only notice it when we are forced to look for it, but it is not hard to find and it never really disappears, does it? Skip the notion of standing in solidarity with the victims of these hateful acts or empty gestures. You can have the solidarity; we will keep the change.

Real change, not the change that makes you feel good for a day but change that advances societies to the next evolutionary step of progress. Change that alters norms forever, substantial change. To the men and women who have suffered and those who stood with them and continue to stand with the oppressed, you are my heroes.

You are who I wish to become. Humankind need not create fictional superheroes to stand up for what is right. All that is required is to look at one another, right now in this very moment. Your moment, our moment, their moment.

Judgment is not passed in the moment or during the circumstances surrounding the events but graded by those who follow us later. Yet the trauma, pain, and consequences are not felt by later generations but by those who continue to endure.

For those who know me; know I am a roller-coaster of raw emotions and at times it consumes me. I do not have an issue with saying what is on my mind, nor do I have an issue standing for what is right, standing for what is fair, or standing for what is just.

I was old enough to remember what it felt like when I watched police officers beat a man named Rodney King. I knew it was wrong at 10 years old and I know it is wrong now. What have we become as a country, as a society, as a people? I barely recognize the country I love or the people who represent what America is supposed to be.

I also remember the L.A. riots on the television and asking my parents what is wrong with people. Now my child, niece, and nephews are privy to the same violence, the same destruction, and the same type of people disguising their actions as just and somehow a way to move forward.

Our behavior is not okay nor is it reflective of a civilized people. In case people need reminded that all positions can be twisted to the narrative of selfish bias people.

"Let's be clear, we said: Black Lives Matter. We never said only Black Lives Matter. That was the media, not us. In truth, we know that All Lives Matter. We've supported your lives throughout history. Now we need your help with Black Lives Matter, for black lives are in danger."

*Gene Testimony Hall*

What about those words offend you? What about those words make you want to destroy the very same community that you must live in? Or is it the fact you don't respect people, property, and the Rule of Law?

Some people may not understand what it is to be empathetic. That is who I am. I cry for others. I feel their pain. I do not have an issue putting myself in the shoes of others. Please do not mistake this for weakness. I have no issue expressing emotions for victims and outrage at their suffering, neither should you.

Why must we be outraged by videos alone? Why aren't we motivated by the thought of—that could be me or that could be my children? Is it not enough to know a person is suffering or an injustice is occurring to a person? Shouldn't the very mention of this behavior sound the alarm, create change, and unite an entire people?

Why do we have to sit back, and watch people shut down highways as if they have the right to do that. That is not peaceful. That is not progress. That is chaos. Why are cities under siege and politicians playing political leverage games with civility. That is not honorable. That is not just. That is shameful.

This is a very supercharged emotional issue. And people must remain capable of following the laws in a time of crisis. You do not have the privilege to remove a person's right to be free of harm because you are angry. You do not have the right to burn property. You do not have the right to take a life because you do not possess the authority to do so.

At the very core of what is occurring, it is racism. That combined with incompetent leaders who lead by party and likeness or similarities. Do not fan the flames. Stand with one another. The pain, the true loss, is only felt by the loved ones who lost that special person in their life. Not the thieves begging for money or the thieves looting to satisfy a selfish desire. The pain is owned by those who lost not those who create a fictitious loss. Not to dismiss what happened or to minimize the trauma and pain they suffered, but this is bigger than them.

Not because those people do not matter, they absolutely do matter. The loss of their lives has sparked a revolution and what happens next is the change previously mentioned. This is bigger than race, this is bigger than hate. The larger picture; the means to the end. This is about the people taking their power back and putting the world on notice.

I continue to watch my countrymen murdered, beat, and treated less than humans. Have we grown so callous self-absorbed that we forgot what it is to be an American? We all should be civil rights activists and stand for anyone who is under attack.

Whether it be from a government, its actors, businesses, or individual actions, we should not tolerate any type of discrimination or selfish actions when it creates hardships for free men and women.

We cannot allow people to lose focus and destroy or cause decay to our values, our beliefs, and our peace. Please use passion when protesting, not anger. Please use words when getting a point across, not violence. Let us not forget why we are here. But also let us not forget we must support the Rule of Law, while supporting the police, so they can support the Black Lives Matter movement.

However, this moment, what is occurring right now, is about race and we should be mindful of that. This is about the way a group of people are affected. This is about their pain and the way they feel. All should be wise to remember that. Not because white people should fear offending what it is to be black in America but because they need us, they are us, we are Americans, and we are people.

Until true equality exists in America, we can never truly recover from slavery. Slavery is morally and ethically wrong. It is also unconstitutional, and we fought a bloody war to finally end the atrocities of that culture, but have we truly changed anything? It seems as if every other generation finds a new way to inflict their will on a people as they continue to oppress what is different, while ignoring what is similar.

I have remained relatively quiet as I watch the country, I love slip into yet another round of chaos. It hurts to see all the pain and anger all around me. I imagine in some sort of way it is my fault. I wish I could do more. I fear that it is arrogance in my belief that I have the answers and can solve the issues that continue to threaten the very existence of this nation that I love.

How disrespectful of me to the leaders who are doing the right thing as I elevate myself to a position of authority in an attempt to somehow convince myself that I have the answers. I am consumed by illusions of grandeur thinking this will solve anything or offer a bit of guidance. Maybe it will maybe it won't, but I can no longer contain what I believe is the issue and the threat to our very existence as a civilized society.

I have grown tired of the lack of leadership and the incompetency of those with authority. I was always under the illusion that the people appointed to govern and lead us would always do the right thing as they deliver us from evil. How naive of me to believe a standard would exist in the White House, the halls of Congress, State, or local level of government. Shame on you all.

We will have to do this without them. People generally do not agree on every topic, nor will they always compromise or find common ground; however, there are things we must agree on if we are to be a united people. Everything has a purpose, and the purpose must be protected at all costs. We can all agree that treating each other as we would want to be treated is the floor of basic human interaction.

The best way to govern people is the system we are currently blessed to be a part of. We must ensure that all people have equal rights. That is something we can all agree on, unequivocally. People are asking for understanding and consideration. That is what we must give them.

The oppressed are not asking for anything other than being treated the same as white people or at least an understanding of that. Nothing more, nothing less. We can do better; we must do better.

~Give me your tired, your poor, your huddled masses yearning to breathe free~

It may be difficult for some to understand but stand back and think critically, observe your surroundings, and listen to those who informing the world that the system is broken. Equality is the only way we can transcend to what we are destined to be. Treating the unequal equal. Not to make it easier to succeed but allowing those who are willing the ability to succeed.

That is social justice and that is the norm we should all strive to be a part of. Remember once we achieve this, we still have a lot of work to do. So do not get lazy and forget that. If we are going to do it lets do it big. But first things first, let us hold our black community up and let them understand that we do love you and you are just as important as anyone else.

Below I have seven topics that must be addressed to restore balance and to prevent the destruction of our way of life. These are not an exhaustive list nor are they complete based on the heading. Feel free to add to or substitute my thoughts. Please think of these as a way to assist us in our struggle to coexist. Shouldn't that be the goal of each and every one of us? Let us all leave this place just a little bit better than the way we found it.

## LEADERSHIP MUST BE PRESENT

This of course seems very odd to acknowledge since we are a society of advance cultures, progressing and making improvements as we go. For some reason it seems we have stalled and actual stopped moving forward to enhance the lives of all who seek protection from persecution. We need leaders to stand and return some normalcy to our daily lives. Where are you?

To the people, use your most powerful tool, your voice. Let your leaders know how you feel. Protest, organize, and for the love of this wonderful Nation vote. We are not informed enough, nor do we participate adequately as a people to take care of our duties as citizens. When this occurs, we fail America and each other.

It seems that the United States may have a minority of people in our population that probably shouldn't vote or even run for positions within the government, but here we are. The United States has close to 220 million registered voters. Think about those who failed to vote in 2016 Presidential election. The absent registered voters would have surpassed and outnumbered the total voters who participated by nearly 90 million.

Our failure to put in leaders in positions of authority who possess the skills and competency has led to the continued decline of our country. Our two-party political system is broken and does not adequately reflect the will of the people anymore. No one cares about party lines, if they do, they are the minority. Most reasonable Americans would like to see guidance and leadership from a professional not bound by party lines that do nothing more than divide us.

Something needs to change. It is odd to me that we live in a country where people are homeless and suffer through inadequacies such as lack healthcare, lack of proper nutrition, or a livable wage so people can provide for their family. Yet someone can spend over $1 billion dollars to lose an election or spend $450 million dollars to drop from a primary race only after a month of campaigning.

We must put the proper leaders in a position to lead us from the front. Americans are less than impressed with the current situation. How is it reasonable that people get paid $174,000.00 a year to be a Senator or a Representative only to not accomplish what the people so desperately need?

Do not vote by party lines, likeness, or how famous or well known a person is. Vote for character and what they stand for. United States' citizens pay entirely too much money in salaries to not see a return on our investment. Isn't that what we are doing? Americans invest everything we hold important in our elected leaders, and we must hold them accountable.

Sometimes I think I can do a better job than what we are forced to choose from...

GEORGE FLOYD'S TRIAL MUST BE FAIR, EXPEDIENT, AND HAPPEN SOONER THAN LATER

In consideration of the state of affairs in the United States our government must expedite the trial and hold those accountable to justice. Due process cannot be violated, and an ending of the continued corruption or protection of the status quo must end post haste.

This will allow our country and its people to heal. We cannot delay and we must not sacrifice what is fair, just, and allowed under our Constitution for a quick verdict. However, this is the most important trial in dealing with America's people. The world is watching, do not take this lightly or fail in your duty to seek justice for George Floyd and all those voices who have been silenced in the past.

TRAIN, TRAIN, TRAIN, POLICE, POLICE, POLICE

Police must be trained continuously and must remain disciplined at all times. The job of a police officer is without a doubt quite difficult and the amount of stress that one must endure is no doubt overwhelming. However, is it not your job to serve and protect? You set the standard of public interaction and what must be done.

I am not a police officer, so I do not have the authority, luxury, or experience to aid in the process of creating a better police force or what is required to accomplish such a difficult and complicated task. Nor would I be so arrogant to think the powers that be should listen to me, although, we can all agree on what should be appropriate and inappropriate to do as an officer who upholds the law.

The aggressiveness and the illusion of a police officer's authority being absolute is part of the symptoms fueling the anger and unrest among our citizens. Nothing will change until those in power recognize the issues and change it from within. Be the heroes and stand against corruption.

If you are a police officer, you should be appalled and disrespected that one of your own is abusing their authority. No one is above the law and even the perception of such a belief is enough to deteriorate the legitimacy of what the police force should stand for.

I do not want to criticize and attack the police as I respect them and the Rule of Law. Police officers are not all bad and those who are, are an exceedingly small minority who do not represent what the police force stands for. Stand up against police brutality, especially in your own ranks.

Those who are clamoring for the disbanding and defunding of police are mistaken. The country cannot count on people to police themselves. There is no way to protect what we all treasure so deeply without them. WE MUST SUPPORT THE POLICE and at the same time support all WHO HAVE THEIR RIGHTS VIOLATED BY AN INDIVIDUAL WHO DOES NOT RESPECT THE LAW.

Let us hold those accountable for their misdeeds and support the ones doing the right thing. Together we can create a better policing force for America. Do not wage war against the police. Imagine the chaos that would happen without them.

It brings my heavy heart great joy to see officers around the nation stand with protestors and stand up for what is right. You are the standard, the ones we look to when we are in need. You are the brave ones who stand firm when others stumble, and we need you now more than ever. Be that standard

## LEGISLATE

Create legislation punishing those who try to blur the line of what is right and wrong. Not everything is justified. Make a special governmental agency that investigates and determines exactly what actually happened. This agency should not be part of the police force and should not report to any other authority except their own.

However, we must keep in mind that the evidence they find must be weighed in a trial and the due process that protects every citizen should not be offended. We must not sidestep what is just for efficiency and convictions.

Create legislation that funds the training that police officers need to properly protect and serve the people and society who need them. Allow them to train as they fight so when they are put in a situation that is highly stressful, they are more likely to succeed and less likely to make a mistake.

For the love of everything stop militarizing the police force. No one should fear the police. Transforming the police force so they resemble the military with training and military grade equipment is not okay. How many departments really need an armored vehicle that is used for neutralizing a threat in a combat situation?

It is time to review, rebuild, and create a system that can serve competing interests but represent fairness, justice, and the Rule of Law.

## STANDARD OF RESPECT

Is too much to ask to treat each other with a standard of respect all are able to receive and enjoy? Have your parents failed to teach you basic principles and values. As I observe the continued failure of human interactions, I think to myself a few more ass beatings may have changed the way some people's children are acting.

Have we forgot that each of us have the duty to teach and prepare the next generation that is to inhabit the earth after us? Did we give up on the goal of raising our children to be better than us? Do we want to continue raising children who do not respect each other?

I was under the impression that all the adults had a mutual understanding to create a better generation than what they were in. It saddens me to think that a number of children are without a proper role model in their home. And when that is missing from the home, school is where it must be learned.

We removed the importance and value of what our education system had the ability to do. We stripped religion, we stripped patriotism, we stripped the ability for our teachers to create stand up Americans. We stripped anything valuable that would allow our teachers to create wonderful young men and women. Those who would later grow up to be community leaders, police officers, politicians, and basic tolerant human beings.

## TOLERANCE

In the event that a misunderstanding or false narrative exists, you do not have the right to tell someone their way of live is wrong and yours is somehow superior. In what version of the Constitution of the United States of America did you read, "I am guaranteed to have my way of life or beliefs respected above all others and if theirs offends me, I will cry and elect leaders who are willing to violate the basic freedoms of others."

Not one race, religion, gender, sexual orientation, ethnicity, or country is better than or above one another. The list provided are all equal and cannot claim superiority over the other. Unless the actions and character of one allow the others to hold them to a standard of which the world agrees is necessary to coexist.

I believe in life there exist all but one absolute, it is death. Other than that, everything else is simply word association and nothing more. However, because humankind has always created what was previously nothingness, for its creation to exist certain limited internal absolutes must be present If these were to fail their creation would cease to exist, collapsing on itself. Whether or not we agree, these variables must be constant for continued existence.

We are all blessed and present in this wonderful life and cohabitate the world together. We must create rules and beliefs that all must follow regardless of if you agree to them. This allows us to live a life free of persecution and the threat of harm. It also allows us to grow together and progress as a people, so we can accomplish greatness that was never thought possible. For when we are united, nothing is impossible.

## THE GOLDEN RULE

Live it, love it, teach it.

Please, do not give up on America, it is pure. America is an idea. It is not a place, it is not a government, it is not a people, and it is sure as hell not a race. It is greater than all that. It is vision that allows people to coexist and fight for what is just, what is right, and what is fair. People perverse things. America is not broken, the people who control it are.

What America represents, the ideas it expresses, the changes it has made across the world must endure and outlast any people or society. It is pure and we must continue to filter out the sediments that threaten to erode all we have achieved.

If you made it this far, that is a good is a start. Complaining, watching, doing nothing, offering no solutions is part of the problem. We are all in this together. Remember, we will need one another to get through this. We must work together to heal our fractures. We need each other.

Greatness and the unachievable has always needed the best of us and this is no different. It may seem difficult, and others may dismiss the belief that we can coexist or live peacefully in spite of our differences, please ignore the static.

Please remember; the pursuit of success, achieving a goal, and doing the impossible is not and has never been contingent on others believing in you. Neither is the difficulty of what lies ahead when deciding to pursue a vision or inspire change. Stay the course, believe in each other, and stand for what is right.

One last thing, yes BLACK lives do matter, POLICE lives matter, and ALL lives matter. How can you find that offensive? Let us stand by the two groups who are at odds, as we all are American. You need not kneel on you own any longer, take my hand and stand beside me as we fight these injustices together; once and for all.

I pledge allegiance to the Flag of the United States of America and to the Republic for which it stands, one Nation under God, indivisible, with liberty and justice for all.

I am not sure what I thought I could accomplish by writing those words. I am just tired of people intentionally forcing problems and not getting. Our people must work together. All people. We must come

211

together especially those who have the affluence to do so. Americans should better one another and offer tolerance to their people.

If people truly wanted equity, equality, and justice, they would create it because they have the power to do just that. The black communities who are well off and the religious leaders and entities who are equally wealthy could lift the world out of poverty by providing civil, constitutional, and economic justice for all. Listen to your own words, "no justice, no peace." Until that is "actually" understood and practiced, there will be no justice and no peace because people choose every determinative outcome consequences flow from.

And just like the Nile, you can damn it up, but it will always flow as that is the purpose of both water and consequences because if you can control it, it is yours to own. Controlling outcomes and water both serve as a means to represent a good end, but an illusion of harm is just that, a consequence of ignorance. People fail to understand because the truth is deeper than what ignorance allows

Justice starts with those who can give it, not those who can take it. Kneeling for God and kneeling for societal changes are identical but assumed to be an insult to people. Both represent justice and peace, but neither side really wants it. Kneeling is a symbol of something, it may insult some, but it also represents something different to the ones choosing to kneel. Maybe it's the necessary change the world needs. I am not sure though. My thoughts on kneeling, "you can find many people and things down there, but I will never be one of them."

The problem in this country is our whiteness and blackness, but they are both equally causing destruction in kind. As equals in America—equals in destroying—they must be recognized as equals in correcting these issues, becoming allies not foes. Because our ancestors are both oppressors and the oppressed, our job is to acknowledge neither of those people is present, not that it doesn't occur or that it doesn't happen. Still, our willingness to set aside to forgive and to accept will mend what those in the past caused. Stop creating a divided country based on skin color or a ruse that a political party has your best interests in mind. A very violent history shows what happens if people segregate by color and lead with powerful selfish desires.

The same thing can occur and will occur if people fail to heed the advice of the past. The need is here, so too must be the desire. People must choose. Does society want a hateful country *divided* or a peaceful country **United**? What makes people uncomfortable are the things society must address. We must discuss what we don't understand so we may address what others would like us to see.

We must speak about the rebel flag. The many different meanings of the rebel flag seem to be at odds with each other. Please consider the symbolism on both sides. The flag represents such a divisive time in our history and an incredibly divisive time presently. But it also means something more to others. Please be more considerate when having these conversations, as we are supposed to be mature adults representing what we would like our children to become. We should not allow the impressionable to regress and internally rot being left to decay. Ask the questions, seek the answers, nothing but the truth.

Was the flag a banner for treasonous people? Was it a movement that represented protection of the status quo with the intent to not conform to an accurate interpretation and understanding of a written document meant for progress through the growth of a race and evolution of a species? Does it represent failure—a privilege to not evolve with the changes in society because the minority felt a central federal government should not tell a free white man that they cannot own a human being?

What does the flag mean to you? Please explain exactly what it represents. If a person can justify it through logic, then do so. However, it does represent multiple things, and recognition or consideration of that should be given. It is not too far of a stretch to associate flying the confederate flag with using the "racial slur" or "owning slaves." Is this what it means? Is that hate? Is that what is represented by such a symbol? Or does it mean something else? Can there be two meanings, and should people consider such a position?

I guess if that is what you want to be associated with, then be associated with that ideology, but these ideas will most likely cause confrontation for all people as the symbolism is clearly a distraction to unity. Ask yourself these questions:

Am I a rebel for flying the confederate flag?

Am I a protector of culture?

Do I seek anything other than controversy?

Does the flag represent an expression of anything positive?

Does it also represent imbecilic beliefs and ignorance of the hateful kind?

Does this help, or does it push the divide deeper?

Do I want a united America?

Do I believe in, equality?

Or do I believe black Americans are less than white Americans?

These questions are essential because that is exactly what that flag means to some people. I am not saying you are wrong or represent those questions posed; I am merely trying to understand and clear the air because it is particularly polluted. However, only you can define who you are, and only you have the power to enlighten those who may misunderstand your position. However, southern heritage and the pride of this flag seem to be connected to racism and hate for many Americans. I am unsure of the truth because people will always believe in whatever they accept. So, I guess the answer is, whatever is in your heart, but consideration should be there as well. And the willingness to have conversations about what it means to others can bridge a gap between our people.

I will support your right to freedom of expression and die for it. But the celebration of what it represents may be misguided. The purpose, design, and symbolic representation are sad, negative, and reflective of a somber time in my people's history and my Nation's growth. What did its creator intend it to mean? What is the truth? The truth I guess, is whatever the user subjectively wants it to mean. Many intelligent people debate controversial topics such as this, but everyone ignores the intent. Understand what purpose it served and what purpose it still serves. It has evolved over time, but I fear the intent may have been to intimidate or represent a destructive meaning with purpose.

If what you want is a banner to wave and proclaim a rich southern heritage or being a rebel to express not conforming and the want to have unrestricted freedom to do so, design one that is not also tied to the rape, subjugation, and ownership of a human race because of a skin color. Apply logic, be honest, and ask yourself how do other flags make you feel? How does a flag you have disdain for make you feel? Not that they are equal or comparable, but it has an emotional response, just as it does to them. Pick a flag. Associate that with the attempt to overthrow the United States through death, murder, and division.

It may represent positive things to you, but it also represents a long history of negativity toward black Americans or other Americans whose families were forced to kill each other because of the policies of the rich. It is not considerate of what occurred, nor is it considerate to them. Imagine Americans owning your ancestors and seeing a reminder of it all the time. It is not very kind. We are better than this. America must represent something greater together. In addition, we already have a national flag. It was defended and must always be defended.

And, southern heritage, the pride it contains, how wonderfully rich it is, and the greatness of the people contained is worth celebrating, just not all of it or all of them. Let us practice a bit more consideration of each other. People may feel it is not necessary to do so, but it is necessary to save our Nation.

In addition, to all people, quit saying the N-word regardless of what flavor it is or what flavor of your skin is.

To black Americans and other black people, it is a word. It does not describe you or your people. It is reflective of hate and used indiscriminately out of anger because those who use it do not know any better or use it for selfish reasons. It is used to insult and achieves this purpose magnificently. It targets with specific intent, it will never leave, and is working as desired. The reaction is always what is sought, effectively drawing controversy and division just like calling people any other ignorant terms with a loaded meaning, especially one connected to a learned emotional response.

The word is a racial slur used to invoke a feeling of inferiority or to create an emotional response of fear. It is a trash word used to insult, usually spoken by intolerant, hateful people or based on an irrational emotional response used to insult and target a specific type of people. It is not necessary and is very divisive. It represents the division of this country and serves that exact purpose. The words have many negatives and must be properly understood to give the consideration necessary to solve what people cannot seem to recognize.

I imagine it says more about the people who say it than those it is directed at. This results from differences trying to coexist. It is no consolation, but I am equally disgusted and honestly surprised that it still can possess that much meaning. However, it cannot harm. It does nothing but creates a response that those who use the word seek. Being called a racial slur is a sign of disrespectful intent created for that purpose.

Those who use the word most likely do not deserve your respect anyway, and reacting in a way that is filled with unapologetic retributive anger is not okay. People will say ignorant and offensive things. The use of the word increases the division of our people, and so too is the way we act. One of my favorite sayings is, "When they go low, we go high." It is powerful; although it may not feel as good as the alternative, the effect is greater, and the change it can create—is much more meaningful.

The world recognizes just how offensive this word is. It is extremely offensive to the black community in America and others around the world, for that matter. It is also the only racial slur that enjoys the protection of not spelling it. It is more often than not commonly referenced as the N-word or N*****. Is that not represented by the high amount of respect and understanding society has for the black community?

A word, the only word in the world, which is given that type of consideration for feelings is for your people. That is a large amount of respect and a way to honor your feelings and recognize the atrocities of the past. Unfortunately, people are cruel, and no matter the amount of good a person represents, they will so often be treated with unkindness and described with words that are offensive. Remember Jesus Christ was executed as was Martin Luther King Jr.. Hate has no bounds, especially with words.

But a racial slur is a racial slur representing a racial slur. Being black does not entitle a person to more offense. It is the same disgusting behavior represented by intolerance and hate no matter the person or race being targeted. It may eventually lead to the belief that one type of racism is less offensive than the other or that it is not possible for others to be racist, and it may already be here. Stop targeting people because of the skin on their back or allowing others not like you to be targeted.

I've had friends and family who were M-worded and R-worded or M***** and R***. Logically speaking, does the writing of or saying the word represent or create more harm than being murdered or raped? Is slavery not worse than the racial slur or the many acts that occurred to a race? Or are we only trying to be considerate of emotions to satisfy a need to virtue stand? The word is simply that, a word. Ignore it as much as possible and prevent its power from growing or controlling. Recognize it as an identity; theirs, not yours, one that you do not want to be around. Now you know the bad guys—the ones who probably should not be granted your attention in the first place.

In addition, the word Nigger and Nigga are different terms used to express other things and applied in various ways. These words do not possess different meanings when the person who uses these has a different skin color. That is not how definitions work. This creates irreparable harm as people start offending without knowing because the language rules are different based on skin color. The meanings must be absolute all the time. It cannot be subjective or protected to mean other things when different races use it and promote it. This is another way to separate our people even more.

If you want to own a word, delete it from your vocabulary, that's power. If hate is taught and can be unlearned, the equal is true for offense. Offense is taught and can be unlearned. An example of things being taught to be offensive are her, him, she he, ma'am, and sir. The intent should be the only controlling device used to measure purpose. If the intent was not meant to be cruel, do not use subjective-triggeredy for selective creation to become a victim and punish people for talking. Your virtue standing only creates more people who are likely to want to avoid your existence altogether or not care because what you are becoming is toxic, even for the innocent.

Do not be that person. Do not be offended. Do not let that ignorance have power. Do not teach children to be offended; teach children to grow to ignore the ignorance of words. As the division grows, so too will the separation of language and meanings used to create more division. Find harm where it was intended and understanding where it was not. It is a huge ask and most likely will create hatred toward me, but the status quo is not working, and our people must figure out something before it is too late. I am not excusing behavior; I am trying to balance what will always occur to create a better outcome.

I don't know what the answer is but taking away its power may be a good start. Wear the rebel flag as a symbol of southern heritage and let cruel people use the words of ignorance until nauseum. Doing so will remove the harm associated by both. I do not support either because I believe the symbolism of each represents an extreme negative and is wrong. I only wish people would care more about one another. I promise I love without limits and support appropriateness over vulgarity.

I am angered and tired of the same unnecessary behavior. I am trying to figure it out, but offensiveness is applicable only to children who have not yet developed emotional and intellectual maturity because they were taught to have these limits by people who promote these limits. The answer is complicated but solvable. Addressing these concerns must occur, regardless of how uncomfortable it makes people. Freedom of expression is a very difficult concept for people to understand and many times it divides simply because expression does not care. The difficulties our races face are real, and no matter the aggression, the ignorance, or the anger, we must be able to speak to what divides us.

But are we capable? Are Americans able to stand up and fight for righteousness? What is the answer? I know what it is not, and allowing an emotional curriculum to spur a political crisis does nothing but alter elections. Be careful what is taught, as resorting to fallacies in the curriculum has unintended consequences. Especially pushing ignorance in the form of argumentum ad nauseam, ad numerum, ad populum, or ad verecundiam. Do not permit people to promote falsities. This is the sustenance of despicable leaders, and their words are used to ignite destruction—the weapon needed to control our species without remorse.

Our Nation is dying and decomposing from internal rot. It is because the history of the black and white community is based solely on lies motivated by hate or retribution both sides cannot seem to escape. We are countrymen, and we are a family, and we are equal. My experiences in America are as different as the differences in America. I am not an enemy to those who are different. But it seems like as time grows, so too does the division. I cannot speak on the topic of race because it offends, or I am too ignorant to do so. Even my patriotism for the country I love is now insulting because it is often recognized and taught to be white privilege representing a racist declaration of white supremacy.

The articles I read, and the words they speak, are extreme falsities used to promote negativity and intolerance towards white people, but because I am white, it matters not. Because they are black or support what is not white, it matters a lot. I must learn to deal with their hate for my country and my beliefs because my existence is offensive to them. Good white people exist just like good black people exist. I just wish we could identify who a bad black person is as easy as we can identify bad white people. But I guess the character our flesh covers is irrelevant when there is an election to win or money to raise.

As Terrell Jermaine Starr said, "Patriotism is for white people." When I read his article, a piece of my heart broke because people of all diversities can love their country. However, attacking a race usually is an indicator of racism, at the very least, hate. I wonder what he thinks about this statement? — "White people used their privilege and their patriotism to free black people from slavery." Although it is of no significance what he thinks, they are supposed to hate me and my kind no matter how much we share, no matter the commonality, no matter the care given. Unfortunately, we continue to target each other based on race because it is easy, especially for those who conflate issues, to gain influence. I think he is wrong and anyone who believes such a position has clouded bias. Also, by any definition of the word, as I understand it, it is simply racism.

I'm not sure where to begin with people who believe that. They do not want dialogue to discuss their points of view. They only wish for supremacy because their identity is somehow superior and others, or mine—inferior. They have excellent writing capabilities and substantive points but often, their logic is flawed, as it offers no alternative for the human condition, maturity through growth, and patriotism for a nation built to correct deficiencies. More importantly, it offers no respect for my people's many sacrifices. White people went to war with themselves because they believed in something worth fighting for.

Why give no alternative to being white and having a sense of patriotism or love for this country without being a racist? If you love this country, you are a racist. If you joined the military out of a sense of pride or duty, you are a racist. Can you be a patriot and love America without being a racist? According to some people's logic, no. In response to his article, I wrote the following after reading his words.

It read:

America is the greatest country in the world not because of our location, people, wealth, or power. It is and will continue to be the greatest because of an idea. This idea transcends race, religions, sexual orientation or any other difference between us. Freedom.

Our way of life is so unique and influential it has changed the world. Our freedoms have been integrated into societies across the world for the last 150 years and arguably longer. America and her freedoms are infectious, so much so, people still die trying to get here.

It is true that the United States of America has its issues, I will concede that. However, I take offense to your cheap insults and your blanket statement of word association between patriotism, white people, and racism.

We have ongoing problems, but we are working towards a greater tomorrow. I am a veteran, a patriot, and contrary to your belief, not a racist. Please stop spreading half-truths and fabricated lies that continue putting our future in jeopardy.

I am white and because of this I am not black and do not know, understand, or have any way to fully insert myself into your shoes. What I can do, is tell you I love you and I do respect the concerns of black Americans in this country. I recognize the atrocities against my fellow man. The reason I joined the military, the reason I am a patriot is because what my America represents. What it means to me and many others is standing when others kneel. Some people fail to protect those who are in need, I am not one and neither is my race.

I love you because you are black. I love you because you are an American. More importantly, I love you because you are human.

I do not support police shooting innocent people and agree when the individual police officer was in the wrong, they should be punished. I do not support racism, sexism, or any other ism that creates hate and continued divisiveness in this country. Because of this, I cannot support your foolish leaders as they use short-sighted campaigns that are also divisive.

I do get upset by when people kneel as the national anthem plays or when people are burning the American flag, but that is their right and we must protect that right. I will protect that right because I am a soldier. I believe in our way of life so much my disagreement is irrelevant to what is more important, freedom of expression.

I get angry but not because I'm white and a racist. I get angry because it hurts to think that you do not think highly of me because of my skin color or the flag and the country that bled for you. I get angry because the intolerance shown to the country and the Rule of Law that continues to bleed for you and will always bleed for you. You do not know me and certainly are without knowledge of the content of my character nor the character of many others like me.

What America is, represents a symbol of our freedoms and all those who sacrificed so we can be at this very point in history. This symbol, what it represents—is in our National Anthem and the blood-stained flag that you are so quick to disrespect, the many white people who died, not for white supremacy but to protect and represent a standard worth dying for, a country worth dying for, a people worth dying for, and the many differences represented in America. You do not owe anyone anything. Not a race, not a religion, and especially not a people. But you owe this nation everything especially the ones who are patriotic and willing to die for your freedom. Again, this is America and because we value our freedoms, I would die for you and that flag so you can call me a racist.

That is about as good as I can express what and how I feel. But my words and what I believe in are irrelevant because the racial problems we have in America are controlling. I know I am a good man and stand for good things. If it were not for black people, America would surely be a lesser place, and the same is true for white people if they were absent from society. Why am I made to be the enemy? Why are we made to be the enemy? Is my lack of comprehension an indicator of white privilege? My white brain cells cannot digest black feelings; therefore, I am unimportant and grossly outdated. Why is my opinion or inclusion in a conversation met with hatred and lack of respect? Even when attempting to stop misinformation by correcting a falsity that can be used to power the creation of more hate, my race is attacked.

I try to engage honestly and in earnest with everything I do, no matter the difficulty of discussions. However, sometimes I cannot see the point of view others are enforcing. Disparities in sentencing are real, but sometimes they are not. People frame ignorance to create and inflict an emotion. The influence and what is caused after consuming is exactly the intent, whether it is good or bad. The following is an attempt to clarify what I felt was an issue with a Facebook post of a meme depicting sentencing disparities benefiting a white person.

It read:

The issue isn't if its fair or not based on race, it's a difference of fairness of statutes by states and the type of law broken. Race has nothing to do with the sentencing when comparing these two specific cases. I concede and recognize the disparities of sentencing or incarceration between white people vs all others as numbers and statistics do not lie. When I was in graduate school for criminal justice, I was aware but utterly shocked and disappointed to know just how big of difference it was. I do not support any type of racism and it is more heinous when this is done by government actors. Also, mandatory minimums lead to a large amount of unjust sentencing causing the truth to be even more muddied.

First issue here is the difference of state laws. One occurred in Michigan, DUI death, the other occurred in Georgia, distracted driving. It is never easy to discuss or have open dialogue discussing what deaths are worse as all deaths are tragic. The latter case involved a teen, 17 at the time, hit three people crossing a road without a crosswalk and the state had the burden to prove without a reasonable doubt that she committed the alleged acts brought by the prosecutor. In this case they did not. It becomes a constitutional issue at this point. A person cannot be punished for a crime they are not convicted for in a court of law. Further, a judge cannot sentence more than the maximum allowed by the statute in question. He or she does not possess that authority and for good reason— separation of powers is important. Legislators write the laws, and the Judicial side interprets law and enforces sentencing.

The former case involved a woman who was drinking and driving while her son was in the vehicle. An accident occurred and unfortunately she lost her child. The court found that she was driving the wrong way, ran a red light hitting a vehicle head on, throwing her 3-year-old through the windshield and then she ran over his head with her car. She had two other children in the vehicle who were unhurt. She was sentenced to 3-15 years. It is very unlikely that she will serve more than the minimum and rightfully so as she will be tortured and in prison mentally for the rest of her life. I believe she is being punished enough by the thought of her actions killing her son. She had a lapse of judgment and it cost her everything, I feel this should have been a mitigating factor in sentencing.

It is short-sighted to compare items that are not related. Confusing motives based on race isn't accurate in this case. Again, I concede these exist however other information is definitely needed to fully understand this case and all cases for that matter.

His comment and the substantive value in his response were fantastic:

"Well, that's mighty white of you to explain jurisprudence to us"

It was not my intent to create a feeling of superiority toward him. To be honest, I am not sure what my race had to do with the explanation I offered, other than he wanted to make it an issue. What would have resulted if my response had been, "Well, that's mighty black of you to say." Same ignorant rhetoric, but one is perceived to be more offensive in the society we both belong to even though it is the same childlike response.

My skin is irrelevant and hardly an indicator of anything except the organ's flavor covering my innards. It does not make sense. Why? Why must we ignore a standard of decency? Creating problems is what people seem to enjoy. Continuously dividing because our skin hates each other, and we do not know another way because our fathers failed each other. Even children are attacked when a logical thought seems to escape the weak-minded.

My son was asked in his 5th-grade class to think about the level of diversity of his friends and use the provided scale to grade themselves on it. The purpose was used to grade the social skills of the youth in class and the diversity it represents. A decent exercise or performance task that I support and see benefits of. It ranked people from a 1- not diverse, to a 5- very diverse. My son's scale and his self-graded understanding were specifically brought to the attention of his class. The teacher asked why he graded himself a five, and my son, a ten-year-old, explained, "because I have friends who are girls, friends who are white, friends who are black, friends who are Hispanic, friends who are Asian. I have a lot of friends who are different." The teacher called my son a racist in class and belittled him in front of his peers, and then allowed other children to do the same. They called him a racist and not once allowed him to defend himself.

This world we are creating will not be kind to the innocent. It will not be kind to those who seek peace. And it will not be kind to factually accurate accounts, nor will it represent any type of logical application. If I had been in the room, I might have been escorted out by the police. What a shame tax dollars are spent on such a worthless human being who belittles children and influences them negatively. I think parents are better off teaching their children at home. What an embarrassment to the profession she represents. But what do you expect from our fathers who hated each other?

I do not blame black people for the way they feel or the reckoning that has finally reached our society. These are consequences of behavior that enslaved and murdered people because of apartheid tendencies. My reaction would be very similar, if not more aggressive. I imagine if a people of a different identity were treating me with hate, hostility, and intolerance, I most likely would have the name of Shawn Paul X. I would violently attack those who seek to make me an enemy. But, I would always stand for what is right and protect what represents decency. I will always defend myself and others when necessary because I fear nothing, especially ignorance.

I do, however, reject any premise that labels me the root cause of race issues or the inequality and racism that is represented in our modern world. It is extremely difficult for me to acknowledge that people can blame me for simply existing. If I attempt to defend myself or disagree in any way it is toxic white masculinity. My actions, what I believe, or my identity is not the enemy. Not only am I confused, but the creation of simpletons representing my likeness, the following created by ignorance, apologizing for atrocities not associated with actions, is not only embarrassing to the truth but short-sighted and will only further a divide between people, encouraging nothing but conflict.

If black Americans are in denial that they are not in possession of authority, power, or influence, they are ignoring the fact that the last 150 years have created a tremendous empathetic following that is finally encouraging to see in this country. All change has been for the better nothing in this society has gotten worse, nothing. Progress has been made for all people. In addition to this progress, the ability to have access to education, money, and representation in government also gives you access to corruption, selfishness, and ignorance in your leaders or lack of motivation in your people. They will do nothing but let you down and divide your likeness and Americans more. Welcome to the club. You are only united because now you share a common perceived enemy—poor blue-collar white people and America.

Your race is filled with toxic people, as is the white race. Do the bad actors speak for the entire race? If they do, what does that say about your race? Do the actions of a few notate a rule and not the exception? There exists a truth within every people, whether the people are of a race, religion, sex, sexual orientation, or nationality. The talented tenth will always be the ones who guide the many, creating a more equitable society. W.E.B Dubois and other people knew this. It is a pretty obvious assessment measuring who does what.

Believing this theory, does the premise allow a further inquiry into the ones who are not the talented tenth? Meaning, if they are not creating change, influencing progress, or changing lives for the better; what are they doing? Can we, as a group, decide what the other 90% are called. And please let us identify these people so they know just who they are. But is it an elitist thought? I do not believe so. All people can be the tenth; they choose not to be. So, the ones who choose, the ones who decide to become something, are extremely rare—most likely these people represent less than the tenth of the population regardless of the identity measured. I think it is more accurately measured by the people who not only recognize something must be done but stop at nothing to end what afflicts their people.

Many people complain, do nothing, consume distractions, and live a life of selfishness because they only ever care about themselves until election day. Their ignorance destroys any type of cohesiveness. People create hardships, and it is not exclusive to any one identity. Therefore, it is imperative to hold those accountable for the misdeeds of their actions and only them. However, our species attacks likeness as it is the root cause and it is not. Good people transcend identities to solve problems. Bad people scream, yell, and blame others for creating problems. This has been on display ad nauseum because technology is advancing too fast while incompetent, ignorant, and irresponsible imbeciles are wielding its power, yielding cataclysmic consequences.

Believing identities are the issue without generational context will remove any type of sustainable peace. What plagues our modern society is different than every decade before it. Substantial progress has occurred and is continuing to happen. Is it enough? Only future generations can tell us that. The standard for success lies in the future, ignoring the past and the present. Bad people will create hardships in every timeline of our species regardless of what race they are from.

They do not represent the identity in its entirety. At one time, white people murdered their own family, friends, and countrymen to benefit black people. They did this to right a wrong during a time that the atrocity was accepted, normalized, and protected. Moral outrage influenced moral growth altering the status quo forever. Sympathetic actualization created empathetic actualization which in turn, not only challenged the status quo, but altered it forever. There are no slaves in America. There are no a people focused solely on keeping an identity down. How many white people are you willing to defend in your war for justice without peace? How sympathetic are you to the consequences of your actions when they demonize the innocent? Remember, empathy creates the pathway to equality and equity.

The problem is we, all of us, are selfish and only ever think about how life affects our world. We never stop to think about how someone else will feel about what we say, what we do, and the selfishness reflective of those decisions. We are not kind to what is different because an idiotic symbol in our lives led us to believe we must have enemies, and they are them. As a result, people are unable to think about more than their life, their likeness, and their feelings.

Stop normalizing suffering. People need each other. Our issues are not what we think. We must focus on detrimental behavior and call it out in our group-identity when it occurs. Being white does not give you an excuse to ignore what we can change. And being black does not give you an excuse to ignore what you have the power to change. Yet we believe our power is either to ignore the sufferings of others or to create suffering for others. We drink the Kool-Aid because some big fat pompous gluttonous container filled with a blue or red flavor told us to, or that is the only flavor we serve around here.

Do you not see the corruption and foolishness of these endeavors? Self-segregation is occurring at an alarming rate. We must work together to destroy what is left of the past inequalities. Emboldening and empowering only selective identities in a generational period will have the opposite effect on those excluded in the name of racial justice. All people born are without sin associated with societies that have made many mistakes. Teach history, yes, but do not subjugate forced recognition of an advantage not applicable everywhere and attached to all simply for being born.

Whiteness should not be made to offend, dismissed because of animosity, or weaponized to create an enemy. For every action, there exists an opposite and equal reaction. A continued trajectory of this course will start, is starting, a race war. History seems to encourage pressing the repeat button. It divides the white race into extremes that may prove too difficult to reign in. Failure to see what is or could occur does not allow growth between people and empathy for differences. It instead invites chaos.

It is not wrong to want justice, equality, or equity. Nor should modern society or its inhabitants run from it. But actions dividing a free people will accomplish tribalistic behaviors pushing people into factions as the only way to defend themselves. Seeking likeness through grouping created kingdoms and encouraged wars against foes who looked, thought, or believed differently. The time to decide what Americans choose is slowly approaching.

We are not enemies. Our races or ideologies are not at war. But if you continue to see me as an enemy, eventually, I will become one, and our races and ideologies will be at war. Not because of a need but because of a want, a desire, or an ignorant belief that we are enemies. A cultural war is occurring because leaders encourage and reinforce division. The truth, what I know in my heart to be factually accurate, I hope I am aware when the need to remove respect is upon me. When those who see me as the enemy attempt to take my life, I hope to recognize peace's end. I wish for nothing but the chance to defend my life. I do not fear what is necessary, either by words or the sword but knowing when it is time is a challenging proposition to contemplate and even harder to recognize, especially if you are a victim.

America must heal the race issues in this country. We cannot continue down this path. America must have accountability. Death alone does not deter ideology, as is the case for the movement people are willing to kill for. Our system will only sustain peace if we choose to nurture it. A key to preventing the collapse is accurate, appropriate personal accountability concerning the critical perspective. No matter how difficult it becomes to understand or apply, if we decide to move away from all applicable information needed for the truth, we destroy ourselves and create the opposite of personal accountability.

Through accountability, people can share in the progress society will create, and we can change perceptions through the leaders who demand accountability. People must be willing to engage with each other, even if it seems futile.

However, engaging is only part of the equation to solving the detrimental distance from one another. People must be willing to create a place where all people feel accepted, or all people will be divided. How easy would it be to include some of the most outstanding black leaders in America's structures? There are plenty of black people who deserve to be immortalized with their white counterparts, or other races for that matter. It is evident that a reason why the black and white communities are so distant is the intent to keep that distance.

Put Martin Luther King Jr. on the twenty-dollar bill. Commit to whatever century we are headed into for the allowance of the leaders from prior generations to have more than a street, road, or boulevard named after them. Do not let those less than deserving become martyrs nor allow people to worship the worst of their people. Lift decency up within each community and celebrate this decency together as this is our identity. Share in the greatness of such beautiful achievements and their devotion to what is just, equitable, and worth fighting for.

It is time to change a few things, and if this change can bring us closer, what are we waiting on? But if you don't respect America or what she stands for, I will not support you, let alone respect you. I understand the issues, but they are to be blamed not her. We need to start building trust in one another, and patriotism for our Nation. We can do this by selecting the correct role models. The ones we shouldn't follow, these people create a void in our hearts and an abscess in our character. Only follow and promote those who are worthy or those we wish our children to be like when they are adults.

There is a man who I see myself being. A man I see myself mimicking if I were in his shoes. A man that I would die for and die with. A man I wish my children to grow to be. This man deserves to be a part of America's structure. There is a scene in one of my favorite movies, The Patriot, where Mel Gibson's character sees the line failing and rushes to save it by grabbing the American Flag and pushing forward through harm, inspiring those who need to be reminded. There is a feeling that scene evokes, a fire that burns deep in my being. Something makes me wish I could be a man like that, a leader like that, a Patriot like that.

Although people believe that type of behavior is a made-up Hollywood script, I assure you it is not. There are people in the United States and the world who represent all that is good in us, virtuous in us, and brave in us. Those people inspire others to go on, even when it seems hopeless. Even if many of us fail to be those shining examples of exemplary courage, they do exist. Not Benjamin Martin. Of course, all legends require a name but let us all recognize the actual name, the true hero, and the true identity.

The man I refer to is Sgt. William Carney—the first black American to win the Medal of Honor. He is my hero; he is a man I can see myself being. A man I see myself mimicking if I were in his shoes. A man that I would die for and die with. This man deserves to be a part of America's structure. Rename Ft. Jackson after this man.

Of course, this is my opinion but if I had the power, I would make such a change. Although, I believe any renaming of Forts should be done by the soldiers past or present who are alive. Allow these brave men and women to choose who they would go into battle with by honoring a past soldier with immortality and the recognition they deserve.

It should be hands off to a bunch of congressional weaknesses and politicians who send others to die in their steed. The decision and honor to rename military property should be given to those willing to die to defend those who are not willing to. It seems odd to allow a group of people this privilege when they know naught of personal courage or selfless service. It should never be reserved for a type of people who neither represent what is required nor understand what is required.

Is it logical to allow politicians to decide whose namesake is worthy? Only soldiers, sailors, airmen, and marines, are aware of what is worthy. And it is time for worthiness to have a very different skin tone. This change must occur. Allow his legacy to inspire millions as his actions inspired thousands. I have a few more choices I think our collective sacrifice would appreciate as well. Let us not miss an opportunity to create a better tomorrow. A tomorrow that includes all of us.

Can we succeed where others failed? It depends; what are people motivated and willing to do? Like anything in life with an understanding of human capabilities, skills and knowledge are utterly worthless unless combined with motivation. What is to become of society when people lose the motivation to solve our issues? People will most likely reject the critical perspective.

They will also dismiss alternative points of view and counter-arguments that were once used to find, strengthen, and promote progressive understanding; or, in other words, truth. When did offering these become insulting or counterproductive to a free society, especially one that not only encourages discourse but has this form of expression protected in the Constitution?

I find flaws in many people's lifestyle selections, although that does not make me evil or hateful. It simply allows me to make my own decisions and my own selection that is appropriate in my life, for my life, represented by freedom, not permission. I do not pursue a campaign to irradicate or silence those who are different, nor do I wish to. I do not seek to create enemies, yet it seems one day I may be forced to.

What I see is a runaway train headed for a bridge that has yet to be completed because society is not working together to finish this project. My opinion, lifestyle, and likeness are being taught to be the root cause of all the world's problems, even though I was born without a connection to or responsibility. I was born innocent without sin as many before me, those who came after, and those yet to come.

The question I ask myself constantly is my identity, what I believe to be both true and accurate, everything that makes me who I am as a man—my convictions, principles, and spirit. Are these—a representation of bigotry? Have I betrayed myself and what I believe in because the critical thought necessary to see my faults cannot pierce my bias, bigotry, or racism? To be honest, I doubt that I am any of those things, but am I the one who decides whether the inclusion of my identity for those descriptors is warranted?

Meaning, in my writings past and present, I am sympathetic, empathetic, and supportive of all movements encouraging people to stand for what they believe in protecting their likeness, and I stand with them. But at times, I feel like, "whoa!!", that is too much protesting, and it is becoming counterproductive to society in general, detrimental even. When does it turn into complaining and unnecessary soapbox standing used simply for attention-seeking?

Again, am I wrong for wanting to limit how much, for the lack of a better term, "complaining" society tolerates from social justice campaigns or the lies being promoted that are destroying peace between our people? Not the legitimate concerns and protesting to achieve the desired much-needed change, but sometimes I know it goes too far. Is the allowance for personal grievances defined as what I subjectively think is proper? What is the right way to address concerns of a people associated with identity, and should I, or anyone else for that matter, be the arbitrator when the limit of productive protesting ends?

I seek answers that I am unable to find. Are people stuck in the fringe zone concerning discourse, never being able to create a shared understanding of what is? The new reality represents the extreme of one side or the other, which is final. It is also acceptable to many people, but I disagree with them vehemently, in the strongest way possible. I do not see that as a progression towards existing with diversity, and it surely does not help the situation in the least bit. It is irrefutable that people do not like each other anymore. However, I doubt that generally, they ever did. The difference now, people do not even go to the lengths of hiding intolerance, bigotry, or hate anymore.

Does it have an end game? Not in the pursuit of all things being fair but in the demonization of people who have no responsibility for what is occurring and the continuation of demoting or promoting as the privileged see fit. If I disagree, I am wrong! If I do not support it, I am wrong! If I do not concede, I am wrong! Is that fair? If I showed up from a different planet and looked the same way I do now, should I be granted clemency and leniency from anger, resentment, and the pursuit to silence dissent? Or would they round me up too?

Does that matter? Should I be forced to believe what I have not been convinced of? Can people not have a proper discussion of what is controversial? If what is being promoted is not widely accepted, is that an indicator of racism or a half-truth. Is it possible it is a bit both or just wrong altogether? Is it an argument built on too much emotion on both sides? Are we to believe a people must go on in a perpetual state of submissive posture for behaviors disconnected from a single shred of responsibility or actual harm?

Society must end the self-righteous campaigns of being unapologetically correct because of past grievances while degrading a race, religion, gender, or sexual orientation for the furtherance of a personal agenda. Do not teach children to hate themselves. They are not them, and them are not they. Encourage accurate historical accounts but discourage inaccurate accusations with intent to assign dishonest fault by promoting absolutism.

There are many arguments that are logical and should be given the respect and weight carried accordingly but an absolute belief that a people are guilty and encouraging a "great white reckoning" to combat the "great white rage" only strengthens my position against a one-America. It also highlights the absurdity by recognizing intolerant behavior from all sides of a competing viewpoint is the cause of America's divisiveness.

People are participating in truth assassination and destroying what is known to better suit what they believe in by ignoring the consequences of which ignorance flows. Motivation to participate in such a destructive act is the opportunity to change reality or the controlling arms of society. This increases detrimental unity by recruiting followers to an end of intent. It is strictly emotional and agreed to because of selfishness.

It is created to grow grouped isolationism, spread disinformation, or used to increase reciprocal diversity application. It is altered to represent a modern subjective understanding unrelated to the original word by ignoring the application of a more appropriate word. This creates new false knowledge to encompass what is attempting to be described or an inaccurate account of history by controlling the narrative in a society where detrimental unity is rampant. Definitions, language, or historically accurate accounts in society do not change meaning over time because of an arbitrary decision or a false subjective belief.

It is often done without consideration of others present in society. It occurs without first creating dialogue to discuss what is appropriate or what is consumed without separating truth from their subjective bias. The attempt to assassinate meanings and alter history occurs because of groupthink when society lacks the cohesive structure necessary to defeat detrimental unity. It flourishes when society allows feelings to determine knowledge, later controlling what is true based on selective creation disconnected from reality.

Acceptable knowledge cannot be subjective; nothing can be true if everything is true. Logic and an agreed-upon rationale must dictate what is true and acceptable. Truth must never encompass likeness or diversity. Because whatever we teach children, they always believe. They will become the creators or destroyers in the future, carrying the banner of whatever leadership they choose to follow. Societies must maintain at least a resemblance of agreement between competing groups unless it is nearing the final step in the cycle of destruction.

The same is true when altering historical events on the basis of inaccurate accounts. If successful, it gives people justification to change how the controlling arms of society function or alter what they desire by destroying what the entities stand for. America is pure and can grow to be whatever good or bad people decide to make it by believing what is easiest to digest. But lying about America being racist, republicans being racists, or an election being stolen will create the necessary fractures to end peace.

Destroying meaning and truth destroys peace and understanding. Accomplishing this over multiple generations or election cycles removes truth and creates existential consequences. This new false truth is consumed, repeated, and believed. It is extremely cataclysmic when it is used to target a competing group in a divided nation of excessive diversity experiencing the societal consequences of diversity. Not specific or reserved for any people but at a point in time it can and has been used to alter the world. What people believe or are willing to believe is what controls behaviors allowing a distorted reality to become true.

As I live my truth, I encourage you to do the same, but my truth will never destroy peace. Never expect me to cower to a dictation of truth authored by intolerant ignorance disguised as moral superiority. In reality, it is nothing more than selfishness used to create validation and legitimacy. Do not make me an enemy nor the target of angst; I should be neither. It is highly unnecessary, and I advise against it. I would much rather live in peace rather than in a constant cycle of conflict.

If we are to develop a more inclusive society where all beliefs and people are welcome, then all people and beliefs must be welcome. Not just the ones you feel are important, see a likeness in, or assign appropriateness to. People must quit making their way of life, whatever group they belong to, or their beliefs an absolute. Especially one that is above reproach from appropriate, much needed, and fair criticism allowing the proper discourse to begin and growth to occur.

History has gifted human civilizations advancements through thought, understanding, and equitable social growth by the sacrifices of people who did not have an issue offending, insulting, or destroying what was in the way of progress.

These progressive movements are easily measured through time. They are represented by equal protection under the law, legislation consideration, and most importantly, the cohesive structure of a population contained within a society. Whatever America chooses, the result will be directly tied to personal accountability. It will either be strengthened or weakened, creating a result selected by selfishness or selflessness. Creation and destruction are always controlled by personal accountability.

## Personal Accountability

Personal accountability is essential, especially when government actors are involved, and abuse of authority is the accusation. However, all people are under the necessity to be held accountable. If these people are not being held to the standard required, it is detrimental to the peace and sustainability of society. The example below only speaks to a particular point. Accountability at every level is needed; however, this problem is in dire need of a solution. Consequences exist when accountability is not present. I do not support unlawful behavior, but it is evident to me that its root causes are related to and arise from the lack of accountability. Defend a standard. Not a people, not a profession, and not a movement.

What is Justice? For many, it is merely a hope that a wrong done to them will be adjudicated fairly and the wrong committed recognized. In our civil society, it is a necessity that allows the majority to live in peace with one another. We understand what is right because we understand what is wrong. Without identifying these wrongs collectively, we are left without recourse for our moral outrage. Our power to change, the power to uphold the Rule of Law and seek justice for our fellow man, is predicated on our awareness of such atrocities. If not for moral outrage and the ability to institute justice, many people would be nothing more than conscienceless psychopaths.

What happens if justice is never found? What happens if your daughter leaves your house one night, kisses you goodbye, and unbeknownst to you, she and all she is or ever will be is taken. What happens if your son is murdered? What happens if a thief takes the most important possession in your life? What happens if justice is denied?

You awake to a phone call, and the person on the other end of the phone says, "they're dead!" Half-asleep and confused, you inquire and ask for clarification. And, as your brain digests the reality of what the words mean, your stomach turns as the most important part of your life has been taken from you. Imagine the one thing in the world that gives this chaotic, messy life purpose is gone, forever. What happens if justice is denied?

I have family members and friends who experience this reality every morning, as do many others. There are people all over the world who are left with no answers. It starts when their brain recognizes their consciousness allowing their nightmare once again to arrive front and center. Most cannot imagine losing their child. Some will try to put themselves in their shoes, but the truth is, that horrific event and that emptiness they and other parents have felt can only exist if it has happened to you.

The only way I have been able to get relatively close in an attempt to understand this emptiness and heartache is by closing my eyes and imagining I am holding out my hand. In the palm of my hand is the most wonderful, cherished item that makes me a complete and happy person. Out of nowhere, a person walks up and snatches it out of my hand. At that moment, I lose my happiness forever. What is worse, I am left with no answers, no reasons why, and an emptiness that eats at my soul every day until I am no longer able to hold on to the emptiness.

Searching for answers from the ones who swore to serve and protect is the right thing to do. But it seems they have turned their back on you. Some treat you as a nuisance, dismissing your attempt to make sense of this unspeakable pain. How can they do this? How can incompetency infiltrate the very place where reliance and hope must rest? We live in such a divisive time. People are often offended by questions as the direction of inquiry is the very problem we seek answers to.

Police officers and other professionals will immediately get defensive when they become the focus of questions involving a negligent act. This is fine. Everyone deserves the chance to defend themselves and must have the opportunity to do so. I think it is very unfair and irresponsible to assign blame and a verdict of guilty before the truth is available or force punishment in the direction where the anger should not be directed. This creates a defensive posture and an unnecessary burden on a system and those representing what is important.

The problem occurs when, instead of seeking the truth, they immediately put up a barrier and assume it is an attack on their entire profession or identity as an accusation of guilt and the association of blame. It is a reactive posture promoted and encouraged by an opposite reactive posture that is also promoted and encouraged in kind. Some will insulate the individuals and become their protector, allowing for an "us versus them" mentality to distract from the truth. While others will make enemies out of the entire police force, the Rule of Law, and the United States as a Nation. Neither is correct nor do they represent the truth.

Truth is a very difficult word to understand. Are the ones who serve protected and considered to be far above reproach? Do people suffer needlessly while bad actors infiltrate our system of fail-safes? The police; the voice of the minority, the politicians; the voice of the majority, and the journalist—not all but some—who serve seem to lack the integrity required to hold such a position. Are we even allowed to be upset and seek the answers to our questions? Are everyday Americans entitled to the truth? The more important question is, what do we do when the answers point toward something as serious as corruption? Is it possible accountability could solve everything?

Let's not be naïve and assume that all people in positions of power or influence are good. Anything that has the possibility of a human touch always has the possibility of corruption through the selfishness of perversion. A greater concern would be an attempt to cover up a mistake to protect someone who; we were told was an otherwise good person. We teach our children from a young age to be accountable for their actions. Admit when they are wrong and accept the punishment. But does the need for cohesiveness remove that accountability?

A profession is not inherently bad. The truth is not intentionally offensive. People are creatures of necessity designed to defend, lie, abuse power, or conflate issues for the sake of self-preservation. This is why accountability cannot be fictitious, as it must be applied on-demand where and when appropriate. Human beings are irrational; therefore, accountability must not be. I have witnessed corruption in policing that is not connected to race. I have experienced corruption in the court system that was wrong because it was simply wrong. Not all people are victims, and not all authority exercised is justified.

Contrary to the loud, unruly demonstrations against our brave men and women who serve to protect America's Rule of Law, our society does not have a police problem; it has an individual accountability problem. The police force in its entirety is not putting on the uniform simply to trample on the rights of people. A specific type of people is not the only ones who suffer at the hands of corruption through abuse of power or an egregious error that caused harm.

However, that is what those with the largest and most influential platforms expect our society to believe. This is the reason why public opinion is influenced by those who control the narrative. The reason why athletes kneel in solidarity while a rendition of freedom through music is played represented by our Nation's National Anthem. The reason why businesses jump on the bandwagon of woke advertising and sympathetic marketing. It is to generate income and maintain influence.

And this is the same reason why our entertainment viewing experience is riddled with the unfair depiction of the justice system and with narratives aimed at creating the perception of the exclusivity of injustice. It is never wrong to stand up for what is just, but conflating issues to increase legitimacy and promote self-importance is uncalled for. It also thwarts the discovery of a solution as the many incorrect assumptions destroy any attempt to properly identify the problem.

It is an attempt to produce a narrative reflecting virtue-signaling used to raise money, generate votes, influence public opinion, and maintain or obtain power. These behaviors are not new nor unique to the current state of affairs in society. This is how the power structure is created—applying the correct facts to strengthen a position and minimize the effects of hurtful facts weakening a position. Attorneys make an extremely large profit practicing such an art form, and piss poor leaders resort to this when the solution is complicated, but the blame is easy.

It is nothing more than selective creation. An unnecessary divisive act used to control the narrative. A simple application of all data will suffice to discredit an absolute thought if it is, in fact, the case that the premise is false. For an absolute to be false, only one contradictory piece of evidence must be present when applying the premise.

The entire world, the population base, is operating under a controlled narrative and a campaign of detrimental logic and dangerous precedent. When breaking news occurs of a police officer-involved shooting, in some sort of fashion designed in an attempt to keep the peace, the world hopes the victim is not black, and heaven forbid the police officer is white. Wishful thinking or a prayer in hopes of preventing further unrest or the violence that follows. As if the death of a person not representing the minority's likeness is less horrific, and the death of the white persuasion is more acceptable than the alternative. The loss of life is equally tragic regardless of the identity of the victims.

Is it a fair assumption that policing in America is inherently racist and used only for the purpose of holding the black community hostage while promoting a white power agenda? Is America racist? Is this the narrative and premise that those with influence want Americans to believe? Consuming all the information available at my disposal, to me, it is. That is exactly what both sides want—controlling the narrative, so they are free to defend or accuse, always maintaining power by creating the numbers needed to do so.

People like numbers unless those numbers destroy a perception of being correct. Numbers do not lie and are free from emotional manipulation. Unless, of course, those with influence omit certain truths to sway public opinion unto their liking. They are bending the free will, the free thought, of a free people.

Do all police officers conduct themselves in the same way? Do police officers look the same, act the same, and believe the same? Are police officers a single unit, with a single thought, controlled by a single action?

And if so, does this single unit, a single thought, and single action call for the disproportionate adversarial treatment of blacks in America by police officers?

Are black people the only race who are subjected to police officers' brutality, police officer corruption, and possible loss of life at the hands of a police officer? Is the police force, as a rule, not the exception, abusing their authority, training corruption, and unapologetic for such tyrannical reign? The answer to these questions is no. But has the police force ever committed such atrocities? Do power and authority corrupt?

Sometimes a simple wordplay can change perception and perspective and present other probable conclusions. Removing the word police officers and replacing it with individuals wearing a badge. It quickly changes the understanding that a person is behind the badge, not a profession acting in unison but an individual acting alone, correctly applying fault and responsibility to and for such behavior to the individual.

Let us now figure in and consider other facts. Police officers who, in a professional capacity, interact with civilians kill roughly 1000 people a year. Civilians with exposure to police officers are killed at a percentage of .00030303 a year. Although it is still difficult to cope with and an emotional tragedy to experience, the adverse consequences are not lost on our society. But a person, regardless of skin color, is 50 times more likely to kill themselves than be killed by a police officer in America. In fact, police officers, in contrast to those in other professions, are disproportionally targeted and killed simply because they wear a uniform at a higher rate than their counterparts.

However, if people listen to the news, every time a black American steps out of his house or interacts with a police officer, they will be murdered. Is this true? Is it because the laws in America and its policing force are racist? Is this true? The police force not only represents but supports white supremacy and is characterized by aggressive, toxic male masculinity. Is this true? What is the truth, and why is it this hard to find?

I am unsure, but I would like to see the actual numbers. Not ones manipulated to represent a tragedy or a defense against the tragedy. I want to see real numbers representing the truth instead of a biased interpretation of research reflecting what the researcher wants to find and exactly what the researcher wants to share. What is the truth without race being a factor, and is that possible in a country that is not supposed to see race but offers it as a measurable metric necessary to all arguments? Can society move past race, or must it remain about group suffering or a group being blamed? It should only include the individual who suffered the injustice and the individual who created the injustice.

There must be a way to fix this and submit an understanding or formula that can be used to create a way to make a structured argument, not a position related to an opinion, political party, race, or profession. Applying all facets allows the most accurate conclusion to be drawn. This would give a more accurate understanding to help aid in the prevention of death by police officer, regardless of the emotion, opinion, or motivation of those involved.

My hypothesis is—the greater number of exposures to police officers with consideration to assigned value of listed factors is reflective and relative to the number of deaths by police officers in any area regardless of race. In short, the more significant number of exposures to police officers will equal a higher death of the civilian population per exposure based on a formula used to calculate all accurate and probative evidence. Concluding, race cannot be the only factor when viewing police officer conduct of the abusive kind.

The only way to determine the causal factor of death by a police officer in every occurrence is to apply a quantitative formula. This would create an avenue to help prevent police officer misconduct and properly address its occurrence, allowing for accountability and altering the perception that policing is somehow represented by a negative connotation.

I'm not offering evidence to counter that an issue is not present; I am simply offering formula in hopes of finding the correct issue so that society may solve what has been so costly over the years. Addressing factors applicable to incidents. Solving the problem, not making it worse.

For the sake of accuracy, in the process of seeking an answer and a solution to the problem, the understanding of all factors and the values assigned to these factors must reflect all the relevant considerations. The incident worksheet would have to include a value for each factor weighed against a consideration of how concerning each factor was with respect to the specific incident under review.

Examples are but are not limited to:

Violent crime level in an area, the number of people killed in the area, the local opinion of policing in an area, accountability of past police conduct in an area or likelihood of, types of businesses by value to society in an area, the population of civilians relative to police officers of an area, unemployment of an area, education level of an area, influence of false information consumed, level of diversity of an area, availability of community policing for the area, local gun laws in the area, the militarizing level of the police force in the area, age of the victim, age of police officer, the experience of the police officer, influencers inside the police force, what was the victim doing, was a weapon present, did escalation or de-escalation occur, which actor did what, and time of the incident, day or night, including the proximity of the incident under review in relation to the calendar date of other events around the country.

In addition, to complete the formula correctly, an estimated number of exposures per day, per year, per person, separated by race in respect to the exposure of police officers to civilians must be calculated as well.

If people wanted to create the appropriate dialogue and solve the accountability issue, they could. Society would be able to destroy such a negative premise connected to the police force and greatly reduce the number of these tragic events. Society could also gain legitimacy in arguments by using the critical perspective allowing multiple factors to be considered and proper blame assigned. But they choose not to.

It is not the group's fault being blamed (police officers), and it is not the only group being targeted (black people). It is simply diffused responsibility, lack of correctly applied accountability, and the misguided application of facts to benefit the perception of whatever narrative a person decides to believe. The truth must not be weaponized and used to insult. When it is, it is highly effective but also highly destructive. There are so many issues not discussed connected to controversies because what causes these are difficult to understand. The easiest concept to recognize for the masses is used to create the narrative of choice influencing all who accept such a poison.

Police officers are necessary, and individuals will cause harm. Because of this, accountability must be present. It must represent the truth regardless of the benefit/detriment of the victim or identity of the victim but reflective and solely based on the probative value of evidence offered in defense of or prosecution of the individual accused. Nothing more, Nothing less. Accountability by and through justice to maintain the legitimacy of the Rule of Law.

I hope America isn't as divided as the powers that be want us to believe. We may be different, but our similarities are what matter the most. Having a differing opinion does not mean a person hates you or dislikes you; they just choose a different way to live. I think a question should be asked, specifically if it's possible for people of other religions, races, sexual orientations, and lifestyles to create cohesion instead of tension. We are Americans, and America is a synonym for different.

Do not get caught up in the political mess America has become. Do not let those who want to be famous by grandstanding influence your understanding of what is true. Ignore the sleaze who wants face time on all the social media platforms. Instead, go outside, hug your neighbor and smile at a stranger. Teach your kids tolerance and love. Please instill a sense of understanding that all things are not offensive. Quit looking for something to fight about and hold people accountable. I imagine all an influential leader must do to change the future for the better is create an economic model to change the future for the better.

## Economic Models

Economics is interestingly simple and yet complicated to understand. Further, it is impossible to make fair based on the varying definitions and interpretations or wants held by those informing us what is correct, including the superior model of subjective confirmation bias used to select a preference. Speculating on which system is the best only serves to push for a specific outcome wanted by the person advocating for their preference.

Intelligent people, who are experts on these subjects, cannot agree on what is superior. I am in no way an expert in any sense of the word in dealing with this topic, but I am going to attempt a quick run-through of what would solve the issues I see destroying our Nation. To be clear, I know enough to remain ignorant, well below the ones who are experts, but my thoughts are observations of the limits and benefits of what we know and what people are. And I very well may be incorrect; however, if we had to look to ourselves, I imagine a better system could be built from scratch because we have a history of what is unfair, and we are aware of the many consequences of the present system.

I know that fair represents ownership of what is earned, not what is given. What does that do for the rest of us? The models are based on goals and envy. People belong to two groups, the ones who are happy pursuing success or the ones who are angry at those who are. The people have the power to understand and choose what system we wish to participate in, yet the haves determine the design for us simply because they are in the best position, not because they know what is best. I guess they earned it, but I would argue, people choose something solely on the premise of what benefits them the most. What system or what changes in the current system would help the most people?—This is the question I would ask.

I am most certainly for helping people, but should not the people be worthy of help first? Do they owe charity a character test first? Should they show themselves to be worthy of such kindness? I am not sure what the answer is, but I know these questions cause issues. I imagine if the people who believe helping others is essential would first focus on the collaborative effort locally instead of relying on others externally, a shift of personal accountability would occur. But what standard are we willing to hold people to?

How can we force people to give away 40% of what they earn, but somehow convince ourselves we cannot make people give 100% of their effort to help themselves? They should at least be able to give 60% of what they are capable of if we only allow those who work to keep 60% of what they earn. Is it because good people will always follow the rules, and the bad ones will exploit the good ones to gain power? We are only limited by our choices and growing up disadvantaged does not mean we have to stay there.

America is not a caste system in the sense that where you are born is where you must stay. Unless, of course, you believe the many inequalities and inequities are greater than the opportunities to succeed in America. But it is arguably easier to succeed in this modern America than at any other time in the history of our species. Yet, people are being taught this is not the case, and the system is designed to fail those who try to succeed.

However, this seems to be true sometimes because of the visible generational poverty and the measurable suffering all around.

However, our actions lead to a determinative outcome, and this cannot be denied. Delaying growth or preventing it all together leaves people behind, but that is a choice that is all their own. But that does not mean America is perfect and without flaws. Our Nation can do many more things so others may accomplish what they attempt. But we must respect each other and expect a standard of personal accountability as well.

When does someone's welfare become the responsibility of others? Locally, people must encourage and promote their own people, those in the community, before they ask other people, those outside the community, for help. The problem stems from respect. People will not help or care for others if they do not respect them. Why should they? Society can agree certain people are not worthy of respect. People do this every day in the political realm. Why not reserve this lack of care for individual character flaws preventing growth and the level of accountability a person is willing to attach themselves to?

Americans no longer respect each other because the economic model exploits, rewards, and operates as intended but so do the people contained within. If people stop exploiting the successful to reward the unwilling, then maybe things would operate better. But is that harsh?

I imagine if the system, and those seeking the truth, would look at the schedule of what encompasses a person's day, it would not only shed light on what limits the individual but also highlight the self-inflicted limits that have become part of their routine. However, detrimental behavior is hard for people to recognize, especially when it is of their own volition. Is it ever insulting to people when you blame them for their success?

I did not author this book waiting on someone to do it for me, and the times I decided not to work on it, something unique happened, the book did not finish itself. Am I entitled to have a book complete itself or have someone do it for me and later reap the benefits of what I did not earn? The book may be criticized as horrible, but it is mine, and I worked hard to create this horrible masterpiece.

Working is important as it produces passion and allows people to find what they are good at or what they enjoy. This is important allowing people to pursue what they want to do for a living. Of course, honesty will keep people from certain professions due to limitations, but people possess capabilities and skills that are all their own. Many things can be learned, fined tuned, or discovered by attempting. Only the person attempting can disqualify themselves. They either find a way to succeed or a way to fail based on hard work or the discovery of their limitations. Some limitations can be overcome individually, and others must be met with a group effort. But the desire to succeed and the willingness to work are necessary.

Many jobs in the modern world allow people to exercise and monetize what they are good at with their skills. And that is a pretty good system to be a part of. It creates many avenues to success; however, it does not change how hard you have to work. But sometimes, people want what they cannot have and own what they should not possess. This creates a system riddled with inequalities because people are becoming conditioned to believe all people are deserving of the same equity simply for existing, and that is not true. Everything has a cost, including success. If people are uninterested in paying it, they must never possess the fruits of no labor.

The opportunity to succeed must be protected, encouraged, and given to all people no matter the diversity of those pursuing it. Still, success must remain contingent on how hard a person is willing to work and how long they are willing to work. Failing does not end the attempt; it allows an understanding that the attempt may have been lacking something. Convincing people they deserve what they are not worthy of possessing is a highly irresponsible thing to do. Especially when the government is promoting such a disastrous policy.

This breeds animosity between citizens and will likely alter the population, the nation containing the population, and the peace that is keeping the population from killing each other. I am not sure people actually want peace. People can create equity to solve the animosity between classes, but when convincing others to believe this premise fails, each non-believer becomes the enemy, and we never collaborate. Part of me thinks America will likely remain in a system destined to fight each other until one of our children fight to unite what selfishness destroyed.

But freedom creates selfishness. Freedom allows people to be nothing, do nothing, and become nothing. It also allows those who can change things for the better to do nothing because choosing is the most selfish thing we can do, and these choices separate people by their value. What would people prefer, freedom with pockets of inequities, or equity with zero pockets of freedom? Lack of freedom means no preference, no choice, no variations. Doing, becoming, and owning only what is permitted. That is not freedom and does not belong in America.

A free market backed by capitalism is the only way to complement the amount of freedom associated with America's Constitution and what it represents, including the reason it was created. Suppose a citizen has the freedom to think, create, and live the way they see fit without the interference and control of the government or others. In that case, they also possess the ability to be as successful or as unsuccessful as they choose. This allows people to earn what that choice represents and precisely what they deserve.

However, it is without question that the consequences of America's form of control have started to erode the quality of life for many in a nation that was built to protect them. It is time to adopt changes to adequately reflect what is necessary to sustain peace and prosperity in America for all people.

A system of economics that is top-heavy will die because it eventually loses its extremities from gangrene and vital organs to malnutrition and lack of blood. A system that concentrates all oxygen and blood in the brain will be without what is necessary to function. A system of economics that removes the value of a heart by feeding fingers before the heart has had its fill will also parish. A finger, hand, or arm a person can live without, but a heart feeds the entire body, including the brain.

The system must operate in a balanced manner, not in a way that benefits the lazy or benefits the privileged. Those who fail to succeed are not lazy, and those who succeed are not privileged, but if we are not careful, eventually both will reflect either, and neither will reflect balance.

The consequences and benefits of both socialism and capitalism are available to those who are seeking the truth. America's system is a hybrid one. It must be conditional, as a flux concentrator. It is meant to adjust according to the requirements of efficiency, but operational consistency has never been obtained, nor has what is required ever been identified as the correct definition of fairness is why people disagree.

The economic model practiced has gluttony on one side and sloth on the other. A system of checks must exist to combat each. If not, the success of the system will be in jeopardy. More importantly, these have equal and contrasting consequences. Eventually, these will create the wrath to destroy both. In addition, it will remove the freedom and the protections contained in a system that requires accountability on all sides.

Things created with the hope of greatness must have balance. It also must have the freedom to change if an adjustment is necessary and the proper controls in place to recognize when it is time—the freedom to change means an increase of or decrease to and destruction to or creation of. People should not be insulted by discussing the possibility of a different system. That posture is counterintuitive to progress. Recognizing limits in a system and the consequences of these limits must be the controlling arm of a free people.

True equality represents inclusivity at the expense of exclusivity regardless of the item referenced. But desire is where the limits must start. A desire to succeed must be nurtured for success. A desire not to succeed must be left to destroy the believer, not the system. Promote the ones willing to sacrifice and earn what they seek. Ignore those who seek nothing, as these are ones who are unwilling to sacrifice. But find the ones willing to sacrifice hidden by the many inequities plaguing society. That is the system preventing progress.

Capitalism is the key to a better future. This system is built to encourage decency, promote efficiency, destroy limits, and solve problems. If America would figure out a way to monetize solutions instead of monetizing problems, our people could reach a collective agreement on many issues modern society is suffering from.

There is a problem with wealth in this country, and it is reflective of greed and the unnecessary protection of a system not meant to benefit people. The current system is built to generate vast amounts of wealth based on hard work, which is fantastic, but it was created to control the distribution of this wealth. This increases the obstacles to achieving wealth and independence. Of course, this should be the goal of all people, but it becomes difficult to achieve this independence. Remove profit, remove the problem. If profit must stay, assigning profit accurately allows the assignment of equity appropriately.

Accumulation of wealth, power, and separation from the populous, which the elite are not a part of, are the motivating factors that led free thinkers to conclude a need for America's Declaration and the Constitution assigned to the people for which these serve. It may be happening again.

Do you think these entities and people are not representative of kings as they bask in the glory of their greatness while those beneath them struggle, starve, and die without a chance to possess the basic necessities to survive, such as shelter, and clean water, food, or healthcare? To be clear, I do not think these are rights because rights, in my mind, are beliefs and virtues that do not cost other people something. At least not forcing a person to pay others for it out of their pocket.

However, there are things people can do to provide these necessities. Or at least care more about the people sharing in this beautiful journey called life. Our systems must complement each other by extending equity to promote equality. It must never be done through redistribution of wealth but through the means of compassion promoting opportunity-creation[45] by those who can. This process must remain voluntary outside the force of a controlling government as these represent the consequences of social programs—abuse, corruption, indolence.

Communism, socialism and Marxist theories are not superior, nor do those represent a viable alternative to capitalism as a means to operate in conjunction with America's Constitution protecting the freedoms granted, which are non-negotiable. It is not possible to maintain liberty when people forfeit autonomy. In addition, people are not equal by simply existing and are unworthy of the fruits of another's hard work by creating forced means of compassion. There is nothing fair or equal in the natural order. Their worth or value is based on their competency, production, and output, represented by the compensation earned. But there is nothing wrong with creating the opportunity to allow growth, success, and equity for people who seek it.

The issue is not the existence of the inequities but the value and worth of each individual. People are not created equal and have different worth, creating a spectrum of haves and have-nots or those who wish to pursue and those who choose not to. However, how can society generate a movement to associate value respective of worth and, at the same time, offer equal opportunities for others who would "use" the resources to succeed instead of "abuse" a system built to aid?

---

[45] A commitment to create opportunities through the means of compassion used to increase equity and close the wealth gap by those who have benefitted from capitalism the most.

Or does our society already reflect that? Is the issue the starting point based on the successes or failures of people's parents? These create more obstacles to overcome in one person's lifetime, allowing people to believe that it is unfair because Timmy has to work harder than Tommy, or Tammy has to work harder than Tiffany?

Life itself is not equitable. People are born with gifts not earned and stations in life not of their own sweat. This can never be controlled through any economic model adjustments, nor do the propositions of higher taxes create an easier path to success when the government pursues handouts. Hard work has and will always be an essential part of a person's desire to make a life that reflects their values. It is arguably easier to succeed in this modern day and age, yet people still blame others for their lifestyle choices or lifestyle selections. Legislators and community leaders can ask a better question: "How can we help but first, what are you doing to help yourself?"

Knowing what's best for people and wanting what's best for people is the difference between forced conforming and the seeds of freedom. Consumption, regurgitation, and a desire to apply what is not understood are reckless. Do not copy other people's work; figure it out yourself. Reading a book or reciting quotes of past thinkers does not make a person or those thoughts controlling, nor should it be applicable because it is relatable or compelling. Our lives are temporary; as such, our effects and influence on the living must also be temporary, which goes double for applying thoughts absent of new knowledge. Especially when what we know was not earned but accepted as a truth because we settled on what we wanted to believe.

People can be anything they want to be, anything they desire to become. Whatever work they are willing to put in is what America offers. Many choose nothing, which is the purpose of freedom. A one-party system prohibiting dissent or free thought used as an illusion to create efficacy is a hard theory to swallow. The final stage of human development is freedom, not a classless system. The most appropriate is the ability to be or not be, identifiable as free will and a choice, not a fallacy of singularity designed to inhibit.

Freedom is not contingent on permission from a controlling group disguising themselves as the creators of utopia. Class struggles will always remain because people are either creators or consumers representative of dreamers or believers and separated by thinking or doing. People are not equal and should not be represented by similarity but celebrated for individuality through expressions of love, religion, family, and the freedom to do so. Removing morality is equal to removing meaning. Good and evil exist, and it is not expressed by an immoral society reflected by what is tolerated or not tolerated. The economy is not fairer or superior,

"From each according to his ability, to each according to his need."

This is not the alternative necessary to counter capitalism's limits. America is different; its people are different, and our commitment is different. People are not born to be controlled. And that is the problem. What is needed is never equal and is freely open to be decided by the person choosing. Applying subjectivity to others is always a form of control not interested in the individual's freedom, only a confirmation and submission to authority, a type and form of yet another thought promoting slavery.

Controlling people with the intent to control people will never work. It is impossible to institute as revolutions are to prevent. Elimination is how you control dissenters by gently removing freedom, as socialism's intent is always communism because these ideas are the same thing. Who will control that system, how are they chosen, how much will they get paid, and will they reside on their own property? More importantly, what happens to those who disagree with the people in charge? The problems in a system that requires obedience cannot be ignored.

Helping the disadvantaged is never wrong. The issue is identifying those who choose to be disadvantaged over those who do not want to be disadvantaged. Hard work must be promoted and incentivized. The argument against capitalism should not be the lack of socialism to benefit the many simply because it is about fairness.

Fairness is not represented by giving things to people they should not possess, nor is it an application of assigning equal shares because one has the power to do so. More importantly, a person not willing to work is excluded from a worker's creed. Success should never insult, and neither should hard work. The laws of nature cannot be controlled by man as the selection process for our kind should be more than the passing of wealth from generation to generation.

The argument against capitalism should be its limits but not to destroy, only to correct. A few things could be adjusted to create a much-needed change. We are buying things we do not need because someone is telling us to do just that. Capitalism is driven by envy and only works because products are built to fail or be repurchased. It creates consequences stemming from the over-consuming and over producing the wrong goods. Imagine a world producing too much agricultural output, the good that type of gluttony and production would cause. On a separate note, I would stand with feeding the world and assign a currency to agriculture.

But capitalism's fatal flaw, which could have the greatest effect if adjusted, is failing to recognize property ownership in parts. Basically, who owns the shares of the profit created? The correct argument should be about the continued abuse of profit derived from the ownership of someone else's skillset or labored production because America is seeking equity through peace protected by freedom. The system that protects all people also gives corporations and entities protection because it represents fairness. An unfair system characterized by abuse and power retention causes harm; eventually, destruction as people will always seek a change.

The issue with capitalism is not capitalism itself, it is the assigned profit businesses, or people make from another person's skill and labor. Wages should reflect the amount of skill needed and the specific percentage of profit that particular skill created. The system operates too top-heavy and must consider America as a whole.

People should own the piece of the output their work is responsible for creating and must be compensated as such. Not sharing equally, only what is reflective of their role in production outside of compensation for work performed. If businesses shared in the profit to their employees, the rightful owners of an end result, the consequences of a wealth gap would be minimal, effectively destroying poverty and increasing the quality of life for all Americans.

Not profit sharing as retirement but profit-sharing as compensation through identification, tied to the importance of tasks related to the means of production. People own the authority to change this yet are influenced by the minority to accept the system in place. And the reason is the continued pursuit of wealth because everyone has a number. Still, the number changes when circumstances change, especially when Android Annie Zuckerberg, Space Cadet Jeffery the Delivery Guy, and Elon Mars Musk keep pushing the limits of what is allowed.

As long as profit is a dividend of a combined effort of the workers paid to the controller of means (see above) and not the specificity of task creation of the workers, their wealth will grow. Surely there must be a limit on what people are willing to accept. Remember kings waged wars only if they were able to afford such a pursuit. So the tolerance of wealth at that level will eventually become detrimental and their influence just as bad.

To be honest, I do not have an issue with the success of those three men or any of the other Forbes supermodels. I grew up watching Bill Gates, I remember the Waltons, and I always cheered for Oprah. I thought it was pretty neat and wanted to grow up to be wealthy. And that is what separates the haves and the have-nots. All these people had vison, and I respect that because when they were starting, nobody believed in them. People had zero faith in what they were selling, and they succeeded even when the odds were against them. So preventing them from completing their vision is the same as not believing in them.

But allowing that type of wealth to grow as large as it has is doing nothing for the good of our Nation, especially for the poor communities across all diversities. Until we get the extremely wealthy to start competing with percentage points of wealth transferred to address the inequities in the world, nothing will change. I am not referring to small donations to make conversations at dinner parties—points—as in the 30% to 50% of wealth range. And since that is unlikely to happen, we must change it on the front end with a consideration of the working class.

Profit should represent ownership by creation, not solely on facilitation or management through the ability to do so. Profit is a sharable personal property interest, and the ownership of such a powerful right should be assigned accordingly. It should not be possessed solely by those who control, protected by those who serve. And it most certainly should never grace those who insult its creation. Profit can create equity, and it can protect capitalism by considering those who work to make profit possible. But, unfortunately, profit can also corrupt, as the race to become the world's first ~~billionaire~~ trillionaire has shown us.

All people should be entitled to a percentage of profit based on their skillset, not a minority-heavy system that allows the monetary gain off something of which claimed ownership is invalid. It has and will always belong to the individual. When a court recognizes profit as a personal property interest and an extension of the individual who created the effect, a shift in wealth will occur. A nexus does exist between creation and those who create—But for the actions of the individual, the task would fail to be complete, the product not marketable, existing without value. All workers should control their wage and ability to create personal wealth from such skillset, not the business owner with the means to control the product of economic development.

Our system is created to solve the underlying condition of profit by removing profit from the businesses and assigning a portion to the individuals by way of due process included in the 4th amendment of the Constitution. If the majority are willing to attach profit as a property interest to protect those who create, then the minority would no longer create wealth based on the means owned by the individual. Instead, those who work would own a skillset within their means compensated accordingly, reflective of the percentage of the profit their task created as a personal property interest.

Because of the logistics and managerial skills required to operate businesses, those who represent these attributes should get paid a higher wage because they are worth it. They are reflective of this value and must be compensated as such. Compensation in consideration of risk, vision, and skillsets needed to create, with the inclusion of profit sharing, would adequately maintain the balance in a capitalistic economy but also make life more equitable, completing the final purpose of America's Constitution.

The repetition of identifying and recognizing the problem will lead to a solution. The issue is and has always been ownership of an end result from a labored activity by an individual, not the corporation. Or in other words, figuring out who it is that deserves ownership of an end result of an activity labored for by the individual even though the corporation provides, among other things, the capital. It is not about anarchy, being anti-capitalist, or pro-socialist. It is about equity, fairness, and changing the system in small increments to improve the quality of life for the majority, effectively destroying the opportunity for violence to destroy the status quo.

However, people should get paid differently according to their value. Because each person has a different value regardless of whether the profession is the same, skills are solely owned, honed, and fine-tuned by the individual existing separate from their peers. Basically, better employees get compensated for what they do—higher quality work, higher production = higher wage. Each person can commit to bettering themselves if a higher wage is desired. If they are unwilling, they are also unworthy.

The issue is not the fight for pay equality, pay raises, or equitable distribution of earned wealth but the inability of the majority to recognize their power. The minority profit because of the work of the majority. It is not to say those who create a business and possess a high level of managerial skills shouldn't be compensated. It should be reflected in their salary, not a profit dump by shares or other means to pass wealth off without being taxed as compensation.

If a person is worth 13.4 million dollars an hour, then let that be reflected on the paycheck, appropriately taxed in payroll, not allowing the shelter to forgo taxes. This only creates a larger wealth gap and strains an overtaxed general populous, feeding the other 1/3 expecting handouts. Profit is the enemy of the many and the last detrimental concept for equity in a system that is created and maintained to support Americans from being oppressed.

Capitalism, what a tragic serene cancerous beautiful addiction you are. It is an allowable Ponzi scheme used to create lords not by birthright or good favor of a king as done in the past. It is now represented by a system that feeds itself while enjoying the protection of a free people, but it accomplishes the same thing. It fattens the few while enslaving the many to continue the glutton of selfish consumption. Peasants and serfs should not know wealth, only the privilege to work on "our" land in "our" rigged system.

This is the ending to freedom. It is destructive because it chooses the process of profit and accumulation of wealth over people. Overindulgence while the masses suffer needlessly. It chooses to limit the expansion of growth and wealth by preventing the inclusion of those who create. Those who seek equity and need it the most are protecting an economic model that causes harm to themselves. To prevent self-destruction and a collapse, assigning ownership of profit to the rightful person must occur.

However, people argue the negatives of each system by ignoring what may be the solution and a superior economic model. Mr. Marx was not always correct, but what he did understand eventually, the poor will become tired of being poor, and violence will always destroy the status quo. Instead of highlighting the limits and benefits of each system based on factually accurate understandings, the arguments are always framed to use half-truth gas lighting rhetoric, motivating people to hate and despise any alternatives or blame the system in place. Instead, society should welcome a superior economic model. A model of production complemented by America, one that is for the many, not the few, one that benefits workers, not the lazy, and one that extends consideration of risk, not reliance.

Americans, in general, do not want a fair economic model, one that is represented by the best interest of all. If that were the case, they would demand it. They only want what someone tells them to want. And those who represent a controlling voice in society who can change it or have the influence to inflict change are certainly not motivated to alter what is benefiting their interest. Even the great promoters of socialism or faith leaders are reaping the benefits of capitalism at the expense of their "ideology" and the premise of charity. All power cares for is control. If the transfer of power is to occur, then independence from control must also occur.

People can survive without the economy, but the economy cannot survive without people. But our system, the people who control us and it, will choose the economy over people as it represents wealth. Making the majority wealthy is not attractive to the powerful. The charity needed to promote equity, real charity, is so hard to stomach for people who enjoy classifying or valuing people by wealth. Power with the minority is a premise protected by the establishment and reinforced through control in the form of government. The government is interested in keeping people weak, and the businesses are interested in keeping people dependent.

It represents a need in the form of a necessity provided by an entity because a person is unable. If a person cannot live without those entities, they are easy to control. Control is effortless when people depend on the government to provide protection or rely on Walmart to monopolize food. That is why the vaccination and getting back to normal was about the economy and not people. If consumer confidence and spending remained stagnant, the system would collapse. If people do not participate in the economy, then the ones who control the majority would lose power, also collapsing the system by altering the status quo. Why would people listen to leaders and a government that lost the ability to provide or protect? If they or it would be unable to protect or give us anything, what is their purpose? Is it only to tax people so they may control?

People only matter to entities when they are controlled or controllable. If the government or those with the power to control lose power or control, people lose value to the entity. More importantly, the entities also lose value and the ability to manipulate. When people lose dependency on the government or Walmart, what is meant to control and manipulate will lose its power, freeing people. Permission to live is not granted by a fictitious adaptation of authority of which governments and businesses rely on. Although those who suffer from dependency also suffer from ignorance because reliance is an addiction and so much easier.

It is a form of control. Education, knowledge, including the skillsets to provide sustenance and sustainability create independence. This remains a reason why votes are closely tied to necessity. What do you need of the government, and what can the government do for you? No amount of free compensation in combination with a lack of ambition ever bettered a people in need. Social programs offer dependency and control through manipulation. A station in life is self-prescribed, as is the medicine to cure the affliction. The role of leaders and the purpose of America is to create opportunities for all, regardless of any identifier, not to keep them from achieving their potential to control them.

The goal should be to become independent, providing the tools for success and to continue those childhood dreams. Forcing people off welfare will also provide a shift in the power structure. Not removing the lifeline those in need require but removing those who have grown accustomed to being lazy and those who can work but choose not to. These people are necessary to achieve independence from corruption as a heavy labor participation rate allows value, prevents inequities, and speaks volumes to the citizen value of a nation.

People must be compensated for their value. That premise is what encompasses capitalism. The issue has and will always be greed reflective of profit. If change is what Americans want, if a change in equity is what Americans need, then the system must be reflective of change. The status quo will not create a different result because it wasn't designed to. In a strange reality the people who support the system as is, are the ones who will never benefit from it and are harmed significantly more by it. Politicians and powerful people influenced half of America's voters to believe, "One day you may be rich and own a successful business. How would you feel if people tried to take your wealth?" However, is that not what the government does every day?

Americans are taxed and wealth removed from those who need it the most, but people allow it because a minority deceives the majority to support the gluttonous few who benefit from such a practice. And criticism of what the taxes pay for will nearly start a fight in different parts of the country. It is a process by which the overtaxed system provides benefits and services not needed by one type of voter but given to the other type of voter. Its criticism is different depending on where the recipient is located, not the services provided.

Americans subsidize everything yet receive zero return on investment. In theory, it should be represented by great leaders and equity in all Americans' lives in the form of education, healthcare, accountability through the law, and peace among the populous. However, what Americans have and what America represents are quite the opposite.

The American people are responsible for the prosperity of this country. This does not fall to the wealthy or the politicians who continue to betray their oath and people's trust. They recognized how to game the system and later created a way to not only prevent their likeness from losing wealth but a way to create an unlimited resource by owning a person's skill. Those with power accomplish this through lobbying by influencing legislation preventing a change.

American politicians continue to line the pockets of those who helped secure their seats, and those seats continue to line the pockets of American politicians. No matter what political spectrum they represent, people with power, money, and influence secured their seats for them. Their disconnect from reality is represented by their salary, the price tag on their clothes, and the armed security which protects them, but more tragically by the ones they represent still struggling needlessly in the district that made them millionaires.

Included in the corrupt controlling arm is the well-oiled machine of wealth generation known as the stock market. That is why the stock market was created and is protected—the ability of the wealthy to create more wealth. The elite has created colleges and knowledge to protect and strengthen the integral foundation used to maximize gains and even convinced people of its effectiveness, creating dependency the world cannot seem to shake. The stock exchange is used to maximize profit as it manipulates value to create wealth by exchanging currency for a chance to increase the value of an entity through the funding of private donors who risk all the loss. The wealthy, the businesses, and the politicians who control the masses all benefit from the siphoning of a U.S. dollar, or whatever nation's currency is involved in creating power.

I am not saying the system does not serve a purpose, but the purpose it serves could be more kind to equity and possess value for more than the benefactors on the other side of the exchange wall insulated from loss. The system protected creates vast wealth in the form of opportunities and networking only a few benefit from. Somehow they convinced people to put all their retirement money in a speculative system because lobbying for a specific outcome works, especially in D.C.. The system must reflect balance. It is hard to comprehend a dollar losing value when it is exchanged for something fictitious. The dollar went somewhere, just not in the direction of equity. Currency is absorbed into the festering wealth gap, doing exactly what it was designed to do—be unbalanced, ignoring equity.

The issue of equity within the means of control for labor has always been profit by the minority over the sweat of the majority. When the majority follows rules and laws created by leaders who are influenced by the minority to create a labor-intensive profit production by the majority, an unbalanced transaction of compensation occurs, and so the result of entitled individuals profiting on the skill of the majority is permitted.

Imagine the workers of every state in this great Nation or the world for that matter, embracing the Marxist views to seize the power that is rightfully theirs attacking the minority's interest to consider the majority's output by way of production, sharing in profit equally based on what is inputted. It is not an attack on, nor is it a coup used to address the tolerated wealth gap around the world but an understanding of the detrimental effects of the minority profiteering off the backs of the majority as those with the means continue to create unearned wealth based on the product of workers and their individual labor.

To be clear, I do not believe in communism, or its alter ego socialism. This system will not bring salvation, only more suffering. Although, what do we really know by repeating something else another person thought about? I wish Karl Marx and his financing benefactor were alive today. I have so many questions that I am unable to answer. For example, capitalism has created some unique things, some of which are unbeknownst to them—electricity, automobiles, planes, television, cell phones, and computers.

My question to them, or the believers of such a control, who gets these? How do we decide who drives what, who owns something, or what they are even allowed to own? Who gets to live in the house built on the property at the beach? But am I mistaken for believing these are the creations capitalism permitted and only because capitalism permitted? But for capitalism, would these have existed when or how we know them to be? It is an interesting thought nevertheless, but I doubt socialism would churn out much ingenuity.

Many fantastic marvels have been created, and ownership of these are usually tied with wealth. Whether they have earned it is not relevant; however, is that not the way it should be. The means to own is a privilege, is it not? Is it jealousy that pushes people to take what they do not have or cannot earn? Do politicians, millionaires, and people who are well off really believe in socialism, or do they say these things to influence votes, their way of maintaining all they have, and then some?

I do believe the accumulation of vast amounts of wealth while others suffer needlessly is a bit cold-hearted, but if given a choice, what kind of house, what kind of car, what kind of job would those suffering and those choosing choose? If given a chance to have anything they want, what would they choose? And are they aware of the cost of such things? Or is that irrelevant because what they want should be given without earning?

People are not born equal. There is no equity in a natural selection or the reproductive process. Do we ever consider the consequences of giving to people that which they have not earned? I do not understand. I believe a system that forces equity after the profit is collected destroys innovation, the value of hard work, and eventually the people who were used as an excuse to overthrow what equity could never bring.

Equity can never be forced or given. It is not money. It is the means and the ability to create something others want. Its creation must come from individual value. And if we want to help create individual value, it must be done with the agreement of the haves because this is the only way to destroy the have-nots. Forced removal of personal property is an extremely invasive action and usually has the same result—a taking used to benefit someone who didn't earn it, creating yet again another way society can divide the wealth. Only this time, the proper parties are decided by power, not volition, creating a different type of have-nots.

It is a problem. Regardless of personal bias or individual ideology, something is off. People are not participating in the best type of system. It can be better with small changes. And if it does not occur to us that our capitalistic economic system will destroy our democratic republic, we will lose both. Because this is the way, progress moves forward. It destroys what must be destroyed to create a version of equity people believe in; it just takes an army to do it. When enough time passes, enough people believe, and enough consequences are present, an army will rise to alter what is known. Let us please fix this before it happens.

The system of balance needed requires an understanding of the continued detrimental abuse by those who control and influence the laws. People are manipulated to vote and agree to policies or law contrary to the best interest of the individual—to be a patriot is not to question the control of the masses but instead to abide by the system in place that benefits the minority. How proper is it to never question the millionaires who represent millionaires?

It is a strange realization, once acquired, that the taxes derived to pay for the policing force, the politicians, and the court systems used to control the masses always has been provided by the masses. Our system exists and is supported by law abiding citizens in part because honest people are too afraid to be considered a problem in a society that encourages compliance yet was born from disobedience. The American people fund their oppressors and cripple themselves by removing the chance for equity because they do not want to create friction or have been convinced bootstrapping solves all issues and can create wealth if the person is willing.

The paychecks given to those who are compensated to uphold the law are created by the individuals who follow the rules set by those compensated and influenced by the minority who profit off the labor of the majority. It is a continuous cycle used to protect the status quo by giving people the illusion of power through voting and the possibility of wealth through hard work.

All the system was able to do, all it was able to create, is a reality where a combat veteran is homeless in a country full of freedoms represented by their sacrifice to create fairness, a system that allows the valueless to eat better than the valuable, and the eventual personal net-worth of 35 trillion dollars for those who could help but are too selfish to do so because comparing bank accounts is what the wealthy do. Is that an accurate statement Forbes?

This creates a cycle of uncontrollable wealth given to the minority by means of profit taking from those who control the labor, or the skillset needed to create the product. Which is later taxed by the government to pay for the politicians who support the monetary influence by the minority who benefit from and control the majority. The system is allowed to exist because the intent is to maintain control through observation by conventional dissemination of fear establishing compliance through patriotism.

Any form of control is not contingent on intelligence. Whether or not a smart man believes in a system doesn't automatically make it the correct form. I would posit kindness and consideration are the keys to a correct form of control. Many people with lower intelligence can lead effectively, and many people with higher intelligence can be dangerous in possession of power. Socialism/communism, like all others, only works if all people agree to the fallacy created. Surrendering something to receive something is required. This is the balancing act created and often overlooked when viewing one system over the other.

I think we get what we deserve. But what do we deserve? Is it our wants, our needs, our goals, or is "what we deserve" based on our attempt and how prepared we are to be successful? Those who do less get what they deserve, and those who do more also get what they deserve. Is this wrong? Should a person get more than they deserve? If so, who decides this? I think I decide what I deserve by attempting to succeed. If I do not attempt to succeed or if my preparation to succeed falls short, then I earned what I deserve.

Taking away from those who are deserving and giving what is earned to those who are not deserving seems a bit harsh, and if I may, it is theft. Ownership must be based on what is earned, not what is wanted. Is there an economic model that rewards people for hard work? Or do we want to force people to support theft? Creating artificial compassion for those who are capable but refuse to be successful is ill-advised. They want what they should never possess. Why would we ever give what is never earned? That removes the purpose of everything.

Is this an expectation people should consider? Should the standard represent what you earn? The best system is the system that promotes freedom and encourages charity. This is easily achievable if the correct leaders would emerge, setting the appropriate example by standing instead of kneeling, creating instead of destroying, and sharing instead of hoarding. Capitalism works extremely well but tends to exploit, destroy, and promote wealth for those who have the means.

Communism only works if people are equal without variations of skill or wants. All people have the same needs, but a need is simply what must be had, and a want is what can be had, and neither should be the responsibility of another. No matter the argument, no matter the books written or the experts lobbying for a position, it is a choice of the people, and it should never be decided by the number of people who believe it. Quantity versus quality is a simple truth. But the truth is subjective because what you value may never be worth anything. Quantity is irrelevant because ignorance can be many, while intelligence will always remain in the hands of the few. This allows worth to match value, always associating quality to what is in short supply—hard work.

The reason this must be true is that it takes work to succeed, and most are unwilling to do what is necessary to succeed, failing to earn what they will only ever desire. It is a hard pill to swallow when people realize their own limits, but the truth should never be offensive. My position will never change. The model of creating and consuming that best suits my truth is reflective of, "if you are unwilling, you are equally unworthy." However, some people need help, and we should do that as well. But holding guns to people's heads, forcing them to believe what they are unwilling to accept, seems a bit antagonistic to autonomy and right in line with any controlling arm with a dictator at the helm.

Limitations, negatives, and consequences are often ignored when defending preferences. Bad people corrupt, good people kill bad people, balance is restored, starting the cycle all over again. People will be victims in every system offered. This is the cycle of man. Peace is just the space in between wars; for some, war and fighting are all their identities will ever know. Life and what plagues humanity will not be solved with this book or with a book written without the knowledge of today, nor are we able to understand what is necessary because implementation is required to compare what is necessary to understand.

I respect Karl Marx because he understood that a nation is not the only thing that can oppress people. I loathe some of the ignorant followers his words created because they are unable to comprehend or contemplate the conclusions he reached, nor can they see the consequences or limits of such a system.

Any theory can be made to be extraordinary or genius if it ignores the fundamental truths required to appropriately understand the laws of nature, the laws of human behavior, and how these will forever remain in conflict as society's continued desire to create equity among the population will never occur because people are not equal, each carrying separate value all their own.

This is not intended to ignore or dismiss the pursuit of equity by downplaying the benefits. Nor am I saying groups of people are not equal. I am saying the many groups of people only ever contain a certain amount of value within their members. This creates a staggering level of inequities as the population grows. But what can we do? What is needed to create the necessary changes to alter what plagues humanity? Will equity always be connected to value and what people are willing to extend it to? What people do not value, they tend to ignore. Is this diversity's Achilles heel?

If great thinkers, activists, and protestors want to solve the problems associated with politics, economics, and education (society), they must first solve the people problem causing the issues in politics, economics, and education (society). They must also realize the value of people and the worth to society each possesses with the autonomy to govern accordingly.

The strangest thing to recognize about a free people who can be as successful as they choose to be or better themselves at any given moment, many are satisfied with their station in life. Whether it be their profession, intellect, or both, sometimes their economic situation matches the required effort for either. Some have been unable to move forward, limited by circumstantial hardships or situational hardships making success a bit harder or longer to achieve, but others rather enjoy mediocrity because it doesn't hurt and is always easier.

Of course, there exists not a person who would refuse an increase or promotion in their life identity if it was handed to them without cost. Knowledge without sacrifice, money without earning, power without competency, growth without sweat—these represent the pinnacle of human existence, all requiring forward motion and the commitment of the individual. That is the only force controlled by the individual and the most important as well. A belief or an internal desire to succeed is required for the eventual rise of oneself—forward progress and the commitment to.

It is without question people share different versions of hardships or blessings which either prevent or promote. The difficulties to overcome (circumstantial hardships) or the struggles experienced (situational hardships) are obstacles for which an antidote does not exist. These will forever remain an identity of people. People have been, will be, and are born with advantages that are insulting to others as these were not earned by the individual. People have been, will be, and are born without advantages at no fault of their own and are blamed for their situation.

The successes created from each hardship are lessons for both; those watching and those feeling. These can be used by the watchers to help those experiencing the hardships or be used to inspire those suffering from the hardships. Why do some people fail given all the advantages in life and others succeed only possessing the will to succeed? Is there a correlation between being successful and attempting to be successful or being unsuccessful and trying to be unsuccessful? Is value born of the individual, and no matter the situation, success is inevitable? Or do the circumstances and situations make the person? Is it an acceptance of the identity the person wants to be or not be?

There is nothing wrong with helping people, and there is nothing wrong with expecting people to help themselves at the same time. People will be as successful or as unsuccessful as they want. That is freedom, and unfortunately for America, we have yet to grant freedom to those who are devoid of our likeness. Past, present, and the future, this is the fight.

America is unique, full of intelligent people who have the freedom and opportunity to continue elevating our species like no other society has done before. Our people must quit trying to promote any version of socialism as the solution or capitalism as the best we can do. What I convinced myself of is this:

Socialism and communism are the same. Communism controls and forces relinquishment. It takes what is created or what was pursued by others and gives it to people who had zero part in creating or pursuing. If this was the controlling arm chosen from the start, nothing would be created, our advancements in technology would be minimal, property would not be personal or real, and many things would not be worth dying for because value is what they tell you it is, effectively destroying visions and goals. The ability for people to arm themselves prevents the system from being implemented but as power and influence grow being armed becomes necessary for survival instead of a deterrent. Ingenuity does not occur, or at least it would go unknown or not shared with anyone for fear of seizing for the greater good. The true believers, the biggest benefactors of such a system—those who are willing to surrender autonomy and submit to control because a free market is unsustainable—will commit violent acts because patriotism is simply necessary to protect whatever system you believe in. People work less because of technology, never overproducing nor productive. Communism cannot be without a dictator because people will not submit to conformity and democratic socialism is a step before the same lie and vison is created. If the freedom to be is absent in politics it is not capitalism; it is a ruse designed to permit participation in other free markets generating wealth for a war.

No Freedom.
Forced Equity.
No Dissent.
An Iron Fist.
Corruption

Democracy could not exist without capitalism, and capitalism could not exist without democracy as the power to monopolize coin via fiat grants control. Capitalism allows what was created or sought to be shared with the world by rewarding the person who created and those who seek to purchase what was created. Both take drive and determination to receive a specific outcome. Its consequences can be measured by the varying levels of socio-economic statuses and the wealth gap created by the successful implementation and protection of such a system. It cannot exist without the proper political system encouraging autonomy. If the largest political system that protects freedoms is ever extinguished, capitalism will be destroyed, and so will democracy. Guns are always a deterrent and a powerful negotiating tool for the free market. The true believers, the biggest benefactors of such a system—those who are willing to value wealth over people and commit others to believe the process is working—will do whatever is necessary to protect the status-quo because patriotism is simply necessary to protect whatever system you believe in. Work the same with technology always overproduce and productive. The system develops self-correcting conditioning to survive, always focusing on profit. These errors were foreseeable yet created for the sake of implementation—profit. Will save the world and all the people if there is money to be made.

Too Much Freedom.
Over Consuming.
Over Creating.
Unjustifiable Poverty.
Corruption.

The more I hate capitalism, the more socialism tempts me, but the more I understand socialism, the more I forgive capitalism. But what do I really know? This is my understanding of economic models and the people who tell us what to believe:

It is irrelevant how smart a person is, how many degrees they possess, or the misguided people they follow or lead when offering evidence contrary of something they have already convinced themselves of. All forms of governance or control create issues, and each one has consequences regardless of who is in charge. Our job, our responsibility, is to limit these consequences the best way we can by considering what those before us never considered because they did not possess the knowledge or strength we do.

If a person can ask themselves these four questions and understand the purpose of each question, the system you are in is the correct one for you.

Would you do anything if the price was right?

Would you create something that was going to be taken from you?

Would you create something if it was going to be given to you?

Would you die for and are you willing to kill to change the system?

I have never studied the history of economics nor am I asserting myself as a resident expert in all matters concerning these transactions. But I do see errors and flaws creating issues in our society. Why are these issues not corrected if we have students and scholars of the studies? Or is their role only to observe and document instead of correcting?

If a doctor was unable to correct a medical issue, would a person not seek a different doctor one who has a better grasp of the symptoms and a superior treatment plan? Or would you allow the cancer to eat away at your being because the incompetent advice was what you knew or all you knew? If a person is not well versed in all the particulars necessary to understand a subject, does it disqualify their thoughts or opinions on the subject matter? Something is wrong and it's wrong because we accept it as is.

What consequences or limits are we willing to accept? Every system must have an end game, and every leader must have solutions for these. Those who possess wealth beyond the means of what is necessary must help our Nation and the world. Your inability to see what is killing us is killing us. Please be more kind to equity, if not for strangers, for our democratic republic.

Socialism is coming if we do not adopt a charity spirit and personal responsibility. If it is within our means, we must solve the limits our economic model has shown. This must be done by creating the opportunity to succeed and fostering hard work, never giving handouts but always providing hand-ups. The system from top to bottom needs housekeeping.

In addition, the credit system in America must reflect change. Should this not occur, extreme measures must be taken. A credit score represents likeness, it represents identity, and because of this, it represents personal property. When it is altered by unscrupulous business practices, it has extremely adverse consequences that can take a decade to correct.

This means a mistake, an error; a libel act of dishonesty could require a person over twenty percent of their adult life to fix. No fail-safe exists, not one requirement of evidence to prove beyond a reasonable doubt that it is in fact true. No deterrent presently offered prevents this. It must be the lack of punishment great enough to represent accountability for the consequences of such a corrosive system. Of course, those standards of control to prevent overzealous actors are reserved for the government. But what are the implications of a mistake, an error, a libel act of dishonesty?

A credit score can be used to deny gainful employment, remove the opportunity to acquire housing, limit the ability to educate further, means for rejection to secure financing for necessities, and even the ability to afford a chance to alter a generational wealth gap. This creates different kinds of trauma, all with the intent to discriminate, allowing businesses to profit from errors or life events outside the control of consumers. A way for the rich to maintain a life of luxury on the backs of the poor.

The livelihood of private citizens, the ability to possess life, liberty, and the pursuit of happiness are in the hands of businesses. Does this seem fair? Or is it a type of arbitrary control created with corruptive intent that Americans are okay with? Of course, the fail-safe is our legislators, who most likely are disconnected from any type of understanding of poverty or struggle. In the event they do have experience but choose to ignore the struggle, it is even more disheartening and disgusting, to say the least.

Because a credit score has value connected to a person, it is property. Because it is personal, it is personal property. Because it can lose value by the act of a third party, reflective of extending quality of life to citizens, businesses are stepping into the role of the government. It seems one or two constitutional arguments can be made against such a practice.

Because a person cannot be deprived of property without due process and the ability for businesses to arbitrarily destroy a private citizen's life is present or its ability to prevent a private citizen from accessing equal protection under the law, the process must be regulated before the mistake is made not redressed after the harm has occurred. One mistake, one error, one libel act of dishonesty is so easy to offer as truth yet so difficult to counter as falsity. All because selfishness found a way to monetize human tragedy and add value where it is not warranted.

We must also work on the uncontrollable cost of living. Controlling the cost-of-living controls economic freedom for the masses. Therefore, essentials must be affordable and outside the influence of inflation.

Control inflation control inequity. A drink of water represents the same quench of thirst today as it did one thousand years ago and as it will one thousand years from now. It is representative and defined by a unit of consumption, and the measurement of worth does not change. But someone figured out the thirst possessed and the quench satisfied is relative to the individual's need, not what is consumed, allowing a higher cost for the same thing at a different time or representing of a different need. Basically, profit and greed, the backbone of capitalism or any form of "this for that" representing gluttony.

Arbitrary value prevents definite worth, and inflation is another way to create more value while destroying wealth for others. The entire economic system of capitalism is broken. The businesses benefitting from employees working hard is broken. But what do we do? Who do we turn to? And are the people we turn to the most competent ones to tell us the truth? Will their intelligence bring about our salvation, or will they use what they know to keep us enslaved?

Unfortunately, we allow people who are not the brightest to dictate our path or enable others to benefit while others suffer—each option plagued with selfishness. The answer is not capitalism/democracy, nor is it socialism/communism as we know it. It must be a hybrid system, one that has yet to be created. Something designed to address all our system's shortcomings and limits. A form of governance representing what we wish our people to become because we were unable to achieve it before or ourselves. I think that was the purpose of America. To allow the later generations the ability to grow together as people, not as separate Nations, but as one. If we cannot compromise, if we are unable to solve what is required, the beast is coming.

What we suffer from, what all people balance, inflict, or ignore—the past, present, or future—is the desire to control people or the desire to reject what others are willing to submit to. Each side subjecting the other or rejecting the other. It is battle for control or rejection of. People are either willing to accept one or the other, creating the desire to have legitimacy and the need for representation. Enter politicians.

People start grouping in pockets based on one or two extensive premises. And the representation trickles down from there, packing groups of people into tribes and fluctuating alliances based on how much the group is willing to concede for their inclusion. Because of this, what each group stands for is hard to find. So, they pocket into likeness and create an inbred version of control, and this is accomplished through political incest.[46] Consequences of each system fighting for dominance and to distract the followers of what they truly are.

Both want to control the output of the other because each affiliation is mad at the other for either the success achieved, or they are offended by others for being themselves for many different reasons. One side wants limits from the government allowing people to create, protect, and believe what they want unless it is tied to sexual reproduction. And the other side protects everything, everyone, and any thought created except the other side, including everything, everyone, and their thoughts created. They want to limit success and allow people to share in the successes of others as a group unless that group believes in gun rights or a God. Or in other words, the power to control those who are wrong.

Economics or governance of people is about control. Totalitarianism is what those who despise freedom wish to create, but first, they need their authoritarian leader to emerge. Communism seeks to control work or in other words output. Fascism seeks to control output or self-expression. These are both equally oppressive and void of freedom, yet all people practice a type of this. A version of each can be found and is represented in our politics by party lines with democrats on one side and republicans on the other.

Dictators and what they create are called many things. They can cloak and disguise themselves in any form necessary. Tyranny is a magic trick often ignored for the sleight of hand used to create compliance. In any form of governance self-autonomy is the most appropriate and least invasive; however, resting on one's loins usually creates the spark of tyrannical control. This occurs because the Nation lacks the soldiers and

---

[46] When a politician puts their business where it has zero business being.

the vigilance from citizens necessary to prevent what is despised or overthrow what is required. Participation is a must mixed with a bit of kindness and consideration. What offers the most freedom is the one I want because I am responsibly able to use it and I am sure others feel the same way. But more importantly, I do not bow to power regardless of the names or titles it assumes because I consider it to be the same foe under many guises.

What's the answer? I am not 100% sure, but I am willing to adjust what I know before dismantling and implementing what I do not. Be the change, fight the good fight, and stand for those who are voiceless. That is what my America is. Broken, yes. Fixable, absolutely. Are the people both willing and worthy? Only time will tell. But I imagine putting people in the system who believe in equity and can create it without taking from others is the start we need.

Once again, the people who are many are fighting for equity in a place the few control. The system of currency, credit, and legislation protecting people—workers and consumers—is broken. It is unfair and does not show signs of being altered for the benefit of the majority. It is hard to offer an absolute theory explaining why this is. The only possibility that points to a logical conclusion, is those with power do not want to alter what benefits them the most.

They are not motivated to change it. The incentives to create equity is not present in those who have nothing to gain. So why would they change it or why would it be important to them? Although asking them directly may offer insight, but the truth is as obvious as the overinflated salaries of the politicians who represent the people.

The conclusion is that these issues will not change until politicians create change. Politicians do what they think the people want. Because of this, change will not occur until the people recognize the behavior in question is detrimental, forcing change through accountability. People represent and create the necessary change. Later the politicians reflect this behavior because this is what the people want. But a unique paradox is created when politicians assume they know what is best for the people and when they attempt to control controversies that are not in their purview. Always failing to solve what is vital because they made a platform of it instead—political incest.

Because politicians believe people are too ignorant, they apply their own version of bias, a superior way of thinking, as politicians believe they have become superior. When leaders believe the people are no longer in a position to recognize what is appropriate or good for them, they become something different. The system reflects something different. Politicians tell voters what they should be mad at and how they should live. Is America stuck in an abusive detrimental system disguised as capitalism in democracy? Is this not eerily similar to a communist community rule or a dictatorship always preventing change because it will destroy what benefits the minority?

Although when the population becomes too dependent, too ignorant, and starts valuing worthless people, professions and ideas, it sure makes it easy to manipulate them and even disguise and hide internal corruption from them. Be aware and wary of the politicians who seek power to subvert antonymic interests. Why would the minority change anything unless it's what they are in conflict with?

Kingdoms or dictatorships are easy to create but hard to destroy. These are always the ending of freedom, the downfall of liberty. It will occur because people become too complacent, allowing behaviors, beliefs, and immorality to occur. Eventually people believe others have lost the ability to govern themselves, and a need arises to control behaviors or eliminate the perceived threat.

People should not possess guns; our system will protect them. People should not own combustible engines; our system knows what is best. Eating meat is immoral; only our diet is acceptable. People must be religious; our system knows best. People should possess more money than they need; others are poor because they choose to be. Healthcare is not a fundamental right, only a necessity.

All these may very well be true, but America offers the opportunity to choose, not force, discuss not decide, and prosper not perish. And we must do these things together; Americans need each other. Accepting what America represents is an extremely difficult premise for people to grasp. Freedom is enormously complicated to understand. Division destroys diversity, selfishness secures supremacy, and laziness loses liberty. Not everyone is capable of being free. Not because they are undeserving but because they are unwilling.

It takes work and a commitment between countrymen to nurture peace. A desire and a strong will of a united people to protect. A thirst of knowledge and the dismission of ignorance to grow. More importantly it requires equity, fairness, and a pursuit to create these, regardless of how hurtful the truth is or how difficult the task proves to be. And that is what the foundation of freedom is; many not one, together not alone, united not divided. When leaders promote; freedom thrives. When leaders dismiss; freedom dies.

An ending is always near. The willingness to allow it to occur is always the cause. Dividers forge fire. People who influence to divide seek this end. People who influence out of choice, represent that beginning. Leaders do neither and are forged from this fire. People who influence to unite, seek this end. People who influence out of need, represent that beginning. Recognizing the difference is vital. Both occur from necessity. Delaying the latter, the cause. When politicians mutate from beneficial to detrimental, it must be recognized.

# Politicians

Politicians should never be activists, and activists should never be politicians. This can create conflicting duties and responsibilities; therefore, roles must have different purposes. One creates change and the other signs change into law. Activists need to work with politicians to develop laws and offer guidance to assist society and its people in working together.

A person must lead without bias. They must represent all without identity. Create and strengthen fairness without benefit. Promote understanding without preference. It is difficult to do, but it is what must be done. Our system is built for the best interest of America, not a single group or a permanent location of liberal influence or of conservative influence. It exists to protect the best interest of freedom, not the destruction of freedom because of a personal preference.

If people are ever interested in changing politicians and the presence of incompetency in leaders, all that is necessary, all people must do is represent the change themselves. Become the people who must be personifications of those positions. When the majority operate as decent, kind, and caring people, so will the politicians who represent them.

Incompetent leaders are created when people permit those less qualified than them to occupy leadership positions. They represent the most inept parts of a people. Competent leaders are created when people permit those who are more capable than them to serve. They represent the best parts of a people. Leaders represent whatever version of a person those who follow choose. Control the behavior of leaders by controlling the behavior of yourself. Leaders do what they think people want them to do. Whatever behavior is promoted is the behavior noted. Whatever behavior is prohibited is the behavior prevented.

Incompetent leaders are hard to recognize, but eventually, they become easy to identify. They are nothing but narcissistic hyper arrogant fools with extreme confidence and selfish motivations. The key is to see their truth. Is their truth motivated by what they are not? Are they inclusive, and do they create dialogue through understanding? Or is their truth motivated by what they are? Are they divisive and ignore the opportunity to create dialogue because they are unapologetic about their feelings and dismissive of yours? A new type of leader is needed, and the system is overdue for an overhaul.

Suppose the goal is to create a fairer system to promote the inclusion of different candidates who represent change. In that case, the goal should be to remove the candidates who only represent a minority of thought because their concerns are exclusively for their kind. Our system must allow a greater choice of preference in elections. This means access to the ballot and the availability of resources necessary to be successful.

This can be accomplished by limiting the amount of money that can be spent on a political campaign. One dollar per population count of the seat sought and an allowable minimum of 100,000 no matter the representation of the population reflective of the seat sought.

For example, the most money allowed to be spent on a presidential campaign is equal to the population of the United States of America. If a candidate and their team cannot run a successful campaign with $330,000,000, they have zero business operating the executive branch or influencing taxes in Congress that must have a budget. Instituting a ceiling for funds during a campaign may create a recognition of a ceiling for debt while serving. Understanding a spending limit is an attribute politicians should possess as it will serve the national debt and the people equally well. If you do not have it, do not spend it.

A surplus never means spend more or give pay raises; it means taxes are too high, straining those who are forced to pay. Government employees need not pay taxes, so too is true for those who receive government subsidies. The government is simply laundering money to pay for wish lists of those who were once in power. Taxes are a grotesque form of control and extreme abuse of power. If not operated to be as minimally invasive as possible and the amount reduced to only what is necessary, these can become oppressive. The next depression will be substantially worse and will be more difficult to overcome due to a tax burden that can never be justified.

In addition, the house of representatives and senators in Congress must accept a pay decrease. There does not exist even a single viable argument to the contrary. Higher pay does not recruit better talent in the political realm, especially when talent was not a factor in putting people in their positions in the first place. There are zero prerequisites to becoming a politician, nor must they have competency requirements to hold a seat. If this was the case, most likely, the best of us would serve the rest of us.

Instead, it attracts people who are imposters looking for power, self-gratification, and in this case a paycheck that never reflects the level of competency or value required to earn such a salary. These are the politicians utilizing divisions to gain legitimacy. Representation should be used to mobilize constituents to create a solution to benefit fairness. But it is misused to keep the problem and to keep the need for representation alive—job security. If their lives were connected to the problem needing to be solved, a resolution would likely reveal itself.

Alternatively, the voters can potentially resolve the dilemma of continual suffering by altering how to compensate our representatives. We can do this by adopting a form of compensation represented by the median income of the United States because this is who and what Congress must represent. It is accurately measured by the number of years their seat is protected. The House members would be compensated at a pay scale of 20% higher than the median American income. And the Senate members compensated at a pay scale of 60% higher than the median American. Just an idea, the numbers can reflect any preference but the greater amount of people our politicians can relate to, the better.

Even if the formula is based on their current pay with a 50% reduction, it will remain well above what 50% of Americans earn at $87,000; it still seems inflated but closer to a fair wage. But if the salary is more intricately connected to the actuality of their constituents, House members would earn $44,000 a year, and Senate members would earn $64,000 a year. The alternative is a system that values politicians at almost three times the worth of Americans, and it is grossly negligent, overinflated, and insulting to appropriateness.

For perspective, only 8.3% of the American population earned between $150,000 and $199,000. My observations may be incorrect, but a salary is a significant indicator of what type of life a person has and the particular issues this life represents. The necessities of living such as healthcare, transportation, food, housing, utilities, and education opportunities are quite different when the access to funds is $36,000 a year versus $174,000 a year. Of course, these numbers fluctuate, but the validity of the argument remains. At a point, salary is of zero concern when their wealth is at a substantial amount—affluence matters.

For example, the Representative in the district my home resides in has a personal net worth of 10.4 million dollars. Most likely, our lives have never been the same, and the struggles my family, friends, and others like us share, are disconnected from people of that wealth. Again, I could be wrong, but it seems a person who represents the concerns and struggles of the people are the individuals who should hold those seats; not just a person who sits in the seat as a figure but as a reflection represented by a connection.

Their salary is extremely unreflective of their job quality, but it is also incredibly arrogant to believe they should receive compensation exceeding those they must represent at the astronomical level permitted. When the percentages are that difficult to reconcile, it may be caused by an inflated cost overvaluing their worth. Their life must be as closely connected to the working class so that they can share in the same struggles. They must feel what it's like to know what it's like. When they are finally able to disconnect from the struggles of Americans, it is also time for them to disconnect from the politics of Americans. America has successfully worked for them and their family.

Allowing a continuous connection to hardships would have a fantastic effect on internal motivation to close the wealth gap and would aid in bringing Americans out of poverty together. The harder they work, the higher their pay, finally justifiable. It would create not only an increase in wealth for all Americans but also increase the amount of taxes collected. This would allow social programs to create greater equity in a system that is in desperate need of operating more appropriately. And in the event they are able to generate enough wealth to separate themselves from the day-to-day struggles, if they fail to represent the population adequately, it is time for the struggle to be known again, represented by a new voice.

Lastly, all issues stem from a lack of representation. If differences are not represented, and they believe their interests are continuing to be ignored or targeted, eventually they will revolt because the system doesn't care about them. This must be addressed. Our leaders must balance these interests more fairly without considering party lines as a priority. One is governing the other is mob rule, forcing authority on those without power.

I do know one thing; voting must change if our leaders are to change. And if what is donating money to specific interests is unable to vote, the entity should never infuse corruption into a campaign or on behalf of a campaign. Unable to vote—Unable to donate. Meaning no blood in your veins, no influence—period.

# Voting

Value and worth are important when accessing what is necessary, what is needed, and when deciding what people should do which job or participate in which activity. Doctors require education, competence, and a vetting system before practicing a privilege extended by a governing body. The same is true of lawyers, police officers, teachers, daycare workers, and even fast-food workers. Yet America operates its most vital system in a way that lets every person who is of age to participate in arguably the most essential part of freedom without first proving competency. A system that allows ignorance to vote for ignorance and incompetence vote for incompetence is a system that will fail because it requires more than being the age to vote to do it responsibly and to vote correctly.

Not all people have the same value. America and her citizens must understand the type of people who are able to create a better America or destroy the current America built to protect freedoms. There are three types of Governed Participants[47] in society and three types of citizen participants[48] who are represented by a nation contained within a society. It is not only important to recognize who these people are but vital to understand these people are continuously causing fractures in society. Their behaviors and what they represent reflect the type of unity present between people.

The power to vote represents the power to elect competency used to create or elect incompetency used to destroy. Those who vote have the power to destroy without a failsafe. Should Americans be okay with this? People can read or watch the news and easily identify those among America's population who are most likely to be incapable of comprehending how much responsibility it takes to adequately exercise such a privilege.

Some people shouldn't vote, not because they are undeserving but because they are unwilling. The consequences of incompetent voters and incompetent leaders are not that difficult to find. A government of the people, by the people, for the people, but what kind of people vote and what kind of people, do the people elect? — results that become consequential to all Americans.

Voting is not just filling in a bubble on a ballot and dropping it into a box or selecting the letter (R) or (D) at your local polling station. It is a type of freedom and privilege many died to create. Voting entails thought, knowledge, and most importantly, respect for the United States Constitution as a duty. More importantly, it is not a duty to vote; it is a duty to correctly vote. And quite frankly, every citizen's responsibility. This is, in my view, the best explanation I can share explained by Robert Longley:

> The United States is erroneously described as a democratic nation, when in fact, we are a Constitutional Republic. There is a difference between a democracy and our Constitutional Republic; in a democracy, officials are elected by the majority and pass laws with majority influence. This allows the majority

---

[47] People who fall under the authority of the controlling arms of society

[48] Type of citizens of a nation who fall under the authority of the controlling arms of society.

to do what the majority has always done, leave the minority subject to abuse and neglect.

The system allows voters to elect representatives who later create laws that must comply with the constitution and should be done with the best interest of Americans not political party lines or the opportunity to maintain power. "While the majority still rules in the selection of representatives, an official charter lists and protects certain inalienable rights, thus protecting the minority from the arbitrary political whims of the majority."[49]

To protect our rights as individuals, voters must become informed. It is not enough to be informed on the platforms of the candidates. It is not enough to be informed on how each candidate affects your emotions. It is a voter's responsibility as citizens to inform themselves how each candidate's platform complies with our Constitution.

The 2nd Amendment is a perfect example. It represents the importance of being an informed voter. Candidates play on your emotions to elicit a response to trigger an action. That action is always to vote for them. When a candidate tells you that they will outlaw certain guns, certain magazine clips, ammunition sales, and the like, they are in direct violation of the United States Constitution. However, if you do not like guns and would like to see them outlawed, this rhetoric is music to your ears.

What if a candidate said they plan on writing legislation to prevent women from voting? The LBGT community? Minorities? What if a legislature tries to remove these protected rights piece by piece, not infringing on the right totally, but a long game? A plan to remove the protections of the Constitution slowly while no one is paying attention. Those things would certainly get people's attention, and indeed, an attempt to stop such behavior would occur. Not only because those words and the threat of such an action are morally wrong but also because an effort to create such law is in direct violation of the Constitution, attacking individual freedoms through an overtly discriminatory act.

---

[49] Longley, Robert. "Republic vs. Democracy: What Is the Difference?" ThoughtCo, Aug. 26, 2020, thoughtco.com/republic-vs-democracy-4169936.

So why does it matter? It matters because all Americans must respect that the Constitution protects the individual and not the majority. It protects someone's right to own a gun, regardless of whether someone else likes it or not, but it also protects someone's right not to be discriminated against due to an identity from prejudicial laws, regardless of whether someone else likes it or not. People must uphold the Constitutions as a whole, not in bits and pieces that fit their emotions or what their "ideal" world is, while forcing those biased agendas on those who think differently.

People must do better to understand why their neighbors' right to own a gun is just as important as their right to free speech, for both of these rights are non-negotiable. It is not just or equitable to protect only the rights that align with a voter and ignore the others. Citizens must commit to truly learning about our Nation and not just the abridged version candidates want us to know. And yes, that includes the dirty, inhumane, and atrocious parts of America's past and her people as well.

Without the commitment to be informed and understand the responsibility that comes with citizenship, a vote is simply a decision used to undermine the Constitution and the protections it provides the individual. It is a vote made with emotion rather than rational thought; it is a vote made with feelings rather than knowledge; it is a vote made with fear rather than love; it is an irresponsible vote—one devoid of empathy and reflective of a one-America.

It is also an incorrect vote and a contributing factor to the Nation's state of affairs. When people vote, they must be informed and understand who, what, and why they are voting for as they graciously put a check by a name. People must be able to justify and arguably give substantive reasons why they chose a specific candidate. Not explaining or defending a vote to others but recognizing internally why they decided to cast that ever-important vote granting permission to lead.

It should never be because the candidate is a woman, a man, white, black, religious, republican, democrat, or any other non-essential, aesthetically pleasing, unimportant reason to vote for a person. The most important factors are how they treat those different from their own identity and how competent their ability to lead is. What does the individual stand for, and what are they willing to do to protect decency among a free people? Our society has shown great people come in many different versions and their abilities transcend an identity. And I would vote for any flavor a candidate has if they convinced me of their character, ability to lead, and commitment to our collective greater good.

It is an honor when a voter casts that ever-important decision electing those who can either unite or divide. A standard of decency and competency must exist at every level of representation. If you are not convinced that a candidate is worthy of your vote, force them to offer further evidence that proves otherwise. And never vote by selecting the lesser of two evils as the consequence is still evil. Force all candidates to be better. This will force our elected officials to create a better future for us all.

But people do not care. They are distracted by their entertainment or cannot be bothered because it does not affect them. Everyone who extends unsolicited advice to me always refers to a cliché saying or a prayer. You can't change the world. Practice the serenity prayer, or another nonhelpful type of advice that does nothing to solve the problems Americans face. The issue with these people and the flaw in their logic, they fail to understand the duties and responsibilities of a self-governing people.

They lack the contextual understanding of what it is to be an American. Citizens must participate in our democratic republic. This is non-negotiable. One cannot just simply live their life and ignore the toll of freedom. This self-prescribed luxury is precisely the detrimental selfish behavior that has the ability to destroy freedom and is most certainly a factor contributing to the decline of our leadership.

We live in a society and a governing system that requires participants to prevent tyranny and inequities. The system designed is flawless if operated correctly. The most important cog in this well oil machine is and always has been its people. Being distracted, not participating, or just being lazy should remove some of the privileges of being an American.

We have grown far too large to not hold people accountable, and the consequences of failing to do this have also grown more prominent. Freedoms do not mean you can do what you want when you want to. It means you are protected by this Nation and her laws when you meet specific criteria.

I have grown tired of watching people who do less than others for this Country yet have the same privileges. As if existing as an American is enough of a contribution or should be enough for any patriot. The issues in this land arise from a lack of accountability and lack of care. This must end. For far too long, we allowed people to be less than, and the time of consequences this laissez-faire mentality creates are here.

We are witnessing the destruction of our system and a collapse of unity. People have successfully negotiated away our sovereignty, the Constitutionality of how our government should operate, and removed the notion of justice for all—diminishing the requirement for equitable administration of the law by dismantling and ignoring the importance of accountability. People have successfully removed knowledge and replaced it with ignorance.

I think it is time to be selective on who should get to vote. Not everyone deserves to vote. Not everyone should have this privilege. How can people vote and not prove competency to earn such a privilege? Allow for a competency exam to be given for voting and running for office; a significant change may occur. . . Lack of significant minimal intelligence should be a cut-off standard all reasonable, informed, and participatory citizens can get behind.

Voting is not a right; it is a privilege. Much like driving or practicing law, competency must be proven before people are granted and extended this autonomy. It was not made a right in the original Constitution but was correctly expressed later that applicability to possess the opportunity to vote cannot be denied by discrimination based on a recognized identity such as race, color, sex, or age.

It, however, is silent on the discrimination of intelligence. This should be the standard. If we are to govern by likeness we must discriminate by intelligence. If people believe voting is a right, it should be strengthened and protected so it cannot harm others, as is the case for gun rights. Or any other practice, behavior, and profession that can harm similar to the limitations attached to the freedom of expression. If voting is arguably the most critical thing in a free nation, then why do all people get to vote? There are irrational people among us. They are not worthy of such power. They must earn that privilege, regardless of how harsh that sounds.

Our system has been infiltrated by people who have zero business voting for people who are as ignorant as they are. Education is key. Some form of a civics competency exam should be given before someone is allowed to exercise such a privilege. Do we really want people who do not understand the importance of the Constitution or the Declaration of Independence to vote? A threshold created to assign and prove value before participation, allowing competent, informed, and a well-regulated citizenry of an intelligent kind to influence the direction and path of our Nation.

I am not saying we make it restrictive only to prevent people from voting altogether, but we allow the votes and the influence it creates to come from a different type of voter. Voting is essential and its power substantial. However, we must make it more efficient by educating those who do vote, ensuring what it creates has substantive value, not just aesthetically pleasing. We fix the inadequacies of education contained in our system. A citizen who is more knowledgeable is a citizen who is an asset to a nation designed to enable citizens to protect each other. We are only as strong as our weakest link.

And thanks to the inequities and inequalities in our system, we have a large wealth gap, a large education gap, and a large justice gap. What do you expect when the powerful write laws for the more powerful while protecting entities over people? Greed and power have once again threatened the stability of a people.

Our strength is our willingness to sacrifice for one another and work together to an end of understanding, compassion, and equality. If people are not willing to better themselves, are not willing to better this country, then why do we allow them to participate in something they do not care about. Why should we allow those people to possess such a privilege that they have not earned?

If people, the voting bloc in America, cannot understand and spot ignorance or ignorant people, how are we as a people to fix our issues? How are people allowed to vote for likeness over substance? I see the collapse of our Nation if the status quo is maintained. I blame the system of power that continues uninhibited and under the false premise that this is the way it's always been or the only way it should be.

Change the system to create a better citizen, a more informed citizenry, and a stronger, more cohesive country. The values of freedom and respect for our fellow American is of the utmost importance to ensure our democratic republic survives any threat. The two-party political system has intentionally divided Americans. My entire life, I wanted to see what happens when a leader deliberately unites the American People.

I am unimpressed by the perversion of accountability. I am disheartened to see the disgusting, disrespectful, and downright degrading behavior Americans show each other. We are better than this. I do not want any of that in my country. That is not what America represents, and if that bothers you—there are plenty of songs and sayings that will encourage you and provide you with guidance on how to proceed next. We must do better.

How can our leaders create different "realities" or "truths" that purposefully and intentionally divide by being blatantly dishonest, ignoring actuality? People cannot live a life only surrounded by the truth representing their likeness, themselves, or what they believe the most. A lifestyle or a reality that shuts out others by voting for likeness serves zero purposes but to create intolerance by fueling division. Our truths should never be based on what political party you belong to. I have never been ashamed of America and never will be, but I am ashamed of what Americans have become. We must refrain from politicizing social issues. This type of voting allows what actually harms us to continue uninterrupted.

Substituting knowledge for ignorance, compassion for hate, and progress for destruction is not conducive to protecting the fragility of America. Continuing on this path will push good people to misbehave, as we have already started to witness. I was fearful of America's reality after election day in 2020; my fear was warranted and correctly assigned. I was afraid of any result as our connection to one another had been lost, which makes our way of life too fragile to survive. Imagine the riots if Trump had won.

We are a sad and shameful people. America has all but created the official borders for tribalism. Our leaders have successfully put citizens in groups who hate each other. The most bizarre thing is the representation and identity of the groups. Americans are choosing sides, and it is not solely based on race, religion, gender, sexual orientation or socioeconomic status. It is an ideology of hate pushing our demise closer. It is a thought, not what we look like. These factions are transferring power in a dangerous way.

What is occurring is the successful transformation of a free Democratic Republic with the allocation of power vested in her people to a hybrid form of communism and dictatorship whose leaders use fascism, pitting us against each other to maintain control. What America represents is slowly fading away. People must remove themselves from the continuous bickering and the back and forth arguing, which creates nothing but an illusion of who is right or wrong.

This is the truth; you are all mistaken. If you pick a side in America, you are part of the catalyst destroying this great Nation. Not that you are wrong, but we can do better, and our Nation requires better—it requires compassion, consideration, and compromise. Do not lose yourselves to the call of chaos; fight it. Our way of life depends on it.

In addition, please stop brandishing the rhetorical falsities as factual evidence. Where are the voters who have not been able to vote in elections, and where is the evidence of voter fraud to alter an election? And who are the people that would be okay with either of these disgusting abuses of power? If these types of oppression, tyranny, and treason are not actual, please refrain from encouraging any sort of lies to incite discontent between our people. Yet again, the intoxication of insanity on a person's tongue has left consequences of uncontrollable magnitudes due to the prevalence of misinformation, disinformation, and the intentional propaganda spread by ill-informed people. Unfortunately, American politicians are resorting to campaigns that lie to the world by controlling the narrative and gaslighting their loyal subjects.

It is not a helpful or reasonable message to convey about The United States of America. It will remove legitimacy from the system, continuing to divide our people until violence from the next conflict swallows innocent bystanders forcing unnecessary casualties. Be better and promote better.

I do not see many solutions on the ballot; only the same talking points recycled every election by the same parties who represent themselves. When new leaders are elected, our issues do not disappear. If an election only contains choices represented by the limits that created our societal fractures, why are people not questioning the choices? The same choices continue to yield the same results. We can do better. We the People deserve better. We must Defend America Values.

Vote because you educated yourself and became a competent American who understands the system and the requirements to exercise such a privilege. The type that of American who formed this Nation because they understood what they were creating and why they were creating it. Make sure these people are of the class who will protect this Nation. Vote responsibly for who you feel is the best option for you and your family. It does not matter who you choose, as this is America, and we have the FREEDOM to do just that. But make sure that person is worthy of your vote because they represented competence and earned it. Voting is vital as it carries consequences; use that privilege responsibly. Educate, weigh all options, and make an informed decision. And no matter the outcome, America's system works. The reality is, as voters participating in a system that allows input, no winners or losers exist; only a celebration of FREEDOM!!! At times those we choose can create hardships, be wary of such people. Exercise this responsibly; our future depends on it.

Let us be better today than yesterday, better tomorrow than we are today. Let us show our children how to rise to the occasion when conflict exists and encourage dialogue to solve our issues. Please show kindness where it otherwise would not exist. If you are a Veteran, please stand and say enough is enough. One group must exist outside of the collective self-destructive madness this Nation is experiencing. It must be us—the group of men and women who transcend differences while accomplishing extraordinary things. We are the ones who change history. We are the reason for freedom. And our silence will be the reason freedom fails.

This is one of those moments. Stand with me. Let us Defend American Values and show the world our might once more. If we fail, our differences will no longer be our strength but our weakness, and America; nothing more than a thought read in history books by children who are taught what not to be.

To correct the destructive path, America must educate her citizens to become competent, sensible assets increasing their benefit to our Nation and society as a whole. It must start at a young age but also continue as an adult later in life. This education cannot be influenced by feelings, nor shall it be forced as an absolute when its purpose has identified itself as nothing more than a nuclear bomb fracturing the cohesive unity required to coexist with diversity and competing interests.

# Education

To understand the world around them and nurture equity, people sought knowledge to change what needed to be changed. Eliminating ignorance is the most important responsibility of an informed citizenry. Through this elimination, Americans can create progress and the peaceful existence of diverse free people. America cannot exist without this understanding. If people cannot remove ignorance, they will be unable to create peace, making the ability to coexist with one another unattainable.

America must commit to growing an informed, literate, and tolerant citizenry. Citizens who represent intelligence, not education, independence rather than dependence, acceptance rather than intolerance. This pursuit must create free thinkers, not sheep who are easily influenced by half-truths, a catchy political campaign, or a loud imbecile with a non-profit used to intimidate by destroying discourse.

"What is necessary will always be created." America needs to reinvent itself to transform education into intelligence, people into citizens, and distrust into patriotism. These endeavors would allow competency to exist in the majority, strengthening the resolve of a free people.

Dedicated people must commit to the motivation to remove ignorance to become informed citizens. This duty requires individuals to maintain and understand its purpose. Intelligence should never be used as a tool to create a class system. It must remain an instrument to remove ignorance and teach an agreeable curriculum achieving bench-marks and goals represented by what society reflects at the time and when the path of purpose[50] was developed, always representing what is true, not what is convenient. This knowledge must continue evolving based on the most widely accepted understanding by experts in the fields of study, never influenced by the number of people who believe falsities.

This is where the desirability and strength of liberal arts maintains its relevance as it has no limits. It transcends the idea of goals. It is a collaboration of disciplines and even fosters the hope of creating new knowledge. It will remain absolute, relevant, and outside the creation or destruction of disciplines because it can be used to encompass all knowledge—similarly beneficial and much like the critical perspective.

---

[50] A clear and concise curriculum represented by goals, bench-marks, and connected to a purpose of rationale intent not emotional trauma.

Not without or in place of other disciplines but in conjunction with. Americans can use this knowledge to maintain the balance between competing interests allowing the future generations to solve the past generation's transgressions, finally overcoming their limits. However, the curriculum must always include all accurate accounts of history and be wholly disconnected from nonsense. And accessibility to all people is a priority.

I never felt highly of myself as a child, adolescent, and young man. Still, today, I recognize the same system is in place that made me feel inferior to everyone around me. It made me feel as if I was unworthy of anything positive. It even fostered a feeling of being unaccepted in a place I did not want to be. How can a system, a governmental institution, create such a belief and defeat an innocent child? It succeeded and succeeds because it is a flawed system. It is a system made to promote memorization instead of intelligence. A system used to encourage repetition and discourage free thinking. A system that made me uncomfortable in school. And that very same system is what nearly made me give up because it gave up on me.

I was never able to learn the same way as other children. I do not believe I lack the intellectual capabilities necessary. It was difficult for me to learn anything unless it was taught in a specific way—over and over and over—allowing my brain to digest what was needed to understand what was taught. It was challenging for me to pick things up. Being the last person to understand what was necessary for the class was embarrassing. It was never a pleasant experience having teachers and students stare at me. So, I shut down, ignored what was necessary, and replaced it with something to keep me entertained.

Maybe the system failed me. Maybe I failed myself. Maybe it was a bit of both. I did not pick up on important things. I missed them because the lessons were missing something, or my teachers were missing something. I did not understand the purpose. If we teach children first, "how to learn" instead of "what to learn," the generation that follows will be the generation who changes the world. If bias is removed and these freshly minted souls are left to comprehend things on their own, imagine the problems they would solve, but more importantly, imagine the people they would tolerate.

I never understood the purpose of memorizing things that do not matter, and since our system is extremely kind to those who can remember things over those who can think, the system failed me and millions of others. Learning is a skill that can be refined, but people must be shown how to unlock this entrance and the purpose for opening that door.

I missed the purpose somehow. As time went by, I began to fail and learned I could teach myself to not only ignore my studies but to not care at the same time. I taught myself that it was okay "not to learn" because I didn't understand "how to learn." You see, when people understand that they can teach themselves not to care before someone shows them how to learn, what they talk themselves into is usually detrimental to self-preservation.

Understanding how and why our system operates the way it does is more important than memorizing information that can be easily recalled from a book. If the first lessons are" how we do things" and why we do those things this way, it allows children to understand why it is necessary to learn these things, and it may create suggestions to improve what others who memorize information solely for an exam missed.

The thoughts we use create purpose, which also decides what we desire. That is why purpose matters, and desires can be dangerous. Suppose people cannot see the purpose? Placing children at a young age in front of the appropriate door is important. As people age, it becomes harder because many people are not keen on destroying their comfort zone.

This is what the system does, "compliance over thought," because if you instruct children on the correct way to learn, they may very well change the way the system operates by making it more efficient, equitable, and appropriately beneficial to all people. Maybe that is the purpose, and it is working as intended. Whatever it is, it created unnecessary hardships, but these hardships later turned into wisdom that a teacher couldn't teach me.

The status quo nearly failed me, it succeeded by failing others, and it is permitting the continued failing of other children like me. Our system teaches children to memorize useless information, later promoting, celebrating, and even rewarding those who can prove their memorization skills on a test.

For what? So America's system can create a profit-driven market of educating the masses by adopting easily measurable proficiency exams and testing used to exclude rather than teach. What is even more corrupt and shameful, the external influences of the legislation process allowed the taxpayers to foot the bill. The government stepped in, subsidized student loans, and now Americans possess debt they cannot pay back because those we trusted used a lie to encourage people to believe in the necessity of college. College became funded by the public, and its price tag was no longer a consideration to worry about. This gave value to degrees that are worthless outside the income generated used to pay for ownership of a skill that is equally worthless.

What value does education have when degrees are created for jobs that pay the astronomical salaries of adults and their facilities used to coach other adults to play a children's game or create tenure for people to encourage indoctrination instead of free thought? This creates two problems. The first is that it negatively affects society's ability to value essential things by encouraging others to seek foolish endeavors used to entertain rather than seeking those that help in the bid to survive. The second is that it creates a need for supply represented by an illusion of a demand used to create a price point of education not worth the value paid for. This is a consequence of the monetization of education due to the gluttonous thirst of a capitalist economy.

If the plan is to educate, teach our citizens valuable things. Give lessons that encourage the adoption of the critical perspective and teach the necessary life skills that are valuable to society, such as reflexive tolerance and independent manifestation.[51] Not a curriculum that is aimed at earning more profits to expand the wish lists of the boosters. Schools are designing and using credit manipulation to mandate classes that do not have value but are requirements for graduation to feed the capitalistic addiction colleges have become a part of. A corrupt cycle is feeding corrupt people to protect a corrupt system.

And if I haven't convinced you of the destructive and detrimental purpose of our educational system, allow me to explain further. This book—all the information created, the graphs, charts, terminology, even the words representing my thoughts— would be impossible for me to remember ever again. If I had to take an exam based on this book, I would likely score between a high B or a low B, most likely a C.

---

[51] An education endeavor used to create a more tolerant, cohesive, and responsible citizenry who possess the means to survive without the government.

But the point is, how can a system used to reward intelligence promote people who can memorize knowledge over the ones who created the knowledge. I created it to ensure I would never have to remember it again. I will never forget it because I will forever have access to it, and I can recall it by reading when needed. Yet a person memorizing someone else's useless or useful information is given the greatest opportunities in society. Why? We know why. There is most undoubtedly strange behavior afoot.

Intelligence should never be based on memorization alone. It must be measured by other metrics such as the ability to teach oneself something, the ability to problem-solve, and how easy it is to convince a person of something. Explicit knowledge through education will only create an echo chamber of likeness, removing any progress to the next stage of evolution for society. It maximizes profit margins and should not be used as a viable means to measure intelligence, especially as a tool to promote or assume vocational competency.

Society cannot push those aside who think differently, learn differently, or possess skills, knowledge, and the ability to succeed without having gone to college. It is not equitable to continue educating and rewarding people for their ability to pay for it or those who can attend college because of circumstances. Educated idiots are among us, and they enjoy the benefit of privileged networking offered by a college degree. Not all people have access to these resources to gain positions of power or influence in government, politics, and the private sector, always excluding those who can never access such privileges. Education is a tool, a powerful one. A free people must be in control of this tool, not a private entity or the glutinous elite. Exclusion is not what education is for; its results are but never the access to it.

Each state must have a free system of postsecondary education to promote and encourage education. Not only for the purpose of learning but also for accepting the burden of such a cost. This will create citizens worthy of the freedoms granted, ensuring those who will and can protect this Nation are plentiful. In addition, the federal government should create an education system used expressly for employment in the government sector. Let the private sector control the free market and allow the government sector, states and federal, to manage their market. This would aid in the disparities associated with education, employment, and socioeconomic status and serve as a tool to create generational wealth, forever altering a family's station in life. Using a bench-mark graph would aid in such an endeavor.

The one thing that diversity through identities does more effectively than creating inclusion is to divide the included by category. The friction between what is understood and what is yet to be understood contributes to divisiveness. Ignorance of differences creates a barrier preventing cohesion or stalling the progression of purpose. The additional hardships are our differences represented by diversity. It is easier to hate differences as the decision is easily identifiable. Differences unintentionally divide people no matter the tolerance level of the individual. An education could close such a destructive gap.

Education should not be used to create division. Its purpose is to educate. It must be used as a teaching device to understand the past and apply it to the present, altering the future for the benefit of all people. If it is used to create hatred and encourage confrontation, be cautious, as conflict can arise from the consequences of this type of influence.

# Influence

Influence can be awe-inspiring, or it can be awfully dangerous, even deadly. It can be used to create or destroy, heal or corrupt, and weaponized to spread either the untrue or the true. Society must maintain the truth at all costs. This is what allows peace to be maintained. Society must also allow people to find what is true. What has an influence on society requires a failsafe to lessen the severity of the negativity it represents. A place where the truth is located. This must be outside of partisanship or any other bias that can be used to promote selfishness or corruption.

Influence is difficult to understand and recognize because people often allow it in their lives without even knowing it occurred. They are oblivious to people and the power they have over them as they are blinded by their own ignorance. People subconsciously choose to be ignorant because it is easy, and they cannot help it. They cling to likeness and shelter themselves from truths too offensive for their careless ways.

Many things must be untrue so something can be true. Not everything can be true and not everything can be false, but something must be true. Destruction of ignorance requires truth. The destruction of negativity involves the promotion of positivity. Where can society receive the truth and influence of a positive kind? The answer—it depends. What are they seeking? Is it likeness? Is it the truth? Is it the ease of digestion requiring less work? It may be a bit of everything. Are they wrong? Subjectively, no. They are searching for something, but it is not the truth. It is a group identity that controls self-identity.

Instead of discovering the truth, people prefer to ignore what is known by acquiring what is convenient. They seek a want to reinforce what their truth is but at the same time they seek a want to reinforce a desire to hate. At times it is subconscious; other times, it is intentional. Talk shows on news channels and social media posts are now where the masses get their news. What is worse, those outlets are not in short supply. There are too many places to obtain unverifiable or heavily biased information, readily available, easily consumable, and extremely believable. This information may or may not be accurate, but convincing people otherwise is nearly impossible. People believe in misinformation, practice disinformation, and will not agree on anything in modern society because people are offended by inconvenient news.

News that may attack a premise believed, identity owned, or a lifestyle practiced. And as this is the truth connected to a divided people, nothing will ever be true again because what is now true to a person resembles the person the most. This was caused because those with influence divided and continued to push differences to a breaking point. Spreading hate and unnecessary rhetoric with falsities that have the potential to create existential consequences. This is why influence that is controlled is influence that is exposed. It is vital to limit who influences people in society. However, those who have influence are controlled by those who receive influence. We just cannot help ourselves.

Important people and famous people are the influencers in society. A large difference exists between the two. It is encompassed by a definite value represented by the truth. One of these people society can live without. The other, they cannot. One of these carries a necessity for society. The other does not. One of these invites' fanciful iterations of destruction. The other will not.

I say this with the utmost respect to those doing the right thing and the utmost disrespect to those who are doing less than required. The selfishness of people is highly insulting and dangerous to freedom.

Ignoring what must be done, they continue to bask in the glory of themselves, celebrating anything that is them, doing nothing but creating a narcissistic, self-absorbed society, and the masses are following. Me, me, me, I, I, I. What about me? I am offended.

People allow themselves and their identities to be controlled by negative influence, no matter how illogical or detrimental the behavior is. As long as it makes them happy. As long as others are aware of their existence. As long as someone is paying attention to their greatness. People create videos in the hopes of satisfying the hunger and thirst of the growing monster, which feeds off an internal desire for vanity. But these do nothing but document how complacent society has become making it easy for future historians to come to the conclusion, "no wonder their civilization died off!"

It is easier to dance in unison while filth is playing in the background to achieve fame than it is to educate yourself to be important. When people monetize filth, it creates a worthless population that will be invaded by an external force, or they will eventually die from internal putrefaction because they no longer have value.

All because the next dance flavor on Tik Tok controls the direction of our youth, allowing its trend of perversion and corruption to devour. This is the addiction that all social media platforms offer. People consume it and assume it is important as the views and trends are enticing to mimic what is being done. Monkey see monkey do, including adults. And not one person from these unnecessary platforms sees the sickness for what it is.

The instantaneous knowledge of what someone is doing creates competition for likes, views, and a need to have importance in society; however, what they are doing is not important to society. What is shared, what is liked, and what is viewed must be less and less decent, so it may create more and more interest.

People no longer perform kind acts unless the camera is rolling. If it is not, it will be turned on before aid is given, compassion shared, or the necessary thing is done, all in the hopes that people see how virtuous they are. It is mandatory to document their good deeds, so their perception of self-greatness is known. Altruism is lost on those who seek this and intend to broadcast their kindness.

It is reflective of an addiction replacing worth with value and importance with fame. It is a drug, highly addicting and detrimental to all.

The longer people consume filth, the more filth is needed to pleasure the brain. The longer people stay ignorant, the less it takes to stimulate the brain. People have created the filthiest, most ignorant society in the history of our species. Social media has destroyed society, forever altering the understanding of how humanity lives, what humanity seeks, and what humanity values. The mass production of the temptations of man has destroyed our environment, our peace, and our ability to save ourselves. What occurs will happen, and what happens will occur. What people are responsible for is both.

Let us get back to important people being our children's heroes and role models, enjoying the gratification of our esteem. Actors, entertainers, models, athletes, and social media superstars are famous rich, representing an unneeded, an unimportant, and an undesirable influential effect. They represent no value and live outside the value continuum. It does not mean these people are bad or not important in contributing to society, nor should they be without praise for what they do. It only means they do not possess anything that is necessary as a profession substantively for the survival of people, nor is their absence from life a great loss when comparing what humanity requires from important people within a society.

Take a close look at those who contribute nothing and those who contribute famous things. The value of what they give to society is strictly zero unless you factor in the entertainment value. But they are closely related and almost identical in contribution. Do not let imbecilic people and those with zero value and low worth influence children. The world should mourn the loss of the soldier, the police officer, the firefighter, the scientist, the doctor, the teacher, the thinker, and the leader more so than the loss of the sports player, the album seller, the person with the greatest following, or the greatest superficial prize. To be offensively honest, any identity in the former, no matter the level of competency, is most likely more valuable than any identity in the latter. Celebrating what is worthless over what has value will create consequences as the scales can never balance or reconcile with the truth.

America has an interest in protecting the youth of our Nation to ensure they do not become the plague of our Nation. America also has an interest in protecting those who are granted the opportunity to live such a wonderful life. A balance must be maintained through an understanding of what is necessary and what is a luxury. People must recognize what is required and what is a convenience. The government must protect and promote what is vital by dismissing what is not.

## Covid-19 and The Many Lies Infecting Truth

This book is not the place to discuss the government's many failures, those with influence, and the innocent who believe both. This pandemic is real, a threat to our stability, and is working exactly as intended by those who seek to ruin what they can never be a part of.

Our society can do many things to mitigate the spread of the virus, ensure our normalcy is minimally disrupted, and stand for freedom, so individual rights are protected but at the same time protect those who are vulnerable. We must unite to overcome this threat, but first, we must deal with what divided us in the first place. These are all related and prevent our cohesive structure from solving what must be solved. Sometimes what we know limits what we will never learn or what we will never become.

Being cautious when information is not readily available is important as was the case during the onset of this global pandemic. But contradictory views based on political bias should not occur, at least not in the understanding that one or more answers exist with what is true. Science must prevail, and because science must prevail, truth must also be what guides our society. Our leaders must be able to discuss what is occurring and agree to a course of action benefiting people, society, and what allows us to exist in an economy dependent on participation.

Also, the medical community cannot be divided, and our ability to adjust what we know to better inform citizens remains of the utmost importance. This pandemic was terrible enough; what concerns me is the next one. Rather or not, I am or we are a part of it, history will dictate how the future responds. For our children's sake, I hope they do a better job partly by swallowing their pride and admitting when they were wrong as necessary.

Hopefully, it is as far from election day as possible to limit the political machine's power constantly lying to control the masses by influencing voting. The most important question for the future: what will I do? Will I make the situation worse, or will I aid in solving it? That choice absolutely matters. And because it matters, our leaders must set an example worth following. It can never be different rules for different people. If people observe our leaders not following the rules they set, what is the purpose of any rules, especially the Rule of Law?

In each recognition of what must be altered, upheld, and protected, Americans must come together, putting aside their differences, to protect each other. We must also force the acceptance that people have an interest in protecting their life no matter the consequences or the offensiveness of the means to do so. This permission is not granted by a man, because it is a right earned and created through death because it cannot be taken away, only reinforced by more death.

Lastly, our Nation needs to commit to promoting participation in society and use this participation to add value to an already wonderful way of life. If people fail to participate, resigning themselves to a way of life that is highly vulnerable to toxic idleness, they should be limited to the amount of influence they have. Their existence has neither value nor worth unto a creation that requires both. If they are unwilling to self-promote and create a better version of themselves, influence is something they should never possess.

But freedom is a paradox of limitless alternatives or restrictions, each with the possibility of destroying our way of life. Figuring out how to balance these will always be the fight. And the need has never been greater.

It is time...

# A Place for Your Thoughts:

# CHAPTER IX

## *A Time for Peace A Time for Truth*

In life, obstacles and people are intentionally placed in our way to influence the path we take and the person we become. Our experiences with these events and our interactions with these people can alter life for better or worse. My life has changed, was influenced by, and sometimes even altered by those placed in my path. Either positively or negatively, I was fortunate to meet and cross paths with these people. I am beyond blessed for the gift of simply knowing these individuals. I am better for it with zero doubt regardless of the type of influence their existence provided because each lesson was equally valuable.

This path is continuous, but it is all connected and led me to this very moment at 5:30 in the morning as I am trying to type through sleepy eyes. I do not believe in coincidences. I think that each individual navigates this path, and we are drawn to a specific place in time within our life span. People have referred to it as destiny, fate, God's plan, among many other descriptors, all being used to describe an external force guiding people in a predetermined fashion. Whatever it is, I have always been a benefactor of such a premise.

Even at times when my mind wanted to end the pain, wanted to destroy the pain, and wanted to quit the pain. I tried to make sense of it all and realized I might never possess such an understanding. But I am aware of what is right, what is wrong, what is just, and what is unjust. I am not easily influenced, and because of this, I am able to recognize the ignorance and the destruction it causes or can cause. I also know people can be cruel and incapable of projecting the respect I often give. However, this allows me to clearly see them for who they are, along with their ugly "truth" and equally ugly nature.

This is my truth, the truth I want to be known for, and the truth I seek to create. I made a decision to represent all through an understanding based on mutual respect and a belief all people deserve freedoms by and through a God of their choosing or no God at all. The truth is simple; I am not afraid. I am not afraid to live my truth anymore. I am no longer afraid to voice my opinion. I am no longer afraid to speak my mind. My truth is not selfish, destructive, or intolerant. That is their truth; it will not be mine. The division is their goal; it will not be mine. Hate is their identity; it will not be mine.

I fear the place our people are creating. I one day may no longer be invited nor welcome to live in America and have no idea where I belong anymore. America was meant to work for its people and protect each. Instead, I see nothing but hate, anger, and the internal desire to inflict pain on what is different. I am saddened by the decisions of our forefathers and those who agree to ignore the issues. I don't know what the answer is, but I know the leaders we follow have a great deal to answer for. They either inspire hope and offer solutions to our greatest problems or create issues and exacerbate our worst fears by ignoring the cause of our potential demise.

Weak people stand for what is easy. They divide because they cannot lead. They encourage intolerance, promoting hate for a chance to feel important. They do not possess what is required to alter a path of destruction because they are the creators of such a device. They choose the direction of incompetent manifestation out of a selfish will just to seek legitimacy.

I know great leaders are forged, created, and born of necessity. They do not self-promote and are certainly not concerned with the materialistic tragedy the world is suffering from. They are not scared to promote peace by destroying the wicked. Their motivations are pure, representing the character and the person their path created.

Great leaders defend the Rule of Law. They are not afraid to protect. They are guided by righteousness. A leader does not measure themselves by the destruction caused or intimidation created. They do not support dangerous ideology by encouraging detrimental behavior, nor do they tolerate such a divisive existence. They are not intimidated, nor are they deterred by an ignorant mob of thugs who destroy peace by terrorizing the innocent. And they certainly do not cave to mayhem because a social media platform or its idiotic equal of a news agency promotes a cult narrative backing foolish instigators.

Eventually, those who are tolerated become legitimate and gain exactly what they were looking for. It is equally true that if the government, the people who are put in the position of faith, fail to control havoc by tolerating what is detrimental to a free people, they no longer serve a purpose, and it is time for them to be replaced. By force, if necessary.

America's system of governance, including those with influence, demands intelligence, strength, and thinkers who can properly identify areas of concern and accurately assign fault to the cause and later solve the underlying issue. The world is full of great thinkers and intelligence, yet they chase money, fame, and other pursuits of a selfish nature, ignoring their true calling.

A system that requires growth and accountability must have thinkers who apply new and emerging ideas in practice to confirm or destroy what is considered. Those who lead must be both thinkers and creators. Leaders who unite people to create a better tomorrow by promoting diversity of thought, identity, and convictions allow freedom to flow as it was intended to.

Those who create theories with a point of press through publishing companies do nothing for society but allow ignorance to latch onto half-truths and divide people. Their pursuit of money and fame has clouded their judgment threatening peace. Those people, the chasers of intellectual supremacy, are not solving the issues—they are, in fact, creating issues because they never attempt to solve them in real-time, with real people, with real results.

I have grown impatient observing the failures and willful ignorance of a people, a government, and the incompetence represented by both. Your fear is motivated by a misguided pursuit to appease those who must be ignored. You are allowing the innocent to be held hostage by bad behavior. A time will come when you and they will have offended too much. It is nearing; be forewarned.

Peace is slowly waning as it is from the absence of strong leadership. What is sowed will control. Your weakness may be as costly as your existence in your position of influence. You cannot control what you are unable to stop. Chaos is what awaits. Are you willing to die for the division and destruction you have caused? Modern society is not different than past societies. People will not stand for weak leadership. This is what you represent, and this is what represents you.

I was told I could never lead. Because I do not pick sides, they believe that I am incapable of leading. But I will not jeopardize what I stand for to play their game. I do not seek inclusion in a group that believes they are superior. I do not choose an unnecessary identity because the one I do choose; represents all. What I represent, is America. If I am not good enough to lead because this is what I represent, then maybe it's time I leave America because she does not represent me.

I am many things. I do not pick one over the other and will not participate in that behavior, especially with people. I try to be as open and honest as I possibly can about everything. I will not dismiss differences or competing thoughts, but I will challenge them. People must learn to listen and extend the same courtesy they often demand. Respect is reciprocal and very necessary to the survival of peace. Together people can change the world if that is their intent. Disagree with civility, knowledge, and the commitment to always use both.

Incompetence should not be protected, sheltered, or encouraged. Not a single person should be safe. Criticism and thoughts used to improve ourselves and others are for all and must not discriminate based on factors such as age, race, religion, sexual orientation, political affiliation, or any other identifier.

I am for equal rights and equity. I wish for nothing more than to see progress between people. I want all sides to participate in dialogue, come together, and make a substantial change for the entire world. Everyone is equal and should only be judged by their actions. This is the creator of equality, not group power. There is nothing special about being black or white, nor does a sexual orientation deserve to be celebrated. Those do nothing but separate by identity used to create classes for the purpose of division and separation—Expressio unius est exclusio alterius.

If you do not respect this Country, respect her flag, or respect the Rule of Law, it is time for you to leave. If you are fed up with the freedoms you are not worthy of, take everyone who thinks like you, looks like you, acts like you, and leave. If this bothers you, raise an army, start a war to create whatever nation of people you desire with whatever rules you want to enforce. We have already played this game. I will not sit idly to let it be destroyed by the likes of you.

Weakness is all you represent. You are nothing more than traitors with treasonous intent. People and leaders like you cannot be trusted as your loyalty is not our Nation, containing all differences, but instead to a nation of your likeness. The best Nation has already been created, and it protects us all with freedoms through the Constitution. It was born of brave people whose only identity and belief represented the will to follow the red, white, and blue—an idea of protection and freedom. Our Nation already contains the best race—free people. It took time, but here we are.

It sure as hell was not formed by those who spit on soldiers, burn the American flag, kneel at the National Anthem, ignore the Rule of Law, create angry mobs when events do not represent preference, or shoot police officers because you can. Your actions are misplaced and misguided. Those are representations of toxicity that arise from failed leadership and not from a failed nation. Those behaviors should never occur in this Country. People should love their country, and the nation that offers protection even while she is in the process of growing, but this fact seems to elude the understanding of many. People create hard times. The Rule of Law of this Nation combined with the strength to lead prevent hard times.

I do not want to live in a place, a country, or a world where I constantly defend what evidently protects those who cannot comprehend what is necessary or required to maintain our freedoms. You are second-class citizens, if even that. Not because of your race, religion, political affiliation, or beliefs but because of your actions, you don't deserve to be here.

Why should I be afraid of some ignorant misfit group hell-bent on creating chaos in my Country, stabbing me in the back, attacking my people, destroying our peace with the intent to collapse stability? If the government does not stop it, eventually, the people will. History is a hard lesson to learn when it is felt and not read. Leaders responsible and those who threaten peace will be targeted and eliminated.

Tolerance of behavior that is unacceptable has brought us to this point. People will remember once again that when they have control, what is allowed, is just that. How else do people express concern with the way society is mismanaged? What does history tell us? When the patriots of a nation, those who believe in what she stands for, those who understand that she is worth dying for, when they had enough, they will not be stopped. It is time for peace; it is time for truth before neither of those is present.

People must be open to different perspectives and allow those ideas to exist side by side with their own. A failure to do this will result in the continuation of the status quo, never-changing, always in conflict with one another. Incompetency creates issues that cause unnecessary conflicts and tensions around the world.

For what purpose and to what end? All because my God is different, my parent's skin color is a shade or two lighter/darker than yours, or I love someone you may think is too similar. Have we not watched enough violence and allowed it to have control for most of our existence? People do not have peace because they do not seek peace. We know what hate and anger can accomplish; let us see what love and tolerance can erase.

What is the purpose of continuing to create a path of destruction? Read, learn, understand, share, and repeat. You don't have to agree with people, just acknowledge differences as they may be your own but viewed from a different perspective. From a different perspective and through the eyes of another, you are different. The identity given is nothing compared to the identity chosen.

Does the difference make them wrong, or is it how you perceive these differences? If people learn to love and accept others blind to their visual privilege, imagine the relationships they could build on substance. Think about the relationships you denied simply because of differences. Actions create consequences of intent. If you knew what you were about to do could make the world a better or worse place, would you still do it?

What starts as a small change can transform into something more significant. As people start to see their likeness in differences, they become more willing to participate in the discourse necessary to create understanding. America's Constitution is perfect. It balances competing interests wonderfully by giving ways to protect autonomy and the innocent from persecution and oppression. Still, people must be willing to live with differences to create a single similarity. Yes, our people are different. That is why we are all here, to be protected from groupthink, oppression, and tyranny. America is for all.

History shows us the right way to lead and govern people because we have evidence of thousands of years of doing it wrong. Since we only ever get to be a part of and a fraction of the entire timeline of the human condition, we judge harshly as our reality, and contextual understanding of life before us is limited by words, not emotions. It is easy for us to stand

304

and judge those before us, as it will be easy for those who are right now at this current moment, reading history books of us, judging our actions.

Human beings are flawed creatures and not worthy of leading on their own for the greater good, as selfishness usually destroys any honorable intention. People are learning and growing as a society. It takes time to create the progress people seek. But it also takes the right people, the correct Constitution, and unwavering commitment to do it.

Tolerance is the key to building acceptance and peace, as intolerance is key to building hate and conflict. Do not force what must occur naturally, as this is the evolution of peace. It has been said many times before that what is untrue, unwise, or unkind should never control words, actions, or beliefs, but why the abstinence of these ignorant reiterations is extremely important—these are the tricks of the devil, a way to create conflict and consume the souls of the damned.

The greatest weakness of leadership is a fear of criticizing those represented and the likeness shared because it takes strength to say what is true; more importantly, it takes honesty. Attacking someone or something different from the reflection in the mirror is easy—Hitler-esque even. How often have you highlighted the bad parts of your identity by speaking the unbridled truth to yourself and to your kind?

Society will always struggle to maintain a trajectory of perpetual positivity and inclusion as those who achieve such a wonderful existence are soon gone through the expiration date of life. The ones continuously replacing our wisest are unlikely to follow in the footsteps of greatness since those life lessons are unteachable through the trials and tribulations of others. Nor are the enlightened able to share in the marvels of their life by speaking and paying forward what is finally known.

These are simply empty words without context.

People cannot learn these through instruction. Youth seldom agrees or listens as ignorance is the default setting of humans. What must be learned is not by the hand of those before us or those appointed above us. Our journey can only transfer it. The path, its many hardships inflicted on the individual, and what life has taken, given, and shown has finally opened our eyes and the consciousness deep in our hearts, minds, and souls. We owe this to whatever faith we choose or belief we follow, allowing our enlightenment to encourage equity, justice, and love for our fellow man. Finally, using self-realization to create the best version of ourselves.

Upon discovering that this version of ourselves is only waiting for a commitment to obtain such a pure form of human life, people become aware and highly sensitive to their surroundings. Life becomes so much more troublesome as worries invade our spirit because we are finally aware of the falsities being spoon-fed into the mouths of the willing and the dangers associated with broken people.

What is true is simply acceptance. It is nothing more than what an individual is willing to accept, and usually, the lies consumed are lies repeated. Our leaders do this because they know it is so much easier to rely on others as the available knowledge in the world is infinite. So they and their megalomaniac media goon squad weaponize what is necessary to stir discontent. Unfortunately, not a single person has the time or motivation to become well-versed in what is necessary to destroy all the abounding ignorance.

Instead, people rely on experts, specialists, and those who committed the time to become educated. Still, the fatal flaw in this is the truth they speak is the truth they formed by manipulating information that best fits their bias. This favors their position because it allows the framing and the creation of what they make true to be influenced by lies because people find agreeance in whatever likeness they closely identify with.

It does nothing but encourages those with influence, power, and authority to change laws, alter the education system, and create new knowledge with pieces of information to remake what is known in their image. Gods are what they want to be, and making enemies of innocent people is the first step in purging what prevents success by destroying those who disagree with them.

This occurs because people lack the capacity, competency, or compassion to represent anything other than what they know, what they look like, and their feelings created by the half-truths consumed through selective creation. Differences amount to nothing more than a sickness as these are irrelevant to the survival of their people—mere obstacles to overcome, overthrow, and destroy.

The error of choosing this type of representation is, of course, attributed to the lack of contextual understanding of the failures of civilizations and societal structures of times past. Each representative of the same fight, the same argument, the same selfish desire to not only control but to assume power at any cost necessary:

"For the fate of our system of government demands, we eliminate all who threaten our way of life."

The creation of banners or flags, the raising of an army by inciting discontent with words, and the criticism needed to convince people later to destroy peace so that the violence necessary to alter the status quo can be readily available only waiting on that first fatal shot. Wars usually start with knowledge, but ignorance is another word for what people know.

The decision to work together toward a determinative outcome has always created peace and war. However, each path is sown, created, or made by the same thing, a choice. Eventually, people grow tired of living with one another because weakness in the form of leadership spouts nonsense to those looking for an excuse to live out the fantasy of violence that hides deep in all of us. The intoxication of thoughts from committing injuries behavior on our enemies. It consumes our souls as we watch those who hate us dubiously make falsities and asinine statements as a rallying cry.

You know the type—deplorables, libtards, republiKKKans, Trumpets, and the chant "lets go Brandon" or any other one-sided absolute. But it seems as time moves forward and the inclination to publicly harass those who are different changes. What we attack changes. It turns from specifics to a general group—Christians, white people, black people, Muslims, Mexicans, Men, Pro-this, Pro-that. Not attacking an idea but the group itself including the decency contained within each. Doing nothing but poisoning people for political gain. And this poison releases a particular type of chemical, and the next time the person sees the trigger, a duty becomes evident. And the justification is concrete.

The animalistic urge to defend our pack, our territories, and our way of life is awakened, creating yet another stain for our children's children to read as a sad chapter in history books. But it will quickly be read and forgotten because what we do harms only us. Depending on the outcome of the conflict—what side was able to kill more through the destruction of the military or outlasting the enemy—will eventually force a peace treaty to end hostilities between two parties. This gives the victor and the framers authority to create the narrative of choice for blame and hopefully destroy the ideology accused of treason.

The spoils of war will create a new truth. A truth society will accept as violence solves all things because whatever a person is willing to die or kill for, in the name of whatever they believe, was always right in their mind. The atrocities committed were justified. What is worse, they have convinced themselves of everything they already needed to know. So what the world is left with is the cycle of destruction—continuously forcing innocent people to be consumed by the desires, the diseases, the disgustingness of those drunk with power. Each reckless endeavor destroys the power of choice for those who do not want war. Therefore, we must proceed with caution.

Do not target the innocent. Do not be unnecessarily cruel to those without fault and bear no resemblance to those you shun. Control your tongue, temper, and tantrums as these faults resonate only with those who share these unattractive characteristics, typical in badly behaved and temperamental children who are yet to mature. You must get past these limits at some point in your life by attempting to truly understand those who are different, even though this may be unagreeable with your convictions.

Historians do not engage with deniers, agitators, or the ignorant, nor do they accept less than the truth. These are attributes worthy of divinity. Virtuous people will change the world; it cannot be done by imposters who lack self-control, suffer from entitlement issues, or have ulterior motives of promoting themselves while dismissing and discouraging others.

Their identity should not be promoted higher than all others, and neither should their arrogance be allowed to fill the smallest room or dominate interactions with others. These are foundational requisites of the division required to start a war and the sociopathic playback used to destroy peace among diverse people. What they possess is not strength, nor is it leadership. On the contrary, it represents a position that will always be defended by better people than them on a battlefield. Their weakness will always stand behind both the strength and the blood of the innocent as their character sorely lacks strength's innocent courage.

It is no coincidence that the worst of society and their ignorant, worthless, selfish leaders are responsible for the decline of peace throughout history, owning entire liability for the conflicts and atrocities their behavior caused. Unfortunately, these horrendous acts are never measured correctly. Somehow the totality of the circumstances is forgotten. The cause or what occurred leading up to the breakdown of society is forgotten. However, these fractures cannot be ignored as the structural integrity of even the sturdiest foundational stronghold can be destroyed by the simplest of imperfections. We must recognize these.

These imperfections—emboldened ignorant people who encouraged other ignorant people—lead to the destruction of truth, which leads to the destruction of tolerance, which leads to the collapse of cohesive unity among the people in even the strongest nation. They are in possession of a nuclear bomb created in the closet by extremists who are angry at something but unable to figure out the cause because their small minds prevent an understanding of what is causing it, let alone how to fix it.

So, they blame what they already do not like because they are racist, sexist, anti-capitalist, anti-gun, anti-gay, anti-American, and finally, anti-freedom. They do this because each person who is a hypocritical closet bigot never pays the price of freedom. When the majority fails to bear the cost of freedom, it produces the most spoiled, ungrateful, weakest, and culturally sick members of society that humanity ever allowed. If not altered, this path will create the most devastating revolution in the history of civilization.

I'm tired of the left, I'm tired of the right; I'm tired of the black, I'm tired of the white. I am tired of their commitment to engage in extreme hyperbolic intolerance. Each imbecilic group continues to be unapologetic, either denying truths or making up their own. No discourse, no peer review, only absolutism shoved down the throats of their sympathizers, their deniers, and the most controversial group to each—those who seek the truth, the innocent.

This truth, the truth the innocent seek, is something correct, not emotional. They are looking for a truth disconnected from bias entangled in actuality suspended far above virtue signaling, victim claiming, and unchallenged rhetoric of the irresponsible kind. But unfortunately, people are slowly losing their way. It has become intolerable to watch, disheartening, and deeply troublesome. It saddens me to be a part of a nation that would rather fight than get along and dismiss differences rather than accept them. Somehow we enjoy berating people instead of educating people.

I've grown accustomed to separating myself from people who cling to their likeness as if it is the only version of the truth. They call anyone who looks different or thinks different wrong. Therefore, they are not only inferior but also an enemy who has destroyed a great way to live or are preventing progress. Sometimes the most intelligent people are the dumbest people, filled with so much arrogance that they have corrupted their cognitive powers to the point where they cannot see how flawed their belief systems have become.

Their brains have convinced themselves that everything they believe, consume, and do is correct. It is, in fact, the only viable option when a competing viewpoint presents itself. This type of behavior is not the purpose of our system of governance. These people are dangerous because they convince themselves of something that can destroy our cohesive structure. Each owning positions similarly related to Hitler, those who deny the holocaust was actual or any creation formed out of fanciful illusions of grandeur as they attack what is at odds with their subjective reality.

History is a strange concept. It's viewed differently and is created to be different depending on the perception, participation, and identity of those who consume, educate, or control. But history should never lie. Its feelings cannot be hurt. Its identity cannot change. It cannot even affect what "is" unless people grant permission. It only continues uninterrupted because it is granted authority it has not earned.

History has nothing to do with the currency of existence that people use presently. Sure, it and all the people who participated in actions have put our reality here out of consequences, but history is an ending. It must remain suspended in time, preventing the repetition clause humanity keeps authorizing from activating. It cannot be allowed to repeat. It requires those in the present to understand it in its entirety, and we must accept what occurred to prevent emotional expression from destroying peace.

The future is created from the past, but the past is the only thing used to destroy the future. The future cannot destroy the past, but the past can destroy our future. Unfortunately, ignorant, intolerant imbeciles continue to alter our future because they cannot let go of the past.

Accountability is, of course, a fundamental concept that limits retribution by assigning guilt and issuing punishment. Still, it should not bend to the will of those who wield platforms, power, or possess control of those who encourage conflict, ignore compassion, and dismiss one another for a chance to exact revenge on innocent identities.

To what end are people willing to produce yet another error and stain in history? Has not the account of man provided enough clues and texts citing what occurs when people fail to heed the advice left from those more competent to understand what is on the horizon when division is present? This is not the time to create more friction by removing discourse and encouraging discord. The framers understood what is correctly identified as the threat to freedom, peace, and our way of life.

Of course, America will have internal conflicts and disagreements as we look different, speak differently, pray differently, love differently, and think differently—we cannot control the discrepancies between our diversity only how we respond to and settle what is unagreeable, unappreciated, or unsolvable.

We must love what we cannot understand, not for the sake of acceptance or surrendering personal convictions but to prevent the cycle of destruction of society. Human civilization has been a victim repeatedly since the first disagreement, the first difference, and the first choice to make competing viewpoints or the great many diversities available, inferior to our own.

"I don't like that man. I must get to know him better."

—Abraham Lincoln

What America shares is unique, beautiful, but also littered with mistakes, tragedies, and triumphs. We cannot dismiss the horrible choices in hindsight. Yet, we can neither forget the righteousness fought for nor the history of the undeniable strength and advancements our people fought for by pursuing a greater nation, a greater people, and a greater peace.

No living creature has the authority to forgo mercy or destroy forgiveness upon those many growing pains the world has suffered through, especially at the cost of freedom and the destruction of tolerance. So why pursue such a selfish desire, filled with a superiority complex and the need to be legitimate. A purpose of destroying and waging war against those who have zero responsibility for actual suffering, perception of suffering, or the illusion of suffering.

Do not lie to destroy. Fight the addiction to create a narrative represented by an internal desire to kill one another out of anger. The road being paved will not be kind to our children and very well may destroy their hopes, dreams, and the innocence they possess. We need not pursue conflict as it is unnecessarily cumbersome to the human soul as it rots the potential for everything that can be good in man.

When the United States and the People who represent each difference respectively decide to unite through division instead of uniting through and for peace, freedom dies, and a state of hatred slowly engulfs the soul of our Nation. Even through the turbulent times, what once held us together is an understanding that a people, regardless of where they are from, the attributes they represent, or the thoughts they consider to be reasonable, will always make us stronger together.

The trial for what is just is upon us. What is worth fighting for must be fought for. The people who crave instability have created it. The trail that led us here is disappearing. The path worth fighting for must be fought for. The people who seek destruction have started it.

Who among us will try to disband this wonderful Nation, and the peace our collective union represents?

Who among us will fight to hold this wonderful Nation, together and the peace our collective union represents?

Unfortunately, this is not the first-time divisions have risen. I am troubled by the toxicity of human nature and its perpetuity and propensity to destroy, especially when taking such a path is strongly advised against, strengthened by horrific evidence. We have lessons taught by history's fallen leaders, caused by history's villains, all created by history's prior wars—all representing history's many mistakes. Something must change, and it is incumbent on all Americans to take a stand. The corruption, the intolerance, and the lies must end.

It is time for catharsis in American politics—a way to cleanse the sickness that has developed over the years. The will of equity, equality, and accountability must occur as intended, or all the progress over the last centuries will be for naught. Americans must reach diversed equilibrium if our society is to survive. The world admired what America accomplished. A system of governance and a Rule of Law allows differences and diversity to live in a constant support state. Each willing to defend and die for one another.

I am blessed every day to live in a place that gives me the protection to worship a God I choose. To express my opinions and beliefs, free from fear of retribution from the government or private citizens. This place gives me the freedom to marry and love whomever I want. An interpretation of an original document guarantees those freedoms. One I am willing to die for at any moment because what I have is very special to me.

I will do this without hesitation, even for people who hate that I fell in love with a black woman who is an immigrant from Ethiopia. We share the most fantastic feeling ever experienced, and it is the most important identity I have. This devotion to her and the love I receive is possible only because our system allows it. People fought for it, and to honor what I have and honor those before me, I will die to defend America, and I will not hesitate to kill to protect it. I believe in equality, the freedom to exist, the need to protect, and the desire to change. And I will defend it, all of it.

Weakness grabs power and convinces other weakness to change the natural order so that they feel positive in a world represented by strength. That weakness is consumed by emotions limited by truth. People should be hesitant to allow equality to represent a lowering of the bar so all can achieve. Instead, it must mean the opportunity for participation by allowing all a chance to reach the bar. The standards and benchmarks of success must remain reflective of the amount of work people put in to accomplish success, equal to the difficulty required to succeed, not the ease of passing or giving for inclusion.

That is not equality??? It is a fantastic lie people convince each other of because a modern understanding of equality still represents the costumes people wear instead of the actions that define a particular person. Its cause is the need to create representation to obtain, maintain, and acquire power that they are unworthy and equally undeserving of.

A continued effort to force equality where it is not merited is ultimately detrimental—actions, character, content, control equal; it is never a gender, race, or religion. People should not forget this, as the package we cover our soul with is irrelevant to the value contained within.

Equality allows people, regardless of their differences, to succeed in a world filled with perceived entitlement. The chance that the underdog slays the giant. The ability of the minority to rule the majority. A pursuit of oneself against the backdrop of overwhelming odds. Equality represents a chance to pursue.

A race or a gender does not make you superior or weaker. So is true for the bank account one has the luxury of access to. Regardless of how hard the human species tries, they cannot change what they cannot control. Outside emotions and feelings are where the natural order of life must remain. Those who are weaker are entitled to equal treatment in society concerning access to amenities, protections, and freedoms. But when it comes to holding positions that require the ability to achieve and ownership of competency, the stronger should be unequivocally favored.

America's way of life can change in a blink of an eye. The system we have can be disrupted and completely removed in a matter of minutes, collapsing the ability of the weak to survive. Essential life skills, the strength to survive without conveniences, and possessing knowledge outside what the majority practice must never be absent.

In a world without conveniences, will someone's feelings matter when the necessity of food is based on the ability for it to be obtained by the individual?—if a person cannot get it, they will not have it. Goodwill and giving represent can, not shall. Weak people need strong people to survive. Do not weaken or demonize the strong for the value contained on social media with views and likes reserved for a selfish endeavor motivated by virtue signaling, so other people think highly of you.

Strength must remain and the natural order protected. Do not make people weaker to save or protect their feelings and inclusivity. Encourage them to be stronger so they can survive in the event they must. There exists a world outside of grocery stores, therapists, frozen yogurt, and the ability to stream imbeciles on reality shows. It is always around the corner and a dangerous proposition for the weak.

It is an absurd premise and against logic to convince people that everyone is equal as their value and worth is neither. People are not equal, but all should have the opportunity to be more than those around them if they so choose. Unfortunately, modern society has blindly ignored the consequences of such a proposition.

Protection of the strong is equivalent to the protection of the weak. Convincing people that strength is toxic will serve only to enslave them by dividing them into classes according to likeness. The natural order controlled by truths is unaffected by those who seek to find offense in the actions of others. Feelings are irrelevant to survival.

It is also true that weakness is created, as is strength. There is a reason why great militaries and accomplishments of history's past cared not for feelings but represented a condition associated with strength and the desire to overcome. A decision to view society in a coddled vacuum is a decision to see—only what an illusion is. This poses a threat to a people's survival. The further away from the truth people travel, the further away from the strength they will be.

People must adapt and overcome, not try to control what's uncontrollable. Believing people are victims in life creates more victims. Tragedies are simply a day living or dying. This is the birthplace of survival. It is neither right nor wrong, just a consequence of living. Did we have so much peace, so much freedom, and too many amenities we forgot?

Is this what's destined to reoccur? Is this what war is? Do people become too weak because everything has been made easier for the newer generation, so the time once used for survival is now used to fight one another?

Has society as a whole ever wondered or cared why we are destined to destroy as people continue to plummet into the same toxic behavior as those before us? Even when people believe they are on the superior side of evolutionary thought and logical inferences, it does nothing but add to the chaos that pushes peace to the limit.

Speaking down and dismissing people as irrelevant or their thoughts as unimportant concerning a perceived elevated status is detrimental to tolerance. No matter the differences, people believe and form an opinion for a reason. People must recognize this and offer patience and understanding instead of anger and discontent. Respect the foundation of the thought-forming process before executing a verdict of inferiority. Freedom of expression gives people the ability to express externally, not think internally.

Most people seldom think of a competing opinion as equal and certainly pass judgment upon those who took the time to either express it or stand by it. Should we not offer recognition of respect and extend understanding to those brave enough to stand against a populous thought or those who voice their opinion? Can we respect the courage to stand no matter the side of elitism the stones are hurled from? At the very least, offer a chance for dialogue so competing views may have the opportunity to develop an understanding and mutual respect for one another.

Is it too much to reach into the depths of our cognitive machine and work the problem correctly before blurting out a short-sighted answer without showing our work? All this does is create animosity while concluding a different solution or identity is not only wrong but offensive? This does nothing to help America's cohesive structure, only further dividing what must be united.

Issues will arise as people cling to a moral and ethical high ground while casting those who fail the purity test to misfit island. Showing them no mercy as superior beings perched high above the serfs, forever casting them as inferior. In reality, all this does is nothing but create a generational enemy who possesses a continued reason and purpose to hate. This eventually creates the soldiers who make up the army required to fight the war inevitably upon the horizon created by intolerance. It is closer than ever as we needlessly create friction instead of togetherness.

It's fine though, is it not? Each willing participant in the generation in question justifies and creates zero remorse for their actions, somehow convincing themselves being an asshole is ok. It seems humankind is and always has been meant to kill. They have been doing nothing but destroying differences along the way to hand over control to corrupt leaders who created the conflict in the first place so they may benefit from the postwar power grabs.

How do we establish decency and reestablish the original purpose of this great Nation? What solutions can bring about sustainable change? If society, more specifically America, is to survive, a forced purge of incompetent leaders must occur.

Are people confident in the system and the status quo currently controlling? The two-party political system and partisanship are the cause of America's division. Those who are interested in the division are continuing to make it worse. Yet people vote for the same people time after time. The same failed leadership over and over those who identify problems yet have zero solutions.

People must follow those who make us better. We are Americans and must respect the system and each other. Dividing our Nation into multiple regions is not a viable solution; it would work for a brief period, only delaying what I believe is inevitable—accomplishing nothing but tolling the conflict for another generation. This would not solve the issues but only pass accountability to those innocent of our many mistakes. So, what do we do?

If our leaders have lost the ability to engage in constructive dialogue, then it is time to change the system or time to change the leaders. Tribalism is creating fractures in our society that we may never recover from. The consequences of this continued behavior will be catastrophic. This will not end the way people think. We must not allow controlling groups in our system. That is not what America represents. We can do better.

People must stop acting as if differences are our enemies. America's differences are the solution. Americans should not attack people because of these differences. These words are not to identify blame. Neither one side nor the other is right or wrong. We all can do better. Better today than yesterday, better tomorrow than today. Forgive and move on by supporting growth and self-discovery.

People must be able to move beyond their mistakes, and society not only must encourage this but nurture forgiveness for those mistakes since past. I am not suggesting we forget, but we should forgive. People are not their mistakes, but they are limited by them. If society forever holds them to the person they were, forever they will remain.

To gain mercy, one must first give mercy. To give mercy is a recognition and acknowledgment that we are ready to move forward together. These are values of my faith and something I believe people need more of. This is what will unite America. This is what will create an environment conducive to peace. A place where people can create the best versions of themselves. A place of forgiveness. A place where truth can prosper.

Regardless of what drives our fate or our path, people have a responsibility to each other. Not necessarily to care for one another but surely to prevent a chaotic depressive form of resentment that eventually turns into selfishness and later weaponized as hate used to destroy peace and the diversity this hate is aimed at.

The sadness we all come to bear because of a great many lessons of history, what is witnessed through the eyes of the persecuted, or by the ignorance born through the hands of our intolerance is happening simply because evil conquered love. This shows how dangerously close the world is to reaching an unnecessary violent point satisfying the desire to hate.

The prophets, the politicians, and the professors can tell us a great many things, but what we decide to believe is simply a choice neither right nor wrong, nor is it superior to others or what they believe in. The question becomes, what are you willing to die for? And the answer to that will most likely be an undeniable truth to the individual wielding the most destructive weapon ever created.

It hurts my heart, clouds my mind, and stirs the restlessness in my soul. The disgustingness inside the willing may prove too great to overcome as no cure for this sickness exists. At least not one the majority will listen to because the lessons are recorded, always there for the taking to those who are willing, but it seems to fall on deaf ears or ignored, but the effects are the same.

I feel the burden, and it is the weight of the world that is crushing me. Although my responsibility and duty to such a feeling are neither assigned nor appointed to me, it hurts so deeply because I wish to change what can never be altered. I wish nothing more than to give a piece of my empathetic existence to those who are without.

But the truth of this strength is learned, felt, and fought for. I am by no means a perfect structured vessel of the teachings I follow; however, the foundation is there, only waiting to be completed. I am guilty of a great many things, but it is my hope that others can forgive me so I may do the same. I take everything to heart and store it deep in my consciousness simply because I am a glutton for punishment, and my penance is a lifelong commitment to suffering and absolution just a day away, but this day never comes.

My struggle in the pursuit of peace is the same struggle America has always borne because I and everyone else know there is greatness within. The shade of blue in my eyes will always fight for what I believe in and what I feel is necessary, but it is exhausting, lonely, and often times dismissed by those who see me as the enemy or a naive person dreaming of changing the world—the error of my convictions.

Something very important was instilled deep in my soul before self-awareness took hold. It has been there ever since I can remember. The tears I have shed over the years and continue to do will always be a part of my life in service to others. Even when these others call me the enemy, I will be there to answer the call as my family, my Nation, and my God requires me to do so. This I know, is non-negotiable.

When a large part of a population in society does not endure the cost of freedom and is without knowledge of this commitment, personal suffering, or the struggle to survive, they become disconnected from reality because their fanciful existence is cancerous to the soul of a nation. Especially when they ignore fault is due from their misguided lifestyle as was their inability to grasp the eerie similarity between the ailments afflicting our society and the internal causes for the collapse of Rome. Internal rot is represented by elites, the privileged, and the lazy becoming too fat, too happy, and too complacent, outliving and overstaying their usefulness or purpose.

If you are not willing to hold yourself to a standard, how can you expect anyone else to do the same? Be better, pursue better, achieve better. My standard is my faith. The teachings of Jesus Christ can create potential as the consequences of love, equity, and justice are a fantastic place to start. Not for religious purposes, if a person is apathetic to faith, but as a standard of decency and the way to treat fellow man. If not Jesus, Martin Luther King Jr. is another fantastic person to learn from. Many people can be examples of appropriateness and a standard to pursue, find one. Each expected better from themselves and others, and I challenge you to do the same.

Eventually, the world will accept you for who you are, but first you must do the same thing. Who you are is simply an entity you created right, wrong, hated, admired, promoted, or dismissed. However, you can be neither of these until you are honest with yourself. A choice of indecision is a choice of insanity. What you feel is true; no amount of convincing will show you otherwise.

It's not what you have; it's who you are, your convictions, and what you stand for. It's not the skin tone, the size or stature of your being, nor is it the attractiveness of the flesh upon your bones. It is the character inside, the soul contained, and the honesty committed to the truth that matters. Do not lie to others or yourself. This creates consequences both internally and externally. The further away from God the world gets, the worse the world becomes. It is not a coincidence, nor is it a surprise. What you seek is what you shall become. There is no glory in selfishness; only death and despair, lonesomeness and emptiness, hate and toxicity.

If a person has yet to figure out that the sins of the flesh enslave, weaken, and compromise judgment, they neither should lead nor pretend their existence is one that should command influence as they are neither worthy nor in possession of value. Anger, laziness, conceitedness, and gluttony; all make the most qualified person unqualified and a danger to their team or anyone they represent because their character is compromised, always embellishing the truth or ignoring it altogether.

The greatest lie contains the greatest amount of truth which makes the lie harder to identify. The greatest truth contains the least amount of lies which makes it easier to ignore. People are drawn to what is untrue for the same reason the truth is ignored. The truth is always insulting but is always a lie when ignored. Whatever lie you convince yourself of, do not force it on others, for the consequences of many liars can destroy the strongest truth.

I found a lot of truth on the golf course. My closest friend and I spent a large part of our lives trying to figure it out, trying to beat the game, trying to control what happens. It led to many mistakes, many successes, and much back pain for a back that was already in ruin, but such is life. It is the darndest thing, isn't it? How a person can get up, go to the golf course, do poorly or well, feel pain or pleasure, and choose whether or not to be honest with themselves at the end of the day. More importantly, a chance to do it again tomorrow.

The unique thing about golf is how closely related it is to life. A golfer can mess up, fix the mistake, come back tomorrow and correct the deficiency. A golfer can lie or embellish the truth making him or herself look better than what they are. And a golfer can make the course their heaven or hell. All representing choices, all representing self, all representing life.

The strangest thing occurs when a golfer decides to not get better. Not better in the sense of a particular score or compared to other golfers but not being as good as they can be on the scorecard and in reality. It is the only game in which you can lie to yourself and feel better and be better. Golfers basically have the ability to exist through the course by the scorecard and make themselves more or less desirable in the eyes of others. All representing choices, all representing self, all representing life.

They are related, but they are both so far apart. One is a game, and the other is not. One truly matters and the other does not. Both are temporary but have the ability from an individual perspective to make it a less pleasurable experience for other people. However, only one being played wrongly can have cataclysmic consequences to the innocent representing no peace and no truth.

Being ignorant is easy; being informed takes hard work, including a conscious effort to remove this ignorance. Our children's future very well may depend on our ability to accept responsibility for our continued irresponsibility.

This is the final warning…

# A Place for Your Thoughts:

# CHAPTER X

## *The Final Warning*

There is a pecking order when it comes to dangerous men. It starts with bad men who fight for control, creating chaos, and then worse men who value freedom and fight for peace. Crossing either is extremely consequential and detrimental to one's health. Only one of these men will fight to protect the weak; the other fights to control the weak. When bad men no longer fear the Rule of Law, good men must remind them the purpose of the Rule of Law is not to protect the innocent from bad men but to protect those who would hurt the innocent from the real bad men.

These men, those who will destroy evil indiscriminately without care or limits, are extremely dangerous and if the Rule of Law becomes unimportant to society, what occurs next is a failsafe with unimaginable consequences. A good man is already aware of what he must do. A leader relies on good men to reinforce or change his mind against what is necessary for the greater good. Good men will not follow a great man until that decision is made. Good men must step up and create these great men.

It is now offensive to be an American. It is offensive to be patriotic. It is offensive to have pride in your Country. The very thing that gives freedoms is being attacked by people who want to change everything America is, what she represents, and what she stands for. The system is built to evolve together with the appropriate steps with the appropriate people at the appropriate time.

If a people go so far, when do Americans not represent America anymore? Isn't that the purpose of a strong citizenry, to protect their home? Why are people okay with changing what shouldn't be changed? If people decide America is not the country they want, are they trying to create a separate nation? More importantly, should they be stopped? America has lost the battle. The war is coming that will decide where our Nation will go from here.

The thoughts and a belief in what are inferior and superior destroy what it means to be an American. It attacks the very fabric of our existence and threatens the cohesive structure of our system. However, there may very well be things other people cannot objectively be subjected to, and I think our people, Americans, will fight the next war of humanity. It will decide what is allowed in the understanding of freedoms.

How long and how much tolerance for ignorance, tolerance for the lies, tolerance for the shameful, should all others be subjected to? The internal rot and decay represented by an attack on the foundation, which was created to protect. All because of ignorance and hate. All because of improper leadership. All because people decided to put value where value should not exist. All because people protected a lie.

Just because you convinced people who look like you and think like you of a truth does not make it so. The test is convincing those who have yet to accept the thoughts promoted by an understanding you and your kind have agreed to. Work harder to convince them, not demonize them. If you are unable to do so, look inward. It is likely what you believe is not a truth, just a convoluted opinion being passed as a moral standard for all to follow. You're being a tyrant and eventually a target to be overthrown or eliminated.

What are men like me to do when picking a side to fight is not only required but necessary for survival? Where do I turn? Who do I follow? I have no place among the divisive characters and dismissive actors. These tyrants, any one of them, would not allow me to be free as I cannot follow the banners they wave. Each one is representative of selfishness and purity, but all require their followers to lose a bit of themselves and compromise their souls simply to comply, as dissent among what is their truth surely cannot be tolerated.

This chapter is for those who have zero value and are more costly than their worth. Those who choose to be ignorant. Those who lead the weak-minded and those who follow the weak-minded. These words are meant for you.

The people you follow, what you believe, and what you have in common will cost you your life and destroy peace. Your ignorance of history combined with your ignorance of freedom multiplied by your misguided pursuit to destroy is nothing more than a traitorous desire. What you promote, what you represent, and what you value—mean nothing.

The decision to ignore those who work, those who protect, and those who are without will not go unpunished. Hardworking people fund professions whose only purpose is to entertain, creating false idols; or fund incompetency resulting in the creation of bad leaders and false prophets. The truth is separated by the illusion of importance in an economic system used to value fame over importance, the unnecessary over the necessary, and the worthless over the valuable.

How can the lavishly wealthy and professionals such as entertainers or politicians assume importance when their value is not among the set of values necessary for survival or developing productive competency? They arrogantly assume this and accept payment from those who work to produce what is actually needed for society to survive.

It is detrimental to people and society to promote nothing over something. It is detrimental to people and society to put people in positions they should never be in. It is detrimental to people and society to allow excess wealth to accumulate in the hands of the few while many starve. It is the actual value of importance versus the perception of importance. It is my understanding that those with little value offer nothing to society as a necessity but receive wealth, status, and preferences offered over those who do represent value.

If the world were to wake up without those who give no value to society or take value from society, nothing would change. Yet if the world would wake up without those who give value, everything would change. An understanding of this is important to recognize worth and position on the value continuum. Promote worth over value, necessity over luxury, and decency over vulgarity.

Do not allow those without decency to grow more important than the ones who do have decency. It is not hard to find the cause of our issues in society as they are a direct reflection of the influence those who lack decency possess. Those who are poor do not matter to those who are well off. Those who are voiceless do not matter to those who are heard. Those who try to unite are demonized by those who divide.

White people cannot say anything to black people, black people cannot say anything to white people, and neither can say anything to police officers. Their selfish illusion of greatness emboldens each. Allowing a fictitious belief that when criticism is necessary, it is because they are being racist, trying to cancel expression, or are plainly anti-cop.

Democrats turned everything represented by republicans into an enemy likened to white supremacy and hate. Republicans turned everything represented by democrats into an enemy likened to communism and being anti-America. But both are patriots protecting "their" version of one-America. Hating each other because trying to understand one another and what they "actually" stand for takes too much work. Everything is being overshadowed by the fringe on each side, and progress has stalled for failing to call out the worst of their identity.

Women are upset men do not respect them. Cops are upset people do not respect them. White Americans are upset because people do not respect them. Black Americans are upset because people do not respect them. All people are mad because others do not respect them. The list goes on and on. Be someone worth respecting, and that will change. Where is society heading, and why have we chosen this path, this behavior, this ending?

How are people to grade the actions of police officers, black Americans, white Americans, or others who need to see the truth? How else is accountability achieved but by criticism directed to those who are deserving? The species has created the opposite of accountability. They have promoted violence instead of justice, division instead of togetherness, ignorance instead of knowledge. People have created immorality that is boundless, intolerance that is controlling, and hate that is destroying.

The kink, the filth, what is best left in the darkness should remain. When it is normalized and promoted, it affects the innocent who are yet to decide what or who they will be become. It also affects the society containing the innocence that will be destroyed. What is immoral should not control, and neither should it be an objective standard used for the interpretation of appropriate behavior. The earth is on fire; a virus is upon us, and the deadliest war is nearing. This is what selfishness breeds. This is what selfishness creates. And this is what selfishness represents—choice. The desire to create has intent. Choose wisely as a sinister version of ourselves is slowly approaching.

Both man and God give human beings laws to maintain peace, not to destroy, not to decay, but prosper together, promoting the best of humanity. Be the change and bring about good in the world. There are things in life worth protecting, worth defending, and worth dying for. Seek guidance to recognize what these are, from whatever source promotes decency.

Participation is not discretionary, nor will the lack of it create a desirable outcome. People now believe removing care makes freedom, but it actually enslaves. The serenity prayer and other cheap proverbs are not to be used for permission to not participate in life, especially in a self-governing society. It was created for a specific type of person in a specific situation who cannot control the outcome giving permission to let go and accept peace or let God deal with it.

It was not meant to prevent accountability. Society needs those who are unafraid, value responsibility, and who will attack the status quo to stand up to fight injustice, immorality, and ignorance. Americans must search for the truth. They must decide what is important to them. They must decide what matters to them; they must decide if America is important and does she matter to them. Is their way of life worth protecting? Is America worth protecting? If it is, they must find the truth.

America, what she represents, the people she protects, and the freedom given is not for a single race, a religion, nor is it only for the powerful elite. It exists for equity, equality, and fairness. She represents morality, is meant for righteousness, and must be pursued to that end. Americans must bring back American exceptionalism by seeking leaders who represent that. This is the enemy of ignorance, the enemy of intolerance, the enemy of alternative structures, either economic or political—American exceptionalism is how we create a better version and destroy all who are uninterested in bettering America and themselves.

A time will come when patriots must do something. If you are not for America and what she stands for, what she represents, and what she can be, you have zero business living in a country with other Americans who are trying their best. Every day over 300 million hardworking decent Americans and others are surviving, pushing forward, working their hands to the bone either through pursuits related to education or a thankless job—some do both—and are doing what they think is right. Those who represent the minority are causing the problems. The ignorance you spread and the divisions you create threaten this Nation and the world.

I have watched this game play for the last 30 years, and I have grown tired of it. You and your people represent far less than what America is. The reason why America is failing is because of people like you. Those who do not want to be held accountable, those who refuse to help, those who ignore a standard of decency, and those of you who ignore the Rule of Law. Scream, yell, burn, destroy, consume, collect, and create the worst version of yourself. Continue to act in a manner promoted and encouraged by imbeciles.

Decorum, respect, and dialogue must be present, or the opposite will be. America is not about a side, a political party, a race, or any other irrelevant identity. Do not ignore the warning signs. Do not continue the trajectory of this ill-advised journey. This path leads to destruction because the respect for truth and accountability has been removed by those offended by it.

Those who encourage and invite chaos are trash. You and those like you do not belong in this Country. It is time for you to decide. Your actions represent who you are, your actions represent what you believe, and your actions represent your ending. Nations form to protect a belief, an idea, and a people. If you want to destroy this Country, burn the American flag, sow chaos because of a belief you have somehow entitled you to do so, tread carefully.

The time will come when the wolves are released. These people are dangerous, extremely violent, and are created by necessity. They will recall skills earned through experience or training used to eliminate enemy combatants. There are those who will remember and those who will learn. They will destroy everything that is threatening their way of life. It will not matter who you are or what you look like. It will not matter if you pray to God or follow a design of human creation. It will not even matter if you are an American. If you stand in the way of peace, promote destruction, divide for relevancy or legitimacy, your existence will be threatened because you threatened theirs. Your fate will be the same as what you represent and what you created—destruction.

Dialogue is always preferred, but it is not necessary. A time will come, a time is nearing, and a time to defend will arise. My Country, my way of life, and my people have once again been threatened and liberty attacked. A plague of ignorance has arrived on the doorstep of patriots. The threat is not a race; it is not a religion; it is not even an army. It is a cancerous stench, a filthy habit, a miscarriage of freedom. It is represented by nothing more than the continued protection of people who are unworthy of living in such a wonderful Nation. This goes for their leaders too. Each pursuing or supporting power over purpose creating an end result defined by THEIR SELFISHNESS.

I keep repeating over and over and over one thing that all people know; what history has taught us and what all futures are created from—the first shot is the most difficult, but after that, they all become a bit easier. I have asked myself; how will you know it is time? When did the Founding Fathers know? When did all righteous wars begin? And is there such an animal? What is more important, the past or the present? Does the future always exterminate the less evolved version of our species? And has my time come?

I don't think a war is ever righteous, nor do I believe people will ever know the right time or when it's time; it just happens. It sweeps the innocent, destroying both them and the wicked before they are aware. However, I do not believe we are there yet, and although many do, I will fight to maintain peace because the fight to create or establish peace after it is lost is much more violent and a world I wish my son, my niece, nephews, and my friends' children never see.

Although I will never shy away from conflict, I try to never be the aggressor as they are equally in error and both are responsible for unnecessary destruction, but justifying action becomes easier as situational awareness indicates a choice not to is no longer an option. Are preeminent strikes and overtly violent acts only something permitted by the government representing the authority only it can exercise? However, are these not people? People, flawed men, and women control the government.

Because of this, what is worth fighting for does not solely rest in the hands or the purview of those who are in charge. That can change relatively quickly. Certain leaders are designed for certain times. People who lack the competency and capabilities required to fix our Nation should not be sitting in those seats, especially when these people are blatantly violating what is necessary to maintain peace. The one-America each traitor is encouraging other traitors to create will be a catastrophe when that final line is crossed. Freedom, autonomy, and the right to protect both are not contingent on a political party controlling the Legislative, Executive, or the Judicial Branch. That authority is granted through the consent of a people who are growing ever so tired of incompetence.

Am I wrong? As long as I continue to ask this question, my thoughts will remain steadfast in my mind, and they are committed to peace. This is something many people should practice as their behavior and actions will be responsible for atrocities this society has never witnessed. Maintain decorum, focus on tolerance, and share in the enjoyment of life with a stranger. Do not encourage violence; it is unnecessary, unwarranted, and unwanted.

When I am convinced peace is no longer an option, it will be an acknowledgment that I must accept a hard unkind truth—my part in history will be one I wish not to occur, nor do I want to participate in. I will belong to a group of many in the past who did not choose as well, but the ability to choose has been removed by ignorance, weakness, and by the people, I will now call my enemy. War is never the answer. It is a mere act of turning the greatest of people into the worst of people. In the event this occurs, may God have mercy on our souls because what is in my mind has zero place among good men.

For as long as I can remember, I have feared death except in circumstances that require a sacrifice to defend what I believe. For these, I am prepared to die. If this is what I was built for, I will gladly lay down my life swearing allegiance to America and the freedoms she represents, allowing the peace for all people to prosper, together, united.

I will keep my faith in my God, my Country, and my family. I will never roll over allowing the threat of incompetency to grow, treasonous behavior to control, or an apathetic demeanor to destroy what so many people have sacrificed over many centuries through generations of brave men and women. If you remain unmoved because your selfishness and ignorance drive your existence, you will be a target of my patriotism to this Nation, loyalty to my God, my family, my friends, and the steadfast commitment to not only decency but the protection of others such teachings demand of me.

Finally, your life will be in danger from aggression as a result of the filth, disgust, and weakness you seem to follow and represent. This is not a threat. It is not idle remarks that will go unfulfilled. What I believe in, what I represent, what is demanded of me is something that seems to escape your comprehension and small imbecilic mind. Because I am willing to die for my beliefs, I am also willing to kill for them. Self-preservation, in combination with—standing for what I believe in, will always guide my principles. These convictions allow me to stand for what is just, what is right, and what is required—all of which encompass the truth contained in my heart.

Regardless of the destruction, the means will justify the end, and I will not be deterred neither shall those who believe what is necessary. I can identify exactly the cause of our divisions, our cancer, and I know the cure that will be administered. The responsibility is not solely on those who create friction presently; however, their complicity will not go unnoticed. Accountability will be had, and an ending is nearing if America's course is not altered.

It will not be pleasant; it will not be enjoyable; it may not even be just. War seldom is. Those who crave destruction need to step down. Those who push the divide deeper must cease such behavior. Lastly, those who can change this destructive cycle humanity seems to be caught in must step up and remain united reflective of our governing documents by continuing to fight for the principles contained therein. A time may come when we will not have a choice, but we must remember what we are fighting for, and until it occurs, we must fight to maintain the peace we enjoy.

True power and leadership occur by convincing others that what you believe is a superior and more equitable way to live. Acknowledging peace, freedom, and economic opportunity should be for all is strength. It is not just for the privileged or those with power who remove it from others if they do not like their lifestyle, do not like their opinions, or do not like their freedoms. Remember what the fight is for.

We will be united in peace or united in war. It is incumbent on all citizens to limit aggressiveness and ignore the push to escalate what should never again consume a free people. This may prove to end what many knew would fail. This will take the best of us as the worst of us have completed their task of destroying the peace that is so exceedingly difficult to obtain.

You do not have to agree with what I stand for, but before you dismiss my words, would you die to defend my beliefs? It's not your job to believe me; just let me live in peace before I am forced to live in violence. We are not so different, you and I. Really, how could we be? We are Americans and are asking to live a life free from persecution. That is the American dream. Any day of the week, America's worst reality is still worth dying for.

# The Final Warning

If you're not part of the solution, you are part of the problem. Please remove yourself before you are removed without your consent. If that struck a nerve, you are exactly the person I am speaking to. You might not be asked again, and it will be without consideration to your feelings or your wellbeing.

This is not a warning to a race, religion, gender, or sexual orientation. It is a warning to those who dismiss the Rule of Law. A warning to those who lead with the intent to sow chaotic selfishness. It is a warning to those who follow weakness and those who should never lead. It is a warning to those who pursue a one-America trying to create a no America. It is a warning that may save your life. This is the final warning before there is no time for peace because there was no time for truth.

Sir, you are not the only one...

# A Place for Your Thoughts:

# CHAPTER XI

## *One Last Thing*

D o not hate me for thinking out loud. Do not hate me for not agreeing with you. Do not hate me for searching for a truth reflective of truth. I think people should question everything and accept nothing. Ignore those who tell you, "They know what is best." They must give you the space and freedom you require to figure out "what is best." These people are dangerous. Their dangers can be limited by a want and a desire to know what they wish to keep a secret. Their secret, what they never want us to know, "they cannot control us." It is wonderful because of the many different variations of what exists, which all can be applied willingly, independently, and under our own volition without the discretion of any authority.

This is what my book is about, change. Through **Individuality**, **Togetherness**, and the **Freedoms** a united citizenry must protect. Fight for freedom and be willing to die for it because those who are against it will kill to extinguish it and anyone who believes in such a divine creation. Stay united and follow the truth. Stand and fight for a standard, control what you consume, and exercise caution before believing in anything. How much thinking did it take for you to believe what you know? If you have zero thoughts of your own, it is likely you do not think anything; you choose instead to follow, believing whatever they tell you. Caution should be your next step. But how can anyone find what is necessary?

First and foremost, seek to educate yourself; being informed is important. It is for you and something that may always be built upon. In a way, it is for your ancestors and your descendants as well; they would be proud, and so should you. It is also a duty and responsibility as an American Citizen. To be honest, being educated, informed, or intelligent is needed to maintain and grow. It is a type of attractiveness created by representing the willingness to possess awareness.

The alternative, not so much. If knowledge is lacking, change is always possible. A thought is not a singular expression. It evolves because people evolve—ever pursuing, everchanging. If a person can control their desires, they would possess something far greater and experience what those desires could never provide. Your body will tell you what it needs; however, your brain will deceive you and misplace a want as a need. Always be mindful of this.

This change, an understanding of something you may have failed to realize, represents enlightenment. Do not be scared; growth is somewhat painful but, in the end, worth every penny. It is always us who decide to follow a path. Many paths exist, and our life is reflective of the path we take, represented by the person it created. Our path is not only for us but also for others as we are all connected. We can change the world for the better if we would just work together. But it is a choice and only ours to make.

We are the creation of our tragedies
We are the tragedy of our creation
When will we recognize what we have become
When will we see the solution to ourselves
We have found nothing
We have found our ending
We are the cause
We are the enemy
When will we stop
When will we quit
We are nothing
We are everything
We must create a path
We must create a unity
We must create the future

A future of prosperity. Not in the selfish inwardly satisfaction but in a spirit of necessity to create good in the world. Our realities are surrounded by only what we see as the truth, what we are willing to accept as the truth, and what reality we are willing to create with those truths. Use your understanding of this to create a better future for all children of whatever

God they believe in or do not believe in. This posterity will create tolerance for those in the society yet to come.

Choose wisely when seeking happiness. Happiness is easy. To achieve this pure form of assentation, one needs only to seek the truth, honesty, and acceptance of things. Keeping happiness is the difficulty humanity faces on a day-to-day basis. It also proves more difficult to find happiness the more one cares, understands, or because of the company they choose to keep.

As society and the population continue to grow, so does the inability to achieve this wonderful feeling. Again, the more one cares, understands, or because of the company they choose to keep, the more difficult it seems to find happiness. In plain words, people suck. And the more people in the world, the more likely these imbeciles will adversely affect our happiness, and the more likely happiness will be out of reach. Recognize this, those types of people, and the type of information that will lead to a cancerous soul. Be in your happiness and your happiness alone. Do not hurt others to achieve happiness, as you will be the representation of all things cancerous but understand your happiness is in your hands; choose wisely.

Form an opinion that is kind, one which promotes the best version of yourself. Build relationships with differences and see something other than the reflection in the mirror. Promote that which the world needs more of and show future generations the acceptable approach to conflict resolution. Stand for righteousness over selfishness and remember to fight for a cause with the same decency as you are trying to create.

At times the paths we travel seem to be overwhelmingly against what is fair, what is just, and what is right. However, this must never grow our hearts bitter, our souls weary, nor can we allow it to destroy what we know in our hearts to be true—we need each other. Our peace is predicated on our cohesion and a collective spirit of the greater good.

Seek counsel, seek guidance, seek understanding. These endeavors will serve peace exceptionally well, allowing more than stains to be left in the pages of history for the acts of selfish desire. A bitter heart cannot survive, so too is true of the person who nurses this bitterness. Eventually, those two forces will devour one another, never solving, only destroying. The ending is always available, and it is a prelude to unparalleled peace for the generations that follow.

Adversity and challenges create a better version of people. If someone has never failed, what have they achieved? Most likely, nothing, as everything, including the opportunities necessary to succeed, was given, not earned. The path that creates a person represents one of two things, the ease or the difficulty of such a venture. This can lead to consequences when they are tested, as struggle creates strength.

Success is and should never be contingent on others believing in you, but it sure does help to have others who do believe in you. People must be supportive of each other. Encouraging, defending, and forcing others to believe in themselves is the ethos Americans must live by. Do not cast negativity upon one another, hoping they will fail or by doubting they will succeed.

I can foresee the consequences of actions based on the ideas of traditionalism, lack of empathy, and the inability to move forward together. When people normalize this behavior, it creates hardships and catastrophic tragedies among the innocent subjugated to live a life of inequity.

Look not unto your actions but further as it can lead to generational limits as ignorance never dies with life, it is quite the opposite. It is given a breath of its own surviving century after century, creating or destroying the society where truth is absent. Shield yourself from this ignorance. Do not weaken society out of laziness, the position of or enjoyment thereof. Use the time spent wisely as foolish choices serve only to enslave us all. Your misdeeds are our misdeeds. In the stead of weakness, create strength.

Truth must never be made false. A collection of falsities creates not only a collection of dangerous people but also a collection of dangerous people who are intentionally dividing, disguising themselves as leaders. No good can come from those who wish to spread untrue beliefs.

These acts can only sow destruction and chaos. Humanity cannot afford these reckless endeavors. We all are faced with the confrontation of these dangerous people who choose to spread wickedness and bias. Do not bend or cower in fear, as these foolish people must be stopped.

Humanity depends on those who are righteous and those who will stop at nothing to protect society from this cancerous growth. Remember, ignorance is the enemy. It feeds on the weak by giving strength to the heartless. It lessens stability and gives influence to those who should never possess it. It divides with intent and removes peace by design. Ignorance has ignore in it for a reason. The less attention these fools are paid, the less legitimacy they will possess.

Run from ignorance but do not attack ignorant people. Educate with a compassionate intent. Those will be every generation's most important battles. Conflict is inevitable among men but a just cause to prevent unnecessary cruelty to the innocent. Be wise and remember conflict is only two competing thoughts, not competing people. Ignorance divides, and ignorance conquers. To defeat ignorance, replace the untrue with the true.

People must seek that which is true. The truth is not reserved for the entitled. It is a gift, a way to self-enlighten. Knowledge should never be protected in a way that prevents further understanding. Nothing is worth having unless it is the truth. Be forewarned; ignorance creates peace while understanding creates isolation of the dreadful kind.

A mind has the power to enslave, but at the same time, a mind has the power to set free. If a person is a slave to one's thoughts, this prevents freedom; on the contrary, a free mind forever protects itself from mental slavery. A mind has the power to destroy, but at the same time, a mind has the power to create. A person who seeks destruction will find destruction. A person who seeks peace will find peace.

Do not be so arrogant and assume those who are ignorant cannot change. Do not blame, for this will lead to a defensive posture. They may be wrong but not your enemies. Explain with truth, compassion, and understanding. Represent with patience, kindness, and a commitment to understanding. Educate the ones who are willing.

Create togetherness with this understanding. Allow for individuality but prevent inclusivity. The ascent of those who seek to elevate themselves above others will only lead to division and the eventual collapse of whatever society this behavior is attached to.

People are governed by whatever they so choose to be controlled by. The law of man is temporary, yet the Law of God is everlasting, for all humanity shall rejoice in the Lord in their search for meaning and the truth.

Do not fear weakness or flaws. Do not judge thyself too harshly, as we are all sinners, and that is what it means to be human. Rejoice in knowing that we all can be saved if we choose to be governed by the truth. The truth is in our Lord. Do not allow the creation of man to run your life.

Celebrate in the complexity of the natural order. Stay grounded and connected, not only with your surroundings but also with the people contained in those surroundings, no matter the contrast between what was chosen or what was given. The Lord is our Shepard. Look to Him for understanding.

Allow the truth to pierce the armor of ignorance and allow it to destroy the selfish worldly form that limits our souls. For with Christ, we can extinguish ignorance. We can wage war with our demons. We can heal our trespasses and our past. With Christ, we can be saved.

Is it not enough to simply open your eyes and see the beauty of our Creator? Do not be fooled in the pursuit of greed but rejoice in knowing fulfillment in life is free. Do not fall prey to the act of self-celebration. The accolades of selfish men have zero meaning. Seeking to be famous or important will lead to the destruction of oneself. Instead, seek to live a life for others influenced by the teachings of Jesus Christ.

Do for others more than yourself. Maintain balance and keep a sharp mind to recognize those who will take advantage of kindness. People disappoint you because they do not respect you. You respect them so much that you have not figured it out yet. Do not hate those who practice this or those who are lost but pity them for the truth eludes their ignorant ways and does nothing but limit their capacity to withstand selfishness.

Lead by example, and others will follow. Do not practice words with a wicked tongue, as this behavior only serves to enslave the best of us and creates more of them. Speak to others as you would to thy father and mother or a child that is in your care. Do not run from the truth; instead, embrace it no matter the harshness contained within. The truth is everything, and the opposite is nothing. Embrace the truth and embark on your journey.

Recognition of the truth proves difficult to swallow. Acknowledging it will only reveal a failure of your own doing and not disappointment from our Lord. We all are granted a life to shine with eternal light. Christ cannot forsake us, as God will never do so. As such, and because our actions will nevertheless fall short, we are never alone.

But we do not fail; quite the contrary. We grow, learn, and eventually love ourselves once again when we know the Lord has never left us. May this grant you peace knowing that our Lord's love is everlasting and cannot die as we can never truly die. It is our relationship with Christ that is permanent, as is His love.

Forgive yourself as all is forgiven. Embrace the gift of everlasting life by removing all that has prevented the purpose of peace and love given by our Savior. Forgive those around you as well. At times this may seem impossible as the anger we retain seems to prevent our soul from doing so.

These trespasses will serve not only to strengthen us but also to free us. Forgiveness destroys anger. Why hold on to the darkness as it serves only to send us to eternal damnation. Forgiveness creates peace, peace creates love, and from this love, joy emanates.

Continue to stay vigilant and protect the peace you have received. Do not forget the love peace brought to you. Do not forget the joy love brought to you. Use this joy to forgive those who trespass against you so they too may experience peace.

I recognize that my limits are mine alone. These are created by me and must be destroyed by me. With the truth, I shall find the Lord who will grant peace. With this peace, I can extend forgiveness by creating love for all I am in contact with so they, too, can experience joy.

No man can take this from me as it is a gift from my Creator, protected by my faith in Jesus Christ and granted by the love contained within.

The limits we face as humans are represented by worldly objects and are easily identifiable with a connection to our flesh. This can be understood by selfishness in the form of impulses, urges, and desires. Selfishness is bred into all living creatures as, first and foremost, a survival instinct. It serves us well so we may survive.

But our selfishness seeks to destroy us too. It is not until we find true love that we are able to override this survival instinct contained within and given by our Creator. We cannot simply hold our breath to extinguish the light in our souls, our instinct for survival will not allow it.

The selfishness all men have is only controlled by true love. We possess the ability to destroy self-preservation by a deep connection to someone. In other words, we do not fear the sword in the protection of others.

It is love that can do this and love alone, but hate is very powerful as well. Hate is a selfish, unnecessary emotion. Hate can remove love by increasing the self-preservation in us all by destroying our ability to not harm and create a desire to harm. Hate is destructive as love is constructive. Finding love extinguishes hate creating empathy.

Heaven and hell are both created by the decisions of human beings, and their actions represent the hastening or delay of the rapture. These are motivated through love or selfishness, respectively. The location of a soul is inconsequential as the location of heaven and hell are both worldly and supernatural. People create their own heaven or hell, both of which are represented by choices in a person's lifetime.

There is a small bit of truth in everything. Search for it, find it, and assemble it. These pieces are not available at the same time. It is a process representing the meaning of life. It will elude those with hate in their heart and ignorance in their mind because selfishness is a sin, and true love—divine.

Gods' religion is language—find the meaning—find the truth.

Heavenly Father,
Allow us to have
Knowledge, so we may understand;
Faith, so we may believe;
Kindness, so we may fulfill;
Vision, so we may execute; and
Strength, so we may endure.
Let us be your rod and deliver these attributes so others may see your light.
Grant us your presence to create something where there is nothing.
Let us prosper in this life together so we may not perish in this life alone.
Bless us for we are weak and riddled with sin in your absence.
Forgive us when we are without your guidance and stray off the path of righteousness.
Let our choices be connected to the best version of ourselves and allow This version to influence others.
This we ask for, this we require, and this we believe.
In Jesus' name, we pray,
Amen

Finally, in closing, I sincerely hope you enjoyed the words of a man driven by his truth, assembled and presented respectful of, and in consideration of others and their truth. If I offended you or insulted you, it was not my intent. I am searching for the truth, and I believe it is missing because of the prevalence of selfishness and a desire to use emotions to destroy logic, ignoring what "is." The world is without truth because the world is without faith. People should be free to choose, but decency and the standard of morality have never been controlled or created by man. This type of morality is easily bought or sold, everchanging, as it is the intent and design of human nature because selfishness controls fools who seek influence or those who desire to be influenced.

The system designed to protect peace is failing, its people are failing, and our leaders are failing. I want the people who may read this in the future to know; that it was not a specific group that destroyed freedom and peace. No, it was not a people. It was not a race, it was not a gender, it was not a religion, and it was not America. What destroyed peace and any hope for differences to live side by side was what we believed. We decided collectively at some point in time that we do not care who we insult, we do not care to promote decency, and we do not care for morality. Americans sidestepped accountability and the standard owed to one another to maintain peace—later, the world followed. You see, when a beacon is missing, when the example of what "to be" becomes what should never be, when our parents stop growing, their children are without proper guidance. And when this cycle continues, we all suffer.

Our incompetent leaders lead us right where they wanted us to be and those who followed never questioned, never changed course, never—not even once—gave a slight consideration that what they are doing may be wrong. What people want; they will always create. My people, the generations contained in my lifetime, those who chose conflict, were limited because of our past. But we failed because those who could extend mercy and equity decided those are things only our likeness should receive.

And bit by bit, every time we intentionally disrespected each other, the scales tipped that much closer toward war. It was not one thing; it was all things.

The past creates future problems, and the people who refuse to change create the consequences that society must unravel presently. The lack of accountability is the cause. The lack of a standard is to blame. Ignorance is making it worse; our divisions are making it worse; our leaders are making it worse. I am afraid. Not because I fear confrontation, nor do I fear violence or an ending of life. I am worried because we may never realize at what point it became enough.

No, it was not our differences. Those identifiers add more difficulty, but differences can live in peace, working together and accomplishing great things. I have been doing this my entire life, and it hurts to think that for the remainder of my life, this may not be possible. One commonality is all we need. One reason to change, one reason to love, and one reason to ascend. People must see this commonality contained in us, and society must recognize what can change everything for the better—**US**.

**OUR** species is the commonality—it is not a measurement of diversity used to divide and put people into categories. Do not do what our fathers instructed us to do. Please, make it work. Make it work for my children and my children's children. Make it work for the world's children. Make it work for those you do not know. It will take courage, strength, and determination to commit, execute, and succeed where my generation and the generations before me failed. It will take forgiveness and the desire to simply get along. Decide and choose as our lives depend on it.

Current societies are always limited by the capacity of choice and the emotional competency preventing cohesive structure. They are also limited by the bias attached to what they believe in and the leaders they follow who see nothingness because they are blinded by likeness. Blinded by the falsity of a truth they internalized, blinded by the falsity they were the right ones to lead, and blinded by the falsity of a one-America they tried to create. Existential consequences are now upon us.

If I could give you one piece of advice, if I could share one piece of wisdom, it would be this; teach your children empathy. Find a way to instill this in their hearts. And always wear hearing protection because I cannot hear a damn thing.

I have ideas to change the world for the better, I hope you do as well...

# A Place for Your Thoughts:

# Terminology

**Antonymic Interest**- The interest opposite the person using the Tolerance Continuum, or the two interests in conflict plotted by a user. These are conflicting identities represented by two positions on the tolerance continuum in competition for legitimacy. Does not indicate correctness nor tolerance level, only a position opposite to another position represented by identities in conflict with a countering truth, belief, or a subjective understanding of life.

**Assumed Originality**- A belief that a person's thoughts in relation to external factors are original and should be considered original. Applies to logical thought that occurs naturally in relation to observations. It is a false belief that an expression is owned by the creator of cognitive actions prejudiced through the senses of design and influenced by the emotions of design chosen by the individual. An example is experiencing something with sight and sound that makes a person angry, sad, happy, or scared and later documenting these thoughts creating a record of expression.

The ability to articulate observations is not knowledge, it is the journal of life. Different yet similar interpretations of a subjective nature will occur that are not influenced by a similar kind but are of a similar kind. If the same conclusion can be drawn by different people in different times, represented in a different way but containing the same meaning or identical purpose, it does not represent creation stolen only observations expressed by language from a need to understand what is occurring. It is created by the ability to articulate a sound argument well and exists irrespective of the diversity in the world.

Examples of this include languages of different people, Gods of different people, or stories of different people. These are all made to do the same thing but created by different people not influenced by one another but born of individuality through singular thought as a self-expression with the emotions of design and the senses of design. When ten people view the same event or are charged with the task to describe a cognitive understanding through a categorical response, similarities will control literal comprehension, but self-expression will control assumed intelligence creating the illusion of assumed originality. Eventually someone more intelligent will create the exact same assumption but with greater articulation with greater knowledge. If all knowledge is destroyed or becomes unknown, it will be recreated similarly to what once existed without knowing what once existed. Knowledge is always expanding upward and outward based on needs and the senses of design influenced by the emotions of design chose by the person creating. Creation will always occur regardless of influence, regardless of time, regardless of originality. It is unable to be stopped.

**Assumption of Offense-** Misinterpreting intent to create a social response. Assuming what occurred, what was read, what was experienced was in fact without viable alternatives, even though evidence is present, was meant to be offensive. The intent has been changed, improperly applied, and redirected to cause harm without the consent and outside the original intent of the person communicating what was expressed. It is a consequence of ignoring the duties and responsibilities of a United States Citizen by allowing triggered citizens to create triggered leaders who use selective creation to advance detrimental unity. Can be, but not always, an example of exceptional privilege.

**Benchmark Graph-** A personal analysis of where a person started, where they are, and where they want to go. The graph is not concerned with situational or circumstantial consequences. It operates under the premise all people have dreams, had dreams, or are working towards achieving dreams. It is used to identify what an individual wants and indicates what society must do to minimize the limits preventing growth. It is used to assign value to the citizens of a nation focusing attention to promote creative participants and to minimize the destructive participants.

**Causal Sum-** The sum of the epitomized attachment score attached to the antonymic interests on the tolerance continuum.

**Circumstantial Atrocities-** Being born in a period of suffering bearing no responsibility of reality. The result of existential consequences that prior generations created effecting those who are innocent. Identified by events throughout history that required the need for human intervention by those encouraged to create a better way. These moments in history changed the landscape of society and were born of consequences by those who removed decency among people. These events are suffered through by the innocent and are notated on the cycle of destruction as conflict or war.

**Citizenry Value**- An impartial rating of a nation's citizens willingness to participate in its form of governance and the benefit or cost objectively represented.

**Cognitive Laziness**- When people assume those who share likeness possess knowledge. This allows what is promoted to be accepted with little or no attempt to verify the accuracy of information. It is a detrimental choice to assume what was consumed is absolutely correct without the need to obtain the critical perspective. Trusting the source removes the need to verify information. When people rely on a source in a position of authority, the end results are fractures in society represented by division, intolerance, and hate. Relied on by leaders who take advantage of the good will in people.

**Cognitive Rules of Growth**- A continuous process from infancy up until death influencing identity and judgments. The influinci consumed affects all aspects of human interaction, human growth, human evolution which alters thought processes, identities, and emotions through and by exposures in a person's environment. This knowledge, experience, and self-identifying process can occur at a personal level, group level, generational level, or societal level forever effecting behavior. This process occurs continuously with or without the knowledge of the individual.

**Cohesive Structure**- Represented by the type of unity present in citizens. This structure is vital to maintaining peace in a diverse society. Two types, creative and destructive. When creative values are present among a diverse society, cohesion occurs creating tolerance, understanding, and the possibility of acceptance. When destructive values are present among a diverse society, fractures occur creating tension, conflict, or the possibility of war.

**Cohesive Unity**- A positive type of societal unity fostering growth, tolerance, and also encourage the necessary actions which are required in order to solve the problems facing society. This type of unity seeks truth, accountability, and equity.

**Competing Existence**- The continuing struggle and relationship of the governed participants in society. Measurable and identifiable with the use of the tolerance continuum.

**Conflict Encouragement**- What is required by an influential leader to push the cohesive structure to the point of no return allowing war to consume the innocent.

**Controlling Arms**- Entities, organizations, and beliefs people have allegiance for and surrender autonomy to.

**Convenience Evolution**- Science used to create an advantage to be pampered more efficiently

**Creative Participant**- Believes in and swears allegiance to the controlling arm of authority but commits to alter what is unjust or fights to protect their interests. This type of participant works to create cohesive unity in society by lobbying for change. Listens to those who are trying to maintain cohesive unity. Promotes diversity, their own interests, and negative participants. Will break laws as long as it is not violent or a felony; however, negative participants will distract from original purpose and commit crimes disguised as creative participants.

This allows other negative participants posing as creative participants to attack their identity or interests as a type of detrimental unity because they each recognize what the other is. Can be both negative and positive depending on the consequences of behavior and the type of promotion practiced by the participants. Identifying destructive participants is controlled by properly addressing concerns effectively creating cohesive unity.

**Creative Structure**- High cohesive structure represented by peace in diverse society.

**Cycle of Destruction**- It is a timeline represented by peace or no peace. The cycle is repeated as is the destruction of society. The timeline is relative to the population size and the diversity of thought, the friction of these competing views, and the commitment to kill or coexist within the race, nationality, or ethnicity type competing for resources either through competition with the human species or the competition representing the natural order uncontrolled and ignored by a system of human design.

The most important factor is the desire of the population to remain civilized through decency and an empathetic will or uncivilized through selfishness and hate. The system, the means of control, regardless of the forces used to group people for compliance against chaos will always fail. Human beings as a species can only be measured by the negativity created. The consequences of one will always be greater because the effect is greater. The positivity measured and used to correct consequences is simply reactive, never altering, never preventing, only delaying the ignus fatuus.

People, their existence, is represented by corruption. It is by ruin through selfishness—the void of empathy—that the plight of the human species is doomed to represent the repeated cycle of destruction until earth is no longer habitable. The irrelevancy to and the pursuit of good means nothing in relation to the species, only the individual. A life has great meaning not the existence of life. Peace is obtained and owned solely as a cognitive possession of the individual. It is for the individual not the species. Influence can inspire peace and must be found because it cannot be given, only lost or destroyed. It is not known exactly when peace was lost or if the cycle has crossed the point of no return as history is silent on this; however, the people living are well aware of its existence.

**Definite Value**- Value assigned to people, professions, or ideas who/that have a vital and important role in the survival of the human species. Celebrating

**Destructive Participant**- - Does not believe in and refuses to swear allegiance to the controlling arm of authority. Is aware of the authority of the controlling arm but commits to alter what is perceived to be unjust without respect to civility, laws, or the operational integrity of society. This type of participant creates detrimental unity in society by creating chaos.

This type of participant works to increase the destructive structure in society. Will listen to creative participants if it benefits their agenda. These people believe maintaining participants are the enemy and the creative participants who are not like them are as well. Extremists fit in this category. Cannot live with diversity. No laws apply to them.

**Destructive Structure**- Low cohesive structure represented by conflict in a diverse society.

**Detrimental Tolerance**- It is a sympathetic extension of tolerance for detrimental behavior by those who share intimacy or an identity with the person(s) or group(s) who are participating in ignorance and/or behavior unacceptable by the norms of society or moral standards of a reasonable person because their likeness is applicable. It occurs in two forms, soft tolerance and hard tolerance. It usually exists to maintain cohesiveness over conflict or in the defense of likeness against unlikeness.

**Detrimental Unity**- A type of societal unity by a citizen of a nation existing only to destroy accountability and dividing people by identities or uniting through similarities.

**Emotions of Design**- What humans use to create. These include the emotions people have when experiencing an event in the environment they are a part of. In combination with senses of design and influinci, these form identity factors.

**Empathetic Actualization**- An empathetic view towards competing identities on the tolerance continuum. The recognition of imbalances relative to those who are experiencing actual harm. Always will alter the authority of the controlling arms in society.

**Empathetic Will**- A conscious decision to reinforce empathy on a continuous basis. It is measured not only by the amount, but by the difficulty in doing so. Each person may find evidence to dismiss their capacity to extend, represent, or consider empathy for differences but their empathetic will is the determination to represent this thoughtful act without care to the perception of justification. It is formed by seeing a human being instead of an identity.

**Enematic Characteristics**- The negative visual or known characteristics of the enemy applied to people simply for possessing a resemblance of likeness associated with and identified by an ignorant application of a perceived threat. These characteristics can be magnified by the modern use of technology by one-America demagogues who seek to control the media's narrative, available truth, and level of cohesiveness within society with the use of societal wedges. Is parallel to empathetic will.

**Epitomized Attachment**- The 8-step process that attaches a competing interest on the tolerance continuum through the eyes of the individual perceiving what is in conflict with their existence later influencing the language, behaviors, and actions towards antonymic interests. This placement is controlled by 1) Exposure, 2) Knowledge, 3) Affects/Effects of the Cognitive Rules of Growth 4) Influinci 5) Computation Limits 6) Intelligence Level 7) Identity Factors 8) Judgement, which in turn are used to justify the desired behaviors and actions that follow. The cognitive rules of growth control the placement of the competing interest on the tolerance continuum recognized by the individual perceiving the value of the interest being judged aiding their decision making which influences behavior.

**Equitable extension of remedies**- These occur because of atrocities committed against a people and must be present to prevent detrimental unity. Represented by the recognition of rights, opportunities to succeed, and the inclusion of their creations of expression by the former oppressed assimilated into the society once controlled by the oppressor in the form of education, businesses, knowledge, influence, art, and most importantly legitimacy. Allows for the cohesive structure in society to be positive and peaceful coexisting successful.

**Equitable social growth**- An end justified by the means to create a more equitable society for the purpose of inclusivity, individuality, and togetherness. Measurable by lack of rights to the granting of rights in the form of equal protection of the law, legislation consideration, and most importantly, the cohesive structure of the population contained within society. When the cohesive structure is high and positive, equitable social growth is easier to obtain and an exponential social growth curve can be achieved.

**Exceptional Privilege**- A type of privilege abused by individuals whose likeness has been promoted above others due to egregious acts in the past by selfish actors. It is applied and used against the similarly related identity of whom committed the wrong when discussing, criticizing, or participating in free thought or actions that others who are not them disagree with. All races, genders, religions, and people use and are or can be in possession of this privilege; however, it is most potent in the hands of those whom history has been disproportionally cruel to and intolerant towards most recently.

In addition to and like other types of privilege, those accused of this unrecognized privilege get extremely angry and confrontational upon informing them that they are in possession of this, even denying it exists. All privilege is unrecognizable by those who are in possession of it because it must be accepted and believed to be appropriately applied upon demand or continuously because a victim is extended such consideration. Abraham Lincoln warned of it but could not describe it.

It is a response to and consequence of past civilizations conquering colonizing people or places, the creation of norms in society, events resulting in discrimination, oppression, and the tolerance of injustices. To counter such a divisive type of privilege society must attempt to resolve egregious acts and pursue the means to end circumstantial consequences in earnest effectively destroying a factor of detrimental unity and limit the prevalence of destructive participants.

**Excessive Diversity**- A point in society's timeline that is over stimulated and infused with a detrimental level of diversity that creates the inability to achieve the cohesive structure necessary to build cohesive unity and maintain peace. Not to be viewed as negative only consequential resulting from the type of unity in society.

When the varying levels of identities are present, the need to strengthen the desire to work harder is of the utmost importance to cohesiveness to prevent existential consequences. The recognition of this measurable difference will prove necessary for the diversity of a society to coexist. Lack of empathetic will and the presence of cognitive laziness exacerbates the consequences of excessive diversity.

**Existential Consequences**- Consequences that are extremely cataclysmic and have the ability to alter society and the people it represents. These events change governments, create revolutions, and seek to end absolutism or create it. These occur as people in society fail to seek actual truth and substitute the truth known for the lie believed. The lie is one that represents their likeness, their bias, or their want and need to satisfy a selfish desire. It is an intentional egregious lie that requires serious and often violent intervention to alter or change its effects. Often represented by the result of ideological differences as diversity grows excessive diversity can become consequential. It occurs because the lie creates division and eventually a means to an end used to silence competing views or eliminate a perceived threat.

**Expectancy Degradation**- A situational hardship occurring as a result of Excessive diversity. Representing a condition of honesty, compassion, understanding, and empathy towards fellow man yet never reciprocated. It is condition of morality represented by a standard of decency motivated by compassion and used to create inclusiveness for those who are different.

Eventually the heart of the most giving and most caring will recognize the detrimental behavior from others is too much to overcome. This will cause a person to forever remove tolerance because of societal self-preservation.

**Exponential Rate of Intolerance**- A rate of change within groups that is magnified by population growth, generational identity, time, occurrences of and perceptions to intolerance and oppressive behaviors. A factor of existential consequences.

**Forced Cultural Belief**- An increasingly detrimental way of thinking reinforcing the need for division between diversity and fracturing the cohesive structure in society. May be used for the purpose of securing a platform by virtue standing/signaling, increasing a person's tolerant attractiveness, and problem creating instead of problem solving. It is a way to create detrimental unity by those with influence. It is used to push the bounds of what a people can cognitively understand beyond that of a reasonable person standard or without the attempts of generations to prove ideas correct or incorrect.

Creation is key as the truth must be easily relatable to an already existing idea; therefore, it is important to be closely related to a truth. This ensures it is more likely to get attention, gain traction, and finally become a truth for those willing to believe. If it is too far disconnected from something society believes, the idea will be dismissed. Always contentious to society and has the potential to increase the likelihood of conflict between the controlling arms in society.

Respect is never reciprocal because those who push this perception of correctness are not looking to coexist but to exterminate the differences. This cult mentality is at odds with freedom but in line with communism. Not to be confused with progressional knowledge. A factor of existential consequences.

**Governed Participants**- People who fall under the authority of the controlling arms of society. Three types, creative, destructive, and passive. Does not indicate right, wrong, just, unjust, superior inferior, only a competing existence of interest. People can either be aware or unaware and accept or reject based on the identity factors of the individual. A controlling arm does not have to be established or defined as it can be internalized as good or evil, right or wrong, superior or inferior because all living things are governed by an identifiable or unidentifiable source both of which recognize parameters accepted by the user. A factor of existential consequences.

**Group Identity**- The identity closely related to self-identity that allows for the inclusion into a group, entity, or organization. Can be used to defend likeness, deflect accountability, or encourage a one-America ideology. Allows for the growth of soft tolerance, hard tolerance, and detrimental unity separated from logic and disconnected from decency.

Can form group perceptions creating grouped isolationism which later can develop into exceptional privilege allowing the application of enematic qualities. The more group identities multiply in society, the more

353

consequential excessive diversity can become. A factor of existential consequences.

**Group Narrative Perceptions**- Experiences and beliefs passed down by groups from generation to generation regardless of and with zero respect to the truth allowing divisions between diversity in society to grow uncontrolled adding to the exponential rate of intolerance and the later effects of grouped-isolationism. A factor of existential consequences.

**Grouped-isolationism**- Not specific to any group—it is an effect of, consequences to, arising as a condition associated with the failure of assimilation by minority groups and lack of acceptance by majority groups. These thoughts and behaviors lead to internal conflicts within a peaceful society.

Detrimental to the sustainability of a diverse people, these unintended consequences are a direct result of and relating to intolerant acts towards differences which in turn creates a sense of unnecessary tension by a false-belief and need to create a one-America.

This occurs when interests or identities recognize the group's independence from all others and does not need diversity to survive. The group must possess the means, resources, and ability to survive without the aid of the controlling arm in society. A factor of existential consequences.

**Hard tolerance**- Is the tolerance of ignorance and/or behavior unacceptable by norms of society or moral standards of a reasonable person because a sympathizer has a similar identity or shares likeness to the person(s) or groups(s) of the individual who is participating in the detrimental behavior. Represented by exceptional privilege. A factor of existential consequences.

**Identity Factors**- Used to create self, knowledge, and truth by being stimulated with influinci in combination with the senses of design and senses of emotion.

**Idiocy schism**- A teaching practice used by educators to inflict their will on students. Motivated by self-importance, tragic dismissal, and the intoxication of authority to promote a self-identity or group-identity. Relying on the fear of being insubordinate, disrespectful to authority, or being labeled intolerant, these practitioners of perceived legitimacy push a selfish agenda on children or young adults newly separated from their parents who are easily influenced. Emboldened by the belief their authority is absolute therefore their words will not be challenged. A factor of existential consequences.

**Incremental Destruction-** Occurs as a result of those who benefit from the sacrifices others made and born with no cost to live in the privileged state better people created.

**Inferiority Cycle-** An internal belief held by a group identity used to discredit another group identity passed to younger generations highlighting a half-truth but later reinforced when it is heard outside the home or when an experience occurs giving legitimacy by firsthand knowledge. Maintaining this posture allows for the creation of reciprocal diversity application and a continuation of status quo feeding the cycle of destruction. A factor of existential consequences.

**Influinci-** Any item, information, behavior, or other measurable exposure large or small that consciously or subconsciously is able to influence the actions, beliefs, understandings, or other measurable actions of individuals effecting self or group behavior.

**Influinci Recognition-** A necessary tool used to combat misinformation, disinformation, and detrimental unity by associating what is read, what is said, and what is done against with the purpose of what was read, what was said, and what was done. Not everything consumed is true and not everyone who influences is honest. Ignorance recognition creates truth recognition and encourages proper discourse destroying irrational hijacking.

**Intolerant Regeneration-** The continued enematic perception against differences past down from generations with the purpose to create friction, intolerance, or hate in society. The foundational requirements ensuring the inferiority cycle continues.

**Irrational Hijacking-** A form of deceptive discourse to create and maintain detrimental unity among the population of a people. Premises used may be related to logical inferences but largely contain incomplete or half-truths misinterpreting causation with correlations to create angered tropes designed to divide. Controlled by virtuous movements by weak leaders. The foundational requirements ensuring forced cultural beliefs continue.

**Legitimacy Ladder-** A ranking of differences in society based on the importance to an individual. It is a subjective application of value used to discriminate against diversity. Typically, the value assigned will be reversed and mirrored identically when the antonymic interest is assigning value. A higher placement represents more empathy a lower placement less empathy. When ranking occurs those using such means fail to see people as equals.

**Legitimacy of Importance**- Assignment of respect to feelings, beliefs, and/or positions that are in direct conflict with or are contrary to what is owned by other people when participating in dialogue, conversations, and discussions in a pursuit to achieve equitable social growth. A requirement to create cohesive unity and a greater cohesive structure within society.

**Longevity Evolution**- Science used to create an advantage to extend life more efficiently.

**Maintaining Participant**- Believes in and swears allegiance to the controlling arm of authority. Aware of the authority of the controlling arm. This type of participant works to maintain cohesive unity in society and listens to those who are trying to create cohesive unity. Appreciates diversity and concerned with negative participants. Will listen to and encourages those participants looking to create a positive structure. Follows the Rule of Law and will protect all who do.

**Means of Compassion**- A necessary tool to balance the adverse consequences of capitalism by directing resources to combat the concerns of a wealth gap and the likelihood of a violent correction to. Those with obscene amounts of wealth and the resources available must recognize the limit capitalism possesses and impending doom it can create. What is owned is always transferrable either by choice or force.

Social programs controlled by the government and non-profits controlled by the private sector are inefficient and cost more to operate then the goodwill they create. The failures represented by both exist because human corruption controls the cycle of destruction through selfish endeavors. A collaboration must exist to maximize efficiency but also to destroy waste. The best use of resources is a combined attempt to achieve the same goal not a broken system compensating nepotism often wasting money through redundant tasks.

**Naught Value**- Value assigned to people, professions, or ideas who/that do not have a vital and important role in the survival of the human species.

**Necessary evolution**- science used to create what is needed to survive more efficiently.

356

**Negative-Participants**- People who produce a destructive structure. They participate in either detrimental unity or passive unity in the form of a destructive participant, valueless participant, or shirking participant.

**one-America**- An intolerant belief that America should be one-sided skewed to a personal bias or selfish understanding inconsiderate of all others without care to consequences of divisive rhetoric in effect and with the intention to subvert the meaning of the Declaration of Independence or the Constitution of the United States of America.

It is not limited by a one-America through culture, country or people but defined through and represented by an extension of intolerance similarly related to historical instances of Nationalism, Fascism, Left wing Extremism, Right wing Extremism, Authoritarianism, Totalitarianism, which leads to Dictatorship or a sympathetic Communistic view of socialistic intent used to remove autonomy, ownership, and the destruction of the current controlling arm in society simply because freedom offends those who refuse to grant it to others.

Though not admitted by proponents, a pursuit of these beliefs cannot coexist with a democratic free people or a capitalistic market driven economy. The very purpose is to remove the freedom to own free thought or free enterprise that is in conflict and at odds with absolutism theories. May be disguised as equity or necessary actions by groups to protect self-interest and likeness but created to eliminate perceived threats by surveillance removing privacy to destroy dissent.

**one-America Demagogue**- Individuals or entities with direct influence over a large populous in America who deliberately attempt to divide by likeness, destroy by differences, and weaponize information to sway public opinion to obtain or maintain power over people facilitating legislative changes of a selfish kind.

These advocates of destruction skew one-sided representation of personal bias or selfish understanding, inconsiderate of all others, without care to consequences of, their/its divisive rhetoric, in effect and with the intention to subvert the meaning of the Declaration of Independence, the Constitution of the United States of America or any other controlling documents designed to create peace by maintaining cohesion. Will work to destroy compromise by enforcing mob rule to destroy what prevents total control.

All participants are subjectively correct and are protecting their America. Not to be viewed as correct or incorrect, this is the nature of society's actors and a consequence of diversity through visual differences, lifestyle preferences, and intellectual development or intellectual decline.

Examples Include (not limited to) Former President Donald J. Trump, Former Secretary Clinton, Speaker of the House Nancy Pelosi, Majority/Minority Leaders Chuck Schumer and Mitch McConnel, Alexandria Ortega Cortez, Bernie Sanders, Joy Reid, Tucker Carlson Fox News, CNN, Washington Post, TYT, BNC e.g..

**one-America Indoctrination**- Used by the controlling parties of whatever entity, organization, or any other influential actor to create an understanding of what America should look like without consideration to the diversity of a nation. In combination with specific intent this ideology creates enematic characteristics recognized at a young age for the use to identify perceived threats and create animosity towards differences as the user and learned trait grow in time.

It is the opposite of reflexive tolerance and used to that end. By developing societal wedges at a young age, this type of indoctrination allows division to thrive, cohesiveness to parish, and threatens peace by removing tolerance. Creates detrimental unity, allows for an increase of selective creation, and other societal consequences of diversity to thrive. Similar to intolerant regeneration but this attacks the competing interests of the controlling arms in society by leaders.

**Opportunity-creation**- A commitment to create opportunities through the means of compassion used to increase equity and close the wealth gap by those who have benefitted by capitalism the most. Not representative of the type of opportunities made but encompasses all in the category of creation. These types of kindness are motivated by a high level of empathetic will to ensure a peaceful coexistence can remain. These will counteract the legitimacy of socialism or the need of. These selfless acts will continue to address the shortcomings of capitalism adding to the efficacy of hard work and determination represented by the freedom to choose attaching value to the individual not an economic model.

**Passive Participant**- Believes in and swears allegiance to the controlling arm of authority. Only does what is required when it is required. Listens only to those they agree with or share likeness with. Can live with diversity but not negative participants. These types of citizens participate when necessary. Follows the Rule of Law.

**Passive Unity-** A harmful type of societal unity represented by the diffusion of responsibility by citizens of a nation. Reinforced by the belief that others will correct deficiencies or a belief that participation as a citizen is not necessary and is of zero concern to an individual counter to the purpose of a self-governing people. This type of unity creates consequences and is the least desirable to any nation because the citizen expects protections but will not protect expectations.

**Participatory Unity** A positive type of societal unity existing to reflect what is and protect what is through an understanding that participation in society is only needed when necessary. Can be categorized in destructive structure as a negative type of unity. Not for the type, but what negatives can occur because of lack of vigilance.

**Perceived Legitimacy-** A belief that greatness has been acquired, respect must be given, and what is spoken must be accepted without hesitation. It is a form of privilege disguised as entitlement. Never earned, never tested, represented by offensive arrogance at nauseum. Usually associated with influential people who create loud words who lack contextual understanding without consideration to alternate or competing thoughts.

**Positive-Participants-** People who produce a creative structure. They participate in either cohesive unity or participatory unity in the form of a maintaining participant, passive participant, or creative participant.

**Progressed Societal Self-image-** The way modern society views its norms either ethically or through morality compared against the norms of prior generations.

**Progressional knowledge-** An extension of thought upward and outward encompassing knowledge types that are based on rational inferences, logical conclusions, and heavily connected to science or the critical perspective involving generational attempts to prove ideas correct or incorrect. Not to be confused with Out-wokening culture.

**Progressive Behavior-** Behavior encouraging peace, increasing cohesive unity, allowing discourse that aids in delaying the cycle of destruction.

**Progressive Offensiveness-** Offensive behaviors from actions or words written or spoken that were accepted by generations prior and are progressively being labeled intolerant, hateful, and a willful attack on people who represent the likeness of offense. Not used to classify what is accurately identified as offensive, just a representation of changing norms from one generation to the next.

However, if not adequately represented by a majority of people, the offense will not carry as much weight on the societal fulcrum and will be dismissed as selective creation in the form of subjective-triggeredy. Societal Consequences of Diversity will continue until the movement of the fulcrum comes to rest at a balance point and constructive dialogue is resumed or conflict forces movement of the pivot point by altering the weight of the population.

**Quantitative Value Scale of Citizens**- Metrics used to identify the value of individual citizens relative to actions taken towards unity against the standard of responsibilities or duties required for protections granted through and by a nation.

**Reciprocal Diversity Application of Hate**- All issues applicable by assigned liability can be associated with the alternative belief or narrative promoted. Example: All white people are the problem, or all black people are the problem. America is the problem, or the world is the problem. Democracy is the problem or Communism is the problem. Capitalism is the problem or socialism is the problem. Christianity is the problem, or no religion is the problem. Each are identical as a subjective truth and can be believable as an objective truth, but all are fallacies not associated with the actual problem in a diverse society.

It is the continual protection of detrimental unity and the creation of negative participants who share a likeness to hate a perceived threat or the actual cause. It is caused by the lack of accountability or inability to conform to a standard of decency required to survive in the controlling arm of whatever society and time people exist.

**Reflexive Tolerance**- An education endeavor used to create a more tolerant, cohesive, and responsible citizenry. Introduced at the earliest stages of cognitive understanding, it creates the reflexive response to differing ideas based on personal preferences or information unknown to the individual. This becomes more effective and most needed in areas lacking diversity. The challenge becomes teaching children at a young age to gain the critical perspective before offering a verdict of what they know against what they do not know or preferences to verses preferences against.

The authority of control should be cautious and never force a self-preference on youth in the form of personal bias relating to politics, religion, lifestyle preferences, or any other modern disagreements society is working through. It is not used for a one-America indoctrination but a way to consider differences of the unknown weighed against the knowledge or information known.

**Regressive Behavior**- Behavior encouraging conflict, increasing detrimental unity, and promoting the cycle of destruction.

**Selective Creation**- A type of sensory blindness used to create, change, or control the narrative of public opinion. These behaviors, often subconsciously, are done purposefully to enhance the emotional response of people with likeness against differences irrespective of the critical perspective. This type of detrimental influinci is used to shape a one-America ideological belief by those willing to engage in detrimental unity.

**Self-position**- A position on the tolerance continuum, or any other self-reflecting exercise, that a person plots to better understand their location in relation to a measurable dependent. In this case the tolerance for a specific variable to measure the level of tolerance represented.

**Self-Identity**- All characteristics, qualities, and representations of people, chosen by the individual or those they can be identified with. Used to create personal convictions, belief systems, lifestyle choices and are used for the inclusion to or exclusion of a group for and by the purpose of cohesiveness. Developed as a survival instinct and used to create a group-identity.

**Senses of Design-** What humans use to create. These include everything people are, their experiences, and the environment they are a part of. In combination with emotions of design and influinci, these form identity factors.

**Shawn Paul Cosner**- A person who creates so much conflict in himself because he is trying to be someone he can learn to love. He believes true equality is simple and is defined by an identity encompassed from the empathetic will towards others, labored thought reflective of logic, and a desire to gain the critical perspective—regardless of the package it comes in.

He is a white, male, Christian who does not care what he looks like or the lifestyle he decides to live because he is an American belonging to the human race and the freedom to be is granted not by man but by faith. Men do not possess this authority. The obedience towards men is neither, required, necessary, nor logical as man seldom has anyone's best interests in mind except his own.

**Shirking Participant**- Is not concerned with or is unaware of, does not believe in nor possess allegiance to a controlling arm of authority. May or may not be aware of the authority of the controlling arm. Suffers from circumstantial or situational hardships preventing participation. Commits to their existence alone. Listens to no other participants. No laws apply to them.

**Singular Progression**- The promotion of one identity over all others. It is a focus to further likeness above all else by intentionally ignoring competing identities. Singular progression occurs by not properly balancing interests in society appropriately and operating without the commitment required to create equity and a positive cohesive structure. Represented by the identities who have authority in the controlling arms of society and the types of benefits extended or removed by the ruling class with power.

Can also occur when aligning loyalty with differences to maintain or create power successfully as a grouped effort. These are witnessed in history and presently identifiable from the consequences of diversity. This commonly occurs in the final stage of the cycle of destruction as consequences from tragic dismissal.

**Social Group-Identity Sensory Blindness**- A type of sensory blindness to behaviors, actions, or words used by likeness encouraging detrimental tolerance within a group. It is a consequence of diversity in a society from competing identities, thoughts, and/or beliefs. The detrimental tolerance of behavior creating division will form grouped-isolationism.

**Societal Consequences of Diversity**-        These are consequences from excessive diversity occurring in society and are reflective of or caused by competing identities, thoughts, and/or beliefs. The prevalence of and danger to society is based on many factors including but not limited to; the level of tolerance in society, intelligent level of a people in society, socio-economic status, population size, number of recognized differences or level of diversity in society, the need for representation, and time since last conflict; including how destructive the result.

The further away from conflict society grows the greater and more consequential the behaviors between diversity contained in society become. These are more extreme the closer to conflict society becomes and are less prevalent following blood shed that ends in a treaty or the elimination of the threat causing harm. It is a recognition that those who experienced war, those who remember war, and those who were informed by the former, do more to prevent conflict and war by those who have not experienced war, those who don't remember war, and those who weren't informed at all. And the cycle starts all over again.

After altering the status quo through conflict or upon the cycle of destruction through war new categories of people are created that follow the norms of the specific generation that created the new status quo or the norms that fought to destroy a new status quo. The first is a person who chooses to believe "what is" as enough and destroying the threat was all the progress necessary. The second is a person who becomes a new minority who believes "why not this too." Eventually they grow in numbers, influence, and power continuing to alter the status quo shifting the societal fulcrum until the two groups are equal in power and equal in influence—society's participants at an impasse. This represents the cycle always repeating because people enjoy controlling others and telling them they are wrong.

**Societal fulcrum-** A continuous shifting set of values and morals contained within a societal structure that allows or prevents behavior by balancing what carries more weight for society. It is not until the majority of the populous is ready to shift does the behavior in question become accepted as appropriate or dismissed as inappropriate. Normalizing behavior controls which way society shifts based on the position of the fulcrum and the amount of weight given for any represented idea.

Not representative of right or wrong, just applicable of what society is willing to tolerate. As society progresses what is tolerated and accepted shifts allowing the fulcrum to move, and the less weight required to carry on the side of change. The point of contention arises when the fulcrum becomes stagnant and people in society are unwilling to move the pivot point to the left or right creating a conflict of competing interests. When this occurs, dialogue must continue to create the outcome sought peacefully.

Respect of differences involving morals, values, and traditionalism needs awareness from all citizens but at times it is believed to be unnecessary. War is possible when people do not see the need in changing their way of life to entertain competing viewpoints or alternatives which attack their way of life. All societies reach this point. It is represented by growing population and diversity of thought and/or appearance caused by societal consequences of diversity.

**Societal Self-preservation**- The decision to survive with those who represent likeness the most. A point in history always presents itself for self-preservation. As detrimental unity rises, so too the need for preservation. All people, regardless of identity, as a species are trying to survive. They are doing the best they can with the available information at their disposal in relation to their intelligence level and the leaders they decide to follow. It is irrelevant to pick a side by choosing a way to live or decide what control is superior as all are nothing more than a way to control the masses to interrupt violence between periods of peace.

An answer to what is right or wrong is always subjective but readily available. People will continue to force others to defend their way of life or beliefs up to including their life. Peace can never and will never be obtained because a standard of what is required will never be forced. The tolerance of ignorance and the will to remain small without intellectual, emotional, and physical growth will forever limit the species as it is always a choice; the internal decision to be less than what is possible.

**Societal Wedges**- Any form of influinci used by means of media narrative, information dissemination, or stimulation created by one-America demagogues to increase the perception of a threat by attaching enematic qualities to innocence strictly for the purpose of controlling, maintaining, or gaining power by division.

**Soft tolerance**- Tolerance of ignorance and/or behavior unacceptable by the norms of society or moral standards of a reasonable person because a sympathizer has an intimate relationship or a close relationship with the individual who is participating in the detrimental behavior.

**Subjective Cruelty**- A choice motivated by intolerance allowing for a ranked placement with the purpose to create love or hate, support or opposition, and knowledge or ignorance. The ladder orientation for competing views will be flipped but nearly identical in a diverse society with more detrimental unity than cohesive unity.

**Subjective-triggeredy**- Can be an introductory form of fascism disguised as a necessary social movement by an overstated perception of offense or fear of competing interest used to create a victimhood status of the

364

personal kind or group kind. Defended by the premise that the offensive actions, words, or people threaten the livelihood of the victim(s) resulting in the removal of the offensive expression or the desire to destroy the trigger by the triggered. Should not be used as a basis for the application to describe the appropriate level of offense to be taken. It represents the sensitivity to on a subjective level and what occurs after.

**Sympathetic Actualization**- A sympathetic view towards competing identities on the tolerance continuum. The identification of imbalance relative to those who may be experiencing perceived harm. May start the process of empathetic actualization.

**Termination Evolution**- science used to create an advantage to kill more efficiently.

**Tolerance Continuum**- A sliding scale used to identify, apply, and understand personal bias. Used to increase efficacy of tolerance when addressing differences or competing positions on a personal level. Self-identifying allows the user to plot a current position based on ignorance or knowledge of competing interest. The tolerance continuum when used in conjunction with the cognitive rules of growth, creates a recordable basis for personal growth of what is unknown or not understood. All facets and information that is truthful needs identified to accurately use the continuum honestly.

**Tolerant Attractiveness**- A belief that people will find attractiveness in a higher level of tolerance for acceptance of ideas they themselves may not agree with but agree to thereby increasing cohesiveness with the group wanting to belong to, their perceived attractiveness, and the detrimental unity created. A continuous cycle of encouraging and increasing the types of tolerance available will increase the perception of being more attractive thereby showing virtue of acceptance versus hate by disagreeing. The tolerance shown may or may not be real as is the belief of the truth followed. If what is accepted and tolerant to an individual-identity or group-identity is not accepted nor tolerated by the competing identities, societal wedges can form creating detrimental unity in a diverse society.

**Toxic Benefactors**- Entitled people who are unable to comprehend what is necessary to keep what is and too selfish, ignorant, or incompetent to understand how it came to be.

**Toxic Honesty**- A false truth created by a group-identity used with the intent to inflict harm by attacking the cohesive unity in society.

**Tragic Dismissal**- The anti-empathetic view that competing identities, beliefs, or experiences are irrelevant and are not worthy of respect nor is their/its existence necessary.

**Trajectory of Conflict**- A directional path representing the point of no return. This path leads to war if the trajectory is not altered. Requires a tragic event and strong leadership to either prevent or promote war.

**Trajectory of Intolerance**- A directional path signifying regressive behavior is present forcing detrimental unity between antonymic interests by destroying the cohesive structure in society. This trajectory permits the cardinal point to settle in the zone of conflict.

**Trajectory of Tolerance**- A directional path signifying progressive behavior is present promoting cohesive unity between antonymic interests by creating cohesive structure in society. This trajectory permits the cardinal point to settle in the zone of peace.

**Transcendent Summit of Harmonious Existence**- The absolute goal of our species' existence.

**Tree of Life**- From one to many, singular to plural, birth to destruction. These describe the foundational structure of thought. The progressive momentum of thought and the growth of different thoughts is representative of a tree. As a tree grows so too does the expansion of its existence. It continues to grow upward and outward creating a new but identical tree as time moves forward. It is equally true as time moves forward so too does expansive thought, adding to what was already there.

The longer a tree grows the bigger the tree becomes. The larger the tree, the larger the reach indicating more mass and different mass. The longer thought grows the bigger thought becomes. The larger the thought, the larger the reach indicating more thought and different thought. The larger something becomes the more of something it can contain.

Because human growth is exponential so too is the knowledge people possess. The issue of expansive thought and the continuation of knowledge created by people, or the knowledge believed by people, is the ability to coexist with the competing version of itself on the other side of the tree of knowledge. Eventually the tree will suffer rot from internal decay and a new tree must be planted containing zero falsities and zero people who caused the rot. This process represents the birth of truth or as a consequence to diversity—war.

At one point thought was singular. It existed in a vacuum and was not changed but for the first disagreement or discovery creating a chain reaction of knowledge growth expanding identically as a tree does—upward and outward. People are only aware of what they know to be true and what they accept to be true. They are limited by the maturity of the tree of knowledge and the maturity of where in time the tree of knowledge is located. What society knows today represents what was wrong in the past. What society will know in the future will represent what was wrong today. As the tree of knowledge grows, a more accurate truth begins to emerge. Out of consequence from humanity, those who are not persuaded of the truth believed by other people grow as well. This can create conflict.

What was the first thought or the second thought that created controversy sparking a never-ending cycle by sense of wonder? Fire or no fire? God or no God? Is earth is flat? Because knowledge is altered by the death of those who believe in its truth or by the discovery of a new thought and later the acceptance of this new knowledge, it proves difficult to remove a truth once it is believed.

The number of thoughts or belief systems is likened to the number of people in the world in addition to those who are no longer in existence. The more thoughts, the more people, the more differences that exist, the more likely conflict will occur. Issues will continue to arise in society but balance between competing thoughts is a must. If tolerance is absent from the tree of life, the knowledge (truth) existing on the specific part of tree (people) who believe the thought and in its existence can be removed forever destroying the knowledge and the people who believed it.

There are many ideas and people that/who are no longer present because their truth and they were unimportant and exterminated because the tolerance shown towards them was equally unimportant. The tree of thought is applicable in different understandings of beliefs representing, individuals, relationships, families, governments, nations, or societies by the creation or the destruction of truth through birth, learning, discovery, discourse, civil war, revolutions, and death.

The further the thoughts are from the middle of the trunk of the tree or centerline; the further away people are on the tolerance continuum as individuals or in society. It is vital to continually weigh and balance competing interests and competing truths. Failure to accept this is a failure to alter the cycle of destruction our species creates, maintains, and encourages.

**Truth Assassination-** This occurs when a person, without authority and without respect to the original creator of truth or the accurate account of history, decides to change the word or an event to fit a representation of the narrative of choice more appropriately. As the human species grows so does the need to change what is around them to better suit a subjective truth. This can strengthen or weaken an argument and is accomplished by controlling what is taught of history, what is taught by educators, or what is read by those seeking a truth.

**Value Spectrum-** A scale used to grade and plot the usefulness of people, professions, or ideas that contained in society. Location of these indicates if they/it have a vital and important role in the survival of the human species. A position inside the value spectrum represents a vital and important role in the survival of the human species. A position outside the value spectrum represents neither a vital nor important role in the survival of the human species. Celebrating positions and the importance of placement on the scale is a normal response when society values people, professions or ideas. Issues arise with the efficacy of society when value is not equal to worth.

Having a false belief that people, professions, or ideas—that are not vital and important to society is a necessity and worth more than—people, professions, or ideas who/that are vital and important to society, will cause people to value people, professions or ideas that are not needed to survive and weaken the ability for society to achieve autonomy from what forces dependency because the fascination with the valueless and worthless creates an interest in becoming what they are.

When enough people pursue valueless jobs a tipping point eventually occurs, and animosity is created between the ones who work and the ones who play work. Play working occurs when the final product is designed for leisure time—a consumable entertainment experience. This is the result of peace and prosperity. Real work provides a product for an end user. This is required for society and an economic model to operate. When those with little or zero value possess more influence and importance than those who are vital and important to society consequences threatens stability.

**Valueless Participant-** Does not believe in and refuses to swear allegiance to the controlling arm of authority. Does not believe in accountability and refuses to accept the responsibilities required of a citizen belonging to a controlling arm of society. Is aware of the authority of the controlling arm. This type of participant works to create destructive unity in society.

Difficult to distinguish from destructive participants; however, their effects are the same and are valueless in a society that requires participation. Listens to creative participants lobbying for change, maintaining participants who listen to creative participants, and destructive participants sowing chaos. Can live with diversity. Some laws apply to them.

**Villainous Scrutiny**- Demonizing differences to create detrimental unity.

**Virtue Representing**- A way to imply how moral and ethically superior a person is by demonizing competing interests. Increases one's social status in the group they belong to or are seeking to belong to. Caused by selfishness and a lack of consideration due to ignorance disguised by knowing what is absolute.

**Zone of Conflict**- Any behavior, structure, societal unity or participant representing apathy, stereotypes/prejudices, or hate identified by the location of interests when plotted on the tolerance continuum or experienced in society.

**Zone of Peace**- Any behavior, structure, societal unity or participant representing apathy, acknowledgment, understanding, or acceptance identified by the location of interests when plotted on the tolerance continuum or experienced in society.

**Zone Graph**- A visual representation of the minority's and majority's cardinal point indicating the type of cohesive structure in society, and the level of hate or acceptance between antonymic interests, and the consequences caused by the type of unity that is present in society.

# POSTSCRIPT

## *The End*

Not only was what you read a collection of subjective words describing a personal belief but also an honest attempt to look through the eyes of people who are participants in society's cycle of destruction. People are in extreme denial of what the truth is, what the plight of man represents, and the consequences representing the continued lack of care for others in their lifetime. These consequences are the faults of our fathers and mothers. This will later become the sins of our sons and daughters. A cycle of trust which ignores decency simply to teach without mercy and certainly no care for who we are not.

We must ensure those we choose to follow and those who choose to lead, do so from a place of peace. Peace is being comfortable within your own thoughts and is simply created by ignoring the thoughts of others. These thoughts do not necessarily need to be good, nor must they be in consideration of others, but collectively for our species, let us hope the choice is not selfish. Peace is simply you versus no one. No arguing, no convincing, no confrontation, only agreeance with yourself. However, peace is never hurting others to feel good about the way you think.

It is certainly not an excuse to be a bigot whether your hatred is centered, left, or right. Be wary of what you convince yourself of as consequences flow from this form of perversion. People are unable to contemplate, comprehend, or consider what is decent because the intimacy within their own minds prevents the critical analysis necessary and the care needed to see the humanity in others. Our ability to maintain peace has always been predicated on our ability to represent a standard of decency and by holding people accountable when they violate their duty of responsibility to others. This book, what our Nation requires, my message—create **peace** and change what is necessary.

The chapters are titled representative of how I think and show the locations in my mind of how I organize thoughts or are used to describe what I believe in. I have expressed my opinions by showing my work instead of repeating talking points as is the standard for weakness and the easily influenced because they have been conditioned to self-remove entirely from the luxury of free thought or individuality—Sheep. Remember, an idiot is a fool who believes their ignorance is absolute. And wisdom is experiencing history with emotion combined with the knowledge gained by the practice of seeking the truth.

If people cannot recognize what is occurring, how can they stop it? If you take nothing away from my words, please take this; understand my purpose and goal were to highlight the importance of equity, equality, and encourage tolerance towards one another. It is also a warning against idiots influencing, idiots voting, and idiots leading. Society can no longer afford such ignorance in areas it should have never entertained. This book is for the world and people who seek more than selfishness. Do not let this sickness continue. Create the leaders of the future, not the villains of our past or the monsters from our nightmares. Americans must accept that each of us has a duty and must recognize what we can accomplish when we are united—the strength to prevent, create, and solve.

I am nothing more than a soldier. A blunt instrument built to protect or destroy. A soldier completes these tasks simultaneously when they commit to it. All I know is what my heart is telling me and what history reminds me—what is coming is an ending. An ideology will be destroyed. If weaker men have always sent my family to fight a war for a just cause, I know when it is time to fight. Consequences are nearing, and there is certainty only in action. Do what you feel is fair, just, and kind because no one else is telling you the truth. But we know what is right and wrong; our children's eyes never lie.

This book was not designed to create a right or wrong. It was only to inform. A way to explain the system is broken, right or wrong. What people choose will always be that—a choice. And we all have a choice. I am neither convinced nor persuaded that anything will change unless people change themselves, but they must have a reason. I will not pick a side by choosing an incorrect version of superiority simply from a reflection in the mirror. I will not assume my existence is the correct version of absolutism. I will; however, stand and fight to **Defend American Values**. I do not fear death, nor do I fear violence. My only fear is losing the one I love, but it is my hope she recognizes what must be done. Those who betray what is worthy of value will pay the price. The belly of the big ugly beast is not a thing; it is a place we create and is utterly worthless.

If there is a breath in my body, if my heart can beat, if I can create logic with my mind, I will stand for what is decent and fight against what I perceive as the enemy. I will not do this out of anger but guided by what is critical and necessary to maintain sanity in a world that has developed a taste for insanity. Although I may be out of my depth, I believe a path forward is possible because modern America is enough. We all must take a step towards tolerance to limit the destructive force that occurs when people unite through hate. This is a thought process for all and can be used to create a time for peace and a time for truth. One last thing, this is the **Final Warning**.

May the future be kind before it is cruel...

# A Place for Your Thoughts:

"What is written in the past is a prophecy. It is understood because what is felt, lived, or inflicted gives firsthand accounts of suffering. If we ignore the wisdom we are in possession of; we are fools and deserving of whatever comes our way"

—Shawn Paul Cosner

# *Patriots Poem*

I look around heartbroken at what I see
When I realize America is not what she should be

Understanding we are all to blame
A pursuit of money and dreams of fame

Continuing to divide joyfully
Celebrating in the selfish atrocity

I sit and wait for patriots to proclaim
The soul of the country we must reclaim

It may never happen or occur
never believe something so absurd

We must unite and fight as one
Never quitting until the work is done

It may seem hard or impossible
But together we are unstoppable

Never forget our history
As our success is no mystery

Stand up and flex your might
It is time to continue this fight

I am no longer heartbroken at what I see
I just needed reminded of what we can be

# How do you Defend American Values?

# Book Description:

The disaster awaiting a divided nation through the eyes of a soldier. The creation of divisiveness is weak leadership but its cause, its purpose, and its intent are flawlessly being executed destroying the peace of a free nation.

A timeless example of patriotism to a nation and a dedication to decency. Regardless of if you are an American or not, the author offers insight into tolerance, compassion, and understanding to create empathy in a diverse society. Discussing the necessary path forward, he highlights the cause of destruction, and the reason it occurs, and offers solutions a divided people desperately need.

Describing the decline of American Democracy, a Veteran takes the time to think and question, "Why are things and people the way they are"?" Is it hate, selfishness, or purposeful intent?

Seeking the answers becomes a problematic endeavor because the truth is almost impossible to find when societal divisions run rampant. The lies we tell each other to create happiness are the same lies we tell to hate. Each contains a part of a truth, but never the entire truth—only enough to keep ourselves happy while targeting those we do not like.

This book ponders why it occurs and whether people will be able to fix it. Or is this the latest attempt to control people that ends in the same bloody cycle of destruction as each form of governance before it? Many questions are asked, yet few are answered. Most must be considered by the reader.

Can we fix what is broken? Or must people suffer as selfishness will always provide an ending for those willing to accept hate? And finally, where do we go from here?

The book also challenges the reader to see their "own" truth for what it is—just another way to maintain the cohesive unity within a group they share a likeness with, even if it means hating those who are different.

The book's theories and words may be controversial to some, even challenging to consider, but worth a read. It is the author's hope that understanding can be created before the destruction of tolerance occurs. America's existence could very well depend on it.

# To Us

Thank you Mom, Dad, Jennifer, and Richard. We have come a long way from that trailer in Pisgah. No matter the distance or where my life takes me, my heart will be tied to a much simpler time and a much simpler place—

"A time and a place wherein I was naive enough to believe that people were inherently good…"

Made in the USA
Columbia, SC
14 August 2022